SOUTHEAST
ASIAN FOOD

SOUTHEAST
ASIAN FOOD

Rosemary Brissenden

*CLASSIC AND MODERN DISHES FROM
INDONESIA, MALAYSIA, SINGAPORE,
THAILAND, LAOS, CAMBODIA AND
VIETNAM*

PERIPLUS

Published by Periplus Editions, with editorial offices at 130 Joo Seng Road #06-01, Singapore 368357.

Text © Rosemary Brissenden 2003
Photography © Robert Ashton 2003

First Periplus edition, 2007
First published by Penguin Books, London 1969
Revised edition published by Penguin Books Australia 1996

Library of Congress Cataloging-in-Publication Data

Brissenden, Rosemary.
   Southeast Asian food : classic and modern dishes from Indonesia, Malaysia, Singapore, Thailand, Laos, Cambodia, and Vietnam / Rosemary Brissenden. — 1st Periplus ed.

      p. cm.
   Americanized version of: South East Asian food. Hardie Grant Books, Victoria, Australia, c2003.
   Includes bibliographical references and index.

ISBN-10: 0-7946-0488-9
ISBN-13: 978-0-7946-0488-2

Photography by Robert Ashton
Cover photograph courtesy of Getty Images
Cover and text design by Cheryl Collins

Distributed by
North America, Latin America & Europe
Tuttle Publishing
364 Innovation Drive
North Clarendon, VT 05759-9436 U.S.A.
Tel: 1 (802) 773-8930
Fax: 1 (802) 773-6993
info@tuttlepublishing.com
www.tuttlepublishing.com

Asia Pacific
Berkeley Books Pte. Ltd.
130 Joo Seng Road #06-01
Singapore 368357
Tel: (65) 6280-1330
Fax: (65) 6280-6290
inquiries@periplus.com.sg
www.periplus.com

Indonesia
PT Java Books Indonesia
Kawasan Industri Pulogadung
Jl. Rawa Gelam IV No. 9
Jakarta 13930
Tel: (62) 21 4682-1088
Fax: (62) 21 461-0206
cs@javabooks.co.id

First edition
12 11 10 09 08 07   10 9 8 7 6 5 4 3 2 1

Printed in the United States of America

In Memory
R.F.B.

CONTENTS

Acknowledgments

In addition to those mentioned in the original edition of *Southeast Asian Food*, I wish to thank the following people without whose help, generosity and skill this latest version would never have materialized: Dick Aitken, who could not have been more generous in his willingness to act as sounding-board and appraiser of my prose whenever called upon; Jean Thompson, whose patience and understanding of food made her the perfect typist of my messy drafts; Jean Kennedy, whose scholarship and enthusiasm were pivotal when compiling the multilingual Chart of Ingredients on p. 58; my daughter Venetia for putting together the bibliography and for proofreading help; Helen and Nick Hammond for generous help with printing and computer problems during the course of the project; and finally all those good friends who dropped everything to proofread the final manuscript and galleys.

In Indonesia I thank Widarti Goenawan, Editor of Femina magazine, and members of her staff—in particular Roos Suyono, Sisca Soewitomo and Odilia Winneke Setiawati—who arranged contacts for me and with whom I had useful discussions in Jakarta. I am particularly grateful to Hiang Marahimin, William and Lucy Wongso and their cook Nah, Tjoe Thee, Bridget and Zainal Tayeb, their cook Warmi, Mama Siar and other members of their extended family for their hospitality, for sharing their special knowledge and for their wonderful practical help. My thanks to Janet De Neefe, teacher of Balinese cooking in Ubud, for her ready advice and her permission to include two of her recipes. In Australia Elaine McKay and Tati Achdiat were once again extremely helpful with briefing and orientation; Robyn Coventry and Dick Aitken produced great eye-witness reports from the field.

In Malaysia thanks are due to Mrs Twinkle McCoy, Mrs Rose Gill, Mrs Pooma Tharmalingam and Che Zaniab for their guidance in contemporary Malaysian cooking and that of their respective communities. Thanks, too, to Sandy Collett for her hospitality. In Singapore I am particularly grateful to Ananda Rajah—cook, thinker and, together with his wife Elizabeth, most generous host; to Mark and Angela Sng and to Celine de Souza. In Australia I thank Christina Benjamin and Nesa Eliezer for sharing many of their families' recipes with me; Professors Virginia and Barry Hooker and Professor Tony Milner for their help with reference material.

My lasting debt in relation to Thai food is to my friend Bunjong (Toi) Miles, in whose company I have learned much of what I know about the techniques of Thai cooking. Though recipes we have worked on together do not appear in this book, the chapter would be much poorer had we not done so.

In Thailand special thanks to Khun Tuanjit Kannang and Donald Gibson, Khun Sawart Pongsuwan, Khun Pricha and Khun Chantima Watanyoo, Dr Suthiporn Chirapanda, Professor Kamala Nakasriri, Khun Pasu Pettanorm and her family for their hospitality and for sharing their knowledge of the food of particular regions; Associate Professor Sasikasem Tongyonk for easing my way in Bangkok; staff and students in the cooking and hospitality section at Suan Dusit Institute; and Bob Satterly and his wife, Khun Pen, for their generous response to some long-distance queries.

For the Thailand section of the book, I have had great help in Australia with recipes, contacts and advice from Sumana Aitken, Suparb Delaney, Khun Weena Sutcharitkul, Dr Ted Chapman and Adam Aitken. Dr Donn Bayard and Khun Niti Pawakapan spent long hours correcting mistakes and inconsistencies in the transliteration of Thai words. Drs Noel Barnard, Tony Diller and Peter Grave were generous with their expertise in response to some historical queries though they should not be held responsible for any of my wild conjectures. Thank you, too, to Bill Forbes for carrying messages to and from Bangkok.

For cooking and food advice in Vientiane my thanks to Michel Somsanouk Drouot, Khamphanh Phachomphonh and his family and May Vhan and Boonti. Thanks, too, to Claudia and Geoffrey Hyles for their kindness and hospitality in Vientiane. I am extremely grateful for the help I received from Seng Rangsi in Canberra who made herself endlessly available to me, and from Pinkham Simmalavong and Souvenally Vongthevanh in Sydney.

Without the chance to visit Cambodia, it is the cooking of Naysin Hac of Canberra that I have recorded here. I cannot thank her enough for her endless patience with me and for allowing me to share in some of the care she lavishes on her family. I am also grateful to Christine Chan of Canberra and Rami Yit of Sydney with whom I was able to discuss Cambodian food and ingredients.

My thanks to Dorothy Button of Vietnam Ventures Pty Ltd in Melbourne for kindly accommodating my project and my special culinary interest on one of her Reunification Railway tours through Vietnam. Few other experiences could have allowed me so rich an initiation into the food of the Vietnamese in their homeland. I owe deep gratitude to the catering crew assigned to the tour by the Vietnam Railway Catering Service, in particular to the two brilliant cooks Mrs Nga and Miss Hat, and to the many restaurant staff who freely talked to me along the way. I am grateful, too, to Pham Thi Tuyet Trang of the Melbourne office who took me home to watch her mother cook, and to the company's representative in Ho Chi Minh City, Christine Hong, who arranged a private demonstration with her cook. In Hanoi great generosity was extended to me by the Hanoi Women's Association, in particular Vice-President Eng. Duong Thi Vin and cooking teacher Nguyen Thi Bích Liên. I was given much help there, too, by Nguyen The Hùng, the manager of a small local restaurant, and spent many happy hours eating and researching local food in the company of Lisa Drummond and Gill Tipping and their Vietnamese friends.

In Canberra I have been the grateful recipient of the cooking, language and friendship skills of Do Van Dung and his wife Thu Oanh and have received special help with recipes from Aisha Minh Thu Ajkic and Mrs A. Nguyen.

How to Use This Book

Recipes in this book are arranged according to the style of cooking rather than by main ingredient. The format is designed to enable readers to construct reasonably authentic menus for whole meals taken from a specific national or sub-cultural cuisine. For this purpose simply make sure, in the cases of Indonesia, Thailand, Laos, Cambodia or Vietnam, that each recipe you select comes from a different section within the chapter as well as featuring a different main ingredient. In the case of Malaysia and Singapore, do the same thing within the sections dedicated to Malay, Chinese, Nyonya, Indian and Eurasian cuisines.

Always consult the index to find individual recipes by title (given, for the most part, in the English language) or to find recipes according to the main ingredient. Consult the index, too, for page references regarding unfamiliar ingredients when you encounter them.

Measurements

Unless otherwise stated the recipes in this book serve 3 people generously when you are preparing only one dish with rice; 6 people when there are two dishes; 9 when three, and so on.

Implements used contain the following measures of liquid:

1 cup	=	8 fl oz (250 ml)
1 tablespoon	=	¾ fl oz (15 ml)
1 teaspoon	=	¼ fl oz (5 ml)

Introduction

It is almost forty years since the original edition of this book was written. It was the first of its kind that attempted to discuss and characterize the food of the whole Southeast Asian region. When it was published, Southeast Asian food was relatively unknown and exotic, sought after only by people who had lived and worked in the area during colonial times or by rare food adventurers who were prepared either to hunt for the uncommon ingredients required or to find substitutes for them. The search often called for a great deal of effort and imagination and remained a labor of love.

It is a measure of how little was known and published about the gastronomy of the area until quite recently that the original edition remained in print until the late 1980s.

Now, of course, the situation has changed vastly. Economic growth and prosperity in the West in the 1960s and 1970s stimulated a dramatic growth in tourism and air travel to Southeast Asian countries and, with it, a broader interest in their food. Refugees from the region who settled in the West in the 1970s opened restaurants and moved into food retailing. Their knowledge combined with modern techniques in food production, transportation, preservation and marketing to make a huge variety of Asian ingredients available throughout the world. Today multitudes seek out Southeast Asian flavors and dishes and there are many who wish to cook the food at home. An array of how to books are currently published to help them.

Like its predecessor, this new edition aims to be both a how to book and something more. I believe cooks feel most comfortable when they know something of both the culinary and cultural contexts of the food they are preparing. Many find pretty pictures of prepared food daunting unless they are aware of its surrounding logic. For different cooks, of course, needs will vary: one may be satisfied with a clear explanation of processes and techniques; another happier to know that the dish is one of a whole category employing similar flavors and transferable skills; a third will be helped by discovering something about the social and cultural context in which the dish is normally prepared and served. Some will benefit by recognizing familiar culinary patterns across and between cuisines.

This revised edition of *Southeast Asian Food* is a total rewrite and an expansion of the original book, taking into account the many changes that have occurred in the intervening years. Important ones that have shaped the book are these: Laos and Vietnam (inaccessible in 1965) have now opened up; many cooks born in Southeast Asia live in Australia today; my own knowledge and experience has grown and so has the global marketing of Southeast Asian foods and ingredients.

Laos, Cambodia and Vietnam are covered in this new edition, as well as the Indonesia, Malaysia and Thailand of the original, and there are many new recipes from the countries included in the original book. While not all of the recipes from the first edition appear again, most of the classics remain. I have, however, often updated those that do to accord with current practice, and I have added any ingredients that could not be included in the first place because they were not available abroad at the time.

Quite profound social and economic changes have occurred in Southeast Asia since the first edition. It was in 1993 that I visited Vietnam, Laos, Thailand, Malaysia and Indonesia solely to prepare this book. As before, I watched and cooked with friends and had many discussions with both practical cooks and professionals about their cuisines. Some of the changes in eating and cooking habits in the countries I had known of old—particularly in the cities—both surprised and alarmed me. Of course there were shortcuts, new fashions and modern embellishments and techniques; that is not surprising in countries that have become as integrated into the global economy as these "tiger" countries now are. Nor is it unwelcome. But there were disappointments too: loss of domestic heritage, loss of time to resuscitate it, loss of skill and of culinary control.

I learned much from people who went out of their way to create opportunities for me in their busy lives, and I am extremely grateful to them. I also realized how endangered domestic traditions have become with the vast number of households now caught up in the hurly-burly of middle-class, urbanized daily life. Many parents and children now leave home at the crack of dawn in order to reach the office on time. They eat in the city at night in an effort to escape the evening traffic, or they buy supermarket or street-vendor take-out meals in their lunchtimes or on the way home. This, together with the proliferation of pizza, hamburger and hot dog parlors and their obvious popularity, convinced me that I should take the risk of looking old-fashioned and retain many of the traditional dishes recorded in my original book, albeit updating them. They are dishes that could be lost before too long.

Few cuisines can be more attractive for the adventurous home cook than those of Southeast Asia. The finest Southeast Asian dishes exhibit that respect for the innate qualities of basic ingredients that is the hallmark of Chinese cuisine. At the same time they are characterized by a blended subtlety of fragrance and flavor that, though unique in every case, displays an affinity with Indian food.

Each country has its own culture and cuisine, of course, though political boundaries sometimes intersect particular cultural and ecological ones. First and foremost it is individual cuisines that this book celebrates. It explores the food of Indonesia, Malaysia and Singapore, Thailand, Laos, Cambodia and Vietnam: the techniques involved, the ingredients employed and how to acquire them, the role of the dishes in different settings and, often, the socio-cultural context surrounding their preparation and consumption.

But there is an overall regional character recognizable in Southeast Asian food as well. Given the common historical, cultural and ecological experiences of the countries concerned it is not surprising that this is so, though they share no one language and have never been united in a single state or empire.

Historians write of a widespread cultural "Indianization" in Southeast Asia in early times. This process spread not only Indian patterns of kingship and political organization throughout the area but also introduced many shared herbs and food plants such as tamarind, garlic, shallots, ginger, turmeric and pepper from or via India. Great Southeast Asian empires arose based on the adopted political tenets and their territorial expansion would have seen the spread of plants indigenous to one part of Southeast Asia, such as lemongrass and galangal, across the region as well.

Most modern Southeast Asian nations include within their territory areas that were important coastal states or ports caught up in the vast sea trade in spices and forest products which once extended from China to India, the Arab world and subsequently to Europe. It was this trade that brought spices such as coriander and cumin, fennel, cinnamon and cardamom into the region and spread localized spices like cloves and nutmeg around more broadly. The trade introduced strong culinary influences from Muslim India, the Arab world, China and to a lesser extent Europe. The wok and the Chinese practice of frying came to Southeast Asia in this way, as did Arab kebabs and spicy Muslim meat dishes. The Portuguese brought the chili, a native of South America.

From an environmental point of view, Southeast Asia is the area of "mush" growth compared to the "husk" of north and west Asia.

Conditions in the former dictate the growing of rice and fruit and vegetables rather than dry grains; the climate is regular rather than dramatically seasonal. The region's warmth, high rainfall, abundance of rivers and proximity of sea coasts have produced lifestyles that revolve around rice farming, forest subsistence and a heavy reliance on fish as a source of protein.

All Southeast Asians eat rice as their staple food and revere it greatly. A meal without rice, be it plain or glutinous, is no meal at all. Their cuisines feature some fragrances and flavors that are unique to the area: lemongrass, galangal and a fermented fish or shrimp paste—the latter developed to preserve protein in a hot climate, the former widely cultivated in house gardens. Used on their own or in combination with items mentioned previously, with other fermented ingredients such as fish or soy sauces and sometimes with coconut, they create a set of flavors that is both recognizable and characteristic.

Echoes of particular dishes resound throughout the region as well. Some such as noodle dishes and noodle soups that are similar, chicken rice and rice porridge are, of course, directly attributable to the settlement of Chinese in modern times. Some like the various meat *kurma* that appear in the Malay area and their close relative, the Thai *Kaeng Matsaman*, can be traced to Muslim trade influences. Others are more directly Southeast Asian in origin: the sour soups or stews, often fish, which are a common everyday dish in every country from Vietnam to Indonesia; spicy fish mixtures steamed or baked in banana leaves; raw vegetables served with a chili dip or condiment.

A noticeable characteristic of Southeast Asian food is its color. This is the result not only of its variety and abundance but of the meticulous and often ritualistic manner in which it is presented. Seasonal and cyclic festivals associated with the planting and harvesting of rice still occur in the countryside (though less so in the face of modern production techniques than was the case forty years ago), and animistic ceremonies and festivals are still included alongside more orthodox religious ones. When these occur, food and the arrangement of food is always involved. In many situations, even today, long and patient hours go into the skillful art of food decoration. Most of the dishes that I have described would show this were they prepared in their traditional settings.

In this new edition I have excluded two countries on opposite edges of the region, each for a different reason. The first is Burma (Myanmar)—not because it does not belong but because it remains generally impenetrable to foreigners. The second is the Philippines, which I find atypical in culinary terms. It does not show the impact from cultural Indianization or from the spice trade which are important in the other Southeast Asian cuisines. Vietnam, which I now include, though considered to possess a "Sinicized" rather than an "Indianized" culture, does share some common culinary influences, inherited no doubt from the Khmer and from the empire of the Chams.

The book closes with a few favorite recipes for sweets and desserts. They are few because main meals in Southeast Asia traditionally do not include them. Sweets are usually enjoyed as snacks and between-meal indulgences and warrant a book of their own.

With the world now full of same-tasting instant approaches to Southeast Asian food through packets and jars, this book aims to serve as a guide to cooks who wish to enjoy its true freshness and variety by cooking it at home. If it also conveys a sense of a rich and diverse set of culinary traditions I shall be more than happy.

Utensils

When the first edition of this book was written in the mid-1960s, there were virtually no ovens, gas grills, gas rings or electrical appliances in Southeast Asia. Most households cooked on small charcoal-burning stoves made of clay in a kitchen separated from the main house. The poorest families used a simple fire outdoors. Very few people in the cities—and these were the really wealthy ones—owned multi-burner kerosene stoves. This is still the case in some parts of the north, in particular in Vietnam, Laos, Cambodia, probably Burma, and in some rural areas. But gas rings, wok cookers, upright stoves and a plentiful supply of electrical appliances are now a normal part of the *batterie de cuisine* in many households in the south.

The nature of the traditional equipment still shapes the cooking habits of much of Southeast Asia. Oven-roasting and oven-baking are seldom employed; grilling over charcoal—sometimes in banana leaves—is the method used instead, though in some places this is increasingly abandoned in favor of deep-frying in a wok. Other cooking methods involve boiling or simmering, steaming or stir-frying on top of heat.

No major problems accompany the conversion of a Western kitchen to enable Asian-style cooking. It is a matter more of ignoring equipment than of adding to it, and all methods of Asian cooking may be adapted to what is on hand. Items that should be charcoal-grilled may be cooked under the broiler or in an oven if necessary and those that call for cooking in banana leaves will not suffer too much in many cases if wrapped in heavy aluminum foil instead. Such adaptations will not often be necessary, however, since you can now buy banana leaves in many Asian food stores and the Western love affair with the barbecue and the charcoal grill is widespread.

The equipment vital for Southeast Asian cooking is a **wok** made from heavy aluminium or lighter sheet iron, complete with a **spatula** for stir-frying and a **wire rack** for deep-frying; also some kind of grinding apparatus—either a **food processor or a stone mortar and pestle.**

All over Southeast Asia the wok is a basic and very versatile utensil. It is perfect for stir-frying, allowing plenty of room to toss ingredients around so that their entire surface comes in contact with the heat. The spatula should have a wedge-shaped blade with a slightly curved edge that will fit snugly into the wok's contours. The wok's shape allows for just the right kind of fairly rapid evaporation that is required when making dry curries. It also nicely accommodates the initial frying of spices needed before main ingredients and liquids are added. It is excellent for deep-frying too. You use much less oil than you would otherwise, and the temperature remains more even and predictable. Make sure, however, that your wok is not stainless steel, as the heat conductivity for this metal is not adequate.

Unfortunately, a proper rounded wok cannot be used on the rigid elements of an electric stove. And while flat-bottomed woks are now available, you lose many of the advantages of the round-bottomed kind. Furthermore, an electric wok won't give you fast enough heat control or distribute the heat properly. Gas heat is ideal, and many gas stoves come equipped with a good double jet and the right-shaped bracket for wok cooking. For older gas stoves you can buy a special metal frame to put over the jet to keep the wok steady. If you don't have a gas stove it is possible to buy a small cooker with a double ring of jets, with a gas cylinder attached made specifically for woks. I still have one of these built into a mobile cupboard under a bench at just the right height for me in an otherwise all-electric kitchen. I pull it out when I cook with a wok and have the bonus of easy access to the bottled sauces, which stand beside the gas bottle on a shelf underneath. A stove like this is not expensive and can be kept especially for Asian cooking.

In Southeast Asian cooking, spices, both dry and fresh, are usually ground down to a paste. The traditional, and still the best, utensil for grinding spices is made of granite, its shape varying from country to country. In Indonesia an angular wooden or stone pestle is rubbed hard against a plate-shaped stone base. Malaysians have two different implements: a stone roller on a flat base, still preferred by Malay traditionalists for their wet pastes, and a bowl-shaped stone mortar and pestle that is easier to use. Other countries use the Thai bowl-shaped one, and you will often find these for sale in Asian food stores with a Thai, Lao or Vietnamese bias. The Thai and Lao have a second kind of mortar and pestle as well: a larger one made of clay with a wooden pestle. These, too, are sometimes stocked in Asian food stores, but do not buy them for grinding. Their purpose is not to make curry pastes but to bruise and mix ingredients lightly for northern salads.

In the first edition of this book I recommended an electric blender to make curry pastes. I don't advocate this for the purpose anymore: its jar is too big to hold wet spices in place, its blades are set too high, and the resulting paste is too mushy. The air whipped into a mixture blended in this way seems to me to work against the chemical changes that occur when a properly made spice paste meets hot fat or oils in cooking.

Many modern cooks in Southeast Asia use small attachments for food processors now available for this purpose. These seem specifically designed for Asian spice pastes: they have blades that sit flat on the base of a small container to allow them to pick up limited quantities; they have heavy-duty motors to take the strain of grinding spices, tough herbs and roots; and they are easy to clean. While small grinding attachments for food processors and hand-held blenders can be bought in most countries, few of the ones available outside Southeast Asia are as good but given the current enthusiasm for Asian cooking throughout the world their proliferation is emminent.

For making quality curry and spice pastes, many years of Asian cooking have taught me that there is no real substitute for granite and old-fashioned elbow grease. An electric blade will always *chop* rather than pound, no matter how finely it does so. Even though you may end up with very small particles in your paste, the flavors will remain "chopped" and separate rather than merged. Pounding spices into each other one by one in a stone mortar and pestle does a more complete job of extracting all their oils and causes the old spice to absorb the tastes of the new, until the flavors are completely melded.

Thai cooking in particular, calling as it does for the reduction of spices into very fine pastes, demands the mortar and pestle pounding treatment. Even in Indonesia, where it is felt that spice pastes should retain a little texture and graininess, traditional cooks still choose to use the flat stone mortar and pestle. While I acknowledge that it is not practical to ask a cook to possess each different kind of mortar and pestle, I would recommend acquiring one of the Thai variety, now readily available in Asian food shops. Both traditional and modern approaches are acceptable in the recipes that follow.

The other modern appliance widely embraced by Asian cooks is an **electric rice cooker,** and I do recommend buying one of these if you can afford it. The difference between rice cooked this way and rice watched on the stove does not seem to me to be so great as to counteract its "set and forget" advantages.

Additionally useful in the kitchen devoted to Southeast Asian cooking would be at least one **medium-weight Chinese cleaver,** and preferably two of the same size and weight. You will find all sorts of uses for your cleavers. Chinese cooks use them for everything. They bone chickens, slice things, mince and chop with extraordinary facility, no matter how delicate the operation. The rapidity with which they work is quite terrifying to watch, although they never seem to lose their fingers.

Cooking Methods and Techniques

The following is a description of some basics you may find helpful when you cook from this book.

EATING MEALS IN SOUTHEAST ASIA

Meals in Southeast Asia do not proceed in courses but comprise a number of dishes all served at the same time as the rice. Rice is the basis of the meal, and you should take a good serving of this on your plate first (or your host will serve it for you). Using the serving spoon supplied with each dish, take a spoonful on to the edge of the rice on your plate in whatever order you prefer, but do not pile everything on at once. The Thai, Vietnamese, Lao and Cambodian practice is to take a spoonful of a single dish at a time, each to be savored separately, with the host or hostess watchfully passing new ones to try. This is the general pattern adopted for modern Indonesian and Malay meals as well. There, however, it has been a practice traditionally for complete ritual meals to be served from time to time, which consist of a title dish together with accompaniments that customarily go with it. They are then all arranged around the edge of the rice on a single plate.

CONSTRUCTING MENUS FROM THIS BOOK

Recipes in this book are arranged according to the style of cooking rather than by main ingredient. Though it may be disconcerting at first, this format is designed to aid menu construction. It should enable you to construct any meal in the manner you choose. You can build reasonably authentic Southeast Asian menus simply by making sure the recipes you select come from different sections and sub-groups and by using a variety of different ingredients. You can also construct Western-style lunches, dinners, barbecues and party menus in this manner.

FLAVORINGS IN SOUTHEAST ASIAN FOOD

The individual flavorings in Southeast Asian dishes never lend themselves to precise measurement, but are the result of each particular cook's artistry. Not everyone reacts to a particular flavor or combination of flavors in the same way, and some people will be happier with one rather than another. The same ingredients, moreover, can vary in taste according to size, age and quality.

For Southeast Asians there is no such thing as a correct amount of any additive in cooking: everything is worked out through tasting and adjusting according both to the nature of the ingredients they are using and personal preference. There may be a general expectation about striking a balance between, for example, sweetness, saltiness, sourness and/or chili heat, but the specific amounts and proportions that are used will always be the result of a cook's own judgement.

There is a clear message here for the readers of this book: accept the amounts of flavoring I set out in any given recipe as a *guide only,* and be ready to taste and adjust for yourself at *all* times. Many people find, for instance, that they cannot taste other flavors if they have too much chili in a dish. If that is the case for you, just reduce the number of chilies in the recipe. Many Thai or Vietnamese people would almost certainly use a heavier balance of sugar and fish sauce than I have here, and the strength and saltiness of the fish sauce they would be using could be different as well. Diabetics, on the other hand, will not want to use any sugar and may want to reduce the amounts of salty fish sauce given. Feel free always to taste and adjust to what suits you.

Southeast Asians, it must be remembered, are first and foremost rice eaters. It is the plate of rice that is the meal; other dishes on the table are there to add interest to the rice but not to dominate it. The way non-Asians approach rice is quite different. Our habit is to treat it as an accompaniment to meat, fish or vegetable dishes, and we view the latter as the core of the meal. Try though we might, this is the practice our culture constantly leads us to adopt. While it is perfectly acceptable to proceed in this way, there is an important consequence of which every Western cook should be aware: it is that the flavoring Southeast Asian food may often be too strong when the food is eaten in a Western way. If you do not adopt the rice-based approach of Southeast Asians, you may wish, sometimes, to adjust flavorings to a milder taste.

COOKING RICE

PLAIN RICE

People in Southeast Asia always eat white rice rather than brown and that is the rice to which these instructions refer. You may, of course, use brown rice if you wish, but do not serve it to an Asian, who is likely to feel—as a very good Thai friend of mine once told me she did—that such food is only fit for prisoners. Brown rice addicts will know already how to cook it so no instructions are given here.

Evaporation method

The evaporation method of cooking rice is the one that is most often used in Southeast Asia, and it is the one that I recommend if you do not have an electric rice cooker. Once you have mastered this method you should find that it never fails to yield a good, clean mound of rice in which the grains are soft but separate and not at all sticky.

Select good-quality white rice (Thai jasmine rice is the one I prefer for most purposes because it is at once fragrant and full of flavor). Put the rice in a heavy-bottomed saucepan that has a tight-fitting lid, pour plenty of water over it and stir well with your hands to dislodge the loose starch adhering to the grains. Strain and repeat as many times as necessary until the water to be discarded is no longer cloudy.

Add fresh cold water to a level approximately 1 in (2 cm) above the rice. No matter how much rice you use, nor how large the saucepan, this level always represents the right amount. Do not add salt as it spoils the flavor of the rice.

Bring to a boil over high heat. Cover loosely, reduce the heat just enough to stop the rice from boiling over, and simmer for about 10 minutes or until the water is absorbed and the steam is escaping through holes in the surface of the rice.

Adjust the lid to fit tightly, and reduce the heat to very low for another 10 minutes or so. Then, without stirring the rice, wrap the entire saucepan in a kitchen towel, and set it aside for another 20 minutes or until you are ready to serve it. The beauty of this system is that the rice will not only cook perfectly but it will also stay hot until you are ready for it and allow you to focus your attention on the other parts of the meal.

Electric rice cooker method

Electric rice cookers cook rice basically by the same method as that described above. If proper care is taken they produce a result that is indistinguishable from rice cooked by the evaporation method.

Wash the rice according to the instructions provided for the evaporation method and cover it with fresh cold water to a level approximately 1 in (2 cm) above the rice. The machine will do the rest. Make sure to make one further adjustment, however. When the machine stops cooking (it will usually emit a loud click at this point), lift the lid and shake off the droplets of water that have condensed there from the steam. Then take a clean kitchen towel and drape it over the top of the cooker before you fit the lid back on. This will absorb any excess water while the machine automatically switches on and off to keep the rice warm, and will prevent any drops from wetting the rice again. Leave the rice in the cooker on "keep warm" until you are ready, then transfer it into a bowl, loosen it, and serve.

GLUTINOUS RICE

People in the north and northeast of Thailand, in Laos and sometimes in North Vietnam eat glutinous or sticky rice in place of the plain white rice of the south. The method of cooking is quite different from that used for ordinary rice. There are two ways to do it—one being the traditional way and one using an electric rice cooker. The first is a bit tricky but gives a better result.

Traditional method

You will need *either* one of the deep clay or aluminium pots made especially for cooking sticky rice and the conical bamboo basket that goes with it *or* a saucepan fitted with a perforated steamer and a lid that fits snugly on top.

I have found using the pot and basket the best method. You can often buy these quite cheaply in Asian food stores. Proceed as follows:

Put 3 cups (750 g) glutinous rice into a bowl and cover it with water to a depth of about 2 in (4 cm). Soak it overnight.

The next day put at least 3–4 in (8–10 cm) of water into your base pot and bring it to a boil. Soak the rice basket. Drain the rice and wash it thoroughly until the water runs clear. Put the rice into the basket and drop it into the pot, covering it with a saucepan lid. Steam for half an hour or so until tender, tossing the rice a bit after about 20 minutes. Remove the basket and tip the rice out onto a tray or a large platter. Using a wooden rice spatula or spoon, turn, lift and thoroughly separate the grains of rice. Spoon it into an insulated rice bucket, cover and set it aside until it is needed, or place it in a warmed and covered pot and wrap it in a kitchen towel. (The resting stage is important and should not be omitted.)

If you are using a saucepan or metal pan fitted with a steamer to cook the rice, line this top section with a wet cloth or napkin before you add the drained soaked rice. As you fit the steamer over the water-filled base, wrap another wet cloth, called in Thai the "pot's trousers," around the junction so that steam does not escape. Cover with the lid and proceed as above.

Glutinous rice is usually served in individual woven baskets, each with a covered top, and it is eaten by hand. Uncover your basket, take a bite-sized clump of rice between your thumb and fingers and mold it into a ball. The ball of rice is then dipped into the food on your plate and eaten.

Electric rice cooker method
This method takes a little more practice and experimentation to perfect. Put the drained soaked rice into the rice cooker and add water. Switch on and let the machine cook it. When the "cook" switch clicks off, stir well, put a dry cloth under the lid and switch to "keep warm" for at least 15 minutes.

MAKING AND USING COCONUT MILK

In all of the countries of Southeast Asia except Vietnam, dishes that use coconut milk are common. Generally, two strengths are used, sometimes three or four, though the third is not much stronger than water and may be replaced by it. The first is generally referred to as thick or first squeeze coconut milk. After this there is thin or second squeeze milk, and sometimes, though only rarely, even third squeeze. Sometimes, too, with Indonesian and Malay recipes you will simply be instructed to add coconut milk. This all-pupose variety is available canned and can also be created by mixing one part thick and two parts thin coconut milk.

Occasionally a Malay recipe will call for the addition of coconut cream (*pati santan*). This ingredient imparts a rich oiliness to dry-cooked dishes and is not to be confused with thick coconut milk. Coconut cream is the liquid squeezed out of fresh grated coconut (it must be a mature one but not old) *without adding any water at all*. It does not appear often in these recipes.

Different forms of coconut milk are widely available these days but the following are the various methods for making your own, some of which, as will become clear, I find preferable to others.

FRESH COCONUT
This is the best but most laborious way to make coconut milk. Break open a mature coconut that is still young and fresh enough to have water

in it. You should be able to hear the water when you shake it; the water will probably not be nice enough to drink but may be used in some Vietnamese recipes. Grate the flesh finely in one of three ways:

1. Use a sit-on grating stool or "rabbit" (Indonesians, Malays, Thais, Lao and Cambodians all have these). With the flesh and skin still adhering to the shell of the coconut scrape out the meat, turning the coconut until it is grated down to the skin. Scrape out the final residue with a spoon.
2. Remove the flesh from the shell and leave its skin attached. Cut the flesh into four pieces and holding the pieces with the skin out use a round grater to grate finely. Grate as closely as possible to the brown skin but do not include it.
3. Cut the skin off the coconut flesh and cut the flesh into pieces 1-in (2-cm) square. Using a powerful food processor or blender, grate or chop the coconut until it is finely and completely grated.

To 1 lb (500 g) of grated coconut or 1 whole grated coconut, add ½–1 cup (125–250 ml) of warm water. (Depending on how juicy the coconut is this should yield about 1–1½ cups/250–375 ml *first squeeze* or thick milk.) Knead and squeeze this thoroughly or process it for 2 minutes to extract as much of the nut's juices as possible, and then squeeze dry, setting the pulp aside. (A piece of muslin or cheesecloth will make the squeezing easier.) Reserve the first squeeze milk and repeat the process with 2 cups (500 ml) of warm water for the *second squeeze*, or thin milk, and again for *third squeeze* if you need it.

CANNED COCONUT MILK
Convenient though it may be to use the cans of coconut milk now readily available in Asian food stores and on the shelves of some supermarkets, great care has to be taken with this product. Until recently virtually all brands of canned coconut milk or cream were thickened with dextrins, caseinates or emulsifying agents. They would look thick and luxurious when you opened them but they often lacked flavor and would not make a proper substitute. When cooking Thai dishes, which rely on the oil that comes out of reduced thick coconut milk to fry spice pastes, once evaporated, the milk would often yield no oil. Thin diluted milk from the cans, moreover, unless diluted to the point of no flavor, would always result in a curry that would be far too thick.

The situation has improved with some brands producing a purer product, but you still have to be vigilant. Look carefully at any cans you see to make sure that the ingredients state something like "coconut milk/cream only" or "pure creamy coconut." It is acceptable if the label declares the contents to have water only added, but do not buy anything that contains caseinates, preservatives or emulsifying agents. It helps, too, if something like "AAA grade" is included on the label. As a final test shake the can—you should clearly hear liquid slopping around inside. If you do not there is every chance that the contents have been thickened and have solidified in the can.

For thick coconut milk open a can that has rested unshaken for a while and skim off the top half, using it undiluted. For thin coconut milk (second or third squeeze) add 1–2 cups (250–500 ml) of water to the remainder according to the thickness required. For all-purpose milk mix the two strengths in the proportion of one part thick to two parts thin.

If you are using the thick coconut milk from cans for Thai cooking and you find the oil will not release to enable you to fry a spice paste, it will not hurt to add a little oil to the pan to fry the spices while still imparting a coconut flavor from the residue of the canned coconut milk.

DRIED COCONUT

For me dried coconut is a reliable way to produce a coconut milk of the right consistency and oiliness when you do not have access to fresh coconuts. Coconut milk made by this method definitely "breaks" when boiled, producing a good amount of oil in which to fry curry pastes for Thai food and achieving the process I describe as the "oil coming out" of a dish's sauce at a certain stage of cooking. Make sure, though, that the dried coconut is unsweetened.

For thick coconut milk, pour 1½ cups (375 ml) of boiling water over 1 cup (250 g) of dried coconut in a bowl and set aside to moisten. If you have a blender or food processor, transfer the coconut mixture to it and process it on medium speed, while you count to twenty. If you do not have a blender, let the coconut soak in the hot water for 20 minutes. In either case the final step is the same: squeeze the mixture into a bowl through a fine strainer or a piece of cheesecloth, pressing the coconut hard until no juice remains. This should yield at least 1 cup (250 ml) of thick milk. The coconut pulp, treated the same way again using 2 cups (500 ml) of water, makes thin coconut milk.

For all-purpose coconut milk combine the two or make it according to the instructions above using 3½ cups (725 ml) of water.

When cooking with thick coconut milk there are two things to remember: always stir it as it comes to a boil, and do not cover the saucepan while cooking. If either of these precautions is neglected, the dish will curdle.

Coconut milk does not keep longer than 1 to 2 days in the refrigerator but it may be frozen for up to a week.

MAKING AND KEEPING SPICE PASTES

USING A BOWL-SHAPED MORTAR AND PESTLE

The bowl-shaped mortar used by Thais and Malays requires a pounding action. Add the ingredients for a spice paste one by one, smashing the pestle down vertically time and again until you pound each ingredient into a paste. Add the next item and repeat, producing a composite paste. Proceed in this way with each ingredient until you have a fine, thoroughly mixed, complex paste. This is the desired consistency for Thai curry pastes in particular.

Mash the soaked dried chilies first, adding salt, as these need to be pounded on their own to mash thoroughly, then add the other ingredients in the order of those most hard and dry—for example, lemongrass after chilies, galangal after lemongrass, then coriander roots, kaffir lime skin, shrimp paste, garlic, and shallots last. If dry spices are involved—for example, coriander seeds, cumin seeds, or peppercorns—either grind these separately in an electric grinder and add them last or grind them by hand before you add the chilies.

USING A PLATE-SHAPED GRINDSTONE AND A BENT PESTLE
(FOR INDONESIAN FOOD)

Indonesians prefer their spice pastes grainier than Thais do, with a little texture retained. Their equipment makes this possible in a way that the Thai bowl-shaped mortar does not. The Indonesian action is not a pounding one but a rubbing, grinding one, as the equipment dictates. Items are generally put on the stone in separate heaps, and dealt with in the order above, but they are ground rather than pounded and mixed in together a little more roughly. Grind the dry spices first, add the hard roots, then the fresh chilies and the garlic and shallots last.

USING A FOOD PROCESSOR

A food processor is more suitable for Indonesian spice pastes than for Thai ones. Grind the dry spices first and then grind everything together. You may add a little water to keep the ingredients rotating around the blades if you must, but do *not* let the mixture turn into mush. The water must first be evaporated before you fry the spice paste.

KEEPING SPICE PASTES

Freshly made spice pastes will keep in the refrigerator for at least a week covered in plastic wrap—and for longer if covered with a thin film of oil under the plastic wrap. They also freeze well—particularly the Thai ones.

STOCK

Many Asian recipes call for the use of stock, either in soups or to moisten other dishes. If you have a freezer it is a good idea to save all non-fatty scraps and bones from trimming raw chickens and meat for making a basic stock. Accumulate these in separate bags according to the source and when you have a good supply proceed as follows.

> 1 lb (500 g) chicken (neck, wing tips, back) or pork bones
> 4 cups (1 liter) water
> 1 shallot (a green one with stalk preferably)
> Salt to taste

Combine all the ingredients and bring to a boil. Simmer for 10 minutes and skim any foam that forms off the top. Reduce the heat and simmer gently for about 1½ to 3 hours, skimming frequently until the stock is clear. Strain. The stock may be stored in the refrigerator for up to a week. It may also be frozen in ice-cube trays, the cubes removed and kept in labelled plastic bags for use where small quantities are required, or it may be frozen in large containers for use in soups.

FRIED ONION OR GARLIC FLAKES

Fried onion flakes and fried garlic flakes are an important garnish in Southeast Asian cuisines. Fried onion flakes are made from small red onions (shallots are the best substitute). You can usually buy fried onion flakes in plastic jars or packets in Asian food shops, and I recommend doing this as their preparation requires a bit of work and it is always good to have some on hand—at least until you are using them in sufficient quantity for buying them constantly to become too expensive. Fried garlic flakes are also sometimes available from these sources but you probably won't use them as often and it's not such a bother to make these yourself.

Both the shallots and the garlic cloves should be peeled and sliced lengthwise thinly and evenly, and then spread out and set aside for a few hours to dry if possible. Heat a little oil in a pan or wok until it is hot. Add the sliced onion or garlic, reduce the heat to low and brown them lightly (remember that they will go on cooking for a bit after you remove them so do not overcook). Watch the pan closely throughout to make sure that the onions fry completely but do not burn. Remove and drain on paper towel.

When the onion or garlic flakes are cool and dry, store them in a glass jar. Salt the portion required just before using.

GRILLING INGREDIENTS FOR ADDED FLAVOR

Traditionally in this part of the world, onions, garlic, chilies, some meats and other fresh ingredients were first grilled over charcoal to bring out their flavor. Today, in most places they are fried instead, but the practice of grilling still persists in some areas in the north.

When roasting chilies, garlic, shallots and most herbs over charcoal, thread them on to a skewer for easier handling.

VEGETABLES IN SOUTHEAST ASIAN FOOD

One of the greatest virtues of Southeast Asian food (as well as Chinese food) is the vegetables used emerge from cooking with a crunchy texture and with their vitamins intact. You will often find in these recipes an instruction such as "simmer (or stir-fry) until the vegetables are tender-crisp." This means that they should have absorbed some of the juice of the dish but should still retain their crisp texture.

Some of the recipes talk about forming chilies, radishes, tomatoes and green onions into flower shapes *for garnishing*. Thais are particularly fond of doing this. Here are the instructions:

Chilies Push a sharp knife blade through the chili about ½ in (1 cm) from the stem, and pull it along sideways to the other end of the fruit so that the chili is bisected except at its stem end. Remove the seeds and core, then repeat the process with the knife until there are 6 or 8 "petals." Soak the chili in iced water and the petals will curl up. (You may wish to do this one side only at a time, detaching the sides from the seed core and leaving the seed core in as a "pistil.")

Radishes   Treat long radishes the same way as chilies. With small round radishes cut about 5 thin slices part of the way into the flesh around their circumference. Soak in iced water until the flesh curls.

Tomatoes   Using a very sharp knife peel the skin of a medium-sized tomato horizontally in one continuous strip about 1 in (2½ cm) wide (with a wavy edge if you can manage it) from top to bottom. Curl the strip around itself, pulling the top outwards, to resemble the shape and general appearance of a rose.

Green onions   Cut a piece about 3 in (8 cm) long from a thick green onion. With a sharp knife, cut fine shreds down to about 1 in (2½ cm) on both ends. Soak in iced water until the cut ends curl into a tassle.

Cucumbers   The skin of the cucumber can be cut into the shape of a leaf. Peel a wide but not too thick slice of skin from the vegetable and carve it into the shape of a leaf, etching out some white ribs.

TECHNIQUES FOR CUTTING VEGETABLES

Generally speaking, cylindrical and/or crisp root vegetables are cut into matchsticks about 2 in (5 cm) long (Indonesian and Malaysian), into flower-shaped slices (a Vietnamese favorite), or are roll-cut (Chinese). To achieve flower-shaped slices for carrots, Japanese radishes or cucumbers, first peel them and then cut out three or four small v-shaped strips down the length of the vegetable. Finally cut across into thin slices, each of which will be flower-shaped. To roll-cut put the vegetable on a board and make a 45-degree cut through. Rotate the vegetable a quarter turn and cut again, repeating the process all the way up. For matchsticks, cut thin slices and then stack these up and slice across into matchstick or julienne strips.

Leafy vegetables, both leaves and stalk, and green ones such as beans, are cut into bite-sized pieces, often diagonally.

To make vegetables fresh and crisp soak them in water to which you have added a pinch of sugar.

CHOOSING AND PREPARING CHICKEN

Free-range chickens have the best flavor and texture for most Southeast Asian cooking, although battery hens are now very common. At the very least always choose fresh rather than frozen fowl. It is better, too, to choose roasting or frying chickens. This is certainly so for Chinese cooking, where nothing remains on the fire for very long, and with curries as well. Though you can sometimes leave curried dishes to simmer until the meat is tender, your concentration is often caught up in achieving the right thickness of the gravy. Stick to roasters so that you can be fairly sure, no matter what, that your chicken will be tender enough.

While it is convenient to buy chicken that is already disjointed, in single pieces and already boned, it is better to have a mixture of parts in a dish, and people may still find it useful to know how to cut whole chickens for different purposes.

The following ways to prepare a bird are referred to in this book.

CURRY PIECES

Disjoint the chicken: legs in two, wings in two, breast in two lengthwise and once across if large, back in three crosswise. Chicken is best skinned for curries, particularly the rich coconut milk variety.

FRYING PIECES

This method usually applies to Chinese recipes. Since the purpose is to prepare pieces of chicken that can be handled with chopsticks, they are smaller than curry pieces.

First remove the legs and wings from the trunk at their connecting joints. Chop the wings again at each joint, and then across diagonally once between the joints. Spread the leg and thigh out to form a v-shape, and chop diagonally across through the bone in about ¾-in (2-cm) strips. Chop the trunk right through slightly to one side of the sternum and backbone to produce two halves, one slightly bigger than the other. Place each half face up on the chopping board, and chop cross-wise so that you have a number of clean strips, about ¾ in (2 cm) wide and 2–3 in (5–8 cm) long, with the bone, on which the meat has been cut across the grain. You can treat chickens this way before cooking, and you can also apply this method to chickens that have been steamed or roasted whole. In the latter case, it is usual then to arrange the pieces neatly on a serving dish in the shape of a spread out whole chicken.

PANGGANG PREPARATION

It is best to use small chickens weighing about 2 lb (1 kg) for these dishes. Sever a whole chicken down the sternum only and bend it back flat, breaking the rib bones at the back to make this possible. Pin the legs down level with the tail by inserting a skewer across the back of the chicken. Keep the chicken flattened out as it cooks and serve whole in this way.

BONING AND SHREDDING A WHOLE CHICKEN

Cut the flesh of a whole chicken down each side of the breastbone and down the center of the back and pull the flesh off half the bird at a time, releasing the thigh, bone and all, from the body as you go. Remove the skin and quarter the body flesh. Bone and skin each wing and the leg. Dip the pieces of meat in water and cut across into thin escalopes. Finally slice these escalopes across the grain into strips.

MINCING AND SLICING MEAT

MINCING
A most efficient way to mince meat or shrimp for Asian cooking is to use two cleavers of equal weight, one in each hand. Chop down alternately on the ingredient until it chopped as finely as you need it. This may take a little practice, but it will pay off in speed, cleanliness and lack of waste in the end. A food processor will also do a good job of mincing and by all means use this method if you prefer.

SLICING
To produce meat slices for Chinese cooking cut a thick piece into 1½ x 1½-in (4 x 4-cm) strips first along the grain and then cut each piece into thin slices across the grain.

THAI BITE-SIZED PIECES
Most Thai curries these days call for boneless meat or chicken that is cut into bite-sized pieces. Cut the meat into about 1½-in (4-cm) strips along the grain, about ¾-in (2-cm) thick. Angle the knife (it should be sharp) outwards at about 45 degrees and cut a strip about ½-in (1-cm) wide at the top to produce a substantial almost triangular-shaped shred. Angle the knife 45 degrees inwards and cut again, repeating these movements until all the meat has been sliced in this way. The pieces, while being only bite-sized, should end up thick enough to have some "chew."

CONVENTIONS IN CURRY COOKING

Curries are either wet (with lots of gravy) or dry (with little or no gravy). Those that aim to be dry usually require the evaporation of the sauce as the curry cooks. Sometimes it may evaporate completely, leaving behind a residue of oil in which the meat or vegetables that remain are fried, thus sealing in their juices (Indians call this process tempering).

Curries made with coconut milk are not usually covered as they cook. This not only prevents them from curdling but also enables dehydration, at least some of which is generally called for in Southeast Asian curries.

Many of the Indonesian and Malay recipes in this book instruct you to simmer a dish until the gravy has thickened. When you are cooking with coconut milk this unmistakably happens as the dish simmers unstirred and sufficient water evaporates out of the gravy. When this occurs the curry is neither really wet nor entirely dry: it is thick, with colored oil visibly floating on top.

The first step in making a curry is always to aromatize the spices in some kind of oil before adding beef, chicken or whatever other main ingredient is to be used. The Thais, who do not like their food oily and who traditionally possessed no native oils, do this differently from everyone else. They first put thick coconut milk into a wok or a pan and let it boil hard, stirring, until it has evaporated to the point where its oil has separated. The spices are added and "fry" in the oil released from the coconut, often assuming a rich reddish hue as they absorb the coconut residues. At this point the main ingredients and the thin coconut milk are added and the dish simmers until it cooks, thickens a little and the oil floats on top. Indonesian and Malay curries, on the other hand, proceed the other way around. The spices are fried in oil (until recently this was always coconut oil), the thin coconut milk is added first and the thick milk is added just before serving to produce extra richness and creaminess.

After frying the spices, curries are cooked on a medium heat.

PREPARING SEAFOOD

MAKING SHRIMP CRUNCHY

To firm up raw shrimp before they are cooked first determine whether they are fresh or have been frozen and defrosted. In either case remove the shells and devein. If the shrimp are *fresh*, they will become wonderfully crunchy if you soak them for 10 minutes in water with a pinch of sugar. If they are *defrosted* and soggy, rub them with salt and rinse them thoroughly to freshen the texture. In both cases, dry well before cooking.

PREPARING UNSHELLED SHRIMP

Wash thoroughly and cut off the feelers. Remove the vein by inserting a needle or a toothpick into the area where the body and tail join. Position the pick under the vein and lift gently. The vein should pull out of the tail.

ASIAN-STYLE SQUID PIECES

Slit the squid tubes down one side, open them out with the inside facing upwards and wash them, removing any adhering membrane. With a knife make diagonal score-cuts into the flesh every ¼ in (5 mm) right across the body, taking care that the cuts only penetrate halfway through the flesh.

Turn and cut across again at right angles to the first set so that you end up with a fine diamond pattern. Cut the tube straight across into ¾-in (2-cm) slices and cut the slices into 1½-in (4-cm) pieces.

DEEP-FRYING WHOLE FISH THE ASIAN WAY
When cleaning and scaling fish, leave the head and tail on for appearance but remove the gills, which would otherwise impart a bitter taste. Slash the fish across its body 3 times on each side to allow for shrinkage and flavor penetration. Dry it with paper towels so that it will not spatter in the oil.

A wok is the best utensil in which to fry a whole fish as its shape will accommodate sufficient oil to produce a crisp crust on the fish without having to use too much. Put enough oil in the wok or pan for one side of the fish only to be immersed. If you use a flat pan the depth would need to be about 1 in (2½ cm). Heat the oil until it is very hot before adding the fish, then reduce the heat to medium and cook until the bottom side turns golden brown and crisp. Turn over carefully and cook the other side. Hot oil may be ladled over the top, the head and the tail to ensure even cooking. Lift the fish from the oil, drain and then transfer to a serving plate. Spoon or pour sauce over the top.

COOKING OIL

Until recently different countries and ethnic or religious groups in Southeast Asia used different kinds of oil for cooking. Indonesians and Malays used coconut oil; Malaysian Indians used ghee or gingilly oil; the Chinese, Thais, Lao, Cambodians and Vietnamese used liquid pork fat. While these fats are still used in some places, with a few people reluctant to abandon the particular flavors they impart, lighter, poly- and mono-unsaturated vegetable oils are increasingly used and are promoted by health authorities. The vegetable oils used vary, with no particular one standing out. There is only one oil that is not at all suitable in flavor, and that is olive oil, the current darling of the gastronomic world in terms of health. Peanut oil, which is congruent in flavor, has been used in the past. Canola oil is now frequently recommended, and it is close to olive oil in it nutritional value. The decision remains a personal one in which the various qualities of the oils available should be judged together. For me canola is a little too thick to be totally satisfactory, and I use the lighter, though less healthy, peanut, sunflower or safflower oils.

SHORTCUTS

As one who has always tried to live about five lives at once, I am very aware of the importance of quality shortcuts for most people in today's busy world. While I believe that people using this book should be happy to immerse themselves in cooking for its own sake, this does not mean that there are no shortcuts available. Indeed there are and they are increasing every day. I cannot recommend all of those available (I do not like the sameness, the industrial taste and the final lack of depth that comes almost inevitably with the instant mixes now flooding the shelves of supermarkets and some Asian food stores), but the following are worth considering:

- Always go through the recipes you plan to cook beforehand. Assemble all the main ingredients for a dish in separate containers, measured out and prepared according to the ingredients list. Measure and prepare the separate spices for a paste, setting them out on a single plate. Grind them into the paste using your chosen technique and transfer the completed spice paste into its own dish ready to go. Make enough coconut milk for all your dishes in one step and have it ready to measure out for individual dishes. In the end you will save time overall and be able to give your full attention to the creative process.

- If you plan to cook a lot of Asian dishes for a party or within one week of each other, chop, slice or mash the spices individually in bulk and keep them in the refrigerator. Note how many teaspoons, tablespoons, etc. equal a measure normally used in these recipes (for example, whole shallots, cloves of garlic, whole chilies, chopped galangal, chopped or sliced ginger), and measure out the amount you need for each dish. Busy Indian cooks whom I have met do this all the time. As a result they can produce a meal for the family very quickly and painlessly, and they can cope happily with an unexpected rush of guests.

- Jars of prepared single items, for example, mashed garlic, onion, sticks of lemongrass in water, fresh coriander (cilantro) paste, are commercially available and are not too bad for convenience. The overall message to remember with packaged items is that the closer they are to the single fresh ingredient the better they are likely to be. This rule at least makes it possible to cook Asian food sporadically without having to seek out and buy up fresh exotic items every time. Another Brissenden rule is that soup mixes seem to be marginally better than curry or dessert mixes. I suspect it is so because they are comparatively simple in their makeup and rarely allow for any profit-enhancing, flavor-confusing "thickening." Tamarind soup base can be substituted for fresh tamarind to make a supply of tamarind water, and the odd *tom yam* cube can make a quick and acceptable Thai soup from time to time.

- Many things can be pre-prepared at a convenient time and then frozen successfully. For example, try freezing **stock** in ice-cube trays. You can decant the cubes into plastic bags in the freezer and use them singly when a splash is required for a recipe. **Tamarind water** can be treated the same way—freeze any left over and store in a plastic bag in the freezer. The cubes can be quickly defrosted in small, usable amounts.

  Crushed or finely sliced lemongrass, chopped galangal, grated kaffir lime zest, shredded kaffir lime leaves—most herbs that are to be cooked rather than used fresh as a garnish may be pre-prepared and frozen. **Curry and spice pastes** can be handled the same way. Make a practice of doubling quantities when you prepare them, wrap what is left over in plastic, label it and store it in the freezer.

- There is no doubt that electric appliances can save labor, in spite of the noises I make about *high-quality* spice pastes on p. 9. Even in the case of spice pastes, top quality can sometimes be compromised in favor of convenience.

  By all means use a food processor to make curry pastes if you are in a hurry; use it, too, to make coconut milk or to grate fresh coconut, to whip up batters and to blend sauces. Use your microwave for steaming and for cooking pappadums and Indonesian *krupuk* (they only take a minute and there is no frying mess to clean up), or a fan for drying off marinated poultry, meat slices, etc., before you deep-fry them. Curries and spicy dishes in fact make near-perfect convenience food in combination with the microwave. Most of them only improve with keeping and can be stored in the refrigerator for days with single portions being heated up at the convenience of family members or people who live alone.

NOTES FOR VEGETARIANS

While I have not provided separate recipes for vegetarians in this book, there will be few recipes here that cannot be adapted for them. People in Southeast Asia are adept at making such adaptations themselves according to whether meat or fish is available or not. Here are a few of the suitable substitutions that come to mind:

- light soy sauce for fish sauce
- tofu or Indonesian tempeh (fermented soy bean cake), plain or fried green beans for meat, fish or eggs
- mung-bean vermicelli may be mixed with herbs, spices and flavorings in place of meat or shrimp in stuffings or salads
- mushrooms, baby corn, soft tofu, sometimes slices of pumpkin instead of shrimp, fish or meat in soups
- chopped mushrooms and chopped tofu for chopped meat in traditional "dressed" dishes; tofu alone for fish
- shrimp paste or country fish paste products may be omitted
- meat, shrimp or fish used for flavoring in predominantly vegetable stir-fries may be omitted.

Ingredients

Techniques such as smoking, salting and fermenting have been used in pre-industrial societies for many centuries to preserve and break down food. They are still important in Southeast Asian cuisine though more these days for their contribution to flavor than to fulfill their traditional function of enabling the storage of valuable and often scarce supplies of protein. Where once the techniques were used by individual households, the foods now tend to be produced industrially.

This is also the case with most of the other fragrances and flavors that distinguish Southeast Asian cuisines. The difficulties of keeping food fresh in a tropical climate encouraged the cooks of Southeast Asia to enlist the help of a wide range of aromatic herbs and roots growing in the area to mask any symptoms of deterioration. Access to the spices involved in the sea trade route between India and China combined with the adventurous use of local flavorings to produce cuisines graced with remarkable vividness and complexity of flavor.

We are fortunate that both industrial food processing techniques and a rapid growth of communications make most of the essential Southeast Asian ingredients available in the West. All kinds of canned and processed goods from Southeast Asia now enter our markets as a matter of course and fresh tropical produce is imported by air into non-tropical areas. The store cupboard of the region has been brought within easy reach and there is very little that home cooks might need which isn't now available to them. Whole Asian shopping districts, emphasizing the food of a local population and carrying a broad range of regional products, now exist in many cities, while individual Asian grocery stores appear randomly throughout the suburbs.

Here is a list of the ingredients you will encounter in this book and some advice on how you might identify them in Asian food stores.

Agar-agar   A seaweed powder used to make dessert jelly in Southeast Asia. Available in packets in Asian grocery stores.

Amaranth   (*Amaranthus* spp.) A very common plant in Indonesia used in *sayur*. Baby spinach or young silverbeet is a close substitute.

Anise   (*Pimpinella anisum*) Anise seed is sometimes identified as *jintan manis*, one of the seeds used in Malay curry powder. *See* Fennel Seed.

Asian celery or **Chinese celery** (*Apium odorum*)   The celery used in Southeast Asia is a small, biennial plant with a thick root and narrow, crisp, juicy, stringless and compacted stems, which remain unblanched.

The leaves of European celeriac root are closer to it in flavor and size than normal celery stalks, but you can substitute celery cut into matchstick strips ¾-in (2-cm) in length or sliced celery tops and leaves. The stalks of flat Italian parsley make an acceptable substitute.

Bamboo shoots (*Bambusa* spp.)   Young shoots of bamboo are collected soon after they appear above the ground. When used fresh they need to be boiled for a long time. Bamboo shoots treated in different ways are available cooked and ready to use from Asian grocery stores. They appear as an ingredient in many Chinese and Thai dishes. Some different treatments and their uses follow.

- Whole large shoots in cans: slice across thinly before adding to a dish (usually added as one ingredient to a composite dish or to soups).
- Shoots that have been sliced across and canned (also usually added as an ingredient to a composite dish or to soups).
- Shoots sliced lengthwise into 2 x ¾-in (5 x 2-cm) strips (cooked as a sole vegetable or made into salads).
- Shoots shredded and cooked in bulk, packed in plastic bags with liquid, or canned (added to meat curries or stir-fried alone with condiments and sometimes egg).
- Shoots soured or pickled, usually in shreds, in jars or cans (mixed into some Thai curries).

When using canned bamboo shoots always rinse them before adding them to a dish.

Banana leaves   These are used to wrap items for baking over charcoal, or for steaming. They keep food moist and impart a slight but characteristic flavor. If you do not live in an area where banana plants grow, you can buy packets of fresh or frozen leaves in Asian grocery stores. Hold the fresh or thawed frozen leaves over a gas ring or electric element, or heat them in a microwave oven on high for 1 minute, to soften before use, then brush the inside lightly with oil. Heavy aluminum foil may be used as a substitute, though it does not breathe as a banana leaf does or have quite the same effect when put on a charcoal grill.

Banana blossom   The young flower of the banana tree, stripped of its tough outer leaves, tips and any developing stamens and stigma, prepared similar to the trimming of an artichoke. The flower is then shredded across and used raw in salads.

Basil   Several varieties of basil are used in Southeast Asia for different purposes. None of them, incidentally, is the Italian sweet basil we are used to, although at least one of them belongs to the same species. Here are the different varieties.

- **Thai basil**, Asian sweet basil or cinnamon basil (*Ocimum basilicum*) is a very heady basil with shiny rich green, slighty serrated leaves, on a purplish stem. The leaves become tinged with purple at the top near the inflorescence, the inflorescence is purple and the flowers when they open are pink. Its fragrance is faintly reminiscent of cinnamon and its flavor of scented cloves. In Thailand, this basil (*horapha* in Thai), is added to curries and fish stir-fries at the last minute as an aromatic garnish; in Vietnam it comes with soups, particularly beef noodle soups for the same purpose. In Indonesian food, lemon basil is the basil most often used (see *Ocimum canum* below).
- **Holy basil** (*Ocimum sanctum*)   Known as *kaphrao* in Thai, holy basil is specific to Thai cooking. (Its Lao name, in fact, translates as "Thai" basil.) It has a pungent, slightly menthol flavor when crushed. Its growth is more bushy, its leaves a duller and darker green than the above and they are slightly hairy. Sometimes the bunches of holy basil that appear in shops have a pinkish stem and are rather twiggy, though the one I grow is soft and all-green. Holy basil needs to be cooked into a dish to impart its flavor.
- **Lemon basil** (*Ocimum canum; O. citriadorum; O. basilicum* var. *citratum*)   Known as *maenglak* in Thailand and *kemangi* in Indonesia. It has smaller, smoother, lighter green leaves than the other two. It is used in some Thai dishes, in Thai Vegetable Soup in particular (p. 342–343). In Indonesia it is used mostly in dishes containing fish where its purpose is to mask any strong "fishy" smell.

All three of these basils are easy to grow in rich soil with full sun. A few plants may be potted and brought indoors for winter use, after which they might even survive for a second year.

Bean sprouts   White shoots sprouted from mung-beans. They are readily available fresh and should never be bought in cans. Pull off any green skins still left on the beans before cooking, and remove any browning tails. For a really elegant dish you might want to take off the beans themselves as well. If you do not know where your bean sprouts have come from and you need to be sure that they are clean, quickly pour boiling water over them in a colander after you have washed and cleaned them, and then run cold water over them. If you like your bean sprouts crunchy as I do, however, and you are fairly confident about the hygiene of your source of supply, just soak them for a while in water to which a pinch of sugar has been added. Drain well before using.

You can grow your own bean sprouts if you want to in one of the plastic sprouters sold in health food shops. Alternatively you could put 8 oz (250 g) of mung-beans in a large bowl and cover them generously with cold water. When the skin has split (about 24 hours later), strain off the water through a colander. Leave the beans in the colander, covering them with a folded kitchen towel and keep them in a spot that is not too cold. Water every 2 or 3 hours for 3 days. The beans should remain wet, but should not rest in water or they will turn brown and smell bad. (Should this happen you will have to start again.)

After 3 days, when the sprouts themselves should look fresh and white, tip the contents of the colander into a large container, fill the container with water, and stir vigorously until the skins float on top. Repeat this process until as many skins as possible have floated off and been scooped out. The rest you will have to take off by hand.

Belly pork   A favorite boneless cut of meat in Laos, Cambodia and Vietnam, where its "three layer" quality (meat, fat and skin all together in one slice) is much admired.

Betel leaves (leaves of *Piper sarmentosum*)   A misleading name given to the leaves of a climbing pepper plant. In Thailand the leaves are wrapped around small cubes of lime, fresh ginger root, peanuts, etc. and eaten raw as a snack; in Malaysia they form a bed for Spiced Fish (p. 251); and in Vietnam beef rolls are wrapped in them and grilled over charcoal. The name probably derives from the fact that the leaves closely resemble those of *Piper betel*, another pepper vine whose leaves are wrapped around betelnut seeds for chewing.

Belacan, blachan or *blachang*   The Malay version of shrimp paste (*see* Shrimp paste).

Broad-leafed mustard   *See* Chinese cabbage.

Candlenut (*Aleurites moluccana*)   A waxy, round nut with a very hard, furrowed shell that is ground with other spices into Indonesian and Malay curry pastes. It enriches and thickens the texture of dishes. Available shelled and raw in packets in Southeast Asian food stores, candlenuts taste bitter in this state and should always be roasted in a dry pan before use. You should also always add a little sugar when you cook with candlenuts, to neutralize their bitterness to some extent.

Macadamia nuts can be substituted for candlenuts—but they do not have the same absorptive, mealy texture. Almonds, which come closer in this sense, may be a better substitute.

Cardamom (*Elettaria cardamomum*)   A strongly scented, slightly bitter Indian spice, cardamom is best bought whole in its green or white pods, which are about the size of a little fingernail. Roughly break these open before adding to a dish. Each pod contains about 6–10 individual seeds. The larger brown Thai cardamom has more seeds that are not so pungent. I have usually mentioned only the number of small pods that are to be added in the recipes in this book. If you have cardamom seeds, not pods, remember the equivalents.

Caramel coloring   A dark brown mixture made in households in Vietnam by caramelizing sugar and mixing it with water. It is used to add the rich color to dishes that dark soy sauce would provide but fish sauce, the Vietnamese substitute, does not. A recipe for caramel coloring appears on p. 527.

Cassia   *See* Cinnamon.

Chilies (*Capsicum frutescens* or *Capsicum annuum*)   There are many varieties of this delectable vegetable, ranging from that tiny ball of fire, the bird's eye chili, to the insipid sweet capsicum, or bell pepper, of the United States. The chili comes originally from South America and was not introduced to Asia until the Portuguese took it there in the 16th century. Once there it was taken up as the favored source of the hot taste previously provided only in one or another form of vine pepper.

Four or five different kinds of chili are used in Southeast Asia for different purposes and effects. They may be green or red, fresh or dried. I have usually stipulated which in the recipes. It is not always clear which species they belong to when they are off the vine, so it is probably best to go by size and color. Two general rules apply: smaller and thinner is

Coriander

Mint

Shallots

Candlenuts

Turmeric

Green chilies

Red chilies

Yam bean

Lemongrass

Mint

Galangal

INDONESIA

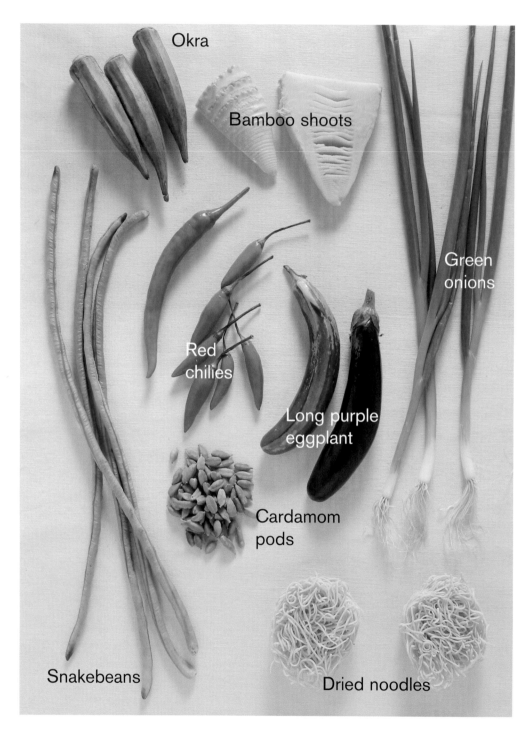

Okra

Bamboo shoots

Green onions

Red chilies

Long purple eggplant

Cardamom pods

Snakebeans

Dried noodles

MALAYSIA & SINGAPORE

Palm sugar

Red shallots

Basil

Kaffir lime leaves

Black peppercorns

Pea eggplant

Mung-bean vermicelli

Mint

Lemongrass

Garlic

THAILAND

Coriander

Water spinach

Dried lily buds

Wing beans

Dried egg noodles

Cloud-ear mushroom

Sugar cane

Taro

LAOS

Dried lily buds

Asian celery

Asian sweet basil

Eryngo (long-leafed coriander)

Chilies

Sponge gourd

Taro

Garlic

CAMBODIA

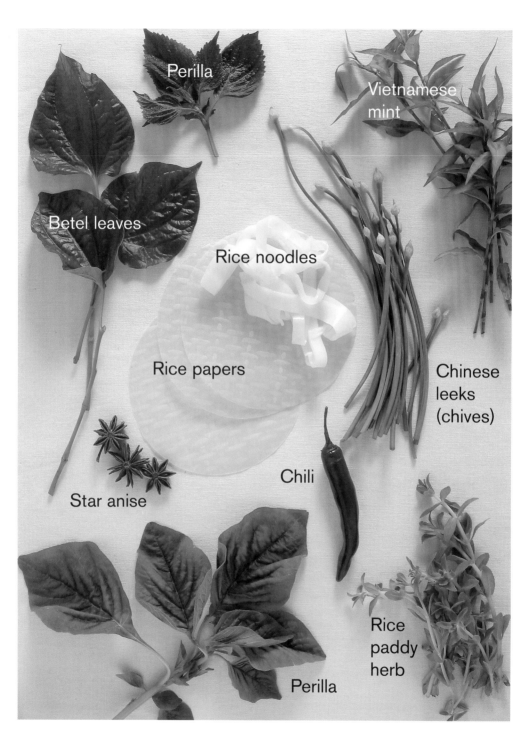

Perilla

Vietnamese mint

Betel leaves

Rice noodles

Rice papers

Chinese leeks (chives)

Star anise

Chili

Perilla

Rice paddy herb

VIETNAM

Bean paste

Sesame oil

Fish sauce

Red chili paste

Light soy sauce

Country fish paste

Dried shrimp paste

Dark soy sauce

Dried tamarind

SAUCES

Thai mortar and (wooden) pestle

Thai glutinous rice steamer

Long-handled spatula

Thai glutinous rice serving basket

Wok

Chinese cleaver

Grater

Mortar and pestle

Indonesian (flat) mortar and pestle

Wire drainer

Bamboo steamer

UTENSILS

always hotter than longer or fatter; and red is usually hotter than green, though also sweeter. The common chilies used in Southeast Asia follow.

- The tiny red or green **bird's eye chili**, about ½ –1½ in (1–3 cm) long, is a variety of *Capsicum frutescens*, with fruits growing erect in the leaf axils. It is the hottest chili of them all and has the most penetrating flavor. You can sometimes buy these fresh, and they are always available dried in Asian grocery stores. These chilies are the ones that are often added whole to cooked dishes as a finishing flavor and a garnish. They are also used in dipping sauces, pickles and side dishes. If you cannot buy them fresh, they are usually available in a jar pickled in brine in Asian grocery stores. Of course the chilies lose flavor when prepared this way, and if you use this type you should be sure to rinse them thoroughly first.
- **Small hot chilies**, about 2 in (5 cm) long, and the most commonly used red chili in Thai food. These are the ones that are dried in the sun and pounded for ground dried chili, chili powder or chili flakes. Most people have access to fresh Tabasco or cayenne chilies, which are the usual substitutes used. If you use the dried ground chili flakes, however, 1 teaspoon of chili flakes equals about 3 fresh chilies.
- **Medium-length chilies**, 4–6 in (10–15 cm) long and still fairly thin. These are the most common chilies in Indonesian and Malay food. They are hot but not too overpowering and look good when sliced in circles or diagonally. You can easily remove the seeds, which are the hottest part, if you wish. These are usually referred to as "red chilies" in Indonesian recipes, since they are seldom used green there, though the opposite tends to be the case with the south Indian food of Malaysia. In Indonesia they are also sometimes misleadingly called "large chilies" to distinguish them from the short bird's eye variety.

  A fatter medium-length variety—still hot—is dried for use in Thai and Indian curries.
- **Large red and green chilies**, which are less hot. In the north of Thailand green ones of this type are roasted and used to make dips. People sometimes recommend banana peppers for this but I have found that seedlings marketed as Masai chili, which you can grow yourself and produce fruits about 6–8 in (16–20 cm) long, dark green in color and as thick as your thumb, are closer in flavor to the ones used in northern Thailand. When red and ripe, though, they are quite hot.

If there is just no way you can get fresh chilies when you need them in a recipe, use bottled sambal ulek (available in well-stocked supermarkets).

This is simply a preparation of blanched hot chilies crushed with salt. One teaspoon equals about 2 red chilies.

Dried chilies come in various forms, as indicated. When a recipe specifies "ground chili," use ground chili flakes.

People who have not cooked with hot chilies before should take care: Don't take a large bite of one to try it out; a careful nibble might even prove more than you bargained for. And wash your hands carefully after cutting them as the juice should not come in contact with the eyes or tender skin.

Chilies have both a taste and a chemical effect. At first this effect may have to be tolerated rather than enjoyed, but once the initial shock has passed they stimulate the appetite, cool the body and bring about a general feeling of peace and tranquility. Once you become a chili admirer it is difficult to resist moving on to addiction.

Chinese broccoli (*Brassica oleracea* var. *acephala*)   A vegetable with leathery leaves on thickish green stalks known in Europe as kale. It is a favorite vegetable for stir-frying in Thailand. Both the stalk and the leaves are used.

Chinese cabbage   There are various types of Chinese cabbage, but some common ones are listed below.
- **Bitter Chinese cabbage,** broad-leafed mustard or *kai choy* (*Brassica juncea*) has pale green stems and leaves and is favored for stir-frying. The Chinese use the large variety, with thick curving stems, for pickling. Use this cabbage as a green vegetable when young, and salted and pickled when larger.
- **Celery cabbage** or *pe-tsai* (*Brassica pekinensis*), is commonly found in well-stocked produce sections of large supermarkets and is used in salads and soups. It can be stir-fried but is watery when prepared this way.
- **Chinese white cabbage** or *bok choy* (*Brassica chinensis*) is sometimes called Chinese green cabbage. It has very white, smooth stems and green leaves as dark as Swiss chard or silverbeet. It is the best cabbage to use in braised dishes.
- **Chinese flowering cabbage** or *choy sum* (*Brassica chinensis* var. *rosularis*) has a delicate long and open stem and leaf and yellow flowers. It is favored for stir-frying.

Chinese celery   *See* Asian celery.

Chinese chives   *See* Chinese leeks.

Chinese keys (*Boesenbergia pandurata* syn. *Kaempferia pandurata*)   This is the English name for *krachai* (Thai), *kcheay* (Khmer) and *kunci* (Indonesian), a yellow cylindrical rhizome with brown skin that grows in a cluster, like a drooping hand of fingers or a bunch of keys. Used in some vegetable soups and with fish in Thai, Khmer and Indonesian cooking. This rhizome has sometimes been called "lesser galangal" but the name is not correct; "lesser galangal" is actually a small variety of galangal from China. Chinese keys are available fresh, pickled in jars, dried whole or shredded, or as a powder in Asian grocery stores. It is usually known there simply as "rhizome" or "rhizome powder."

Chinese leeks (*Allium tuberosum*)   Both the leaves and the flower heads of this plant are eaten. The leaves are used in all countries with noodles, as a stuffing or as a garnish. Leaves of the more common but smaller plant sold here as "Chinese chives" may be used as a substitute. In Thailand, the flower heads may be added to Country Vegetable Soup, (p. 343), or stir-fried with meat or shrimp.

Chinese mushrooms   Also known as shiitake mushrooms, these dried whole mushrooms are rather expensive, but they have a strong flavor and you usually need only a few. Chinese mushrooms give a distinctive taste to the dishes that contain them, so when they are called for it will not do to substitute either fresh or canned mushrooms. Nor would other varieties of dried mushrooms be suitable. Chinese dried mushrooms are readily available in Chinese groceries. To cook them, soak in warm water until soft, remove the hard stems, and slice or use whole.

Chinese mustard (*Brassica juncea*)   *See* Chinese cabbage.

Chinese sweet black sauce   Referred to as *tim cheong*, this is a thick sauce containing flour. Indonesian *kecap manis* may be used as a substitute.

Chinese turnip, Japanese radish or **daikon** (*Raphanus sativus* var.)   A long white root vegetable used as a flavoring in soups or, sliced in round flower shapes, as a decorative salad vegetable.

Chinese vermicelli   *See* Noodles (mung-bean vermicelli).

Cinnamon and cassia (*Cinnamomum* spp.)   A highly aromatic tree bark used all over Asia. Cassia, or Chinese cinnamon, is the version used in Thailand. It is thicker and coarser than the more common Ceylon cinnamon and comes in a solid piece, whereas the Ceylon cinnamon exported to other countries is usually flaked. Cassia is also the cinnamon component of Chinese five-spice powder. Cassia and cinnamon may be used interchangably, though cassia is rougher and less aromatic. A 1-in (2½-cm) piece of cinnamon bark also denotes a 1-in (2½-cm) piece of flaked stick.

Cloud-ear mushroom, wood-ear mushroom or **jelly mushroom** (*Auricularia* spp.)   This Chinese vegetable is black and hard in its dried form, and its common English names are quite descriptive. When soaked in water it becomes soft and jelly-like and looks a bit like black ears. You can sometimes buy it fresh in Asian grocery stores.

Coconut cream   The juice squeezed out of grated fresh coconut. It is sometimes used in Malay food, and is to be distinguished from thick or first squeeze coconut milk. For a canned version use the very top of an unshaken can of coconut milk.

Coconut, fresh grated   Fresh grated coconut is used in different ways in Southeast Asian food.
- In Balinese cooking, a piece of mature coconut is removed from the shell, its skin side held over a flame until the coconut exudes a fragrant smell. If old and tough, the skin is then partially removed (if the skin is younger and pliable there is no need to bother). The coconut is then grated and added to the food, usually a salad.
- In Malaysian and some Indonesian curries, the freshly grated coconut is put into a hot, unoiled wok or heavy pan and roasted, stirring frequently until it is golden brown. It is removed, allowed to cool and then ground as finely as possible with a mortar and pestle or in a food processor before it is added to a cooked dish. The Malays call the final product *kerisik*. It should be the color and texture of brown sugar.

If you cannot find fresh coconuts to grate, you can use dried, unsweetened shredded coconut as a substitute if you steam it over water first for about 30 minutes. The equivalent amount for ½ fresh coconut is 1 cup (3½ oz/100 g) of dried coconut before steaming and 1½ cups (4½ oz/125 g) after steaming.

Coconut juice or **coconut water**   This is the fresh juice found in the center of a young coconut and it is frequently used to add a luxurious touch to dishes from South Vietnam. It comes from coconuts that are young and soft enough to have the top cut right off, revealing a center that is mostly juice with only a thin layer of still jellied flesh. Usually there is little juice left in the husked, brown coconuts sold in temperate climates, and it is not worth buying them for this purpose, although you can occasionally find young juice coconuts in produce markets that cater to Asian clientele. The most available source in temperate climates, however, is the can or carton of coconut juice sold in Asian grocery stores for drinking. However, this juice usually has sugar added, so be careful to reduce any sugar called for in the recipe. A 14 fl oz (400 ml) can holds the equivalent of the juice from about 1½ coconuts.

Coconut milk   Coconut milk is the liquid that results when water is added to the grated flesh of mature coconuts and the mixture is then kneaded and squeezed. There are two other varieties of coconut milk used in these recipes: thick and thin. The different uses of coconut milk and the ways of producing it are outlined on pp. 16–19.

Coriander or **Cilantro** (*Coriandrum sativum*)   Southeast Asian cuisine makes use of the seed, root and leaves of the coriander plant.
- The dried seed is an ingredient in most Southeast Asian curries. It is better to buy all dry spices as seeds and grind them yourself, to ensure their freshness.
- The fresh root is a uniquely Thai contribution to Southeast Asian food. It is used crushed with garlic and pepper to flavor meat and fish and it makes something uniquely Thai out of curries adopted from India or soups taken from the Chinese. Include about ¾-in (2-cm) of stalk when you separate the root from the plant and chop both the leaves and stalk before adding it to the other ingredients to be ground.
- The leaves are used as a garnish. Though they look something like parsley and are often called Thai or Chinese parsley, their flavor is unmistakably different and quite strong. In the Americas, they are often referred to as Cilantro.

Coriander root and coriander leaves are usually available fresh in many supermarkets and in Asian grocery stores. Coriander is easy to grow in temperate climates in spring and autumn. Make sure that the plants are well protected as snails love them. Water well and harvest regularly to stop them from going to seed. The coriander seeds that you buy as a spice are suitable for planting.

Country fish paste   This is my name for the "potted" freshwater fish and its derivatives that are the equivalent of shrimp paste all over the landlocked north of Southeast Asia. In Thailand this is called *pla ra*, in Laos *padek*, in Cambodia *prahoc*. Filleted pieces of the fish are packed into an earthenware pot with rice husk dust and left to ferment. Sometimes, as in the recipe for Green Chili Dip, the whole fish pieces and some of the juices are chopped together and used in a dish. More often they are boiled in water, strained and discarded, and only the liquid is added to the dish. The smell is quite strong, but its flavor is delicious when added to a dish and cooked, and there is no exact substitute for it.

In Thai- or Lao-oriented Asian grocery stores you can buy country fish paste or its derivatives in the following forms.

- The fish itself in its brine, usually available as "Pickled Gourami Fish" or "Pickled Mud Fish." If you are using the whole fish, take the fillets out of the jar with or without liquor as instructed and follow the instructions in the recipe.
- A paste made from the fish itself, called "Pickled Gourami Fish—Cream Style" is sometimes available. This saves a lot of trouble in washing the fish and mashing it when you are asked to use the whole fish in a recipe.
- A number of ready-made versions of the boiled strained water are available. One is called *Nam Budo* or Budo Sauce. Another bottled sauce exported from Thailand for the Vietnamese market called *Mam Nem* seems very close to this as well, though it is stronger than the above versions and you will probably want to add water to taste.
- To make your own country fish paste water, remove one fillet of pickled gourami fish or mud fish from its jar. Put this in a saucepan with about 1 cup (250 ml) of cold water, bring to a boil and simmer for at least 30 minutes, until it has started to fall apart. Take off the stove and pour through a strainer, pressing the solids to strain off all the juices.

The World Health Organization has warned people in northeastern Thailand not to eat gourami fish processed at home because it has been discovered that the fish there sometimes harbors a fluke that is a health hazard for humans. There should be no problem eating the version processed for export, however, and *Nam Budo*, which is made in the seaside port of Samut Sakhon on the gulf south of Bangkok, is probably manufactured from sea fish anyway. People who are worried about this could use *Bagoong Balayan* from the Philippines instead, which is a sauce made from anchovies and is very close in flavor, or any of the Southeast Asian shrimp pastes. Again, water these down to taste—perhaps by about half.

Finally, some Lao, Cambodian and northern Thai people no longer use country fish paste or water made from it at all, adding only fish sauce to their dishes. This is a suitable substitute, though the food does not taste the same.

Cowpea   *See* Snakebean.

Cumin seed (*Cuminum cyminum*)   Cumin is the spice that always accompanies coriander seed in curries. Many spice seeds are of a similar shape to cumin, and this can be confusing in Malay where two of them have the name *jintan. Jintan putih* is cumin; *jintan manis* is fennel.

Curry leaves (*Murraya koenigii*)   Curry leaves are widely used in Indian cooking. It is far better to use them fresh rather than dry as the latter have very little flavor. Bunches of fresh curry leaves are usually available in Indian grocery stores.

Daikon   *See* Chinese turnip.

Daun salam   *See* salam leaves.

Dill (*Anethum graveolens*)   The dill of the Mediterranean is used as a vegetable in Lao food and as a garnish in Vietnamese.

Dried shrimp   Very small shrimp that have been dried in the sun. They are usually soaked and ground or pounded finely before added to a dish to give depth of flavor. Always test for saltiness before grinding as some kinds are much more salty than others and may need to be soaked and rinsed to tone them down a little. Buy dried shrimp in packets from any Asian grocery store.

Dried squid   Whole squid dried to parchment consistency, which is sometimes used to flavor rich stocks for Chinese steamboat cooking.

Dried "tamarind"   Slices often used in Malay and Indonesian wet or clear dishes to provide the sour taste achieved in other dishes through the use of tamarind fruits, pulp or water (purée). The fruit used is not tamarind at all, but garcinia, the fruit called *madan* in Thai and used fresh in Thai food.

Eggplant (*Solanum* spp.)   Many kinds of eggplant are used in Southeast Asian food, particularly in Thai food. They vary greatly in size, color and shape and I have only listed some of them and their uses.

- **Pea eggplant** (*Solanum torvum*) grows in clusters and looks like green peas. This is a favorite in some curries. Some are very bitter.
- **Golf-ball** or **apple eggplant** (*Solanum melongena*) is white, green and purple (in Indonesia), and is used raw in salads, with other raw vegetables accompanied by chili sauces, or quartered in stews.
- **Sour orange** or **yellow hairy eggplant** (*Solanum ferox, S. stramonifolium*), also the size of a golf-ball, used sometimes in pounded relishes for its sour contribution. The hairs are rubbed off before use.
- **Cigar-shaped** or **long thin purple eggplant** (*Solanum melongena*), used in stir-fries or soups.
- **Long green eggplant** remains dry when grilled. Used grilled in a Thai tossed salad or sliced thinly lengthwise, coated with egg and fried. Outside Southeast Asia long purple eggplant may have to be used instead even though it is wetter than the green one.

Eryngo or **long-leafed coriander** (*Eryngium foetidum*) A long, club-shaped green leaf with a serrated edge, eryngo has a flavor reminiscent of coriander but sharper (hence one name "foreign coriander" in Thai). It is used in soups in Vietnam and Cambodia, and raw as an accompaniment to dressed meat or fish in northeastern Thailand and Laos.

Fennel seed (*Foeniculum vulgare*)   This seed is the true Malay *jintan manis*, though *manis* is sometimes translated into English as anise. Fennel is larger, softer and sweeter than anise, but the two are botanically related and are very close in flavor. *Jintan manis* usually accompanies ordinary cumin in Malay curries.

Fenugreek (*Trigonella foenum-graecum*)   Yellowish, small and oblong in shape, this seed is used in small quantities in some Indian curries and pickles.

Fermented soy beans   *See* Soy bean paste, yellow or brown.

Fish-cheek mint (*Houttuynia cordata*)   A perennial herb with heart-shaped leaves and a fishy flavor. It is eaten raw in a salad plate in Vietnam and Cambodia, or as a raw herb vegetable in Thailand.

Fish sauce   A thin, salty sauce fermented from fish and used in Thai and Vietnamese food. It resembles light soy sauce, which can be substituted by vegetarians. Fish sauce is now readily available at well-stocked supermarkets. There are many different brands available, some made in Thailand, some in Vietnam, some even in Singapore. Quality and saltiness may vary between brands, so be prepared to judge by taste as much as by quantities given here. All measurements for quantities of fish sauce in this book are based on the use of a common brand of fish sauce manufactured in Thailand.

Five-spice powder   A ground mixture of star anise, cloves, cinnamon, fennel seeds and Sichuan pepper. Sold in Chinese and Asian grocery stores, it is used to flavor meat in Chinese cuisine. Buy in small quantities to prevent loss of flavor or make your own by grinding the following ingredients together.

> 2 teaspoons star anise
> 2 teaspoons fennel seeds
> 2 teaspoons Sichuan pepper
> 1 teaspoon cloves
> 1 teaspoon cinnamon

Fried onion flakes   A very common garnish used all over Southeast Asia. Thin slices of small Asian red onions or shallots cut lengthwise are deep-fried in oil until they are light brown (pp. 20–21).

Prepared crispy fried onion flakes are available in packets in Asian grocery stores.

Galangal (*Languas galanga* syn. *Alpinia galanga*)   Galangal is one of the characteristic flavorings used throughout Southeast Asia. It is a rhizome with cream-colored flesh and pink lines in the skin with pink emerging shoots when young. The pink bits turn brown after it is kept for a while. A member of the ginger family, galangal possesses a distinct flavor.

Galangal is often available fresh or frozen from Asian grocery stores with a Southeast Asian bias, or you can find it sliced in jars in brine or dried. The pickled slices are acceptable if they are rinsed first. Soak the dried slices in warm water for half an hour before using. When you slice fresh galangal, do so on the diagonal so that you end up with a long slice about ⅛ in (3 mm) thick.

Garam masala   Not a curry powder but an aromatic blend of spices added to Indian food near the end of cooking or sprinkled on after cooking. You can buy garam masala in many well-stocked supermarkets or your can make your own from the following ingredients:

> 3 cinnamon sticks
> 4 tablespoons coriander seeds
> 2 tablespoons cumin seeds
> 1 tablespoon black peppercorns
> 1 tablespoon cloves
> 1 tablespoon cardamom pods
> 1 whole nutmeg or 1 ½ teaspoons ground nutmeg

Break the cinnamon sticks into pieces. In a dry pan roast the coriander, cumin, peppercorns and cloves separately until fragrant and set aside to cool. Remove the seeds from the cardamom pods and smash or chop the nutmeg into small pieces. Grind the nutmeg to a powder in an electric grinder, add all the other spices and grind to a fine powder. Store in an airtight jar or container, but do not keep more than three months.

Garlic (*Allium sativum*)   The garlic grown and used in Southeast Asia is much smaller and more potent than the medium-sized European variety but the latter will do if you cannot get small-cloved garlic. Just adjust the number of cloves as necessary according to their size. For pickled garlic in Thailand whole heads of local garlic are used, but if you pickle your own remember that the Thai garlic heads are small, often containing only about four or five cloves.

To chop garlic, smash a clove with the side of a knife to loosen the skin so that you can peel it off easily, then chop it with the sharp edge. This method gives more aromatic results than using a garlic press.
It should be enough simply to slice peeled garlic cloves before adding them to a spice paste for grinding.

Ghee   This is clarified butter and it is available from Asian grocery stores.

Ginger (*Zingiber officinale*)   The root of the ginger plant, which is of Indian or Chinese origin. For cooking it must always be fresh (not ground) and young. Ginger used for cooking in Asia is always tender and juicy, while the roots we buy are comparatively old and fibrous. When I speak of a slice of fresh ginger in this book I mean a diagonal cut about 2 in (5 cm) long and ⅛ in (3 mm) thick.

Always peel fresh ginger before using it in Spice Paste.

Glutinous or sticky rice   A variety of rice that coagulates when cooking. It is the staple in northeast Thailand and Laos, and is also eaten in North Vietnam. It is cooked differently from ordinary rice—see p. 15 for instructions. A black variety is used in sweets in Indonesia.

Green gram (*Phaseolus aureus* syn. *Vigna radiata* var. *radiata*)   This is dried mung-bean. Used for many things throughout Southeast Asia: to make bean sprouts, flour, Chinese vermicelli, sweets and puddings, cooked as lentils, and so on.

Green papaya (*Carica papaya*)   The fruit of the papaya when very green and still hard is used as a vegetable in Thailand. Peel and slice it thinly for Chili Sauce or peel and shred it for the northeastern salad, Pounded Green Eggplant. To shred it, hold the peeled papaya in the palm of one hand and use a chopping action with a heavy knife to make many fine cuts through almost to the center on the uppermost surface. Sit the papaya upright on its base on a cutting board and slice finely downwards. The papaya should fall away in fine shreds in the area you have treated. Turn the whole fruit around 45 degrees in your palm and repeat, continuing in this fashion until you have enough shreds. Use the same process to shred green mango.

Japanese radish   *See* Chinese turnip.

Javanese soy sauce   *See* Soy sauce.

Jelly mushroom   *See* Cloud-ear mushroom.

Kaffir lime (*Citrus hystrix*)   Sometimes called "wild lime," this is a large lime with a warty skin. The leaves and the skin are used frequently in Thai cooking and occasionally in Indonesian. The fruit itself is not very juicy and is seldom used. The leaves occur as two on a single petiole, but unless otherwise stated "1 kaffir lime leaf" in the recipes in this book refers to a single leaf.

A plant will grow quite well in a good-sized pot indoors and outside in the summer in temperate climates. Water only once a week when in-doors but quite often when outside.

Kaffir lime is usually available in the following forms from Asian grocery stores with a Thai or Southeast Asian bias:

- **Fresh leaves** are sometimes available in plastic bags; if not there will almost certainly be dried ones that you can reconstitute in warm water as you need them. The fresh leaves are always preferable.
- **Lime skin** for use in curry pastes, is sometimes available as whole fruits. Pare off thin slices of the skin with a minimum of pith and chop them finely or finely grate the skin without pith to create zest. Lime skin is also available in jars as thick strips pickled in brine. This is easy to chop and also acceptable.

Lemongrass (*Cymbopogon citratus*) Lemongrass is a perennial herb native to India. The thin fibrous stalks are bruised to release their flavor and then knotted or cut into lengths before they are added to soups and stews. Use only the more tender white part unless otherwise directed, first cutting off the hard root end. Do not throw out the leftover tough green leafy part, however, as it makes a most refreshing and fragrant tea.

To grow your own lemongrass, soak the lower half of a stalk in about 4 in (10 cm) of water, changing the water every day, until the stalk develops roots, then plant it in a pot or in your garden. Once established, lemongrass multiplies easily in most places in the summer months. During the winter in frosty areas it can be lifted out of the ground, potted and kept alive indoors, but it will also survive and grow again in the spring if you cut off about one-third of the top of the plant and let it die off.

Lentils (*dal*) are used extensively in Indian cooking, especially in southern Indian cooking, which is predominantly vegetarian, where they are valued for their high protein content. There are many types of lentils. The most common are the small split green lentils (*mung dal*), tan split lentils (*toor* or *thuvar dal*), brighter yellow split lentils (*channa dal*) and red Egyptian lentils (*masoor dal*).

Lily buds Dried, these have a musky flavor and are used as a vegetable in Chinese food after soaking. They are available from Chinese groceries.

Limes Indigenous to Southeast Asia, the smooth green lime is frequently used as a flavoring in food and in fresh drinks. It is thinner-skinned, juicier and more fragrant than lemon, but you can use lemon if you have to. Two kinds of lime are used in Malay food: *limau nipis* (*Citrus aurantifolia*), the conventional one that is only a little smaller than a lemon and may be substituted with lemon; and the small round *limau kesturi* (*Citrus microcarpa*), whose juice tastes more like a mixture of lemon and orange juice.

To cut lime wedges attractively for an accompaniment or garnish, slice off a section just short of the pithy center to achieve an attractive round that is free of white pith. Cut the remaining piece into two wedges through the pithy center and trim off the white pith in a single clean slice. Pile the two trimmed wedges and the round piece of lime together on the edge of the dish to be served.

Long-leafed coriander *See* Eryngo.

Lotus stems (*Nelumbium nelumbo*) Lightly pickled young stems of the lotus plant are used in Vietnamese salads as a green. Canned lotus stems are available in Asian grocery stores. In shops with Vietnamese or Lao proprietors, freshly pickled lotus stems packed in plastic bags are sometimes available in summer.

Mace (*Myristica fragrans*) This is the dried aril (net) that grows around the nutmeg seed.

Maggi Seasoning Sauce This is an extremely versatile sauce with a distinctive flavor and aroma, used frequently in Thai cooking. It is made with pure vegetable protein and without any preservatives. A few dashes add zest and depth to soups, salads, and vegetables and it makes an excellent sauce for marinating, stir-frying, and dipping.

Mint (*Mentha* spp.) Various mints are used in Southeast Asia although they are usually not what are called "mint" in English by the Vietnamese. The latter are not true mints but fresh leaves of a large number of different herbs and leaves that are eaten raw in herb salad plates as an accompaniment to cooked food.

Mung-beans *See* Green gram.

Mung-bean vermicelli *See* Noodles.

Mustard seed The small dark variety called black or brown mustard seed is often used in south Indian and Sri Lankan cooking. The whole seeds are usually dry-fried before they are ground for curry powder or fried and roughly broken before added as a finishing flavor.

Noodles Many different kinds of noodles are used in Southeast Asia. Recipes in this book for dishes containing noodles usually specify which kind and how to prepare them. The most common dried noodles follow.

- **Fine rice vermicelli**–Rinse or soak in cold water until soft, drain, and dunk for 2–3 minutes in soup stock or boiling water using a strainer. If you plan to keep them aside for later use, rinse them again under cold water to stop them sticking together and drain well.
- **Narrow rice noodles**–These are about ¼ in (5 mm) wide and are called "rice sticks." Soak in cold water for about 20–30 minutes until soft and boil for 1 minute or stir-fry in oil with other ingredients.
- **Dried egg or wheat noodles**–These "Long Life" noodles should be cooked as directed on the package.
- **Mung-bean vermicelli or mung-bean noodles**–A thin, wiry thread-like noodle also known as cellophane noodles or glass noodles because of their transparency. Soak in warm water for 5 minutes or until soft and cut into 2-in (5-cm) lengths before using.

The following noodles are sometimes available fresh in well-stocked supermarkets or Asian grocery stores.

- **Fresh narrow rice sticks** (*Thai sen lek*). About ¼ in (5 mm) wide, cook as directed in the recipe.
- **Wide flat rice noodles** (*sen yai* in Thailand, *kwei tiao* in Singapore, *kway teow* in Malaysia). To make these buy a package of folded flat, uncut noodle sheet and cut across into strips of about 1 in (2–3 cm). Pull them out straight, rinse and separate. Drain well and cut each one across again into lengths of about 3 in (8 cm) for cooking. Cook as directed in the recipe.
- **Egg noodles** (*mee* in Malaysia, *ba mi* in Thailand, *bakmi* in Indonesia) Made from wheat flour and eggs and yellow in color, these noodles are sold in round "cakes," which need to be shaken loose before cooking. Cook them in boiling water as directed on the package.

Other fresh noodles, not so readily found outside Singapore or Malaysia, are *laksa* noodles, round rice noodles about the size of spaghetti. Coarse rice vermicelli can be sustituted instead.

Rice noodles are the noodles predominantly used in indigenous dishes in the rice-eating countries of Thailand, Laos and Vietnam.

Nutmeg (*Myristica fragrans*)   This spice is so well known that it needs no comment, except to say that a whole nutmeg grated when needed produces a better flavor than ground nutmeg.

Oil   For health reasons it is a good idea to substitute vegetable oils for the traditional fats used for cooking in different parts of Southeast Asia. Be careful though not to introduce strong flavors—olive oil, for instance, is not appropriate. Some people advocate canola as the healthiest alternative, but I find it a little thick, if suitably tasteless. I prefer something less thick such as safflower or sunflower oil.

Oyster sauce   A thick oyster-flavored sauce used in many Chinese-style stir-fries.

Palm sugar   A rich, distinctively aromatic sugar made by tapping and boiling the juice of the sugar palm (*Arenga pinnata*). Thai palm sugar is much lighter and more refined than the Malay or Indonesian *gula Malacca* or *gula Djawa*. The latter is richer in flavor, and therefore is the type I prefer to use in sweets. Subtitute dark brown sugar for palm sugar.

Pandan leaf (*Pandanus odorus*)   Also known as screwpine leaves, these are the fragrant leaves of a small pandanus used for their distinct flavor and sometimes for their green color in cooking (largely desserts) in Thailand, Malaysia and Indonesia. They are also the ingredient that gives Ceylon curry powder its unique perfume and flavor. When adding pandan leaves tie them in a knot to hold them together.

Peanuts   Many dishes in this book call for the use of fried or roasted peanuts—coarsely chopped or crushed and used in sauces or as a flavor addition in cooking, sprinkled over salads and dipping sauces, with ginger, red onions and pieces of lime as a side salad accompanying some one-dish meals. Roasted peanuts may be bought in health food shops or raw peanuts may be deep-fried in plenty of hot oil until they are light brown. If you are frying your own, cook them briefly as they will go on cooking after you remove them from the oil. Note that it is best to buy small raw peanuts in their brown skins so that only the skins will get scorched as you fry them. After deep-frying set them aside to cool and rub the skins off between the palms of your hands. Make sure they are completely cold and crunchy before you start to crush them, leaving the pieces big enough to retain some texture.

Pepper (*Piper nigrum*)   White peppercorns are the ones most commonly used in Southeast Asian food. If possible, they should be freshly ground. Another form of pepper, long pepper (*Piper retrofractum*), in which minute fruits grow in a spike about 3–5 cm (1½–2 in), grows wild in the area and is dried and used in Thailand, Malaysia and Indonesia.

Pork skin   This is treated in various ways to add texture and interest to food in the Buddhist countries of mainland Southeast Asia. Important pork-skin products are as follows.
- Boiled shredded pork skin, in which just the rind is boiled until white then shredded very finely into strips about 1½ in (4 cm) long. This is added to savory relishes and some dressed dishes to provide a chewy texture.
- Fried pork skin or pork cracklings with some of the fat attached, used as an accompaniment to northern Chili Sauce (*nam phrik*).

Pumpkin shoots   The youngest and most tender tips of the leaves on pumpkin vines are very successfully used in vegetable stews in north Thailand, Laos and Cambodia. The leaves are rolled in the palms of the hands to remove the hairs before they are added to the dish.

Resurrection lily (*Kaempferia galanga*)   This tuber (*kencur* in Indonesia, *kuncor* in Malaysia, *prohom* in Thailand) looks a bit like ginger but is white inside and has a darker skin. Resurrection lily has a very strong medicinal flavor and is used sparingly in only a few dishes. It is available from Asian grocery stores in dried slices or as powder.

Rice papers   Round white dried crêpes used in Vietnamese food. Sold in clear packets in some well-stocked supermarkets and in Asian grocery stores, they are distinguishable by the lattice pattern they reveal from having been dried in the sun on bamboo trays.

Salam leaves (*Eugenia polyantha*)   A leaf about the size and shape of a bay leaf and used in Indonesian cooking. Available dried in packets from Asian grocery stores, but the dried variety has little flavor. You can, if you must, substitute either fresh curry leaves or bay leaves, but they do not produce the same flavor.

Sesame seed (*Sesamum indicum*)   Roasted sesame seed is sometimes sprinkled over cooked food and indigenous cakes for added flavor, particularly in Laos and Bali. The seed is usually unhulled and quite dark in color.

Shallots (*Allium cepa var. aggregatum*) In Southeast Asian food small red onions are the onions mostly used, not large brown or red (Spanish) onions. Small red onions are drier, more concentrated in flavor and easier to slice and grind than the larger brown or Spanish ones. The dry-skinned shallots that are available here, though slightly bigger than the red onions of Southeast Asia, are the best substitute. If you can, use red shallots, rather than the more common brown (or golden) ones, as they have the dry quality required in Asian cooking. At the end of the season, just before new planting time, these will have become quite distinctly segmented into red-skinned cloves ready to shoot and regrow if planted again.

Red shallots are usually stocked in Asian grocery stores and sometimes the produce sections of well-stocked supermarkets. If you have to use onion as a substitute, use the red Spanish one. The equivalent of one small Spanish onion is 4–6 whole plump shallots. Be careful when you make this substitution, though, for spice pastes that include too much of the large, juicier onions will stew when you try to fry them until fragrant. Try to squeeze off some of the water before you start.

Sometimes I refer to "segments of shallot" in the recipes. These are the dry-skinned cloves that the older red shallots will be made up of at the end of the season.

I also refer to green shallots, which are sometimes called French shallots. These are also a member of the same *Allium cepa* var. *aggregatum* group as the above, and are not to be confused with green onions. They have clump-shaped small white bulbs and green leaves that are separate, hollow and finer than green onions, the latter in their common salad form being straight and even in shape with a composite leaf most of the way up. Green shallots are not always easily available, but may be found in larger produce markets or large Asian grocery stores.

Shrimp paste A basic flavoring made from shrimp that has been salted, dried, ground, rotted, and then formed into cakes. It can be pink, soft and mushy, or darker in color and dry. In one form or the other it is usually available in packets or jars. Once opened it should be transferred to a jar or plastic container with a tight-fitting lid and kept in the refrigerator.

Shrimp paste should always be roasted or fried before it is eaten. If the recipe you are cooking involves frying all the spices, just add it as one of them. If you are not frying the spices, however, wrap the shrimp paste in foil and roast it in a dry pan on top of the stove for a minute or two, or put it in a microwave oven in a small container covered with plastic for a minute. Remove the shrimp paste from the wrapper or container (which will have prevented the smell from penetrating the house) and grind it with the other spices. 1 teaspoon of shrimp paste equals a slice of hard shrimp paste about ¼ in (½ cm) thick.

You can buy the kind of shrimp paste used in these recipes in the following forms in Asian grocery stores:

- in a block labelled either *belacan* or *terasi* (the Malay or Indonesian versions respectively)
- in a plastic container as *kapi* (Thai)
- in a glass jar from Hong Kong called, in English, "fine shrimp sauce" or "refined shrimp paste."

It really doesn't matter which variety you use, although *terasi* and *kapi* are more appropriate for cooking Thai, Malaysian and Indonesian food, while fine shrimp sauce is better for Vietnamese food. In Vietnam, the practice is to dilute and strain a much coarser original mixture called *mam tom*, making the pink refined shrimp paste from Hong Kong more appropriate.

Snakebean, longbean, cowpea or **yard-long bean** (*Vigna sesquipedalis*, V. *unguiculata*) These, rather than the European bean are used as a green bean in Southeast Asia. Often available from vegetable markets, greengrocers and Asian food shops but usually expensive, snakebeans may be replaced by stringless green beans.

Soy bean paste, yellow or brown Fermented soy beans sold in jars or bottles. They are mashed slightly before using.

Soy sauce The following is a breakdown of the different kinds of soy sauce used in this book.

- **Light soy sauce** and **dark soy sauce** (which is thicker and heavier than the former and is described as containing "caramel") are both well known and readily available in well-stocked supermarkets.
- **Javanese soy sauce** is sweet and very thick, called *kecap manis*, or *kecap benteng*, and usually available from Asian grocery stores. If you cannot buy it you can make your own with the following recipe.

1 cup (250 ml) dark soy sauce
¼ –½ cup (75–125 ml) molasses
4 tablespoons dark brown sugar

Combine all the ingredients in a small saucepan over medium heat. Cook and stir until the sugar melts. Store in a covered jar.

Alternatively you can simply use dark soy sauce and palm or dark brown sugar.

- **"Seasoning sauce"** is a light sauce with a soy sauce base combined with other things. It is frequently used in Vietnamese cooking.
- **Japanese soy sauce** is a light soy sauce with a maltier and more "brewed" flavor than the Chinese version. It is used in some Thai fish dishes.

Star anise A dried spice which both looks and tastes as it sounds. Imagine a brown dried apple core cut into a cross section with seeds. This is just what star anise looks like only it is larger. A "point" of star anise includes both seed case and seed.

Tamarind (*Tamarindus indica*) A fibrous pod used in curries and soups for its acidic effect. Tomatoes, lemon juice or vinegar will often do as well. Tamarind is available in Asian grocery stores in a variety of forms.

- Whole green tamarind pods (especially in shops with a Vietnamese bias). Cook in boiling water or soup for 5–10 minutes until soft. Remove, mash them in a bowl with some hot liquid added, strain through a sieve and return the liquid back to the water or soup.
- Ripe tamarind pulp is available in all Asian grocery stores, usually containing some seeds but no fiber. It is used to make tamarind water (see separate entry below).
- Tamarind concentrate is available in plastic containers, exported from Thailand. Already processed, this purée varies in strength, so if you use this instead of tamarind water, adjust the quantity to taste.
- Tamarind soup base is available in instant packets and often used as a base for Southeast Asian tamarind-flavored soups. This is an acceptable substitute if you are in a hurry but the flavors are not really specific enough for the connoisseur interested in local variations in flavor.

Tamarind water To make your own, soak 1 walnut-sized piece of tamarind pulp (with seeds) in ½ cup (125 ml) of hot water, or 3 tablespoons tamarind pulp in 1 cup (250 ml) of water, until soft. Squeeze the pulp repeatedly with your fingers to dissolve it, and then pour everything into a strainer, forcing the liquid through with a spoon. Discard the fibrous material and reserve the thick liquid.

Taro stalks (*Colocasia esculenta*) These are favored as a vegetable in Vietnamese sour fish soups. Known as *bac ha* in Vietnamese, they are usually available fresh in Vietnamese food stores.

Tempeh   This is a solid cake made from fermented soy beans. It is high in protein and is much valued in Java where it is commonly used instead of meat or to help a little meat go a long way. It is available fresh in many well-stocked supermarkets and in Asian grocery stores with an Indonesian or Malay bias. The best tempeh comes in a flat cake that has a white skin similar to that on a camembert cheese. Tempeh is delicious when fried crisp.

Terasi   *See* Shrimp paste.

Tuong   This is a Vietnamese brown soy bean paste that is not salty. It is not to be confused with the too-salty Chinese yellow or brown soy bean paste.

Tofu   Fresh tofu comes in two main forms.
1. A very soft, white unsalted variety, which is cut into cubes and used in soups and Japanese food.
2. A firm, white unsalted variety, which is cut into triangles or blocks and deep-fried. This is a favorite ingredient in Indonesian and Malay salads. Ready-fried cakes about 2-in (5-cm) square are often sold in Asian grocery stores.

A harder, cheesy, compressed and salted version of the latter is also available, which is sometimes (though not always) colored yellow on the outside. This tends to be the one that Thais cut into small dice, fry and then add to fried rice or noodle dishes, or that Malays add to Stuffed Pancake Rolls (p. 269).

All the varieties of fresh tofu come in blocks or cakes and may be kept in the refrigerator for a few days after opening. The soft ones produce whey and the water needs to be changed daily.

Tofu is a common meat substitute and may always be used in its stead in curries and soups.

Dried tofu, used in Chinese cooking, comes in sheets or twists.

Turmeric (*Curcuma domestica*)   A fleshy rhizome used fresh and frozen in curry pastes. Used largely for its color, it is brownish and scaly on the outside and bright orange inside. Often available fresh in Asian food stores but is also available dried and powdered, though the latter has a slightly sour, stale flavor. A (¾–1½-in (2–3-cm) piece of turmeric is equivalent to 1 tablespoon chopped fresh turmeric or ⅓ teaspoon ground turmeric.

Vietnamese mint (*Polygonum* spp.)   Also known as knotweed. This slightly variegated leaf from an erect, creeping plant is used widely. It has a flavor reminiscent of coriander though possessing a slight sharpness, and is eaten raw as an accompaniment to dressed meat (*lap)* or with Chili Sauce (*nam phrik*) in Thailand and Laos, in herb salad plates or mixed into salads in Vietnam (*rau ram*) and Cambodia (*sang hom*), and as a garnish in Malaysia (*daun kesum*). It is available fresh in Asian grocery stores with a Vietnamese bias and often in small pots in nurseries in spring. It grows easily in the garden.

Vinegar   The vinegar used in Southeast Asia is made most often either from rice or coconut water. Its strength is hard to predict in the abstract as it is still homemade in many places, particularly in the less industrialized north. Store-bought rice vinegar and the white wine or spirit vinegars commonly available in the West are often stronger than local or homemade Asian vinegars, and I have sometimes (for example, in Vietnamese salads) recommended dilution to make up for this. The nicest vinegar used in Indonesia, Malaysia and southern Thailand is the one made from coconut. One of the softest of these that is available in Asian food shops in the West, and the one I like best, is a slightly cloudy one from the Philippines reduced to 4 percent acidity.

Water chestnut   A Chinese vegetable notable for its crisp texture. It is available in cans in most well-stocked supermarkets and in Asian grocery stores.

Water spinach (*Ipomoea aquatica*)   A water plant with hollow stems and arrow-shaped leaves much used as a vegetable in soups, stir-fries and salads across the region. Called *kangkung* in Malaysia and Indonesia, *phak bung* in Thailand and Laos, and *rau muong* in Vietnam.

Yambean (*Pachyrrhizus erosus*)   Crunchy tubers that look like a lobed white turnip and taste something like a cross between a mild turnip and a radish. Yambean is eaten raw with chili mixtures or in salads with a sweet sauce (Indonesian or Malay *rujak*). It is native to tropical America where it is known as jicama.

Chart of Ingredients

	BOTANICAL NAME	INDONESIAN	MALAY
agar-agar	—	agar-agar	agar-agar
amaranth	*Amaranthus* spp.	bayam	bayam
anchovy	—	ikan teri	ikan bilis
anise	*Pimpinella anisum*	adas manis	jintan manis
bamboo shoots	*Bambusa* spp.	rebung	rebung
basil	*Ocimum* spp.	—	—
Asian sweet, cinnamon	*O. basilicum*	—	daun selaseh
holy	*O. sanctum*	surawung	—
lemon or hoary	*O. canum, O. citriadorum,* *O. basilicum* var. *citratum*	daun kemangi	daun kemangi
bean curd	—	tahu	tahu
bean sprouts	*Phaseolus aureus*	tauge	taugeh
betel leaves	*Piper sarmentosum*	—	daun kaduk
candlenut	*Aleurites moluccana*	kemiri	buah keras
cardamom	*Elettaria cardamomum*	kapulaga	buah pelaga
celery, Asian or Chinese	*Apium odorum*	selederi	selderi
chilies	*Capsicum frutescens, C. annuum*	cabai, lombok	cili, cabai
bird's eye	—	cabai rawit	cili padi
medium length, 10–15 cm (4–6 in)	—	cabai merah	cili merah
Chinese broccoli (kale)	*Brassica oleracea* var. *acephala*	kol	kai lan
Chinese cabbage	—	—	—
bitter or broad-leafed mustard	*B. juncea* var. *rugosa*	sawi hijau asinan	kai choy
celery or pe-tsai	*B. chinensis* var. *pekinensis*	sawi puteh, pecai	sawi puteh
flowering or choy sum	*B. chinensis* var. *rosularis*	—	choy sum
mustard greens	*B. juncea*	cai sin	sawi
white or bok choy	*B. chinensis*	sawi hijau	bok choy
Chinese flowers *See* dried lily buds			
Chinese keys (rhizome)	*Boesenbergia pandurata* syn. *Kaempferia*	kunci	—
Chinese leeks (Chinese chives)	*Allium tuberosum*	kucai	kucai
Chinese turnip (Japanese radish, daikon)	*Raphanus sativus* var.	lobak	lobak
cinnamon (cassia)	*Cinnamomum* spp.	kayu manis	kayu manis
cloves	*Eugenia caryophyllus*	cengkih	cengkih
coconut	*Cocos nucifera*	kelapa	kelapa
juice or water	—	air kelapa	air kelapa
milk	—	santan	santan

THAI	LAO	KHMER	VIETNAMESE
—	—	chahoy	—
phak khom	phak houm	phti	rau den
—	padek	—	ca chay
yira	—	—	—
no mai	no mai	tumpang	mang
—	—	—	—
horapha	phak i tou	chi neangvong	rau que
kaphrao	i tou thai	—	—
maenglak	hom hor	—	—
tao hu	tao hou khao	taohou	tau hu
thua ngok	mak thoua ngok	sandaek bandoh	gia
bai cha phlu	bai som phou	chaphlou	la lot
—	met nam man	—	—
krawan	ken ka wan	kravaan	—
phak chi lom	phak sen leu ri	khinchhay	can
phrik	mak phet	mteh	ot
phrik khi nu	mak phet noi	mteh kmang	—
—	mak phet ngai	mteh kraachaak neang	—
phak khana	phak khana	khatna	—
—	—	—	—
phak kat khiao	phak kat meo	spey chœung tie	rau cai
phak kat khao	phak kat khao	spey kdaop	cai lam kim chi
phak kwang tung do	phak kat som	spey khiev muul	cai ngot bong
phak kwang tung khiao	phak kat khieo	spey chœung tie	cai xanh
phak kwang tung	phak kat khao	spey saa	cai be trang
krachai	—	kcheay	—
bai kuchai	phak pen	kuu chaay	ne
phak khi hut	hua phak kat	they thav	cu cai trang
ob choei	khe	—	que
kram plu	kan phou	phkar khhampou	—
maphrao	mak phao	doong	dua
nam maphrao	nam mak phao	tik doong	nuoc dua
nam kathi	hoa kathi	ktih doong	nuoc cot dua

	BOTANICAL NAME	INDONESIAN	MALAY
coriander (cilantro)	*Coriandrum sativum*	ketumbar	ketumbar
coriander, long-leafed *See* eryngo			
country fish paste	—	—	—
cumin seed	*Cuminum cyminum*	jintan putih	jintan putih
curry leaves	*Murraya koenigii*	—	daun kari
dill	*Anethum graveolens*	adas	—
dried lily buds (golden needles)	*Hemerocallis* spp.	—	bunga pisang
dried tamarind	*Garcinia* spp.	asam gelugor	asam gelugor
eggplant (aubergine)	*Solanum* spp.	terung	terung
pea	*S. torvum*	takokak	terung pipit puteh
golf-ball or apple	*S. melongena*	terung lalap	terung
sour hairy	*S. ferox, S. stramonifolium*	—	terung asam
cigar-shaped purple	*S. melongena*	terung	terung
long green	*S. melongena*	—	—
eryngo	*Eryngium foetidum*	—	—
eugenia *See* salam leaves			
fennel seed	*Foeniculum vulgare*	adas pedas	jintan manis
fenugreek	*Trigonella foenum-graecum*	—	halba
fish-cheek mint	*Houttuynia cordata*	—	—
fish sauce	—	—	—
five-spice powder	—	—	serbuk lima rempah
galangal	*Languas galanga* syn. *Alpinia galanga*	laos	lengkuas
garlic	*Allium sativum*	bawang putih	bawang putih
ginger, fresh	*Zingiber officinale*	jahe	halia
glutinous rice	*Oryza sativa* var.	ketan	pulot
green gram, dried mung-bean	*Phaseolus aureus* syn. *Vigna radiata*	kacang hijau	kacang hijau
green onions (scallions)	*Allium* spp.	daun bawang	daun bawang
jointfir spinach	*Gnetum gnemon*	melinjo	meninjau
laos *See* galangal			
lemongrass	*Cymbopogon citratus*	serai	serai
limes	*Citrus aurantifolia*	jeruk nipis, limau nipis	limau nipis
kaffir	*C. hystrix*	jeruk purut	limau perut
musk	*C. microcarpa*	—	limau kesturi
mace	*Myristica fragrans*	bunga pala	bunga pala
mint	*Mentha* spp.	merdinah, kresnan	daun pudina
Japanese mint	*M. arvensis*	daun poko	—

THAI	LAO	KHMER	VIETNAMESE
phak chi	phak hom pop	van suy	ngo
pla ra	padek	prahoc	mam nem
met yira	met nyi la	kroap m'aam	—
bai kari	khi be	—	—
—	phak xi	—	thi la
dok mai jin	—	pkaa chek	kim cham
madan, som mawon	som phor di	sandan	—
makhua	mak kheua	trap	ca
makhua phuang	mak kheua khom	trap put gnaong	ca phao
makhua pro	mak kheua pom	trap srouy	ca bat
ma-uk	mak kheng saphao	trap room	—
—	mak kheua ham ma	trap sandaay	ca dai de
makhua yao	—	—	—
phak chi farang, laaw	phak hom nhan	chi rona	ngo gai
—	—	—	—
—	—	—	—
phak khao tong	phak khao tong	chi trey	rau dap ca
nam pla	nam pa	toeuk trey	nuoc mam
—	—	—	bot ngu vi huong
kha	kha ta deng	romdeng	rieng
krathiem	ka thiem	ktim saa	toi
khing	khing	khgney	gung
khao niao	khao niao	angkaa damnap	gao nep
thua khiao	mak thoua khiao	sandaek baay	dau xanh
ton hom	phak boua	ktim slek	hanh tuoi
pisae	—	—	—
takrai	houa si khai	slœuk krey	xa
manao	mak nao	krooc cmaa	chanh
makrut	mak khi hout	krooc sœuc	—
—	—	—	—
—	chan thet	—	—
bai sarana	phak horm	chi mahao	rau thom
—	phak sa ra ne	chi angkam	—

	BOTANICAL NAME	INDONESIAN	MALAY
mushrooms	—	jamur	cendawan
Chinese dried mushroom or shiitake	*Lentinus* spp.	—	—
cloud-ear or wood-ear mushroom	*Auricularia* spp.	kuping tikus	—
straw mushroom	*Volvariella* spp.	jamur	cendawan
mustard seeds	*Brassica nigra*	—	biji sawi
neem tree, young leaves	*Azadirachta indica*	—	—
noodles	—	—	—
dried: egg or wheat (Long Life)	—	bakmi, mi	mee
fine rice vermicelli	—	mihun	beehoon
mung-bean vermicelli (cellophane)	—	sohun	so hoon
narrow rice (rice sticks)	—	—	beehoon
fresh: wide flat rice	—	kueh tiao	kway teow
nutmeg	*Myristica fragrans*	pala	buah pala
onions *See* shallots			
pandan leaves	*Pandanus odorus*	daun pandan	daun pandan
papaya (pawpaw)	*Carica papaya*	papaya	papaya
pennywort, Asian	*Centella asiatica*	pegagan	pegaga
pepper, white or black	*Piper nigrum*	lada, merica	lada
Javanese long	*P. retrofractum, P. longum*	cabai jawa	—
perilla	*Perilla* spp.	—	—
peteh (locust or stink bean)	*Parkia* spp.	petai, peteh	petai
resurrection lily	*Kaempferia galanga*	kencur	cekur
salam leaves	*Eugenia polyantha*	daun salam	—
scarlet vine	*Coccinea grandis*	—	—
sesame seeds	*Sesamum indicum*	bijan	bijan
shallots	*Allium cepa*	bawang merah	bawang merah
shrimp paste	—	terasi	belacan
shrimps, dried	—	ebi	udang kering
snakebean (yard-long bean, cowpea)	*Vigna sesquipedalis, V. unguiculata*	kacang tunggak, kacang panjang	kacang panjang
soy bean paste, yellow or brown (fermented soy beans)	—	tauco	tauco
soy sauce	—	kecap	kecap
sweet	—	kecap manis, benteng	—

THAI	LAO	KHMER	VIETNAMESE
het	het	pset	nam
het hom	het hom	pset kriem	nam
het hu nu	het hu nu	pset trachiek kandao	nam meo
het fang	het fuang	pset chambœung	nam rom
—	—	—	—
phak sadao	phak ka dau	—	—
—	—	—	—
ba mi	mi leuang	mii	mi
sen mi	khao pun	banh hoi	banh hoi, bun tau
wun sen	sen lon	mii su	mienh
sen lek	sen pho haeng	kuy tiev	banh pho, bun, hu tieu
sen yai, kuai tiao	sen pho	kuy tiev kat	banh pho
chan thet	chan thet	—	—
toei hom	teui hom	slœuk toeuy	la dua
malako	mak houng	lhong	du du xanh
bua bok	phak nok	rom chang	rau ma
phrik thai	phik thai	mrĭc	tieu
phrik hang	—	—	—
—	phak meng kheng	—	rau tia to
sato	houa lon	—	—
proh hom	houa ka xai	prah	—
—	—	—	—
phak tamlung	phak tamlung	slœuk baah	—
met nga	met nga	lngor	me
hua hom	houa phak boua	ktĭm krahaam	hanh
kapi	kapi	kaapi	mam tom, mam ruoc
kung haeng	kung haeng	bangkia kriem	tom kho
thua fak yao	mak thoua niao	sandaek ku	dau dua
tao jiao	tao chiao haeng	sĭeng	tuong
si yu	sa iou	tĭk si iev	xi dau, nuoc tuong
si yu dam	—	tĭk si iev p'aem	—

	BOTANICAL NAME	INDONESIAN	MALAY
star anise	*Illicium verum*	bunga lawang	bunga lawang
star fruit (carambola)	*Averrhoa carambola*	belimbing	belimbing
small sour cooking variety	*A. bilimbi*	belimbing wuluh	belimbing buluh
tamarind	*Tamarindus indica*	asam jawa	asam
taro, elephant's ear: stem	*Colocasia esculenta*	tales	keladi
tempeh	—	tempé	tempe
tomato	*Lycopersicon esculentum*	tomat	tomato
turmeric	*Curcuma domestica*	kunyit	kunyit
Vietnamese mint (knotweed)	*Polygonum* spp.	—	daun kesum
water chestnut	*Eleocharis dulcis*	teki	sengkuang cina
water spinach (swamp cabbage)	*Ipomoea aquatica*	kangkung	kangkung
winged bean	*Psophocarpus tetragonolobus*	kecipir	kachang belimbing
yambean (jicama)	*Pachyrrhizus erosus*	bangkuang	sengkuang

THAI	LAO	KHMER	VIETNAMESE
poi kak bau	—	poch kak lavhav	canh hoi
mafuang	mak feuang	spœu	khe
—	mak ta li ping	—	—
makham	mak khame	ampil	me
phuak	bon, kok thoune	—	bac ha
—	—	—	—
makhua thet	mak len	peng pah	ca chua
khamin	khamin khune	romiet	nghe
phak phai	phak pai nam	sang hom	rau ram
haeo chin	hua heo	mœum plong	cu nang
phak bung	phak bung	trakoun	rau muong
thua phu	mak thoua phou	popiey	dau rong
man kaeo	man phao	pek kouk	cu dau

Indonesia

Happy Eating! *("Selamat makan!")* is the ritual toast at the beginning of a meal in Indonesia. Indonesian food, with its variety of taste and texture and an accompanying grace of presentation, has always made eating an event of great joy in that country. This is so, as Stamford Raffles observed, for the foreigner as much as for the family. In his *The History of Java*, published in 1817, he remarked:

> *By the custom of the country, good food and lodging are ordered to be provided for all strangers and travellers arriving at a village; and in no country are the rights of hospitality more strictly enjoined by institutions, or more conscientiously and religiously observed by custom and practice. 'It is not sufficient,' say the Javan institutions, 'that a man should place good food before his guest; he is bound to do more: he should render the meal palatable by kind words and treatment, to soothe him after his journey, and to make his heart glad while he partakes of the refreshment.' This is called bojo kromo, or real hospitality.*

That was nearly 200 years ago of course, and we may well not be able to attain this matchless ideal of *bojo kromo* in the fast and furious world of the present. We should, however, be able at least to approach it. All that is really needed to make a start in the direction of good Indonesian food is a little care on the part of the cook and some patience.

Interest in the outcome are the first qualification, and nothing will stimulate this more quickly than the tantalizing smells that issue from the cooking area as those marvellous spices begin to spatter in the pan.

The most important of these are hot chilies, two kinds in particular. The basic everyday variety, *cabai merah*, are fruit of medium but variable length and size, some claw-shaped, thin and hot, others finger-length, fatter and less hot. You may take your pick. The second group, *cabai rawit* or bird's eye chilies, are very small, erect, green or red in color and fiery. Bird's eye chilies are used whole in pickles or salads or added to some dishes either for extra "oomph" or as decoration. After the chilies come *terasi*, a fermented shrimp paste that contributes a characteristic and irreplaceable flavor; the galangal root, forgotten in the West since Roman and medieval times but still a basic spice throughout Southeast Asia; *daun salam*—the leaves of the plant *Eugenia polyantha*; lemongrass; turmeric (*kunyit*); small red onions or shallots (*bawang merah*); garlic (*bawang putih*); coriander and cumin (seeds only); candlenuts (*kemiri*); coconut milk; tamarind root; fresh lime juice; fresh ginger root;

lemon basil (*Ocimum canum*); and the leaves of kaffir lime (*jeruk purut*). Occurring in some recipes, too, are the dry spices—pepper, nutmeg, cloves, cinnamon and, sometimes, fennel. I have discussed all of these spices in the Ingredients chapter.

Indonesia is a country of great variety—in agriculture, in experience of and contact with the outside world, in social patterns, and in religious and cultural expression. It is nothing if not heterogeneous. At different periods of its history it has been influenced by India (both Hindu-Buddhist and Muslim), by Arab traders and scholars, by trading and immigrant Chinese, in some parts by the Portuguese, and by the Dutch. All these influences manifest themselves in some startlingly different ways in various parts of the country, and all of them are reflected in the food of different areas.

In recipes from Aceh and north Sumatra, for instance, where Islam first took root in the archipelago, Indian and Arab spices and the spices of trade predominate: ginger and pepper, coriander, cumin, cloves, cinnamon, cardamom and fennel. In west Sumatra and Minangkabau a prosperous agriculture has been accompanied by wealth accumulation through traditional out-trading activities on the part of its young men. This advantageous economic position combines with scholasticism and Islamic orthodoxy. Here food is prepared from raw materials in a rather austere fashion, with meat and fish dishes more common than in many other agricultural parts of the country.

Central Java, on the other hand, is a land of intensive rice agriculture, of deep tradition, of pomp and conspicuous consumption as well as of relative poverty, and the religion of the common people remains tinged with animism. Here there is a strong reliance on rich and artistic festival foods to add substance to the simple rice and vegetable-based fare of everyday. West Java, or Sunda, is perhaps the most interesting of all. This area has been close to the inland central Javanese world but has known in its past religious and economic affinity with parts of Sumatra. Sundanese cuisine combines both Javanese sophistication and lightness with Sumatran abundance and solidity.

Encompassing this variety, one can make the generalization that traditionally Indonesian food has been inclined to follow one of two tendencies. The first is the style of what a sociologist might call interior agricultural or agrarian societies; the second that of more outward-oriented trading and coastal ones. In the former, not only culinary but also social and economic influences that come from outside tend to be absorbed and modified in the light of local practice. They usually fail or prevail according to whether the tradition they encounter is in sympathy with them or not. Whichever happens, it is the local tradition that determines the course of events. In the tradelands, however, things tend to occur the other way around: outside influences in food as well as culture play a determining role.

In interior societies simple basic materials such as fresh spices prevail, sometimes arranged in a sophisticated fashion. Recipes from central Java, for instance, a classically interior society, use lots of sugar, which grows there. They also feature galangal, a root characteristic of the paddy areas of Southeast Asia, and *terasi*, a preserved and therefore accessible protein. It is interesting that these are important ingredients in Thai cooking as well, since Thailand can also be described as having a predominantly interior culture.

North Sumatrans are a good example of the second pattern. They use ginger, a plant of foreign origin, rather than galangal. They are more fond of chilies, which came in originally through trade. They use neither *terasi* nor sugar. The spices on which trade was built are the ones that they employ most and these are blended to flavor a single, solid, main ingredient. The orientation of their cooking style is outward rather than inward. It is an orientation that is evident in eastern Indonesian cooking as well, though in the latter case the influence is Portuguese rather than Arab/Indian.

Of course there is little doubt that such differences are bound to fade under the impact of increasing globalization, whichthey are already showing signs of. Researching the new edition of this book more than thirty years later, I found a very different scene from the one I had first encountered. Present-day Indonesia is a modernized economy embedded in a global market. Its cities are urban and sophisticated, there is a large business and professional community, fast communications networks are widespread and the population is increasingly mobile. Few Indonesians nowadays remain unaffected by the world beyond their immediate horizon.

Broad regional differences do still show up in food, however. In most situations meals and styles of eating still tend to revolve around the foods that are cheapest and most readily available. Certainly urban people rely increasingly on industrialized and globalized food products, but rural people still eat local food. Certain kinds of smooth rich dishes cooked with fresh roots and herbs and lots of coconut milk remain identified as "Padang" food, seafood is still a mainstay in the eastern islands, and Java remains the place of inspiration for many of the tasty and delicately executed side dishes which transform a plate of rice into a symphony of flavor and texture. In Jakarta you will find a large outdoor eating complex devoted to the food of particular regions, its clientele made up of homesick migrants who have come to work in the city of opportunity. Most of the swelling Jakarta middle class, forced to spend much of its time in traffic traveling to and from work and losing access to cooks and servants trained by home-focussed grandmothers, relies more and more on packaged, packet and supermarket foods.

As Sri Owen points out in her book *Indonesian Regional Food and Cookery*, the picture foreigners most often have of an Indonesian meal is a false one derived from the *rijsttafel*, a large meal of Indonesian dishes of great richness and variety. The *rijsttafel* was a Dutch invention based on the model of the special ritual meals mounted by Indonesians to mark particular events in their family, agricultural, community or religious lives. For Indonesians such special communal meals were deeply significant but irregular events whose preparation was a collaborative effort; the Dutch adopted the format and elaborated upon it, extending its range and serving it regularly in restaurants and for entertaining in colonial households.

Quite unlike the *rijsttafel*, a normal everyday meal eaten in the house of most Indonesian families will feature a plate of rice as the main dish and center of the meal accompanied by a small number of side dishes depending on the circumstance and location. Those appearing most regularly in farming households would be a small amount of fish caught in the paddies, canals or rivers, often dried to be available at any time, and a homemade sambal or chili relish, prepared in the morning with the rice. Other dishes will be added to this depending on what might be available in the house garden, what is cheap in the daily market (if there is money around) or any other bounty that might present itself.

Among the dishes there may be a wet dish of the kind found on pp. 74–93. These employ vegetables and/or a small amount of fresh fish or meat and serve to moisten the rice. Alternatively vegetables may be stir-fried with a little protein as on pp. 118–122. There may also be some raw or blanched salad vegetable with a sambal or a sauce (pp. 143–150), and additional frugal but highly flavored condiments or crunchies such as those on pp. 162–171. The latter are most important, for they often provide the variety and flavor in everyday meals.

Only in urban or wealthy households might you encounter rich dishes such as thick curries, braised, fried or grilled meat, chicken or fish on a regular basis. For the rest such substantial dishes would be confined to special occasions when a ritual or celebratory meal is called for. Animals are often killed for these occasions and food is prepared in large quantities as a family or communal event.

Ritual meals of the latter kind occur in different forms in all parts of Indonesia according to custom and religion. For most Indonesians, as for other people in Southeast Asia, such events are still an important feature of family and community life. In rural Java the common form is the household *slametan*; in Hindu Bali, household, neighborhood or associational feasts are frequently held as well as special temple festivals, where an entire community prepares foods and offerings to the gods. Throughout island Indonesia there are communal feasts based on shared input and mutually understood ritual, obligation and responsibility.

Many travelers have witnessed the splendor and joyous atmosphere of a Balinese temple festival, though not all realize the depth and extent of the communal effort that has gone into its preparation. A whole community will spend days cooking, and there is a strict ritual involved. The preparation is supervised by a ritual cooking specialist—a man—and men do the actual cooking while women prepare the spices. Neither physically nor financially could festival food be the food of every day.

The traditional Javanese *slametan*, less public and lower key in nature, also adds richness, variety and concentrated protein to the simple everyday diet of ordinary people. A *slametan* is held to mark any occasion of importance to a family—weddings, funerals, the birth of a child, moving house, harvesting the rice, circumcision, name-changing, to mention but a few—and to mark important dates or periods in the religious calendar. Food is an essential part of the ritual, with special dishes associated with the particular occasion, among them usually several kinds of meat, chicken or eggs. The meal will include some molded or fancy rice and will be surrounded by a number of hearty main dishes and an assortment of side dishes and garnishes. A share of everything is set out on banana leaves for each guest. After the formalities are over, those present (traditionally the men from neighboring households) eat only a few mouthfuls. They then wrap up the rest of their portion in the banana leaves and excuse themselves, taking it home to share with their families.

To help you create Indonesian menus I have organized the recipes into sections based on style of preparation and cooking. As outlined above, in Indonesia some contain what would be everyday dishes while others would usually be included only on special occasions.

For a normal Western family meal I would serve steamed white rice, two main dishes chosen from different sections, other than the last two (Accompaniments and Special Rice Dishes and Noodles). I would serve at least two accompaniments such as a condiment (sambal), a pickle (*acar*) or something crunchy. One of the main dishes might come from among the wet ones in the first section (indeed if this one contains both meat and vegetable it could stand alone as the only main dish), or it might be a stir-fry. To compliment these, add a richer, drier or more substantial dish. Among the accompaniments, crunchy textures and complex flavors go particularly well with wet dishes; fresh and sour pickles are good accompaniments for creamy coconut milk dishes or rich chili-fries; hot, tangy and slightly liquid sambals suit fries and grills; a roasted sambal goes well with stir-fries. Many accompaniments may be prepared in bulk and stored for later use.

For a more elaborate meal or a dinner party serve a variety of dishes, taking care that each one comes from a different section and that it contains a different main ingredient. Add a variety of appropriate accompaniments.

Sometimes particular dishes are served with a fancy rice for a party or a special occasion. If you want to serve a fancy rice rather than steamed white rice, it is probably a good idea—at least in the beginning—to stick to the accompanying dishes I suggest in the section devoted largely to them.

Happy Eating! (*Selamat makan!*)

WET DISHES
Sayur

Sometimes translated as "soups" in English, these predominantly vegetable dishes are not really soups as we understand them but more like thin vegetable stews. They are served and eaten as supplements to other dishes and to enhance the flavor of the main dish of rice. They are a frequent addition to the basic meal of rice with a little dried, fried or grilled fish and chili condiment that is the daily fare of country people.

SAYUR BAYAM ## SPINACH SOUP

4 cups (1 liter) chicken stock

2-in (5-cm) piece galangal root, sliced and bruised

1 teaspoon shredded Chinese keys or 2 salam leaves (optional)

1 cup (250 g) fresh or frozen corn kernels or 3 small fresh cobs, cut into chunks

1 bunch amaranth or young spinach

Salt

Pinch of palm or dark brown sugar to taste (optional)

Spice Paste

1 small red chili, sliced

½ teaspoon dried shrimp paste, roasted in foil in a dry skillet or heated in a covered container in the microwave for 1 minute and crumbled

2 cloves garlic

4 shallots, sliced

In a mortar, grind the Spice Paste ingredients in the order listed: the chili, shrimp paste, garlic and shallots, reducing everything to a rough paste each time (note that Indonesians like a little texture in their pastes). Alternatively put all the Spice Paste ingredients together into a food processor and grind to a paste.

Add a little stock to the paste and blend well. Bring the rest of the stock to a boil in a saucepan or wok, add the galangal, the Chinese keys or salam leaves and the Spice Paste and simmer for a few minutes. Add the corn and cook for a few minutes, then add the greens and simmer a couple of minutes more. Adjust the seasonings, remove the pieces of galangal and serve.

SAYUR ASAM TAMARIND VEGETABLE SOUP
(Java)

In Jakarta, where this dish comes from, Tamarind Vegetable Soup always includes some leaves and nuts of the *melinjo* tree (*Gnetum gnemon*), the plant from which *emping* or bitter nut crackers are made. In places where *melinjo* is not available a few tiny green olives taken from their brine make a suitable substitute.

1 tablespoon oil
4 cups (1 liter) water
1 thick slice galangal root, bruised
2 salam leaves
4 oz (125 g) beef, chicken or shrimp, sliced or chopped
4 cups (750 g) vegetables (green beans cut into bite-sized pieces; corn kernels or chunks of fresh corn cob; young eggplant or zucchini, sliced into rounds; skinned raw peanuts; jackfruit; *melinjo* nuts and leaves or a few leaves of young spinach; cubed green papaya or summer squash; tomato wedges; a few small green olives)
2 tablespoons tamarind water (p. 55) or to taste (sometimes tamarind leaf is used as one of the vegetables and this may reduce the amount of extra sourness needed)
1 teaspoon palm or dark brown sugar, or to taste

Spice Paste
2 medium-length red chilies, sliced
1 teaspoon dried shrimp paste
2 cloves garlic
5 shallots, sliced

In a mortar, grind the Spice Paste ingredients to a paste in the order listed. Alternatively, combine them in a food processor and blend to a paste. Heat the oil in a saucepan and stir-fry the paste until fragrant. Pour the water into the saucepan, add the galangal, the salam leaves and the meat and bring to a boil. Reduce the heat and simmer into a stock. Add the vegetables in the order they require cooking. When the vegetables are lightly cooked, add the tamarind water and sugar to taste. Stir, return to a boil, remove the galangal and serve.

SAYUR LODEH VEGETABLE SOUP

1 tablespoon oil
4 oz (125 g) chopped or ground beef or chicken, small raw shrimp or 1 stock cube
2 cups (500 ml) very thin coconut milk (third squeeze if fresh)
1 slice galangal root, bruised
1 salam leaf
3–4 cups (500–750 g) mixed vegetables (sliced bamboo shoot; cubed summer squash; sliced zucchini or eggplant; green beans cut into bite-sized pieces; sliced carrot; cubed fresh tempeh; shredded cabbage)
1 cup (250 ml) thick coconut milk
½ teaspoon palm or dark brown sugar (optional)
Salt to taste
1 lime cut into wedges

Spice Paste
4 red medium-length chilies, sliced
½-in (1-cm) piece turmeric root, peeled and coarsely chopped or ⅛ teaspoon ground turmeric
1 teaspoon dried shrimp paste
2 cloves garlic
5 shallots, sliced

In a mortar, pound the Spice Paste ingredients to a rough paste in the order listed. Heat the oil in a wok or deep pan. Fry the Spice Paste until browned and fragrant. Add the beef, chicken or shrimp and stir-fry until it changes color, or crumble in the stock cube. Add the thin coconut milk, galangal and salam leaf, stir and bring to a boil. Add the vegetables in the order that they require cooking. When the vegetables are tender, stir in the thick coconut milk, add sugar and salt to taste. Return to a boil, remove the galangal and serve with lime wedges. Add water if you want a thinner soup.

SAYUR TERUNG ATAU LABU
EGGPLANT OR SQUASH SOUP
(North Sumatra)

2 tablespoons oil
4 oz (125 g) beef or chicken, sliced into shreds
Salt to taste
1 thin slice galangal root, bruised (optional)
2 salam or kaffir lime leaves
2 cups (500 ml) coconut milk
2 small eggplants or 2 cups (500 g) cubed summer
    squash, zucchini or green jackfruit, sliced into wedges or
    diced
Fresh lime juice to taste

Spice Paste
7 red medium-length chilies, sliced
1-in (2½-cm) piece turmeric root, peeled and coarsely
    chopped or ¼ teaspoon ground turmeric
1-in (2½-cm) piece fresh ginger root, peeled and coarsely
    chopped
3 roasted candlenuts or raw almonds or macadamia nuts
1 large clove garlic
5 shallots, sliced
½ teaspoon ground coriander
Pinch of ground cumin

Grind the Spice Paste ingredients in a mortar in the order listed or all together in a food processor. Heat the oil in a saucepan and fry the Spice Paste for 1 minute. Add the meat and salt to taste, barely cover with water and bring to a boil. Add the galangal and the salam leaves and simmer for about 15 minutes or until the meat is nearly cooked. Add the coconut milk and simmer uncovered for about 10 minutes. Add the vegetables and continue cooking until they are tender but not overcooked. Remove from the stove, add lime juice to taste and stir. Remove the salam leaves and galangal before serving.

SAYUR LEMENG VEGETABLE COCONUT SOUP

This dish is similar to a Malay vegetable *lemak*. It is a rich dish and if you make it thick (i.e. use less thin coconut milk) it could be served with a sour poached fish dish such as Sour Fish Stew (p. 87) or in place of a *gulai*. The same is true of both the previous and the following recipes. If you serve it as a stand-alone dish, however, try adding a little sugar and fresh lime juice to taste.

1 tablespoon oil
2 cups (500 ml) thin coconut milk
¼ cup (50 g) sliced fresh young coconut or 2 tablespoons
    dried unsweetened coconut, steamed
    (p. 18)
3–4 cups (500–750 g) mixed vegetables (corn kernels;
    green beans, cut into bite-sized pieces; cubed pumpkin;
    cubed summer squash; shredded cabbage; cubed
    eggplant; sliced bamboo shoots)
4 oz (125 g) peeled raw shrimp
1 cup (250 ml) thick coconut milk
Salt to taste

Spice Paste
1 teaspoon coriander seed
3–4 red medium-length red chilies, sliced
1-in (2½-cm) piece resurrection lily (optional)
5 roasted candlenuts or raw almonds or macadamia nuts,
    coarsely chopped
½ teaspoon dried shrimp paste
2 cloves garlic
6 shallots, sliced

Grind the coriander seed in a spice grinder. In a mortar, grind the remaining Spice Paste ingredients to a paste, adding each one in the order listed, adding the ground coriander last. Alternatively grind everything together in a food processor. Heat the oil in a wok or a saucepan and fry the Spice Paste until it smells fragrant. Add the thin coconut milk and bring it to a boil, then add the coconut slices, the vegetables that take longer to cook, and the shrimp and simmer for 10 minutes. Add the remaining vegetables, the thick coconut milk and salt to taste. Simmer, stirring, until all the vegetables are cooked and the gravy is thick, with its oil floating on top.

SAYUR BUBUR CREAMY VEGETABLE SOUP
(West Java)

This makes a good vegetarian dish if you leave out the chicken stock cubes.

2 cups (500 ml) thin coconut milk
2 chicken stock cubes
1-in (2½-cm) piece galangal root, sliced and bruised
1 stalk lemongrass, cut into 2-in (5-cm) lengths and
  bruised
2 salam leaves
1 cup (250 ml) thick coconut milk
1 bunch young spinach, amaranth, Swiss chard or any
  similar green leafy vegetable
Salt to taste
Palm or dark brown sugar to taste (optional)

Spice Paste
3 roasted candlenuts or raw almonds or macadamia
  nuts, coarsely chopped
1 clove garlic
4 shallots, sliced
¼ teaspoon freshly ground coriander seed

Pour the thin coconut milk into a saucepan, add the stock cubes, the galangal, lemongrass and the salam leaves and bring to a boil. Grind the Spice Paste ingredients to a paste in a mortar or a food processor. Add a little stock from the saucepan and blend until smooth.

Stir the Spice Paste into the saucepan and simmer into a tasty broth. Add the thick coconut milk and return to a simmer. Add the spinach and continue to cook gently, stirring constantly for a minute or two. Add salt and sugar to taste. Remove the salam leaves, galangal slices and lemongrass and serve.

Soto

Soto is a meat-based broth dish that usually includes some mung-bean vermicelli and has its own side dishes and accompaniments. Traditionally *soto* has stood alone as a special between-meal snack bought from hawkers or as a complete meal with rice. I include it here because it is likely to turn up as one dish among many on a party table. Remember, however, that served with a bowl of rice and its own special accompaniments, *soto* is a good meal for lunch or supper for the family.

NASI SOTO AYAM CHICKEN SOUP DINNER

There are as many versions of chicken soup (*soto ayam*) as there are cooks in Indonesia. The recipes included here represent only a sample. My first is an elaborate one pressented as a meal in its own right. The others may be served either separately with rice or as one of many main dishes at a party.

6 tablespoons oil
2 lb (1 kg) chicken or mixed breast and thigh pieces
6 cups (1½ liters) water
2 shallots or 1 small onion, quartered
Salt to taste

Spice Paste
1-in (2½-cm) piece tamarind root, peeled and coarsely
   chopped
3 roasted candlenuts or raw almonds or macadamia nuts,
   coarsely chopped
2 shallots, sliced
2 cloves garlic
Pinch of freshly ground pepper

Accompaniments
Steamed white rice
3 hard-boiled eggs, shelled and sliced
1 cup (250 g) bean sprouts, washed and trimmed
Shredded cabbage, lightly cooked (optional)

2 medium potatoes, peeled, thinly sliced and fried until
crisp then drained on paper towel
4 oz (125 g) mung-bean vermicelli, soaked in water until
soft, then cut into bite-sized lengths

Garnish
Sliced green onions
Chopped celery leaves or chopped Asian celery
3 tablespoons fried onion flakes (p. 20)
1 lime cut into wedges
Chili-Ginger Sambal (p. 159) or store-bought sambal
Javanese or regular soy sauce to taste (optional)

Grind the Spice Paste ingredients. Heat 2 tablespoons oil in a large pot
and fry the paste until fragrant. Wash the chicken and put it in the pot.
Add the water, the shallots or the onion and salt and simmer until the
chicken is cooked.

While the broth is cooking, prepare the Accompaniments. Put the rice
in a large bowl and arrange the remaining ingredients on separate plates
or decoratively in separate heaps on a large serving platter. On another
plate arrange the Garnishes. Put some sambal in a sauce dish and add a
teaspoon for serving.

When the chicken is cooked, remove it from the pot and reserve the
broth. When the chicken has cooled slightly, add three or four tablespoons of oil to a wok and fry either the whole chicken or the chicken
pieces, turning them frequently, until brown. Remove the chicken from
the pan and take the meat from the bones and cut it into shreds. Keep
the meat warm and discard the bones. Pour the broth into a large serving bowl and keep warm.

Set the large bowl of broth on the table surrounded by the
Accompaniments, Garnishes and the sambal and a soup bowl for each
individual person. A little chicken, hard-boiled egg slices, vegetables,
potato crisps and mung-bean vermicelli are all piled on top of each other
in the individual bowls and a little sambal is added to taste. Broth is then
ladled over the top, green onions, celery and onion flakes are sprinkled
on, and lime juice squeezed over to taste. Serve the rice on separate plates
and ladle spoonfuls of soup on to it as you eat.

MADURESE CHICKEN SOUP

SOTO AYAM MADURA

2 lb (1 kg) chicken or chicken thighs and legs
4 oz (125 g) small raw shrimp, peeled and chopped
  (optional)
Pinch each of salt and pepper
6 cups (1½ liters) water
1 stalk lemongrass, cut into three pieces
4 kaffir lime leaves
3 large waxy potatoes, boiled and sliced
4 oz (125 g) mung-bean vermicelli, soaked in cold water
  until soft then cut into bite-sized lengths
1 cup (250 g) bean sprouts, washed and trimmed
3 hard-boiled eggs, shelled and sliced
Fresh lime juice to taste

Spice Paste

1-in (2½-cm) piece fresh ginger root, peeled and
  coarsely chopped
1-in (2½-cm) piece turmeric root, peeled and coarsely
  chopped or ⅛ teaspoon ground turmeric
4 cloves garlic
6 shallots, sliced

Garnish

Asian celery, chopped
4 green onions, sliced
Fried onion or garlic flakes

Disjoint the chicken. Put the chicken and shrimp, with a pinch each of salt and pepper, in a saucepan with the water, the lemongrass and the lime leaves. Bring to a boil and reduce the heat to a simmer. Grind the ginger, turmeric, garlic and shallots to a paste. Add ½ cup (125 ml) of water to the paste and blend it thoroughly. Add the Spice Paste to the pot and simmer until the chicken is tender and the broth is fragrant. Remove the chicken and reserve the broth. Remove the meat from the bones and cut it into shreds.

Arrange the meat on a deep plate with the slices of boiled potato, mung-bean vermicelli, bean sprouts and egg. Remove the lemongrass and lime leaves from the broth and pour it over the meat and other ingredients. Sprinkle the sliced celery, green onions and fried onion or garlic flakes on top, then squeeze the lime juice over top to taste. Serve with Chili Sambal for Soto (p. 160).

SOTO AYAM SPICY CHICKEN SOUP
(North Sumatra)

This soto comes to me from north Sumatra and contains dry spices, a characteristic of the area.

2 lb (1 kg) chicken or chicken pieces
4–6 cups (1–1½ liters) water
1 stalk lemongrass, bruised
Salt to taste
1–2 tablespoons oil
1–1½ tablespoons tamarind water (p. 55), or to taste
2 teaspoons palm or dark brown sugar, or to taste
4 oz (125 g) mung-bean vermicelli, soaked and cut into
  bite-sized lengths
2 pickling cucumbers, unpeeled and diced
Fresh lime juice to taste
Light soy sauce to taste

Spice Paste
2-in (5-cm) piece ginger root, peeled and coarsely
  chopped
1-in (2½-cm) piece galangal, peeled and coarsely
  chopped
3 cloves garlic
5 shallots, sliced
1 teaspoon coriander seed, roasted and ground
½ teaspoon cumin seed, roasted and ground
Pepper to taste

Garnish
Green onion, sliced
Asian celery, cut into bite-sized pieces
Fried onion flakes

If using a whole chicken, cut it into pieces. In a mortar or a food processor, grind the Spice Paste ingredients to a paste. Add ½ cup (125 ml) of water and blend thoroughly. Cover the chicken with the water, bring to a boil, add the Spice Paste, lemongrass and salt and simmer until the chicken is tender. Remove the chicken from the stock, take the meat from the bones and slice it into shreds. Strain the stock and set it aside. Heat the oil in a wok or pan, add the chicken, tamarind water and sugar to taste and stir-fry until the meat is brown.

Place the chicken, the mung-bean vermicelli, the cucumber and the garnishes in the bottom of a serving bowl and pour the strained stock over them. Add a little lime juice and light soy sauce to taste, and serve with Chili Sambal for Soto (p. 160) or Chili-Shrimp Paste Sambal (p. 161).

SOTO MACASSAR ## MACASSAN MEAT SOUP

A great dish for the offal lover. It is not unlike the *soto daging madura* of Javanese hawkers, though richer. Soups made with offal are popular all over Southeast Asia, although this recipe can be made using shin beef on its own.

2 lb (1 kg) mixed shin beef, unblanched beef tripe, intestine, and lung (optional)
6 cups (1½ liters) water or to cover
4 kaffir lime leaves
2 stalks lemongrass, bruised with the side of a knife
1–2 tablespoons oil
2 teaspoons yellow soy bean paste (omit if you use only shin beef)
2 chicken stock cubes
3 shallots or green onions, chopped
¼ teaspoon freshly ground pepper

Spice Paste
1-in (2½-cm) piece ginger root, peeled and chopped
1-in (2½-cm) piece galangal root, peeled and chopped
6 cloves garlic
6 shallots, sliced
1 teaspoon coriander seed, roasted in a dry pan and ground
½ teaspoon cumin seed, roasted in a dry pan and ground
2 tablespoons raw peanuts or 5 roasted candlenuts, raw almonds or macadamia nuts, coarsely chopped

Accompaniments
Chili-Shrimp Paste Sambal (p. 161)
2 limes, cut into wedges
2 cups (500 g) small round raw peanuts with skins, fried in 1 cup (250 ml) oil in a wok until brown, and drained

White rice or compressed rice pieces (p. 206)
Fresh pickles

Prepare the offal by thoroughly cleaning and washing it. To clean the beef tripe pour boiling water over it and scrape it with a knife until all the black parts come off. Trim the intestine of its skin and adhering fat.

Cut the intestines into 1-in (½-cm) lengths and all the other meats into ½-in (1-cm) thick slices then into squares. Put the water on to boil and add the meats, the lime leaves and the lemongrass and simmer for half an hour.

In a mortar or a food processor, grind the Spice Paste ingredients, omitting the coriander and cumin if using shin beef only. Heat the oil in a wok and fry the Spice Paste until it is fragrant. Add ½ cup (125 ml) of water and blend thoroughly. Add this to the soup with the yellow bean paste and the chicken stock cubes. Simmer until the meats are half cooked, about 30 minutes, then add the shallots and cook for 1 hour.

To serve, ladle the soup into individual bowls, mix in the sambal, squeeze lime juice over the top and add crunchy peanuts on the side. On separate small plates place rice and some pickles, and take a bite of rice followed by a spoon of soup and occasionally a spoon of pickles for fresh, sharp contrast.

SOTO BABAT GARNISHED TRIPE BROTH

This is a much blander dish than Macassan Meat Soup (p. 84) and would be a better choice for people who tend to be squeamish about variety meats other than tripe.

1 lb (500 g) blanched ox tripe, thinly sliced
1 tablespoon oil
3 cloves garlic, chopped
2 tablespoons grated fresh ginger root
4 cups (1 liter) beef stock
Salt and pepper to taste
¾ cup (175 g) Chinese turnip or drained boiled bamboo
   shoots, sliced into matchsticks

Garnish
Asian celery, finely chopped
Green onions, sliced

Fried onion or garlic flakes
Fresh lime juice

Accompaniments
Cooked white rice
Peanuts, fried in 1 cup (250 ml) oil until brown then
    drained thoroughly, and coarsely chopped
Shrimp crackers (p. 164), pork cracklings or thick potato
    chips
Chili Sambal for Soto (p. 160), made without the shrimp
    paste

Cover the tripe with water. Bring it to a boil, drain, and discard the water, setting the tripe aside. Heat the oil in a saucepan and fry the garlic and ginger until golden. Pour in the beef stock, add the tripe, salt and pepper to taste, and simmer gently until the tripe is tender. Add the turnip or bamboo shoots and continue cooking until the vegetable is tender but not too soft, then remove from the stove.

Pour the soup into a deep bowl. Add the celery, green onions and onion flakes. Stir in a little sambal and fresh lime juice to taste. Stir well and serve.

Indonesians like to add crunch to this slightly silky and bland *soto*. It is important to offer something like fried peanuts, a plate of shrimp crackers or thick potato chips, which can be crumbled or broken over the top. If the diners are not Muslim or Jewish, you might like to use some chopped pork cracklings.

Fish Stews

PANGÉ IKAN
PADANG

SOUR FISH STEW
(Sumatra)

This dish is a Sumatran version of the sour fish stews found all over Southeast Asia. Compare it with the Malay Hot Sour Fish (p. 181); Thai Stir-fried Sweet Shrimp (p. 504) and Chili-Hot Sour Soup (p. 340); Cambodian Sour Chicken Soup (p. 461); and Vietnamese Sour Fish Soup (p. 489). The carambola used in this recipe are the small, smooth cooking variety of star fruit about the size and shape of avocados.

1 stalk lemongrass, bruised
8 whole small carambola, cut in half lengthwise or 2
    small tomatoes, each cut into 4 wedges
Salt to taste
1¼ –1¾ lb (600–800 g) whole small freshwater fish (e.g.
    trout or pike) or saltwater fish (gurnard, King George
    whiting, bonito, sea perch), whole or cut into steaks
1 thick slice ginger root, bruised
Fresh lime juice to taste (the dish should be sour)
3 lemon basil leaves or 1 salam leaf, roughly chopped

Spice Paste
4–6 medium-length red chilies, seeded and sliced
1-in (2½-cm) piece galangal root, peeled and chopped
1-in (2½-cm) piece turmeric root, peeled and chopped or
    ⅛ teaspoon ground turmeric
3 roasted candlenuts, or raw almonds or macadamia
    nuts, coarsely chopped
3 cloves garlic
6 shallots, sliced

Grind the Spice Paste Ingredients to a paste. Put the paste in a wok or a pan with enough water to later cover the fish, add the lemongrass, carambola and salt and simmer into a tasty broth. If you are using tomato instead of carambola add this toward the end. Add the fish pieces and the ginger and simmer gently over low heat, uncovered, until the fish is cooked. Do not stir this dish with a spoon as it cooks but shake the pan occasionally. Just before serving, add lime juice if necessary to achieve a good sour flavor. Remove the lemongrass and ginger and garnish with lemon basil leaves.

PINDANG IKAN ## SPICED FISH STEW
(Java)

This is a Javanese version of Sour Fish Stew (p. 87). It is quite popular to use large fish heads for dishes like this.

2 tablespoons oil
8 shallots, finely sliced
5 cloves garlic, peeled and finely sliced
1 thick slice turmeric root, peeled and sliced
1 thick slice galangal root, peeled and sliced diagonally
1 thick slice fresh ginger root, peeled and sliced
2 stalks lemongrass, bruised and cut into 2 in (5 cm) lengths
10 small carambola, cut in half lengthwise or 2 small tomatoes, each cut into 8 wedges
2 salam leaves
3 cups (750 ml) water
Salt to taste
1 teaspoon palm or dark brown sugar, or more to taste
Fresh lime juice to taste
2 medium-length red chilies, seeded and sliced diagonally
8 whole bird's eye chilies
2 heads (about 2–3 lb/1–1½ kg) salmon or 1½ lb (750 g) fish, cut into steaks

Heat the oil and fry the shallots and garlic for a few minutes. Add the turmeric, galangal, ginger and lemongrass, and stir-fry until fragrant. Add the carambola if you are using it and the salam leaves and stir-fry a few minutes more. Add the water, and tomatoes if you are using them, and simmer for a few minutes. Add salt and sugar to taste and lime juice if you need it and simmer until the stock is flavorful.

Add the chilies, reduce the heat to low, add the fish and poach gently until the fish is cooked. Taste and adjust the flavors—the broth should be sour. Remove the turmeric, galangal, ginger and lemongrass and serve.

PALLU MARA   EASTERN SOUR FISH STEW

2 large meaty fish steaks (Spanish mackerel, skipjack tuna)

Tamarind water made from 1 tablespoon tamarind pulp and 1 cup (250 g) water

Oil for frying

1 large clove garlic, finely sliced

5–6 whole bird's eye chilies

1 stalk lemongrass, bruised and cut into pieces (optional)

1-in (2½-cm) piece turmeric root, chopped, or ⅛ teaspoon ground turmeric

½ teaspoon palm or dark brown sugar (optional)

Salt and pepper to taste

Wash the fish and cut it into medium-sized pieces, discarding the bones. Cover with the tamarind water. Heat the oil and briefly stir-fry the garlic, chilies and lemongrass. Add the fish and tamarind water, turmeric, sugar, salt and pepper to taste and simmer gently until the fish is cooked. Remove the lemongrass and serve.

PALLU BASA   FISH STEW WITH COCONUT

¼ fresh coconut, peeled and grated or ¼ cup (65 g) prepared dried coconut (p. 18)

1 lb (500 g) Spanish mackerel fillets or steaks, boned and cut into big pieces

1 cup (250 ml) tamarind water made from a pea-size piece of tamarind

1 teaspoon salt

1-in (2½-cm) piece turmeric root, peeled and grated or ⅛ teaspoon ground turmeric

2 cloves garlic, chopped
Freshly ground pepper to taste
Fried onion flakes for garnishing

In a dry pan roast the coconut until it is light brown. Remove it from the heat and grind it very fine in a food processor. Put the fish, tamarind water, salt and turmeric into a pan. Add the garlic and pepper and bring to a simmer. Add the ground coconut to the fish mixture and simmer gently, uncovered, until it is cooked.

Turn off the heat, leaving the stew in the pan for a few minutes until it thickens. Serve garnished with the fried onion flakes.

Semur—Javanese Stews

Javanese stews are similar to the stews enjoyed in the Eurasian community in Malaysia. They are probably European in inspiration, beginning their life in Portuguese or Dutch Malacca.

SEMUR DAGING ## TANGY BEEF STEW

1 tablespoon oil
2 lb (1 kg) stewing beef, cut into cubes, sliced brisket
    trimmed of all fat or lean beef short ribs
3 tablespoons Javanese soy sauce or 2 tablespoons
    dark soy sauce and 1 tablespoon palm or dark brown
    sugar
1 slice fresh ginger root, bruised
2 whole cloves
1 teaspoon grated nutmeg
1 small cinnamon stick
Salt to taste
3 small potatoes, quartered (optional)
1 tomato, cut into 8 wedges
Fresh lime juice to taste
2 red medium-length chilies, sliced in rounds

Spice Paste
3 cloves garlic
5 shallots, sliced
Pinch of black pepper

Grind the Spice Paste ingredients to a fine paste. Heat the oil in a pan and fry the Spice Paste until it is fragrant. Add the meat and stir-fry until it changes color and is well coated with the spices. Add the soy sauce, enough water to cover, ginger, cloves, nutmeg, cinnamon stick and salt. Cover and simmer until the meat is nearly cooked (about one hour). Add the potatoes and simmer until they are cooked. Add the tomato and the lime juice, and more water if necessary. Serve garnished with the chilies.

AYAM SEMUR JAWA — CHICKEN IN SOY SAUCE (Java)

1 2 lb (1 kg) chicken or mixed breast and thigh pieces
Salt to taste
Oil for deep-frying
2 cups (500 ml) water
2 thick slices galangal root, bruised
2 tablespoons Javanese soy sauce or 1–2 tablespoons dark soy sauce and 1½ teaspoons palm or dark brown sugar
Palm or dark brown sugar, to taste
½–1 tablespoon white vinegar, to taste
1 tomato, chopped (optional)

Spice Paste
2 medium-length red chilies, sliced
2 cloves garlic
5 shallots, sliced

Wash the chicken (if whole) and cut it into pieces (p. 22). Rub the pieces with salt and deep-fry them in oil. Remove the chicken and drain it on paper towel.

Grind the Spice Paste ingredients to a rough paste. Fry the Spice Paste in 1 tablespoon of oil until it is fragrant. Add the water, galangal, soy sauce, sugar, vinegar and tomato, and cook the chicken in this broth until it is tender. Remove the galangal and serve. The dish should remain liquid.

RAWON BLACK BEEF STEW
(East Java)

The distinguishing feature of this dish is the *keluak*, a flat nut (*Pangium edule*) shaped like a cockle. The flesh is dark with the consistency of very ripe avocado and has a tart flavor. You can sometimes buy *keluak* meat dried (or even canned) in Asian food stores. The dried variety is usually broken up into pieces—you will need two or three pieces for one nut. Soak the dried pieces in hot water to soften them before adding them to the recipe—you might even need to boil them for a few minutes at the end.

2 tablespoons oil
1 stalk lemongrass, bruised
1 thick slice galangal, bruised
6 kaffir lime leaves
2 lb (1 kg) stewing beef, cut into cubes
8 cups (2 liters) water
1 teaspoon salt or to taste

Spice Paste
2 medium-length red chilies, seeded and sliced
½-in (1-cm) piece resurrection lily, chopped (optional)
1-in (2.5-cm) piece fresh ginger root, peeled and sliced
1-in (2.5-cm) piece turmeric root, peeled and coarsely
    chopped or ⅛ teaspoon ground turmeric
4 roasted candlenuts, or raw almonds or macadamia nuts,
    coarsely chopped
5 *keluak* nuts
4 cloves garlic
10 shallots, sliced
1 teaspoon roasted coriander seed, ground
½ teaspoon roasted cumin seed, ground
1 tomato, coarsely chopped

Grind the Spice Paste ingredients to a very fine paste. Heat the oil in a wok, add the Spice Paste, lemongrass, galangal and lime leaves and stir-fry until fragrant. Add the meat, water, and salt to taste. Simmer until the meat is tender, adding more water if necessary, to keep the dish very saucy. Remove the lemongrass and galangal and serve.

This stew may be served as a complete meal with white rice, washed and trimmed bean sprouts, Marbled Eggs (p. 155), Shrimp Crackers (p. 164) and Chili-Shrimp Paste Sambal (p. 161).

Creamy Coconut Milk Dishes— Gulai Padang

The dishes in this section come from the relatively wealthy area of Minangkabau in West Sumatra, where there has been a tradition of out-trading, capital accumulation and self-sufficient wet-rice agriculture. More fish, chicken and meat are eaten here on an everyday basis than in many other parts of Indonesia. The essence of these dishes is the liberal addition of coconut milk along with the use of the fresh roots and herbs that go with the farming lifestyle.

While *gulai* is usually translated into English as "curry," *gulai Padang* need to be clearly distinguished from the thick or dry curries in Curries and Rich Coconut Milk Dishes (p. 96) which includes a complex mix of both fresh herbs and roots and the dry spices associated with the international maritime trade. *Gulai Padang* are the wet dishes in a meal: they are a frequent and basic main dish in the areas from which they come and for the purposes of menu planning they belong in this section.

Where *sayur* will go well with any of the drier, richer coconut curries and almost any of the more substantial dishes of the second section, a creamy coconut milk dish is best partnered with a stir-fry, a grilled or braised dish or a sour one such as a pickle.

GULAI IKAN PADANG FISH CURRY

1 tablespoon oil
2 cups (500 ml) coconut milk
1 stalk lemongrass, bruised
2 slices galangal, bruised
2 small red chilies, cut in half lengthwise and seeded
2 kaffir lime leaves

1¼–1¾ lb (600–800 g) whole small fish or fillets cut into
   bite-sized pieces (Spanish mackerel, silver trevally,
   bonito, longtail tuna), rubbed lightly with tamarind
   water and salt
Fresh lime juice or tamarind water, to taste
Salt to taste

Spice Paste
4–6 medium-length red chilies, sliced or 1–2 teaspoons
   ground chili
1-in (2½-cm) piece turmeric root, peeled and coarsely
   chopped or ⅛ teaspoon turmeric powder
½-in (1-cm) piece fresh ginger root, peeled and coarsely
   chopped
2 cloves garlic
6 shallots, sliced

Grind the Spice Paste ingredients to a paste. Heat the oil in a wok or a
pan and fry the paste lightly. Add the coconut milk, lemongrass, galangal, chilies and lime leaves and bring to a boil, stirring and simmering
until the broth is fragrant. Add the fish and cook gently, uncovered,
spooning the sauce over and around the fish constantly until it is cooked
and the oil floats on top of the broth. Add the fresh lime juice or
tamarind water to taste and adjust the salt. Remove the lemongrass and
galangal and serve.

   This recipe may also be made with shrimp or chicken and is good
served with Peanut Coconut Garnish (p. 153); a stir-fried vegetable dish;
Plow Sambal (p. 158) and a cucumber pickle.

**GULAI UDANG
DENGAN LABU
KUNING**

SHRIMP AND PUMPKIN CURRY

2 cups (500 ml) thin coconut milk
1 stalk lemongrass, bruised
2 kaffir lime leaves
1 thick slice galangal, bruised
1 lb (500 g) shrimp, peeled and deveined
1½ cups (350 g) Japanese pumpkin or winter squash,
   peeled, cored and diced
1 cup (500 ml) thick coconut milk
Salt to taste
Fresh lime juice or tamarind water, to taste (optional)

Spice Paste

4–6 medium-length red chilies, sliced

6 shallots, sliced

2 cloves garlic

1½-in (3-cm) piece turmeric root, peeled and coarsely chopped or ½ teaspoon ground turmeric

Grind the Spice Paste ingredients. Add some of the thin coconut milk and blend thoroughly. Transfer this mixture to a saucepan or wok, add the lemongrass, lime leaves, galangal and the rest of the thin coconut milk and simmer over medium heat into a broth, stirring constantly. Add the shrimp and the pumpkin or winter squash and simmer gently until almost cooked. Add the thick coconut milk and salt, and cook uncovered until the shrimp and pumpkin are cooked. Just before serving add fresh lime juice or tamarind water (if using) and remove the lemongrass and galangal.

GULAI PAKIS   FIDDLEHEAD CURRY

This dish highlights the newly unfurling head of a fern similar to the fiddleheads native to America. The Indonesian fern is now hard to find even there, but broccoli or water spinach make an acceptable substitute.

1 lb (500 g) fiddleheads, broccoli or water spinach

2–3 cups (500–750 ml) coconut milk

1 stalk lemongrass, bruised

2 or 3 lemon basil leaves

3 thick slices galangal, bruised

2 dried tamarind slices or 2 tablespoons tamarind water or to taste

3 small dried fish (*ikan teri*), washed and heads removed or small dried shrimp, soaked and drained (optional)

Salt to taste

Spice Paste

6–8 small red chilies, sliced or 2 teaspoons ground chili

¾-in (2-cm) piece turmeric root, peeled and coarsely chopped or ¼ teaspoon ground turmeric

1-in (2½-cm) piece fresh ginger root, peeled and coarsely chopped

4 roasted candlenuts, or raw almonds or macadamia nuts,
   coarsely chopped
1 clove garlic
4 shallots, sliced

Wash and chop the fiddleheads or broccoli. Grind the Spice Paste ingredients. Add the coconut milk and blend well. Pour the coconut milk mixture into a wide pan or wok, add the lemongrass, basil, galangal, dried tamarind slices (if you are using them) and dried fish, and bring to a boil.

Boil the broth rapidly, uncovered, stirring constantly until it reduces and thickens. Add the fiddleheads or broccoli, reduce the heat, and continue to simmer, uncovered, until the vegetables are nearly cooked. Add the tamarind water (if using) and salt and continue cooking until the vegetable is done and the oil floats on top. Remove the lemongrass and dried tamarind slices before serving.

This recipe is works for any vegetable *gulai*. Try a mixture of young jackfruit or summer squash cubes, thinly sliced bamboo shoots, green beans cut into bite-sized pieces and sliced white cabbage.

CURRIES AND RICH COCONUT MILK DISHES

The dishes in this section do not have a lot of liquid. They were traditionally eaten only occasionally rather than on a daily basis: animals may have been killed for a special occasion and leftover parts cooked in a way that would allow them to be kept; some life-cycle or unusual event may have prompted the family or someone in the immediate neighborhood to hold a celebration, preparing and sharing appropriate special foods. The dishes are more substantial in both protein and flavor than those of every day and add richness and variety to the diet of the common people.

KARI JAWA JAVANESE CURRY

Javanese Curry is an exception to the special occasion rule. This standard main dish was a specialty among Dutch-trained household cooks in urban Java and passed through them into the vernacular. It makes a rounded meal for lunch or a family dinner served with rice and one or two of the high-flavor accompaniments from pp. 151–164.

2 tablespoons oil
¾ lb (400 g) stewing beef, diced
2 kaffir lime leaves
1 stalk lemongrass, bruised
Salt to taste
1 medium-sized waxy potato, peeled and cubed
¼ very small cabbage, finely sliced
3 or 4 small red and green chilies, bruised
1¾ oz (50 g) mung-bean vermicelli, soaked and cut (optional)
1–2 cups (250–500 ml) thick coconut milk
Tamarind water or fresh lime juice to taste
1 tablespoon fried onion flakes for garnish

Spice Paste
1 teaspoon coriander seed or ¾ teaspoon ground coriander
½ teaspoon cumin seed or ½ teaspoon ground cumin
2 small red chilies, seeded and sliced
2 thick slices galangal, peeled and coarsely chopped
2-in (5-cm) piece turmeric root, peeled and coarsely chopped or ½ teaspoon ground turmeric
1 thick slice fresh ginger root, peeled and coarsely chopped
3 roasted candlenuts or raw almonds or macadamia nuts, coarsely chopped
½ teaspoon dried shrimp paste
3 cloves garlic
4 shallots, sliced

Grind the coriander and cumin seeds (if using) to a powder in an electric grinder. Grind all of the Spice Paste ingredients together.

Heat the oil in a wok or skillet and fry the Spice Paste until it no longer sticks to the pan. Add the beef and mix well. Barely cover the beef with water, add the lime leaves, lemongrass and salt. Cover and simmer until the meat is nearly cooked. Add the potatoes and when they are nearly cooked, add the cabbage, the red and green chilies, the mung-bean vermicelli and the thick coconut milk. Stir until the cabbage and chilies wilt, then and add the tamarind water. Remove the lemongrass and serve garnished with fried onion flakes.

OPOR AYAM MILD CHICKEN CURRY

This is a spicy dish that does not include chilies and therefore is a good choice for those guests about whose chili tolerance you are uncertain. It is a thick special occasion dish customarily served with rice cakes (*ketupat*), but it also goes well with white rice, a *sayur*, some Chili-fried Crunchy Sambal and other crunchy side dishes.

1 chicken
Oil for frying
2 cups (500 ml) thick coconut milk
1 thick slice galangal, bruised
1 stalk lemongrass, bruised
1-in (2½-cm) piece cinnamon stick
2 kaffir lime leaves
1 tablespoon tamarind water or fresh lime juice to taste
½–1 teaspoon palm or dark brown sugar to taste
Salt to taste
1 tablespoon fried onion flakes for garnish

Spice Paste
1 tablespoon coriander seed or 1¾ teaspoons ground coriander
1 teaspoon cumin seed or ½ teaspoon ground cumin
½-in (1½-cm) slice fresh ginger root, peeled and coarsely chopped
3 roasted candlenuts or raw almonds or macadamia nuts, coarsely chopped
3 cloves garlic
6 shallots, sliced
½ teaspoon ground white pepper

Cut the chicken into curry pieces (p. 23). Grind the coriander and cumin seed (if using) into a powder in an electric grinder. Grind all the Spice Paste ingredients to a rough paste.

Heat 1 tablespoon of oil in a wok. Fry the Spice Paste until it is fragrant. Add the chicken pieces and stir fry, turning them until they are coated with the spices. Add the coconut milk, galangal, lemongrass, cinnamon and lime leaves, and simmer gently, uncovered, until the chicken is cooked and the gravy is thick. Add the tamarind water or fresh lime juice, sugar and salt and stir, but do not return to a boil. Remove all the whole spices before serving. Garnish with fried onion flakes.

SPICY CHICKEN IN COCONUT MILK (Java)

AYAM BUMBU RUJAK

The thick texture and heady aroma of this dish together with its rich appearance make it a staple at Javanese celebrations (*slametan*).

1 chicken
2 tablespoons oil
1 cup (250 ml) thin coconut milk
1 stalk lemongrass, bruised
2 salam leaves or kaffir lime leaves
Salt to taste
1 cup (250 ml) thick coconut milk
1 teaspoon palm or dark brown sugar to taste
Dark soy sauce to taste (optional)

Spice Paste
1 teaspoon coriander seed or 1¾ teaspoons ground coriander
6 medium-length red chilies, chopped, or 3 teaspoons
    sambal ulek
1-in (2½-cm) piece galangal, peeled and coarsely
    chopped
1-in (2½-cm) piece turmeric root, peeled and coarsely
    chopped or ½ teaspoon ground turmeric
3 roasted candlenuts or raw almonds or macadamia
    nuts, coarsely chopped
½ teaspoon shrimp paste (optional)
2 cloves garlic
6 shallots, sliced

Cut the chicken into curry pieces (p. 23) or into quarters. Grind the coriander seed (if using) in an electric grinder. Grind all the Spice Paste ingredients to a rough paste.

Heat the oil in a wok and fry the Spice Paste until it is fragrant. Add the chicken pieces and mix, stir-frying until they change color. Add the thin coconut milk, the lemongrass, the salam leaves and the salt, and simmer until the chicken is nearly cooked. Stir in the thick coconut milk and the sugar and dark soy sauce to taste. Bring to a boil, reduce the heat and cook uncovered, stirring occasionally, until the chicken is tender and the gravy is thick.

KELIO AYAM

CHICKEN CURRY
(West Sumatra)

1 chicken

1–2 tablespoons oil

2 cups (500 ml) coconut milk

1 stalk lemongrass, bruised

2 kaffir lime leaves

1 tablespoon tamarind water or fresh lime juice, or to taste

Salt to taste

1 tablespoon fresh grated coconut or steamed dried
    coconut, roasted in a dry pan until golden brown and
    then ground finely (p. 40)

Spice Paste

2 teaspoons coriander seed or 1¾ teaspoons ground
    coriander

½ teaspoon cumin seed or ½ teaspoon ground cumin

4 medium-length red chilies, coarsely chopped

1-in (2½-cm) piece galangal, peeled and coarsely
    chopped

¾-in (2-cm) piece turmeric root, peeled and coarsely
    chopped or ¼ teaspoon ground turmeric or ½ turmeric
    leaf

1½-in (3-cm) piece fresh ginger root, peeled and
    coarsely chopped

3 roasted candlenuts or raw almonds or macadamia
    nuts, coarsely chopped

½ teaspoon shrimp paste

2 cloves garlic

4 shallots, sliced

Cut the chicken into curry pieces (p. 23). Grind the coriander and cumin seed (if using) in an electric grinder. Grind all the Spice Paste ingredients to a rough paste.

Heat the oil in a pan and fry the Spice Paste until fragrant. Add the coconut milk, the lemongrass and the kaffir lime leaves and bring to a boil. Add the chicken pieces and bring to a boil, stirring constantly. Reduce the heat, add the tamarind water and salt. Simmer uncovered until the chicken is tender and the gravy has reduced and thickened slightly. Add the coconut and continue simmering until the gravy is very thick but not dried out. Add water if you wish to thin the curry a little.

NASURAKKO AYAM ## COCONUT CHICKEN
(Sulawesi)

This dish is not as creamy as the Javanese special dishes but the addition of grated coconut to chicken or fish is characteristic of some Sulawesi food and has its own kind of richness.

1 chicken, jointed
2 cups (500 ml) thin coconut milk
½ coconut, skin removed and flesh grated or ½ cup
    (125 g) prepared dried coconut

Spice Paste
2 stalks lemongrass, finely sliced
3-in (7-cm) piece galangal, peeled and coarsely chopped
½ in (1-cm) piece turmeric root, peeled and coarsely
    chopped or ⅛ teaspoon ground turmeric
½-in (1½-cm) piece fresh ginger root, peeled and coarsely
    chopped
2 cloves garlic
5 shallots, sliced
½ teaspoon freshly ground pepper

Grind the Spice Paste ingredients to a paste. Coat the chicken pieces with the Spice Paste and set aside for an hour.

Put the chicken in a wok, add the thin coconut milk, bring to a boil and simmer, uncovered, until the chicken is cooked and the liquid has evaporated completely.

While the chicken is simmering, heat a dry pan and roast the grated coconut, turning constantly until it is golden brown, then grind it finely. When the chicken pieces are cooked and dry, mix them with the roasted coconut and serve.

RENDANG · BEEF RENDANG (Sumatra)

Rendang is a dry curry that owes its origin to a wealthy agriculture, where people can afford to own oxen. In the days before refrigeration this style of cooking enabled preservation of the large amount of meat that would result from killing one of these animals.

This is a north Sumatran version of rendang and therefore quite spicy. You can suit the dish to a milder palate by using fewer chilies. *Rendang* takes a bit of effort to cook and therefore should be made in larger quantities. It is best cooked in a wok, and cooked dry it will keep for at least two weeks in the refrigerator. It makes a tasty meal with rice and a sayur or stir-fried vegetable dish. It is delicious, too, as cold finger food.

2 lb (1 kg) beef topside
4 tablespoons grated fresh coconut or steamed dried coconut, roasted in a dry pan until golden brown then ground finely (p. 40)
3 cups (750 ml) coconut milk
2 stalks lemongrass, bruised
¾-in (2-cm) piece galangal, bruised (optional)
2 kaffir lime leaves (optional)
Salt to taste

Spice Paste

1 teaspoon coriander seed, roasted or ¾ teaspoon ground coriander
9 teaspoons ground chili flakes (this is very hot—adjust to taste)
1-in (2½-cm) piece fresh ginger root, peeled and coarsely chopped

1-in (2½-cm) piece turmeric root, peeled and coarsely
    chopped or ¼ teaspoon ground turmeric
4 cloves garlic
10 shallots, sliced

Grind the Spice Paste ingredients, adding a little warm water if the
mixture is dry. Cut the meat into cubes and mix it with the Spice Paste.

Combine the spiced beef, the coconut and the coconut milk in a wok.
Add the lemongrass, galangal, lime leaves (if using) and salt and bring to a
boil, stirring constantly. Cook, uncovered, until the gravy is almost dry.
Reduce the heat to low and cook until the oil comes out of what is left of
the gravy. Then, stirring constantly, fry the meat and its spices in the oil
until the dish is really dry and the meat has turned dark brown but is not
burned. This last tempering is crucial for *rendang*—the whole quality of
the dish depends on the care with which it is done.

GULAI (Korma)
AYAM

RICH CHICKEN CURRY
(North Sumatra)

What I call "*gulai (korma)*" to distinguish them, are
much more opulent than the wet Padang-style *gulai*.
They are the richest of all the Indonesian curries. Their
origin lies in the powerful trading states, such as Aceh
in north Sumatra, which in the past were involved in
the great spice trade route between China and the
Mediterranean and came under strong Arab/Indian
influence. These *gulai* are characterized by liberal use
of the dry trade spices, such as coriander, cumin, cinnamon, cloves and nutmeg.

1 chicken
2 or more tablespoons oil
5 shallots, sliced
3 cloves or ¼ teaspoon ground cloves
1 small piece of cinnamon stick
1 tomato, peeled, seeded and chopped
2 cups (500 ml) thin coconut milk
1 small stalk lemongrass, bruised
½ cup (125 g) fresh coconut, grated or ½ cup (125 g)
    steamed dried coconut, roasted in a dry pan until
    golden brown then ground finely (p. 40)

1 cup (250 ml) thick coconut milk
Tamarind water or fresh lime juice to taste
Salt to taste

Spice Paste

1 teaspoon coriander seed or 1¾ teaspoons ground
   coriander
¼ teaspoon cumin seed or ¼ teaspoon ground cumin
¼ teaspoon fennel seed or ½ teaspoon ground fennel
10 peppercorns or ½ teaspoon freshly ground black
   pepper
7 medium-length red chilies, coarsely chopped
1-in (2½-cm) piece fresh turmeric root, peeled and
   coarsely chopped, or ¼ teaspoon ground turmeric
1-in (2½-cm) piece fresh ginger root, peeled and
   coarsely chopped
3 candlenuts, roasted or raw almonds or macadamia
   nuts, coarsely chopped
2 cloves garlic
8 shallots, sliced

Cut the chicken into curry pieces (p. 23). Grind the Spice Paste ingredients, adding a little warm water if the paste is dry.

Heat the oil in a pan and fry the shallots with the cloves and cinnamon until the shallots are soft. Add the Spice Paste and fry until it is fragrant. Add the chicken pieces and stir-fry, coating them thoroughly with the spices. Add the tomato and cook until soft. Add the thin coconut milk and lemongrass and stir well until blended.

Add the ground coconut to the chicken and simmer until the chicken is tender. Add the thick coconut milk and the tamarind water and bring to a boil, stirring constantly. Reduce the heat and simmer until the oil floats on top. Stir and serve.

GULAI (Korma) KAMBING

GOAT CURRY
(North Sumatra)

2 tablespoons oil
5 shallots, sliced
3 cloves
1 small piece of cinnamon stick
2 cardamom pods

½ cup (125 g) grated fresh coconut or steamed dried
    coconut (p. 40)
1 lb (500 g) goat, mutton or lamb from the leg, diced
1 tomato, peeled and chopped
2 cups (500 ml) coconut milk
1 stalk lemongrass, bruised
Salt to taste
Tamarind water or fresh lime juice to taste

Spice Paste

10 peppercorns or ½ teaspoon freshly ground black
    pepper
¼ teaspoon cumin seed or ¼ teaspoon ground cumin
¼ teaspoon fennel seed or ½ teaspoon ground fennel
½ teaspoon ground nutmeg
1 teaspoon coriander seed or 1¾ teaspoons ground
    coriander
½ teaspoon poppy seed
1-in (2½-cm) piece turmeric root, peeled and coarsely
    chopped or ¼ teaspoon ground turmeric
7 medium-length red chilies (or fewer, to taste), coarsely
    chopped
3 candlenuts, roasted or raw almonds or macadamia
    nuts, coarsely chopped
1-in (2½-cm) piece fresh ginger root, peeled and
    coarsely chopped
8 shallots, sliced
3 cloves garlic

Heat 1 tablespoon of oil in a pan and fry the 5 sliced shallots over medium heat with the cloves, cinnamon and cardamom, until the shallots are soft.

If using whole spices for the Spice Paste, grind them to a powder in an electric grinder. Grind all of the Spice Paste ingredients to a paste then add the paste to the shallot mixture and fry until fragrant.

In another dry pan, roast the grated coconut until it is yellow. Grind it as finely as possible and put it in the pan with the spice mixture. Add the meat and fry, stirring constantly, until the meat is browned and coated with the spices. Add the tomato and cook for a few minutes. Add the coconut milk, lemongrass and salt and simmer, stirring constantly, until the meat is nearly cooked and the gravy is thick. (Add more water if it gets too dry.) Stir in the tamarind water or fresh lime juice, adjust the seasoning and serve.

GULAI KAMBING JAWA
JAVANESE GOAT CURRY

I have included this Javanese version of *gulai kambing* to show how a basic dish is often adapted to conform to the food habits of the region in which it is cooked. This recipe differs from the previous one in that it does not use the fennel and cardamom that came with a direct involvement in the international spice trade. Instead it uses sugar and galangal, which reflect the Javanese rural lifestyle.

2 tablespoons oil
1 cinnamon stick
1 small tomato, peeled and chopped
2 lb (1 kg) goat or mutton or lamb from the leg, trimmed
   of fat and cut into thin strips
2–3 cups (500–750 ml) thin coconut milk
3 salam leaves
1 tablespoon palm or dark brown sugar, or to taste
1 cup (250 ml) thick coconut milk
Salt to taste
Fried onion flakes for garnish

Spice Paste
1 tablespoon coriander seed or 1¾ tablespoons ground
   coriander
½ teaspoon cumin seed or ½ teaspoon ground cumin
   (optional)
3 cloves or ¼ teaspoon ground cloves
⅛ of a whole nutmeg or ½ teaspoon ground nutmeg
½ teaspoon ground turmeric
2–5 large and small chilies mixed, seeded and coarsely
   chopped
2 stalks lemongrass, finely sliced
1-in (2½-cm) galangal, peeled and coarsely chopped

1-in (2½-cm) fresh ginger root, peeled and coarsely
    chopped
3 candlenuts, roasted or raw almonds or macadamia nuts,
    coarsely chopped
8 shallots, sliced
4 cloves garlic

If using whole spices for the Spice Paste, grind them to a powder in an electric grinder. Grind all of the Spice Paste ingredients to a paste.

Heat the oil in a wok and fry the Spice Paste and the cinnamon stick until fragrant. Add the tomato and fry for a few minutes, then the meat and stir well. Add the thin coconut milk, the salam leaves and the sugar and bring to a boil. Reduce the heat and simmer, covered, until the meat is cooked. Add the thick coconut milk and salt to taste, stir and remove from the heat.

Garnish with fried onion flakes and serve with rice. This recipe can be made with chicken too, but use kaffir lime leaves instead of salam.

CHILI-FRIED SHRIMP WITH COCONUT MILK

SAMBAL GORENG SANTAN UDANG

When coconut milk is added to this dish it becomes a rich and refined one for special meals.

Chili-fries should have a reddish color and to ensure this I have used chopped tomatoes instead of tamarind water to provide the slight acidity required.

1 tablespoon oil
2 small ripe tomatoes, peeled and chopped
1 thick slice galangal, bruised
2 salam leaves
1–2 cups (250–500 ml) thick coconut milk (depending on
    how much liquid you want)
1 lb (500 g) medium-sized shrimp, peeled, rubbed with salt
    and rinsed (p. 25)
Palm or dark brown sugar to taste
Salt to taste
2–3 whole green bird's eye chilies or 1–2 small green
    chilies, seeded and cut in half lengthwise for garnish
    (optional)

Spice Paste

3–5 medium-length red chilies, seeded and coarsely
  chopped
½ teaspoon shrimp paste (*terasi*)
4 shallots, sliced
2 cloves garlic

Grind the Spice Paste Ingredients to a paste.

   Heat the oil in a wok or frying pan and fry the Spice Paste until fragrant. Add the tomato and fry for a few minutes, then add the galangal, salam leaves and coconut milk. Bring to a simmer, add the shrimp and stir, until everything is mixed well. Add the sugar and salt, and continue to stir gently until the shrimp are cooked and the gravy is dark and thick, with its oil floating on top. Just before serving stir in the bird's eye chilies and remove the galangal.

CHILI-FRIED EGG WITH COCONUT MILK

SAMBAL GORENG SANTAN TELUR

1–2 tablespoons oil
1 large ripe tomato, peeled and chopped
2 cups (500 ml) thick coconut milk
1 thick slice of galangal, bruised
1 stalk lemongrass, bruised and cut into pieces
3 salam leaves
6 hard-boiled eggs, shelled
1 teaspoon palm or dark brown sugar, or to taste
Salt to taste
Fried onion flakes for garnish

Spice Paste

4 medium-length red chilies, seeded and sliced
3 roasted candlenuts, or raw almonds or macadamia
  nuts, coarsely chopped (optional)
3 cloves garlic
6 shallots, sliced

Grind the Spice Paste ingredients to a paste. Heat the oil in a wok or frying pan and fry the paste until fragrant. Add the tomato and fry for a few minutes. Add the coconut milk, galangal, lemongrass, salam leaves and bring to a boil. Add the whole eggs, sugar and salt to taste, reduce the heat and continue to cook uncovered, stirring constantly until the sauce reduces and thickens and the oil floats on top. Garnish with fried onion flakes and serve.

CHILI-FRIED VEGETABLES
SAMBAL GORENG SANTAN SAYURAN

This is a good recipe for vegetarians if the shrimp paste is omitted.

1–2 tablespoons oil
2 cups (500 ml) thick coconut milk
2 slices galangal, bruised
3 salam leaves
Salt to taste
3 cups (750 g) mixed vegetables (green beans cut into
   bite-sized pieces; cubed pumpkin, sweet potato, or
   summer squash; soft tofu or tempeh, diced; and/or
   mushrooms)
Tamarind water or fresh lime juice to taste
Palm or dark brown sugar to taste
Medium-length red chilies, sliced diagonally for garnish

Spice Paste
3–5 medium-length red chilies, seeded and coarsely
   chopped
½ teaspoon shrimp paste
2 cloves garlic
3 shallots, sliced

Grind the Spice Paste ingredients to a paste. Heat the oil in a wok, add the Spice Paste and fry it until fragrant. Add the coconut milk, galangal, salam leaves and salt and mix well. Add the vegetables and simmer, uncovered, until they are nearly cooked. Add the tamarind water or fresh lime juice and the sugar and stir until the gravy is thick. Remove the galangal and salam leaves and garnish with chilies before serving.

You can use 2 small ripe tomatoes, chopped, instead of the tamarind water. These would be softened after frying the spices and before adding the coconut milk as in the recipe for Chili-fried Eggs with Coconut Milk (p. 108). In Sumatra, no sugar would be added to the recipe, and the shrimp paste would be optional.

These recipes also work well with chicken livers.

Braised Dishes

The dishes in this section may appear on the table during bountiful times when protein in the form of market meat, eggs or large fish is available or can be afforded.

IKAN MASAK BALI

BRAISED FISH IN HOT AND SPICY SAUCE (Java)

The "bali" in the Indonesian name for this recipe refers to the sauce, not to the island of Bali, as this dish and the two following are in fact Javanese. The spice and flavor of *bumbu bali* is not dissimilar from that of *semur* but the cooking style is of distinctly Chinese heritage. All the dishes here are eaten in small quantities to flavor rice. I have given a range of flavor strengths to choose from— test the strength and the balance to suit your own taste. The flavor should be tangy (sweet–sour) and hot.

2 small fish, about 1¼ lb (600 g) total (mullet, mackerel, trevally, blackfish), cleaned, scaled and slashed two or three times across each side
Salt to taste
Fresh lime juice
Oil for frying
1 cup (250 ml) water
1–2 tablespoons dark soy sauce
1 tablespoon tamarind water or fresh lime juice to taste
1–2 teaspoons palm or dark brown sugar
1 medium-length red chili, sliced, for garnish

Spice Paste
6 medium-length red chilies, seeded and coarsely chopped
1 thick slice fresh ginger root, peeled and coarsely chopped or ¼ teaspoon shrimp paste (*terasi*)
2 cloves garlic
5 shallots, sliced

Rub the fish with the salt and lime juice. Heat the oil in a wok and deep-fry the whole fish the Asian way (p. 26) until golden, turning carefully so as not to break the flesh. Drain and set aside.

Grind the Spice Paste ingredients to a paste. Fry the paste in 1 tablespoon of oil in a wok until fragrant. Add the water, soy sauce, tamarind water or fresh lime juice and sugar, and adjust the flavors to taste. Return the fish to the pan and simmer, uncovered, until the sauce has thickened. Serve the fish on a plate with the reduced sauce poured over it and garnish with chili slices.

STEAK IN HOT AND SPICY SAUCE

DAGING MASAK BALI

I prefer to cook this dish with dark soy sauce rather than Javanese soy sauce, but cook it to suit your taste.

2 tablespoons oil
1 lb (500 g) round steak, thinly sliced
1 cup (250 ml) water
2 tablespoons dark soy sauce
2 teaspoons palm or dark brown sugar
1 tablespoon fresh lime juice
Salt to taste

Spice Paste
6–8 medium-length red chilies, seeded and coarsely chopped
1-in (2½-cm) slice fresh ginger root, peeled and coarsely chopped
1 teaspoon shrimp paste (*terasi*)
4 cloves garlic
5 shallots, sliced

Grind the Spice Paste ingredients into a paste. Heat 1 teaspoon of oil in a wok and fry the Spice Paste until soft. Add the meat and stir-fry until it changes color. Add the water, soy sauce, sugar, lime juice and salt, and simmer, uncovered, until the meat is tender and the gravy is thick. Add more water if the liquid evaporates before the meat is cooked.

TELUR BUMBU BALI	# BOILED EGGS IN HOT AND SPICY SAUCE

This dish is similar to the Thai "Son-in-Law" Eggs (p. 387), though less sweet and spicier.

Oil, well flavored from previous use, for deep-frying
8 cold hard-boiled eggs, shelled
1 tablespoon Javanese soy sauce or to taste
1 tablespoon tamarind water or fresh lime juice, or to taste
1 cup (250 ml) water

Spice Paste
6 medium-length red chilies, seeded and coarsely chopped
¼ teaspoon shrimp paste (*terasi*)
1 clove garlic
4 shallots, sliced

Heat the oil in a wok and deep-fry the hard-boiled eggs until they are golden brown. Lift out and drain.

Grind the Spice Paste ingredients into a paste. Drain the wok of all but 1 tablespoon of oil and heat it. Add the Spice Paste and stir-fry until it is fragrant. Reduce the heat to low, add the soy sauce, tamarind water or lime juice, sugar to taste and water and mix. Add the eggs and spoon the sauce over them. Cook until the eggs are thoroughly heated and the sauce is thick.

PESMOL	# FISH IN A PICQUANT SAUCE

This dish is similar to Pickled Fish from Dutch Java. A Sumatran version of this dish would omit the sugar.

1 whole fish, about 2 lb (800 g) (snapper or other thick white flat fish)
Salt
Juice of ½ lime
Oil for frying
2 salam leaves

1 stalk lemongrass, bruised
1 cup (250 ml) water
1–2 tablespoons vinegar, or to taste
1 teaspoon palm or dark brown sugar (optional)
Salt to taste
8 shallots, peeled
2 cloves garlic, peeled and sliced in large pieces
4 small medium-length red chilies, seeded and halved
   lengthwise

Spice Paste
¾-in (2-cm) piece galangal, peeled and coarsely chopped
¾-in (2-cm) piece turmeric root, peeled and coarsely
   chopped or a pinch of ground turmeric
¾-in (2-cm) piece fresh ginger root, peeled and coarsely
   chopped
5 roasted candlenuts or raw almonds or macadamia
   nuts, coarsely chopped
3 cloves garlic
8 shallots, sliced

Clean and scale the fish, make two or three slashes across each side and rub the flesh with a little salt and lime juice. Heat the oil in a wok and deep-fry the whole fish the Asian way (p. 26) until golden, turning carefully so as not to break the flesh. Drain and set aside.

Grind the Spice Paste ingredients to a paste. Drain the wok of all but 2 tablespoons of oil and fry the Spice Paste until fragrant. Add the salam leaves and lemongrass, water, vinegar, sugar (if you are using it) and salt. Bring to a boil, reduce the heat and simmer for a few minutes, then add the shallots, garlic, chilies and fish. Heat through and serve.

For a vegetarian alternative, replace the fish with some cubed, deep-fried tofu and green beans. Be sure to cook the green beans sufficiently before you add the tofu.

STEAMED DISHES

PEPES UDANG ## SHRIMP STEAMED IN BANANA-LEAF PACKETS

Steaming or grilling in banana-leaf packets is common throughout Southeast Asia. This dish is a steamed version of the popular *pepes*, which are usually grilled over charcoal (pp. 136–139).

1¼ lb (600 g) large raw shrimp, deveined (and peeled, if
  you prefer)
4 medium-length red chilies, finely sliced on the diagonal
3 cloves garlic, chopped
Pieces of banana leaf 8 in (20 cm) square for wrapping,
  or heavy aluminum foil
2 eggs
2 green onions, green part only, finely sliced
Salt to taste
1 small handful of lemon basil leaves

Mix the shrimp, chilies and garlic well. If you are using banana leaves, soften them over a hot electric stove element, gas ring, or in hot water until they are pliable. If using foil, rub one end of a 5-in (12-cm) piece lightly with oil. Beat together the eggs, green onions and salt then stir in the lemon basil.

Depending on their size, place about four shrimp in their chili-garlic mixture about a quarter of the way in from the end of a banana leaf or piece of foil and across it leaving about 1½ in (3 cm) clear at each end. Spoon 2 or 3 tablespoons of egg mixture over the shrimp, roll up carefully into a packet about 2 in (5 cm) in diameter and fold each end into a point. Secure the ends with a toothpick. Steam over boiling water for 15–20 minutes.

PEPES JAMUR MUSHROOMS STEAMED IN
BANANA-LEAF PACKETS

½ cup (125 g) thick coconut milk

1 egg, beaten

3 green onions, green part only, finely sliced

Salt to taste

1 cup (250 g) mushrooms (button, oyster, or soaked
   cloud-ear mushroom), sliced

Pieces of banana leaf 8 in (20 cm) square for wrapping,
   or heavy aluminum foil

Spice Paste

2–3 medium-length red chilies, seeded and coarsely
   chopped

1 stalk lemongrass, finely sliced

2 candlenuts, roasted or raw almonds or macadamia
   nuts, coarsely chopped

1 clove garlic

2 shallots, sliced

Grind the Spice Paste ingredients to a paste. Mix the Spice Paste with the
coconut milk, beaten egg, green onions and salt. Add the mushrooms
and mix well, then spoon the mixture on to the leaves or foil and wrap
up as in the recipe for Shrimp Steamed in Banana-Leaf Packets (p. 114).
Steam over boiling water for about 20 minutes.

FRIED DISHES
Chili-fries

Dry-fried chili-fries are the epitome of the high-flavor side dishes Indonesians love to add to their plate of rice. Those that include meat are most likely to be served on special occasions. Frugal recipes, such as the first recipe here or the "crunchy" version given on p. 117, are the everyday variety.

SAMBAL GORENG HATI TEMPÉ

CHILI-FRIED LIVER AND TEMPEH

2 cups (500 ml) oil for deep-frying
1 cup (250 g) cubed tempeh
2 thick slices galangal, bruised
6 salam leaves
8 oz (250 g) calf's liver, sliced
2 small tomatoes, chopped
2 tablespoons Javanese soy sauce
Tamarind water or fresh lime juice to taste
Palm or dark brown sugar to taste
1 medium-length red chili, sliced diagonally for garnish

Spice Paste
3 medium-length red chilies, seeded and coarsely
  chopped
2 cloves garlic
5 shallots, sliced

Heat the oil in a wok. Deep-fry the tempeh until it is brown and crisp. Remove and drain. Grind the Spice Paste ingredients into a paste. Drain all but 2 tablespoons of oil from the wok and fry the Spice Paste together with the galangal and the salam leaves until fragrant. Add the liver and stir-fry until it is cooked. Add the tomato, the Javanese soy sauce and stir-fry until cooked and not too wet. Add the tempeh and stir-fry to mix and warm through. Taste and adjust the seasonings. The taste should be tangy and a bit sweet—make it more tangy by adding tamarind water or fresh lime juice if you wish. Stir and serve, garnished with the sliced chili.

This dish is also good made with liver or tempeh alone or with green beans. Remember to stir-fry the green beans first and if using tempeh do not add it until the end, to preserve its crispness.

SAMBAL GORENG KAMBING CHILI-FRIED LAMB

I observed the preparation of this dish as part of a special *Buka Puasa* feast prepared communally in the family compound of my Macassan hosts in Bali. (*Buka Puasa* signifies the breaking of the fast after dark during Ramadan.)

Men, women and children were involved in the preparation of the feast and the cooking went on all day. The men of the family who were not at work fetched and carried heavy pots and prepared charcoal fires; the women assembled in one house and made a social occasion of it as they prepared ingredients and supervised the cooking; small children watched everything with wide eyes and older children dropped in from school to help with the chopping.

A whole goat was slaughtered for the occasion and every part of it was used. Saté with Kecap Sauce (p. 138) accounted for the best bits, the stewing meat became Javanese Goat Curry (p. 106) and this Chili-fried Lamb, while the bones and scraps made an excellent base for *soto* and *sayur*. Other dishes prepared were Coconut Chicken (p. 101), some Sulawesi vegetable pasties, various side dishes and Indonesian salads.

Like other *kambing* dishes, this one works just as well with mutton or lamb. While this recipe utilizes stewing meat, you could take a shortcut and use lamb fillets and omit the stewing step. After slicing the meat and marinating it in tamarind water, sugar and salt, put it in when you have fried the spice paste and stir-fry until the meat is cooked, browned on all sides and aromatic.

1 lb (500 g) goat or lamb stewing meat, trimmed of all
   fat and sinew and cubed
2 tablespoons tamarind water or fresh lime juice
1 tablespoon palm or dark brown sugar, or more to taste
Salt to taste
6 tablespoons oil

Spice Paste

3 medium-length red chilies, coarsely chopped

1 stalk lemongrass, finely sliced

¾-in (2-cm) piece galangal, peeled and coarsely chopped

2 roasted candlenuts or raw almonds or macadamia
  nuts, coarsely chopped

3 cloves garlic

6 shallots, sliced

In a saucepan, combine the meat, tamarind water or lime juice, sugar and salt and mix well. Cook over medium heat until the meat is tender and dry. Add no water—the meat will exude its own juice and this will eventually cook dry. Remove from the heat and set aside to cool.

Grind the Spice Paste ingredients to a paste. Heat the oil in a wok and fry the Spice Paste until fragrant. Add the meat and stir-fry until it is browned on all sides—this will take up to 10 minutes. Serve as a side dish with special rice platters or with white rice and coconut milk dishes.

Stir-fries

Apart from cooking rice, stir-frying is one of the most frequent and basic forms of cooking undertaken in Indonesian households every day. Always a convenient way of creating a tasty meal from whatever is in the house garden, stir-frying is also a time-saving method of cooking for the large number of city-based households that attempt to strike a qualitative balance between work and family life. Stir-fried vegetables accompanied by tasty meat sides such as Stir-fried Beef (p. 121) often now replace the more frugal but time-consuming *sayur* in the daily repertoire.

TUMIS   STIR-FRIED VEGETABLES

3 tablespoons oil

5 shallots, finely sliced

2 cloves garlic, chopped

2–6 medium-length red chilies, seeded and sliced

2 thick slices galangal, bruised

2 salam leaves

3 cups (750 g) mixed vegetables (sliced cabbage; Chinese
    mustard or Chinese flowering cabbage, which should be
    cooked separately; green beans; sliced zucchini or
    summer squash; very young peas in the pod; baby corn;
    bean sprouts)

Dash of soy sauce or a pinch of salt

Splash of water or chicken stock (optional)

Heat the oil over medium heat in a wok or a pan and fry the shallots, garlic, chilies, galangal and salam leaves until soft. Add the vegetables and
stir-fry until tender crisp. Add the soy sauce or salt to taste, and a splash
of water or stock if necessary. Stir again and serve.

You can add 3½ oz (100 g) of sliced chicken or small shrimp to this
dish but be certain to add it before the vegetables. If you live in the trop-
ics, try making this dish using shredded green mango and raw peanuts—it
is an especially good combination.

TUMIS LABU SIAM STIR-FRIED SUMMER SQUASH

2 small zucchini or summer squash

Salt

1–2 tablespoons oil

4 shallots, finely sliced

2 cloves garlic, finely sliced

2 slices galangal, bruised

6 small red chilies (or fewer to taste), seeded finely sliced

8 oz (250 g) firm tofu, cut into 2-in (5-cm) square pieces,
    deep-fried and further cut into 4 (optional)

Cut the zucchini or summer squash into fine matchsticks. Put them in a
colander, salt them and set aside for about half an hour to remove some of
their water. Rinse, drain and dry the zucchini.

Heat the oil in a wok and add the shallots, garlic and galangal and stir-
fry until golden. Add the chili and stir-fry for a minute or two. Add the
zucchini and salt to taste and stir-fry until cooked and coated with the
spices. Add the fried tofu, heat through and serve.

STIR-FRIED WATER SPINACH WITH YELLOW BEAN PASTE

TUMIS KANGKUNG TAUCO

This way of cooking water spinach is also popular in Bangkok.

2 tablespoons oil
4 shallots, finely sliced
6 cloves garlic, chopped
2 tablespoons yellow bean paste
1 bunch of water spinach, trimmed of the tough stalks,
  coarsely chopped, washed and drained
Salt to taste
Splash of chicken stock or water

Heat the oil in a wok and fry the shallots and garlic until golden. Add the bean paste, water spinach and salt and stir-fry until coated with the spices. Add the chicken stock or water, cover and cook until the spinach is slightly wilted.

STIR-FRIED CABBAGE WITH EGG

ORAK-ARIK

2 tablespoons oil or butter
1 clove garlic, chopped
1 large onion, cut in two across and thinly sliced
  lengthwise
14 oz (400 g) cabbage, finely sliced
Salt and pepper to taste
2 eggs

Heat the oil in a wok and stir-fry the garlic and onion until they are soft. Add the cabbage and salt and pepper and stir-fry until cooked but still crisp. Push the cabbage to the edges of the pan and break the eggs into the center. Break the yolks and stir the eggs only with the edge of the spatula until the white and yolk are mixed. When the egg begins to set on the bottom stir everything together, mixing it with the cabbage until it is just cooked.

EMPAL STIR-FRIED BEEF

1 cup (250 g) thick coconut milk

2 salam leaves

½ teaspoon palm or dark brown sugar

Salt to taste

1 lb (500 g) beef round steak or topside, sliced and
  pounded thin to tenderize

3 tablespoons oil

Spice Paste

1 stalk lemongrass, finely sliced

½-in (1½-cm) piece turmeric root, peeled and coarsely
  chopped or ⅛ teaspoon ground turmeric

1 thick slice fresh ginger root, peeled and coarsely
  chopped

2 cloves garlic

3 shallots, sliced

1 teaspoon ground coriander

Grind the Spice Paste ingredients to a paste, add the coconut milk and blend. Pour the coconut milk mixture into a wok. Add the salam leaves, palm sugar and salt and bring to a boil. Add the meat and cook over medium heat, stirring constantly until the meat is tender and the coconut milk has evaporated. Remove from the heat and set aside.

Wash and dry the wok. Heat the oil, add the meat and fry until brown and fragrant. Drain on paper towel.

This is a very good standby for everyday meals for busy families. It will keep well in the refrigerator for a few days covered in plastic wrap. Reheat in the microwave as an accompaniment to rice with a stir-fried vegetable or a vegetable *sayur*.

EMPAL PEDAS SPICY STIR-FRIED BEEF

1 lb (500 g) tender beef (sirloin or fillet), sliced

½ teaspoon freshly ground coriander

Salt

2 tablespoons oil

1 teaspoon palm sugar or dark brown sugar, or more to
  taste

1 tablespoon tamarind water or fresh lime juice

Spice Paste

3–6 medium-length red chilies, coarsely chopped

½-in (1-cm) piece galangal, peeled and coarsely chopped

1 teaspoon shrimp paste (optional)

6 shallots, sliced

3 cloves garlic

Grind the Spice Paste ingredients to a paste. Rub the sliced beef with coriander and salt and set aside. Heat the oil in a wok and fry the Spice Paste until fragrant. Add the seasoned beef, the sugar and the tamarind water or lime juice and stir-fry. Add a splash of water and stir-fry until the liquid has evaporated.

SEMARANG-STYLE BEEF

LAPIS DAGING SEMARANG

5 shallots, coarsely chopped

4 cloves garlic, coarsely chopped

½ teaspoon freshly ground pepper

2 tablespoons dark soy sauce

Pinch of ground nutmeg (optional)

2 teaspoons palm or dark brown sugar or more to taste (optional)

1 tablespoon oil

1 onion, thinly sliced lengthwise

1 lb (500 g) topside or round steak, pounded thin to tenderize and cut into bite-sized pieces

1 large ripe tomato, peeled and chopped

Grind the shallots, garlic, pepper, soy sauce, nutmeg and sugar (if using) to a paste. Marinate the beef in this mixture for 30 minutes to 1 hour.

Heat the oil in a wok or a pan, add the sliced onion and stir-fry it until soft. Add the beef together with the marinade, and stir-fry for 1 minute. Add the tomato and a splash of water. Stir-fry until the beef is tender, the tomato soft and the sauce is slightly reduced.

To cook this dish to north Sumatran taste, omit the sugar and add a stick of cinnamon and two whole cloves during the last cooking step.

Pan-fries

DADAR JAWA JAVANESE OMELETTE

An excellent breakfast dish or quick family meal when paired with stir-fried vegetables.

4 eggs
1 teaspoon Javanese soy sauce (optional)
2 tablespoons oil
4 shallots, finely sliced
2–3 medium-length red chilies, seeded and finely sliced

Lightly beat the eggs with the Javanese soy sauce and a splash of water. Heat the oil in a pan and fry the shallots and chilies until soft. Pour in the egg mixture and let it sit until half set. Then proceed as you would with a French omelette: either run channels through it gently with the flat tip of a knife or lift the edges of the setting omelette and tilt the pan so that the remaining liquid comes into contact with the hot pan. When completely set, fry until the omelette is golden brown on the bottom then serve.

Deep-fries

IKAN LAUT GORENG FRIED FISH

1 whole sea fish, about 1 lb (500 g) (small snapper or
   other good frying fish)
Salt
Tamarind water or fresh lime juice
1 clove garlic, chopped (optional)
Oil for deep-frying the Asian way (p. 26)

Clean, scale and wash the fish. Make some slashes through the skin on each side. Mix the salt, tamarind water or lime juice and garlic and marinate the fish in this for about 30 minutes, turning it frequently. Heat the oil in a wok. Dry the fish with paper towels and fry first on one side, then on the other, until it is cooked. Turn it over only once, carefully, as the flesh may crumble. Serve with Tomato Sambal (p. 161).

DEEP-FRIED FISH TRIANGLES

TUMPI TUMPI
(Ujung Pandang)

2 large steaks or cutlets of oily fish (skipjack, Spanish mackerel), bones removed
¼ cup (60 ml) water
Pieces of banana leaf about 10-in (25-cm) long, washed and softened, or heavy aluminum foil
Oil for deep-frying
1 egg, beaten

Spice Paste
7 stalks lemongrass, finely sliced
3 shallots, sliced
3 cloves garlic
1 wedge fresh young coconut (about 3 in/8 cm) wide at its center), skinned and finely grated
1 teaspoon palm or dark brown sugar
½ teaspoon freshly ground white pepper

Cut the fish into pieces and poach gently in the water, uncovered, until the water has evaporated and the fish starts to fry in its own oil.

Grind the Spice Paste ingredients into a very fine paste. Add the fish pieces and pound everything together until you have a *very* fine paste. Fold the banana leaves over double and form a cone (or use thick foil doubled). Put 2 heaping tablespoons of the Spice Paste mixture into each cone, flatten the cones out and fold over the top to form a triangle with equal sides, about 2 in (5 cm) in length. Put the triangles in the refrigerator for at least 2–3 hours. The triangles will keep in the refrigerator for up to 3 days.

Remove the fish triangles from their banana leaf or foil. Heat the oil in a wok. Dip each fish triangle into the beaten egg then drop it into the hot oil. When brown, lift out, drain and serve.

FRIED SPICY CHICKEN

AYAM GORENG
BUMBU

1–2 tablespoons oil
1 chicken, cut into curry pieces (p. 23)
Water or light chicken stock
1 tablespoon palm or dark brown sugar

3 tablespoons tamarind water or fresh lime juice

1 stalk lemongrass, bruised

1 salam leaf

4 kaffir lime leaves

Oil for deep-frying

Spice Paste

2 tablespoons coriander seed or 1¾ tablespoons ground
  coriander

⅛ teaspoon cumin seed or ⅛ teaspoon ground cumin

1-in (2½-cm) piece galangal, peeled and coarsely
  chopped

1-in (2½-cm) piece turmeric root, peeled and coarsely
  chopped

1-in (2½-cm) piece fresh ginger root, peeled and
  coarsely chopped

7 roasted candlenuts, raw almonds or macadamia nuts,
  coarsely chopped

4 cloves garlic

6 shallots, sliced

If using whole spices for the Spice Paste, grind them to a powder in an electric grinder. Grind all of the Spice Paste ingredients to a paste. Heat 1–2 tablespoons of oil in a wok and fry the Spice Paste until fragrant. Add the chicken pieces, add water or light chicken stock to cover, sugar, tamarind water, lemongrass, salam and lime leaves and simmer until the chicken is cooked. Drain and set the chicken aside to dry.

Heat enough oil in a wok to deep-fry. Add the chicken pieces and deep-fry until they are brown and serve.

For vegetarians this dish works very well using firm cubed tofu instead of the chicken.

AYAM GORENG JAWA ## JAVA-STYLE FRIED CHICKEN (Java)

1 small chicken

1–2 cups (250–500 ml) coconut milk

1 stalk lemongrass, bruised

Salt to taste

Palm or dark brown sugar to taste (optional)

Oil for frying

Spice Paste

1 teaspoon coriander seed or ¾ teaspoon ground
   coriander
2 medium-length chilies, seeded and coarsely chopped
1-in (2½-cm) piece galangal, peeled and coarsely
   chopped
½-in (1-cm) piece turmeric root, peeled and coarsely
   chopped or ⅛ teaspoon ground turmeric
2 roasted candlenuts or raw almonds or macadamia
   nuts, coarsely chopped
3 shallots, sliced

Cut the chicken into curry pieces (p. 23). If using whole coriander seeds, grind them to a powder in an electric grinder. Grind all of the Spice Paste ingredients to a paste. Add the coconut milk and blend well. Pour the mixture into a wok, add the chicken, lemongrass, salt and sugar to taste. Stir well, and set aside to marinate for up to an hour.

   Put the wok on the heat and bring the mixture to a boil. Reduce the heat and simmer, stirring constantly, until the chicken is tender and the liquid has evaporated. Remove from the heat and lift out the chicken pieces.

   Heat plenty of oil in a pan and fry the spiced chicken pieces until they are brown. The amount of coconut milk needed for this and the following recipe is variable, depending on the nature of the chicken. Free-range chickens will need more liquid to cook than fresh battery hens.

AYAM GORENG PADANG

SAMATRA-STYLE FRIED CHICKEN (Sumatra)

1 chicken
1–2 cups (250–500 ml) coconut milk
1 stalk lemongrass, bruised
Oil for deep-frying

Spice Paste

2 medium-length red chilies, seeded and coarsely
   chopped
1-in (2½-cm) piece fresh turmeric root, peeled and
   coarsely chopped, or ¼ teaspoon ground turmeric
1 clove garlic
5 shallots, sliced

Grind the Spice Paste ingredients to a paste. Cut the chicken into serving-size pieces and rub them well with the Spice Paste. Set aside for 10 minutes.

Put the seasoned chicken into a wok, pour the coconut milk over them, add the lemongrass and bring to a simmer. Cook, uncovered, for about 30 minutes, spooning the sauce over the chicken pieces constantly until the sauce evaporates completely. Set the chicken aside to cool.

Heat the oil in a wok and fry the chicken pieces until brown.

This recipe is also suitable for a barbecue. Do not let the sauce evaporate, but reserve it for basting the chicken as you finish cooking it on a charcoal grill.

DENDENG BELADO ## CRISP-FRIED BEEF WITH HOT AND TANGY SAUCE

This dish is a favorite pre-dinner appetizer and goes very well with drinks. For a main meal team it up with something creamy but fairly bland like Mild Chicken Curry (p. 98), a mild shrimp dish, or a vegetable *sayur*.

3 cloves garlic
2–3 tablespoons tamarind water or fresh lime juice
Salt to taste
2 lb (1 kg) topside beef, trimmed of all fat and sinew, or skirt steak, sliced along the grain and pounded thin to tenderize
Oil for deep-frying

Belado Sauce
6 medium-sized red chilies, coarsely chopped
10 shallots, sliced
2–3 tablespoons oil
1 ripe tomato, peeled and finely chopped
Fresh lime juice to taste (optional)

Grind the garlic, tamarind water and a little salt together to make a marinade. Mix this tamarind–garlic marinade with the beef and marinate overnight. Dry the beef in a good dehydrator or in the oven (p. 442 for instructions). Heat the vegetable oil in a wok, add the meat slices and deep-fry until they are brown and dry. Lift out and drain.

To make the Belado Sauce, grind the chilies and shallots to a rough paste. Heat the oil in a wok and fry the mixture until fragrant. Add the tomato and stir-fry to soften. Add the meat and stir until it is coated with the spices. If you like more of a sour flavor, add lime juice to taste.

To serve as an appetizer, lift out on to a plate. To serve this dish with rice as part of a meal, add a splash of water, stir to moisten and heat it through.

Basic dried beef slices are sold in packets in Asian grocery stores. If you use these you need proceed only from the point where the meat is fried.

TEMPÉ GORENG FRIED TEMPEH

Tempeh, made from yeasted soy beans, is an excellent high-protein substitute for meat. You can buy it fresh in an oblong cake from most well stocked supermarkets. In Java, tempeh has been the common person's most accessible protein other than shrimp paste (*terasi*).

3 small cloves garlic
½ teaspoon ground coriander
1 tablespoon water
8 oz (250 g) tempeh, sliced and scored a little with a fork
Oil for deep-frying
Salt to taste

Mash the garlic and coriander together and mix them with the water. Rub this marinade over the tempeh slices and set aside to marinate for at least 15 minutes and preferably until dry.

Heat the oil in a wok and deep-fry the tempeh slices until they are brown. Lift out, drain and salt them. Serve fried tempeh with a wet vegetable, fish dish or a stir-fry, a sambal and rice for a satisfying family meal.

GRILLS AND BARBECUES

IKAN PANGGANG JAWA ## GRILLED FISH, JAVANESE-STYLE

Grilling the fish over an open charcoal fire produces the most delicious result.

1 small sea fish (snapper or other flat white fish)
1 clove garlic, chopped
2 tablespoons Javanese soy sauce or 2 tablespoons dark soy sauce mixed with 1 tablespoon palm or dark brown sugar
1 tablespoon water
Butter for basting
3 hot red chilies, finely sliced
1 tablespoon fresh lime juice, or to taste

Clean and scale the fish and make two or three slashes down the sides. Mix the garlic with 1 tablespoon of the soy sauce and the water. Marinate the fish in this mixture for about 1 hour.

Put the fish in a fish grill, reserving the marinade. Grill the fish over low heat, basting with a little butter as it cooks to prevent it from drying out. Alternatively, grill the fish on a charcoal or gas grill or wrap it in greased aluminum foil and bake it in the oven for approximately 10 minutes per pound (500 g). You can cook this recipe in the microwave as well. Add 1 tablespoon lime juice to the marinade mixture, put the fish in a microwave dish and pour in the marinade. Scatter the sliced chilies over the top, cover and cook.

Combine the remaining soy sauce, the sliced chilies and the lime juice and spoon this mixture over the cooked fish before serving. Squeeze additional fresh lime juice on top before serving.

GRILLED SEA FISH
(Ujung Pandang)

IKAN BAKAR COLO-COLO

2 relatively oily sea fish (mackerel, bonito, tuna, trevally)
Tamarind water made from 1 teaspoon tamarind in 1 cup
   (250 ml) water or fresh lime juice
Salt
Oil

Soak the fish in tamarind water and salt for 20–30 minutes. Remove the fish from the marinade and dry it with paper towels. Brush the fish all over with oil, make 2 or 3 slashes across the sides and wrap it in banana leaves or place it in an oiled fish grill. Grill over a charcoal fire. Serve with a bowl of Tomato Sambal (p. 161).

SQUID GRILLED IN BANANA-LEAF PACKETS
(Jakarta)

PEPES CUMI-CUMI

A west Javanese dish that has become very popular in recent years.

1 lb (500 g) baby squid or cuttlefish, with ink sacs if possible
1 large bunch of lemon basil leaves, Asian sweet basil or a
   few green leaves of spring onion, chopped
5 kaffir lime leaves, finely sliced
Salt to taste
Pieces of banana leaf or heavy aluminum foil 8-in (20-cm)
   square for wrapping

Spice Paste
5–10 medium-length red and green chilies, seeded and
   coarsely chopped
2 stalks lemongrass (white part only), finely sliced
5 roasted candlenuts or raw almonds or macadamia nuts,
   coarsely chopped
3 cloves garlic
6 shallots, sliced
½ teaspoon shrimp paste (optional)

Grind the Spice Paste ingredients to a paste. Wash the squid, pull them apart and remove their quills, skin, heads and beaks but leave their ink sacks in, if they have them.

In a bowl carefully mix the squid (both bodies and tentacles), Spice Paste, basil, lime leaves and salt. If you are using banana leaves, soften them over a hot electric stove element or gas ring, or in hot water until they are pliable. If using foil, rub a 5-in (12-cm) strip on one end lightly with oil. A quarter of the way in from the end of the banana leaf or piece of foil, put enough of the mixture to make packets about 2 in (5 cm) wide, leaving 1½ in (3–4 cm) clear at each end. Roll up, fold into points at each end and secure with a toothpick.

Boil some water in a steamer and steam the packets over it for 30 minutes. Alternatively, if you are using banana leaves, cook the packets in a microwave.

In the meantime bring a charcoal barbecue to a steady glow. Remove the packets from the steamer or microwave and grill them on both sides over the moderate fire until the banana leaf is brown. If using foil you can cook these entirely on the grill. Cut the packets open neatly at the table.

PEPES IKAN   FISH IN BANANA-LEAF PACKETS (West Java)

You can also use the above recipe for plain fish packets. Clean and scale a small whole fish (it should be a soft one—freshwater fish or mullet). Prepare the banana leaves or pieces of aluminum foil, put the fish on top, sprinkle with lime juice, then spread spice paste over and inside it. Roll up the packets and cook according to same directions provided for Squid Grilled in Banana-Leaf Packets (above).

This recipe is also very good with fish roe—try sea mullet roe. Keep the roe in a piece (about 9 oz/250 g), steam it first and then rub it with spice paste. Wrap into a parcel and finish off on the grill.

PEPES IKAN   MENDANO-STYLE FISH IN BANANA-LEAF PACKETS

10 shallots

3 cloves garlic

5–10 small medium-length red and green chilies, seeded and sliced diagonally

2 handfuls lemon basil leaves

2 green onions (green parts only), sliced

Salt to taste

Light soy sauce to taste

Pieces of banana leaf or heavy aluminum foil 8 in (20 cm) square for wrapping

3 small whole sea fish, cleaned and scaled, or 1¼ lb (600 g) fish fillets

Fresh lime juice

Chop the shallots and garlic finely and mix the herbs, spices and salt together, moistening with a little light soy sauce. Prepare the banana leaves of pieces of aluminum foil according to the instructions in Squid in Banana-Leaf Packets (p. 131).

Put a whole fish or a fillet on leaf, squeeze lime juice over it and spoon the herb mixture around it on both sides and in the cavity if whole. Roll up the leaves and secure with a toothpick. Steam for 10–15 minutes first (or cook it in a microwave if in banana leaves), then grill over low heat until the leaves are brown.

If you use foil, you can cook the packets entirely on the grill.

GRILLED SPICY COCONUT CHICKEN

AYAM PANGGANG BUMBU RUJAK

1 chicken

1 cup (250 ml) thick coconut milk

1 stalk lemongrass, bruised

1 teaspoon palm sugar or dark brown sugar

Salt to taste

1 tablespoon tamarind water or fresh lime juice

Spice Paste

3 medium-length red chilies, coarsely chopped

3 shallots, sliced

2 cloves garlic

½ teaspoon shrimp paste, roasted in foil

1-in (2½-cm) piece galangal, peeled and coarsely chopped

Cut the chicken down the breastbone and open it out in one flat piece with the legs skewered down to the back so that the bird remains flat.

Grind the Spice Paste ingredients to a paste. Coat the chicken all over with the Spice Paste and set it aside for a while enabling the spices to penetrate the skin.

In a shallow pan large enough to accommodate the chicken, add the coconut milk, lemongrass, sugar, salt and tamarind water or lime juice and the seasoned chicken. Bring to a boil, reduce the heat and simmer gently, uncovered, spooning the sauce over the bird frequently until the chicken is cooked and the sauce has evaporated.

Remove the chicken and grill it over low heat until brown, spooning the remaining dried spices over it from the pan as it cooks. This final roasting can also be in a baking dish in the oven, though it will not be as flavorful as the barbecued version.

SINGGANG AYAM ## GRILLED CHICKEN
(Sumatra)

1 chicken
2 cups (500 ml) thick coconut milk
1 stalk lemongrass
1–2 kaffir lime leaves
Salt to taste

Spice Paste
3–4 medium length red chilies, coarsely chopped
1-in (2½-cm) piece turmeric root, peeled and coarsely
    chopped or ¼ teaspoon ground turmeric
1-in (2½-cm) piece fresh ginger root, peeled and
    coarsely chopped
½ teaspoon freshly ground pepper
2 cloves garlic
5 shallots, sliced

Cut the chicken down the breastbone and open it out in one flat piece with the legs skewered down to the back so that the bird remains flat. Grind the Spice Paste ingredients to a paste. Coat the chicken all over with the Spice Paste and set it aside for a while enabling the spices to penetrate the skin.

In a shallow pan large enough to accommodate the chicken, add the coconut milk, lemongrass, kaffir lime leaves, salt and the seasoned chicken. Bring to a boil, reduce the heat and simmer gently, uncovered, spooning the sauce over the bird frequently until the chicken is cooked and the sauce has thickened.

Remove the chicken and grill it over low heat until brown, spooning the remaining sauce from the pan over it as it cooks.

SLOW-COOKED DUCK (Bali)

BEBEK BETUTU

I ate this rich and ancient Balinese dish in 1977 when it was cooked for me by the music and dancing master who had taken the first Balinese music and dance troupe to Europe in the 1930s. Cooked his way, the process took 24 hours. The intriguing flavors lingered in my memory, and I am grateful to Robyn Coventry for supplying this eyewitness account after she saw it cooked in a shorter amount time in 1993.

1 cleaned fresh duck, complete with neck and, if possible, head and feet (about 3–4 lb/1.5–2 kg)
2 cups (500 ml) tamarind water (p. 55)
1–2 tablespoons Javanese soy sauce
1 teaspoon soft shrimp paste (*kapi*)
½ cup (125 g) oil
1 bunch cassava leaves, silverbeet (leaves only), amaranth or baby spinach, washed and cut into strips
Banana leaves
10 salam leaves (optional)
Leaf-sheaths from the betel tree (*buah upih*) or heavy aluminum foil

Spice Paste
Sacred Spice Paste (p. 141)
3 cloves or ¼ teaspoon ground cloves
3 cardamom pods or ¼ teaspoon ground cardamom
2 stalks lemongrass, finely sliced

Pierce the duck all over with a fork or the point of a sharp knife and then marinate it in the tamarind water for 10 minutes, turning it over after 5 minutes. Remove and wipe dry.

Grind all the Sacred Spice Paste ingredients to a paste, together with the additional spices, adding sufficient water at the end to make a smooth mixture. In a separate bowl mix together the Javanese soy sauce, the soft shrimp paste and the oil. Rub the duck vigorously all over with this mixture, breaking its bones at and between the joints and on its trunk with your hands as you go. Stuff the bird with the cassava leaves together with the duck's feet, if you have them, and a little Spice Paste and close the opening. Lay the duck on banana leaves, spread the Spice Paste all over it and fold the head and neck down beside the body, scattering the salam leaves on top.

Wrap everything into a secure banana-leaf parcel, then in two layers of heavy-duty aluminium foil. The traditional material used in Bali is the tough sheath at the base of the leaves of the betel tree (*areca*). First the sheath is moistened, then split and pulled up on the soft inside to make a flap. The duck parcel is put in, covered with the flap and the rest of the sheath is wrapped tightly around and secured with bamboo pins. A second sheath is then wrapped around the first and secured again. The whole package is wet again when ready to be put into the built-up oven.

To cook this dish the Balinese use rice husks and a special earthenware cover the size and shape of a plastic washbowl about 20 in (50 cm) in diameter and about 8 in (20 cm) deep. They first place the duck on two half-bricks so that it sits above the ground then put the cover over and around it to form a kind of clay oven. They mound a pile of dampened rice husks over and around the bowl to the maximum thickness that will stay in a mound and start it smouldering with some pieces of red-hot charcoal placed at the apex. The fire is kept smouldering and burning slowly downwards for eight hours.

This whole process is reminiscent of the Indian style of cooking in a tandoor except that it is much slower and less fierce. The duck ends up slightly smoked, moist and falling off the bones.

I have used two alternative methods to cook this dish, both of which work quite well although they do not produce exactly the same result as the traditional Balinese method. For the first, build a very slow charcoal fire in a charcoal-burning kettle barbecue and when it is ready put in the wrapped duck, cover, and cook for about 5 hours.

For the second method place the duck, in its foil wrapper, in an oven preheated to 350°F (175°C) for 3–3½ hours, reducing the temperature to 300°F (150°C) after 2 hours.

To serve, put the sealed parcel on a plate and bring it to the table where it should be opened carefully in front of the diners so as not to lose any of its marvelous juices. The clouds of aromatic steam that should billow forth as you cut it open along the top are bound to produce the same kind of excited response among waiting diners as does the opening of the mud casing around a Chinese Beggar's Chicken.

SATÉ BANDENG ## STUFFED FISH SATÉ
(West Java)

If you really want to impress a Javanese, just cook this dish successfully!

2 cups (500 ml) thick coconut milk
1 small mackerel or other fish with tough skin, about 8-in (20-cm) long
2 tablespoons oil
1 teaspoon palm or dark brown sugar
1 pea-sized piece of tamarind
Banana leaves or greased heavy aluminum foil

Spice Pastes (per fish)
2 shallots, sliced
2 cloves garlic
½ teaspoon ground coriander
Pinch of ground cumin
½ teaspoon shrimp paste
¾-in (2-cm) piece of lemongrass, finely sliced

Bring the coconut milk to a boil in a saucepan. Boil the milk, stirring it constantly until it has reduced and thickened into a cream. Remove it from the heat and set aside to cool.

Wash and scale the fish taking care not to perforate the skin. Massage it vigorously all over to release the backbone from the flesh. If this is done properly you should be able to break the bone near the tail and again near the head and pull it out through a gill opening. Then press out all the entrails through the gill hole and discard them, followed by the flesh, which you should put aside. Leave the fish skin whole but empty. Turn the skin inside out through the gill opening to remove any remaining flesh, then wash it and push back right side in. Do not displace the head or tail or break the skin anywhere except at the gill hole.

Remove all the bones from the flesh that you have kept aside and flake the flesh with your fingers.

Heat the oil and fry the sliced shallots and garlic until they are browned. Remove, drain and set aside. Roast the coriander and cumin seeds and the shrimp paste then grind them to a powder. Combine the ground mixture with the lemongrass and the shallot mixture, mashing everything to a paste. Blend in 4 tablespoons of cooled thick coconut milk, the sugar and the tamarind. Add the flaked fish and blend everything thoroughly. Fill the fish skin with this mixture. Completely wrap the whole fish in banana leaves or greased foil and grill. It will take about 20 minutes to cook.

Less artistic and less dedicated cooks can split the fish along one side and remove the bones and flesh. After stuffing the fish, the opening can be carefully closed with toothpicks or sewn up. This probably would not do in Indonesia where the fish are grilled in more porous banana leaves, but with a sealed foil covering no juices should escape.

SATE BEEF OR LAMB SATÉ WITH PEANUT SAUCE

Saté on skewers is quintessential street food in Indonesia, and a ritual food at Balinese temple festivals. Cooked on carefully tended charcoal stoves, the fires brought to just the right temperature through vigorous fanning, saté is perfect food to serve at outdoor barbecues. An authentic presentation would include pieces of rice cake (p. 165), cut into chunks, and a cucumber pickle (p. 155), but it would do just as well to provide a tossed salad and perhaps a bowl of steamed rice. Always remember to soak the saté sticks in water for an hour or two beforehand to prevent them from burning on the fire.

1 lb (500 g) beef steak or boned leg of lamb, cubed
Fried onion flakes for garnish
Squeeze of fresh lime juice

Marinade
½ teaspoon salt
2 cloves garlic, chopped
2 shallots, chopped
2 teaspoons dark brown sugar
3 teaspoons fresh lime juice
1 tablespoon tamarind water or fresh lime juice
2 tablespoons dark soy sauce

Peanut Sauce

4 medium-length red chilies

4 shallots, sliced

Oil for frying

½ cup (125 g) raw peanuts, freshly fried, skins removed
 and coarsely ground

1 cup (250 ml) coconut milk

Palm sugar or dark brown sugar to taste

1 stalk lemongrass, bruised

1 salam leaf

Salt and pepper to taste

Soak several bamboo skewers in water and set aside. Combine all of the Marinade ingredients and the cubed meat in a shallow dish or zip top plastic bag and marinate for at least 30 minutes. Thread the cubes on to the wooden skewers to about one-third of their length and grill them, basting with what is left of the marinade. The satés are best when grilled over a charcoal fire, though a gas or electric grill or even a griddle on top of the stove is acceptable. Try using a thick stalk of lemongrass crushed at the bottom as a basting brush: it will not disintegrate in the heat as a nylon brush might.

To make the Peanut Sauce, grind the chilies and shallots to a paste. Heat a little oil in a small saucepan and fry the paste lightly. Add the remaining sauce ingredients, mix well and bring to a boil. Simmer gently until thick, stirring constantly. Add a little water if the sauce is too thick.

Place the satés on a large platter and spoon Peanut Sauce over them. Garnish with fried onion flakes and a squeeze of fresh lime juice before serving.

**SATÉ KAMBING
BUMBU KECAP**

SATÉ WITH KECAP SAUCE

This saté is probably the most common one in Java.

2 lb (1 kg) goat or lamb shoulder, cubed

Fried onion flakes for garnish

Marinade

2 teaspoons coriander seed, roasted or 1¾ teaspoons
 ground coriander

¼ teaspoon cumin seed, roasted or ¼ teaspoon ground
 cumin

2 stalks lemongrass, finely sliced

1½-in (4-cm) piece galangal, peeled and chopped

1-in (2½-cm) piece turmeric root, peeled and chopped or
  ¼ teaspoon ground turmeric

½-in (10-cm) piece fresh ginger root, peeled and chopped

2 cloves garlic

4 shallots, sliced

½ cup (125 ml) tamarind water or fresh lime juice

2 tablespoons palm or dark brown sugar

1 teaspoon salt

pinch pepper

Kecap Sauce

2 medium-length red chilies, seeded and finely sliced

½ cup (125 ml) Javanese soy sauce

1–2 tablespoons fresh lime juice

If using whole coriander and cumin seeds for the Marinade, grind them to a powder in an electric grinder. Blend all of the marinade ingredients together. Combine the Marinade and the cubed meat in a shallow dish or zip top plastic bag and marinate for at least 3 hours.

Soak several bamboo skewers in water and set aside. To prepare the Kecap Sauce, mix the sliced chilies with the Javanese soy sauce and the lime juice. The sauce should be sweet and sour.

Thread the meat on to the skewers to about one-third of their length and grill over a medium hot charcoal fire. Place the satés on a large platter and spoon the Kecap Sauce over them. Garnish with the fried onion flakes and serve.

SATÉ AYAM CHICKEN SATÉ

2 lb (1 kg) boneless, skinless chicken breasts or thighs,
  cut into wide strips

1 tablespoon Javanese soy sauce

Fried onion flakes for garnish

Marinade

2 cloves garlic, sliced

1-in (2½-cm) piece fresh ginger root, peeled and
  chopped

2 tablespoons light soy sauce

Peanut Sauce

4 medium-length red chilies, chopped

½ teaspoon shrimp paste

1 clove garlic, sliced

6 shallots, sliced

1 tablespoon oil

1 tablespoon fresh lime juice

1 cup (250 ml) coconut milk

¾ cup (175 g) fried peanuts, coarsely chopped

Salt to taste

Soak several bamboo skewers in water and set aside. To make the Marinade, crush the garlic and ginger to a paste and then combine it with the soy sauce. Combine the Marinade and the chicken strips in a shallow dish or zip top plastic bag and marinate for 30 minutes. Thread the strips on to the skewers and grill over a low charcoal fire until cooked (about 20 minutes).

To make the Peanut Sauce, grind the chilies, shrimp paste, garlic and shallots to a paste. Heat the oil in a wok and fry the paste until fragrant. Add the rest of the sauce ingredients and cook over medium heat until the sauce is thick. Add a little water if the sauce is too thick.

Place the satés on a large platter and spoon Peanut Sauce over them. Garnish with fried onion flakes and drizzle Javanese soy sauce on top before serving.

MAGBUB # GROUND LAMB SATÉ
(Banten)

2 tablespoons oil

1 lb (500 g) ground lamb

Spice Paste

5 shallots, coarsely chopped

4 cloves garlic, sliced

1 tablespoon coriander seed or 1¾ tablespoons ground
   coriander

½ cup (125 ml) tamarind water or fresh lime juice

4 tablespoons palm or dark brown sugar

3 tablespoons thick coconut cream (p. 40)

Salt to taste

Heat the oil in a pan and fry the shallot and garlic until they are brown and crisp. Remove from the pan, drain and set aside. If using whole coriander seeds, roast them until fragrant in a dry pan, then grind them to a powder. Grind all of the Spice Paste ingredients to a paste. In a food processor mince the lamb, add the spice mixture, and blend into a paste. Add the ground lamb and blend. Refrigerate for at least 1 hour.

Cut several bamboo skewers down to 6 in (15 cm) in length. Soak in water and set aside.

With oiled hands, mold a heaped tablespoon of the meat mixture into a pear shape. Place the meat on the skewer and mold it firmly down to about half of the length of the skewer in a club shape with the broader end at the top, oiling your fingers again if necessary. Brush with oil and grill over low heat until golden brown.

SATÉ LEMBAT GROUND PORK SATÉ (Bali)

This is the famous saté of Balinese temple festivals, always cooked by men. In this Hindu society there is clearly a lingam symbolism attached to it. I am indebted to Janet De Neefe, a cooking teacher at Ubud in Bali, for this recipe. The Balinese treat the coconut in this dish in a special way to release its oils and aroma before they grate it. See the recipe for Vegetables with Roasted Coconut on p. 147.

1¼ lb (600 g) finely ground pork
1½ cups (375 g) grated fresh coconut or dried coconut, steamed for 10 minutes
4 teaspoons palm or dark brown sugar
6 kaffir lime leaves, finely shredded
2 tablespoons fried onion flakes
1 teaspoon salt or to taste

Sacred Spice Paste
½ teaspoon ground nutmeg
2 teaspoons coriander seed or 1¾ teaspoons ground coriander
2 teaspoons sesame seed
6–10 medium-length red chilies, coarsely chopped
2-in (5-cm) piece galangal, peeled and coarsely chopped

¾-in (2-cm) piece resurrection lily, chopped

3-in (8-cm) piece turmeric root, peeled and coarsely chopped

2-in (5-cm) piece fresh ginger root, peeled and coarsely chopped

5 roasted candlenuts, raw almonds or macadamia nuts, coarsely chopped

1 teaspoon shrimp paste

6 cloves garlic

5 shallots, sliced

½ teaspoon freshly ground black pepper

½ cup (125 g) water

Cut several bamboo skewers down to 6-in (15-cm) lengths and soak them in water for an hour or two.

To make the Spice Paste, grind the nutmeg, coriander and sesame seeds in an electric grinder. Grind all of the Spice Paste ingredients to a paste.

Combine 6 tablespoons of the Spice Paste with the remaining ingredients and knead into a sticky consistency (you could use the dough attachment for your mixer). Cover and refrigerate for at least an hour. Refrigerate any remaining Spice Paste for another use.

With oiled hands, mold a heaped tablespoon of the meat mixture into a pear shape. Place the meat on the skewer and mold it firmly down to about half of the length of the skewer in a club shape with the broader end at the top, oiling your fingers again if necessary. Brush with oil and grill over low heat until golden brown.

SALADS AND DRESSED VEGETABLES

GADO-GADO ## VEGETABLES WITH PEANUT AND COCONUT MILK SAUCE

The rich sauce in this dish adds a touch of luxury to the blanched vegetables.

5 or 6 mixed vegetables (5–7 oz/150–200 g per person) (green beans, cut into bite-sized pieces, lightly blanched then rinsed in cold water; amaranth or baby spinach, lightly cooked; shredded cabbage, blanched and rinsed in cold water; bean sprouts, trimmed and washed; cubed tofu, deep-fried in oil until brown and crisp on the outside or pre-fried tofu pieces, quartered; waxy potatoes, boiled and sliced; carrots, cut into matchsticks, lightly blanched and rinsed in cold water; seedless cucumber with skin intact, cut into thick strips)
Hard-boiled eggs, peeled and quartered
Splash of dark soy sauce or Javanese soy sauce for decoration
Asian celery (optional)
Fried onion flakes
Shrimp Crackers (p. 164)

Peanut and Coconut Milk Sauce
7 medium-length red chilies, seeded and sliced
3 cloves garlic, chopped
1 teaspoon shrimp paste
1 thick slice resurrection lily, chopped (optional)
1 tablespoon oil
1 cup (250 ml) coconut milk
1½ cups (375 g) fried peanuts, skins removed and coarsely ground
1 teaspoon palm or dark brown sugar, or to taste

2 salam leaves
Salt to taste
Water
Fresh lime juice or white vinegar to taste

To make the Peanut and Coconut Milk Sauce, grind the chilies, garlic, shrimp paste and resurrection lily to a paste. Heat the oil and fry the paste until fragrant. In a saucepan, combine the fried spices, the coconut milk, the sugar and the peanuts thoroughly. Add the salam leaves, bring to a boil and cook until the sauce thickens. Add salt to taste and enough water to thin the sauce to pouring consistency. Remove the sauce from the heat, add fresh lime juice or white vinegar, stir, and set aside to cool.

Arrange the vegetables in layers on a flat plate with the egg quarters on top and pour the sauce over them. Decorate the surface with a drizzle of dark soy sauce and garnish with chopped Asian celery and fried onion flakes. Serve with shrimp crackers. With or without the peanuts and the resurrection lily, this sauce goes well with hard-boiled eggs on their own.

PECEL VEGETABLES WITH THICK PEANUT SAUCE

1 lb (500 g) lightly blanched mixed vegetables (water spinach, amaranth or baby spinach; shredded cabbage; sliced zucchini or summer squash; green beans cut into bite-sized pieces; bean sprouts, washed and trimmed; sliced waxy potatoes; carrots cut into matchsticks)
3 hard-boiled eggs, peeled and halved
3½ oz (100 g) deep-fried tofu cakes, sliced
1 pickling cucumber, cut into strips
Shrimp Crackers (*kerupuk,* p. 164)
Fried onion flakes for garnish

Peanut Sauce
4–6 medium-length red chilies, sliced or 1–1½ teaspoons ground chili
1 teaspoon shrimp paste
3 cloves garlic, sliced
1 cup (250 g) fried peanuts, skinned and coarsely ground

1 tablespoon Javanese soy sauce or 2 teaspoons dark
 soy sauce and 1 teaspoon palm or dark brown sugar
½ cup (125 ml) or more water
Fresh lime juice or white vinegar to taste
Salt to taste or 1 teaspoon dark soy sauce

To make the Peanut Sauce grind the chilies, shrimp paste and garlic to a paste. Add the peanuts, soy sauce and ½ cup (125 ml) of water and blend. Blend in enough water to produce a sauce with the thickness of heavy cream. Finally add the lime juice or vinegar and salt to taste and blend again. Pour the sauce into a serving bowl.

Arrange the vegetables, eggs, tofu and cucumber in separate heaps on a serving platter. Serve with the Peanut Sauce, a plate of shrimp crackers and a small dish of fried onion flakes. Diners select their own vegetables, spoon sauce over the top, mix everything together on their plate and garnish with fried onion flakes. This dish can be served either warm or cold.

TAHU GORENG FRIED TOFU WITH THICK PEANUT SAUCE

This dish is easier to prepare than the previous one but also uses Thick Peanut Sauce.

3½ oz (100 g) deep-fried tofu cakes, sliced
3 cups (250 g) bean sprouts, trimmed and washed
1 seedless cucumber with skin, sliced into wedges
Chopped Asian celery and fried onion flakes for garnish

Thick Peanut Sauce
See Vegetables with Thick Peanut Sauce (p. 144)

Prepare the Thick Peanut Sauce following the method on page 144.

Arrange the sliced tofu on a platter. Strew the bean sprouts and cucumber wedges over the top. Pour the sauce over the vegetables and garnish with the chopped celery and fried onion flakes. Serve with shrimp crackers or, for vegetarians, rice crackers.

LALAP CRISP VEGETABLE AND SAMBAL
SALAD

This salad is the Javanese version of the Thai dishes
with Chili sauce (*Nam phrik*) and a Malay dish called
Ulam Ulaman.

12 small Asian eggplants
2 or 3 leaves from the crisp heart of a cabbage, cut into
   pieces
1 small head of lettuce, washed
1 bunch (or 6 large sprigs) lemon basil
1 bunch green beans, cut in half
1 cup (250 g) bean sprouts, trimmed and washed
4 pickling cucumbers
Pinch of sugar

Grill the eggplant lightly, preferably over charcoal, then slice them. Soak
the remaining vegetables in water with a pinch of sugar until crisp. Drain
and dry.

   Decoratively arrange the vegetables on a platter. Place the beans, eggplant, bean sprouts and cucumber strips in mounds in front of the leaf
vegetables and around a bowl of Chili-Shrimp Paste Sambal (p. 161).
Diners select the vegetables of their choice and spoon a little sauce on to
their plates for dipping. Serve with rice and fried or grilled fish for a simple meal.

ASINAN SIMPLE VEGETABLE SALAD
(Jakarta)

This quick and popular dish is clearly related to
Thai Pounded Green Papaya (p. 404) and Lao Chili
Papaya Salad (p. 450). It, too, is sometimes made
with shredded green papaya.

3 cups (750 g) mixed vegetables (inner leaves of raw
   cabbage, shredded; small seedless cucumbers,
   complete with skin, cut into matchsticks; daikon, cut

into matchsticks; bean sprouts, trimmed and washed;
carrot, cut into matchsticks)
Pinch of sugar
2–3 tablespoons fried peanuts, coarsely chopped
Sliced cucumber for garnish
Tomato for garnish
Pineapple for garnish (optional)

Dressing
1 tablespoon sugar
2 tablespoons water
3 small red chilies, sliced
1½ tablespoons dried shrimp, soaked in hot water for 1
minute and drained
Salt to taste
2 tablespoons white vinegar

Soak the vegetables in water with a pinch of sugar until crisp. Drain and
dry them and place them in a salad bowl.

To make the Dressing, heat the sugar with some of the water in a
saucepan until it dissolves. Cool. Grind the chilies and the shrimp to a
rough paste. Mix all the Dressing ingredients together, adding a little water
if you wish to dilute it, and toss with the vegetables and the peanuts.
Garnish with cucumber, tomato and pineapple.

URAP VEGETABLES WITH ROASTED COCONUT (Bali)

While this dish is well-known in Java, the use of
dried cowpeas in this version is common in Bali.

1–2 tablespoons oil
4 shallots, sliced
2 cloves garlic, chopped
½ fresh coconut, shelled, aromatized and shredded finely
or prepared shredded coconut (p. 40)

12 oz (350 g) mixed vegetables (green beans cut into
bite-sized pieces and blanched lightly; dried cowpeas
[*kacang tunggak*], previously soaked overnight, boiled
until tender, drained and cooled or adzuki beans
[optional]; bean sprouts, trimmed and washed)
1–2 medium-length red chilies, seeded and finely
chopped
2 kaffir lime leaves, shredded
Vegetable oil, for dressing
Sugar to taste
Fresh lime juice to taste

Heat the oil in a wok and fry the shallots and garlic until brown and crisp. Drain and cool.

Hold the skin side of the coconut over a gas flame or a flame from a wood or charcoal fire until the coconut releases its aroma. If the skin is leathery, grate some of it off, leaving a little behind; if it is younger and more delicate, leave it all intact. Grate the whole piece of coconut.

Mix the vegetables with the fried shallots and garlic. Mix together the coconut, chili and shredded lime leaves and sprinkle over the vegetables. Toss everything together. Add some vegetable oil, sugar and fresh lime juice to taste and toss again.

LAWAR BUNCIS

GREEN BEAN SALAD WITH GRATED COCONUT
(Bali)

This is a sacred dish in Bali, cooked by men under the guidance of a ritual cooking specialist. The first one I ate, in 1977, was taken from a recipe written on a 13th-century palm-leaf manuscript. Substantial amounts of pig or chicken blood were an important ingredient in it. While these are still used in the many versions of this dish prepared today, the following recipe from Janet De Neefe's Balinese cooking school may be a little more to Western tastes. It uses coconut milk instead of blood, a practice that is now quite common.

1 lb (500 g) lightly steamed green beans, cut into small
   pieces
1½ cups (750 g) grated fresh coconut, from a coconut
   that has been held over a flame (p. 40)
3 tablespoons fried onion flakes plus extra for garnish
½ teaspoon salt
2 kaffir lime leaves, finely shredded

Dressing
3½ oz (100 g) ground pork or chicken
3 tablespoons Sacred Spice Paste (p. 141)
1 stalk lemongrass, finely sliced
2 cups (500 ml) coconut milk
1 teaspoon salt
2 whole kaffir lime leaves

Prepare the Sacred Spice Paste and add the lemongrass to it.

To make the Dressing, combine ground pork, the spice paste, the coconut milk, salt and lime leaves in a saucepan and simmer over medium heat until the meat is cooked. Discard the lime leaves and set aside to cool.

Put the dressing into a bowl with the grated coconut, fried onion flakes, salt and shredded lime leaves, squeezing and kneading everything together thoroughly to blend all the flavors. Add the beans, taste and adjust the seasonings if necessary and scatter a few more onion flakes over the top before serving.

RUJAK PUNGENT FRUIT SALAD

This dish is prominent on the Javanese list of special foods for ritual occasions. In Java it has been traditionally served at the *slametan* (the ritual meal to which neighbors, friends and relatives are invited) given by a family before the birth of a first child.

The story behind this dish reveals a fascinating process of culinary diffusion at work. Introduced into Malaysia by Javanese settlers at the end of the 19th century, it now appears in Indian and Chinese street food there, as well as in the classic Malay version.

There are two kinds of *rujak*: one made from the usual Indonesian salad vegetables such as water spinach, snakebeans, cucumber, yambean, and fried tofu, with peanuts in its sauce; the other made from sour and crisp fruit with a dramatically matched sweet, sour, salty and flavourful dressing or sauce. The one given here is of the latter variety, sought after by Indonesians as a refreshing snack.

3 or 4 bird's eye chilies, chopped
¼ teaspoon salt
½ teaspoon shrimp paste, roasted
3 tablespoons palm or dark brown sugar
2 tablespoons tamarind water or fresh lime juice
1 teaspoon Javanese sticky shrimp sauce or *petis* (optional)
3 cups (750 g) mixed crunchy fruit and salad vegetables (sliced wedges of cucumber, pineapple, papaya, green mango, yambean or apple; starfruit slices; pomelo or grapefruit segments with the membrane removed)

Grind the chilies, salt and shrimp paste to a fine paste. Add the sugar and the tamarind water or lime juice and blend until the sugar has dissolved and the sauce is thoroughly mixed. Add the shrimp sauce (if using) and mix well again. Taste and adjust the flavors (it should be quite sweet).

Toss as much of the sauce as you want with the fruit and vegetables and set aside to stand for about 30 minutes before serving. Pungent Fruit Salad is good as a snack or goes well with deep-fried, grilled or rich festive food.

ACCOMPANIMENTS

With an everyday diet consisting of rice, a little fresh or dried fish and any vegetables that are available, Indonesians avoid monotony through accompaniments, which creatively use vivid flavors and surprising textures. The garnishes and condiments here are examples of this creativity.

Concentrated Flavors

Dishes in this first group keep well and can be stored in airtight containers for adding spice and flavor when there is no substantial meat dish in a meal. They are particularly good with white rice. Try a rice meal with a salad or vegetable main dish accompanied by Shredded Crisp-fried Beef, Crisp-fried Beef (p. 152) or Peanut-coconut Garnish (p. 153), some kind of pickle, eggs or omelette, a sambal and shrimp crackers or chili-fried crunchy sambal.

ABON DAGING ## SHREDDED CRISP-FRIED BEEF

1 lb (500 g) topside steak, in one piece
2 cloves garlic
2 teaspoons palm or dark brown sugar
1 thick slice galangal, peeled and coarsely chopped
1 teaspoon ground coriander
Pinch of ground cumin
½ cup (125 ml) thick coconut milk
Salt to taste
2 tablespoons oil, or more
2 teaspoons tamarind water or fresh lime juice
3 tablespoons fried onion flakes

Place the meat in a frying or saucepan and add enough water to just cover it. Simmer gently until it is tender and ready to fall apart. Remove the meat from the water, drain and dry it. Pound the meat to soften it, and then shred it very finely until it is a light nest of fibers. Place in a bowl and set aside.

Grind the garlic, sugar, galangal, coriander and cumin to a paste. Combine this with the shredded meat, coconut milk and salt and knead everything together until well mixed.

Heat the oil in a frying pan, add the meat mixture and stir-fry it until it is fragrant and dry. Add the fresh lime juice to taste and stir-fry until dry again. Remove the meat from the pan and drain on paper towels. Once cool, toss the beef with the fried onion flakes.

The beef may be stored in a glass jar for up to a month and used in small quantities to flavor rice.

DENDENG RAGI CRISP FRIED BEEF
(Sumatra)

1 tablespoon palm or dark brown sugar, to taste
1–2 tablespoons tamarind water or fresh lime juice
10½ oz (300 g) sirloin steak, sliced very thin across the
　grain into small squares
2–3 tablespoons oil
1 cup (250 g) grated fresh coconut or ⅔ cup (150 g)
　prepared shredded coconut (p. 40)
Salt

Spice Paste
1½ tablespoons coriander seed or 1 tablespoon ground
　coriander
1 teaspoon cumin seed or ½ teaspoon ground cumin
10 whole black peppercorns, cracked
3 cloves garlic
5 shallots, sliced

If using whole coriander and cumin seeds, grind them with the cracked peppercorns to a powder in an electric grinder. Grind all of the Spice Paste ingredients to a paste. Add the sugar and tamarind water or fresh lime juice, mix well and combine with the meat. Refrigerate for a few hours or overnight.

Heat the oil in a wok, add the meat without any liquid and stir-fry until it is brown and dry. Lift out and drain. Reserve any leftover marinade and discard the leftover oil from wok. Dry the wok, add the coconut and roast it, stirring constantly until it is golden brown and aromatic. Return the meat to the pan, toss everything together, add salt to taste and any leftover marinade, adjusting the sweet and sour flavors to taste if necessary. Continue to stir-fry until everything is brown, dry and uniformly aromatic without being burned.

This accompaniment will keep well in the refrigerator. It can be added to a rice meal with a vegetable dish for a tasty lift.

SERUNDENG KACANG PEANUT-COCONUT GARNISH

1½ cups (375 g) grated fresh coconut or steamed dried coconut (p. 40)

2 teaspoons palm or dark brown sugar

1 tablespoon fresh lime juice

1½ kaffir lime or curry leaf

⅔ cup (150 g) fried peanuts

Spice Paste

½-in (1-cm) piece fresh ginger root, peeled and coarsely chopped

2 cloves garlic

5 shallots, sliced

1 teaspoon ground cumin

Grind the Spice Paste ingredients to a paste. Mix the coconut, sugar, lime juice, salam leaf and Spice Paste together. Roast this mixture in a dry pan, stirring constantly until all the moisture has evaporated and the coconut mixture is golden brown. Set aside to cool. Mix in the peanuts, remove the salam leaf and serve.

You can also make this recipe with small or tiny shrimp. Peel and devein the shrimp, leaving the tails intact (with tiny shrimp you need not even shell them). Marinate them in lime juice, dry them and deep-fry in hot oil until they are brown and crisp. Remove the shrimp and drain on paper towel and proceed as above, adding the fried shrimp at the very end with the peanuts. This garnish will keep well stored in a glass jar.

Fresh Pickles

Sharp flavors are good with rich coconut milk dishes.

ACAR KUNING ## MIXED VEGETABLE PICKLE

This recipe yields a large enough quantity for serving as a vegetable side dish at a party featuring a spread of rich and spicy food. When stored in an airtight container in the refrigerator it keeps for a week.

1 tablespoon oil
1 onion, sliced lengthwise
2–3 medium-length red chilies, each sliced into 3 pieces
3 bird's eye chilies, each sliced into 3 pieces
3 tablespoons white vinegar
1 tablespoon sugar, or less to taste
½-in (1½-cm) piece fresh ginger root, sliced
1 stalk lemongrass, bruised
1 cup (250 ml) water
1 lb (500 g) mixed vegetables (⅔ cup [150 g] green beans, cut into bite-sized pieces; 2 small carrots cut into matchsticks; 2½ oz [75 g] cauliflower florets; 3½ oz [100 g] cucumber with skin, cut into thin strips)

Spice Paste
¾-in (2-cm) piece turmeric root, peeled and coarsely chopped or ¼ teaspoon ground turmeric
4 roasted candlenuts or macadamia nuts, coarsely chopped (optional)
1–2 cloves garlic

Grind the Spice Paste ingredients into a paste. Heat the oil in a wok and fry the Spice Paste and the onion until they are fragrant. Add the two kinds of chilies, the vinegar, sugar, ginger, lemongrass and water. Bring to a boil. Add the vegetables and stir until the sauce thickens a little and the vegetables are lightly cooked.

ACAR MENTIMUN ## CUCUMBER PICKLE

4 small pickling cucumbers or 1 English cucumber,
  halved, seeded and sliced
2 medium-length red chilies, seeded and sliced
1 tablespoon sugar or to taste
2 tablespoons white vinegar
Water, if necessary
Salt to taste

Mix the cucumbers and chilies together in a bowl. In a small saucepan mix the sugar and vinegar, adding water to taste if you want to weaken the flavor and heat until the sugar is dissolved. Add salt to taste, cool, pour over the cucumber and serve.

ACAR TIGA WARNA ## THREE-TONE PICKLE

3 medium-sized carrots, peeled and sliced into half rounds
6 pickling cucumbers or 2 English cucumbers, peeled,
  seeded and sliced
½ tablespoon salt
2–3 tablespoons white sugar
12 shallots or 2 small Spanish onions, peeled and sliced
Juice of 2 limes

Peel the carrots, cut them in half lengthwise and slice them into half rounds. Mix the cucumbers with the carrots in a bowl. Add the salt and sugar to taste and mix well. Add the shallots or Spanish onion and lime juice, mix again and serve.

Fancy Eggs

PINDANG TELUR ## MARBLED EGGS

8 eggs
A handful of the skins from shallots or onions
2 cloves garlic
¾-in (2-cm) piece galangal, bruised
1 stalk lemongrass, bruised

Place all the ingredients in a saucepan and add enough water to cover. Bring to a gentle boil, reduce the heat and simmer for about 20 minutes, until the eggs are hard-cooked.

Remove the eggs, tap them on a hard surface to crack the shells slightly, return them to the pan and simmer gently for another two hours or so to let the eggs absorb the flavors. Add more water to the liquid if it is evaporating too quickly. Remove the eggs and when cool, shell them. They will have a marbled pattern.

Make a party meal of white rice, Marbled Eggs, Grilled or Fried Chicken, Vegetables with Roasted Coconut, Stir-fried Beef, Shrimp Sambal and Chili-fried Crunchy Sambal. Add a *sayur* if you want to have a wet dish on the table as well.

Patties and Croquettes

These dishes usually appear as a garnish and accompaniment on a fancy rice platter. There is no reason, however, why they may not be piled on a plate and served with other dishes and white rice for an ordinary meal.

PERKEDEL JAGUNG   ## SWEET CORN PATTIES

2 tablespoons flour
1 tablespoon self-rising flour
1 large egg, beaten
13 oz (375 g) corn kernels, stripped off the cob, or canned corn, drained
7 oz (200 g) shrimp, peeled, deveined and chopped or tiny shrimp, shelled
2 tablespoons chopped green onions
1 clove garlic, chopped
2 tablespoons Asian celery, chopped or celery, finely chopped
Salt and pepper to taste
2 or 3 medium-length red chilies, finely sliced
Oil for frying

Sift the flours together and combine with the beaten egg to make a batter. Mix in all the other ingredients, adding a little water if necessary to make the batter smooth. Heat a little oil in a heavy frying pan or griddle and drop spoonfuls of the mixture on to it. Flatten them and fry on both sides until brown.

POTATO CROQUETTES
PERKEDEL KENTANG

5 oz (150 g) ground beef
2 tablespoons fried onion flakes
½ cup (125 g) cold mashed potatoes
1 cup (250 g) self-rising flour
¼ teaspoon grated nutmeg
1 egg
Salt and pepper to taste
Oil for deep-frying

Lightly grease a frying pan and stir-fry the ground beef until it is cooked and dry. Remove from the pan and set aside to cool.

Grind the onion flakes until crumbly, then add all the ingredients and process into a light dough.

Heat the oil in a pan until quite hot. Dip your hands in flour and mold spoonfuls of the mixture into small egg shapes. Fry these in the oil until they puff up and brown. Remove and drain on paper towel.

BEEF AND COCONUT PATTIES
REMPAH

½ fresh coconut, grated or 4½ oz (125 g) prepared dried
  coconut (p. 40)
8 oz (250 g) ground beef
2 cloves garlic, chopped
½ teaspoon ground coriander
Pinch of freshly ground cumin
1 egg
Oil for deep-frying

Grind the grated coconut as finely as you can. Combine all the ingredients in a food processor and mix well. Shape the beef mixture into small balls. Heat the oil in a wok or frying pan and deep-fry until brown.

These patties may be served with Fragrant Yellow Rice (p. 167) or on their own. They are very good accompanied by Chili-Shrimp Paste Sambal (p. 161).

Sambal

If there is one food that is more important than any other to Indonesians apart from rice, it is the sambal. Sambal can always be relied upon to turn a plate of rice into a tasty meal. Be it large, small, splendid or frugal, no meal would be complete without spooning sambal on the side of the plate to give it a final lift.

There are a number of favorite Indonesian sambal that are readily available commercially in small jars. They are produced by various Dutch and Australian companies and can be found in most well-stocked supermarkets. Since these keep indefinitely, particularly if refrigerated, you can always have something on hand for a quick meal, though they are not as good as the ones you make yourself.

SAMBAL BAJAK ## PLOW SAMBAL

Along with Chili-Shrimp Paste Sambal (p. 161), this cooked sambal is the one eaten most often. The "plow" may refer to the rice, sambal and perhaps a little dried fish farmers take to the fields with them.

10 medium-length red chilies
4 roasted candlenuts or macadamia nuts, coarsely
   chopped
1 teaspoon shrimp paste
3 cloves garlic
6 shallots, sliced
2 tablespoons oil
1 teaspoon palm or dark brown sugar
Salt
Tamarind water or fresh lime juice to taste

Grind the chilies, candlenuts, shrimp paste, garlic and shallots to a rough paste. Heat the oil in a wok, fry the paste unti soft, and add the sugar, salt, tamarind water to taste and a dash of plain water. Reduce the heat and simmer for a few minutes. Turn the heat up to medium-high and stir-fry until all the water has evaporated and the spices are brown. Cool before serving.

SAMBAL JAHE CHILI-GINGER SAMBAL

1½-in (3-cm) piece fresh ginger root, peeled and thinly sliced
10 medium-length red chilies,
Dash white vinegar or fresh lime juice
Salt
Dash of chicken stock

Grind the ginger and chilies to a paste. Add a little vinegar or lime juice and salt to taste and moisten with chicken stock. This sambal goes with Chicken Soup Dinner (p. 80).

SAMBAL KACANG CHILI-PEANUT SAMBAL

3 medium-length red chilies
Squeeze of fresh lime juice
⅛ teaspoon shrimp paste (*terasi*), roasted (optional)
Palm or dark brown sugar to taste (optional)
½ cup (125 g) fried peanuts, coarsely chopped
1 kaffir lime leaf, shredded
Salt to taste

Grind the chilies, lime juice, shrimp paste and the sugar to a rough paste. Combine the paste with the peanuts, lime leaf and salt and mix well, adding a little hot water to moisten.

SAMBAL KELAPA CHILI-COCONUT SAMBAL

½ young fresh coconut, for grating, or ½ cup (125 g)
  prepared dried coconut (p. 40)
2 medium-length red chilies
¼ teaspoon shrimp paste, roasted or 1 slice resurrection
  lily, chopped (optional)
2 shallots, sliced
½ clove garlic, coarsely chopped
1 kaffir lime leaf, shredded
Sugar to taste
Salt to taste

Remove the brown skin from the coconut and grate the flesh finely. Grind the chilies, shrimp paste or resurrection lily, shallots and garlic to a rough paste. Mix all the ingredients together and set aside to let the flavors mingle before serving.

SAMBAL PETIS   CHILI-SHRIMP SAUCE SAMBAL

Petis is another concentrated, salty shrimp extract like *terasi*, but black in color, slightly sweet and has the consistency of molasses. You can find it in Asian grocery stores or substitute with Thai fish sauce if you must.

8 green bird's eye chilies, chopped
3 cloves garlic, sliced
1 teaspoon shrimp paste (*petis*)
Salt to taste

Grind all the ingredients to a rough paste. Serve in a small sauce dish with fried noodle dishes, especially those with shrimp.

SAMBAL SOTO   CHILI SAMBAL FOR SOTO

5 roasted candlenuts or macadamia nuts
10 medium-length red chilies
½ teaspoon shrimp paste (*terasi*), roasted in foil
  (optional)
Salt
Javanese soy sauce or dark soy sauce to taste

Grind the ingredients to a rough paste and moisten with a little water or broth from the *soto*.

SAMBAL TOMAT TOMATO SAMBAL

This sambal is very good with grilled fish.

5 shallots, cut into 2 or 3 pieces
4–6 medium-length red and green chilies, sliced
2 tomatoes, chopped
1 tablespoon fresh lime juice
Salt to taste
Small handful of lemon basil

Toss everything together and serve with grilled fish.

Menadonese Grilled Fish (*Menadonese Ikan*)—Grind the shallots, chilies and a thick slice of peeled fresh ginger root to a paste. Fry the paste in an oiled wok until fragrant. Add the tomatoes and stir-fry until soft, stir in lime juice and salt and spoon over grilled fish.

Menadonese Grilled Chicken (*Menadonese Ayam*)—Make the same cooked sauce provided for Menadonese Grilled Fish using 1 teaspoon of shrimp paste instead of ginger root and pour over charcoal-grilled chicken.

SAMBAL TERASI CHILI-SHRIMP PASTE SAMBAL

12 medium-sized red and green chilies
1 teaspoon shrimp paste (*terasi*), roasted in foil and
   crumbled
Pinch of sugar
1 tablespoon fresh lime juice

Grind all the ingredients to a paste. Serve in a small dish with a spoon.

Crunchies and Crackers

Indonesians highly prize bursts of crunchy texture as well as sharp and dramatic flavors as accompaniments to their everyday rice meals. Other dishes will most likely be fairly simple, though nourishing, combinations of vegetables and small fish caught in the rice fields when they are flooded. Crunchies and crackers play an important role, often helping to turn a simple meal into a sensory adventure.

SAMBAL GORENG KERING

CHILI-FRIED CRUNCHY SAMBAL

½ cup (125 g) dried anchovies, heads removed
Oil for deep-frying
1 cup matchstick potatoes or fried potato straws
½ cup (125 g) raw peanuts (little ones with skins) or salted "beer nuts"
1–1½ tablespoons dark brown sugar
Salt
1 tablespoon fresh lime juice or tamarind water

Spice Paste
2–5 medium-length red chilies or ½ teaspoon ground hot chili
1 slice galangal, peeled and coarsely chopped
4 shallots, sliced
1 clove garlic

Dust the dried anchovies so that they are free of debris. Heat enough oil in a wok to deep-fry the potatoes if you are using raw ones. Dry them first and fry until crisp. Lift them out, drain and set aside to cool. Next, deep-fry the peanuts, if using raw ones, in the same oil. Lift out, drain and cool. Fry the dried anchovies until crisp, drain and cool. (Take everything out a little earlier than you would normally as they will all continue to cook for a while afterwards.) Leave 1½ tablespoons oil in the wok.

Grind the Spice Paste ingredients to a paste. Stir-fry the paste in the wok until fragrant, add the sugar and salt and mix well. Add the potato straws, the peanuts and the dried fish and mix well. Add the lime juice or tamarind water to taste and stir. Cool and serve in a bowl.

This is a favorite to have on hand in an airtight jar to serve at an everyday meal (it is particularly good with *sayur*). Make twice the quantity suggested if you want to keep some and do not add the salt until you are ready to serve.

You can use anything crunchy as a basis for a *kering* of this kind— potato straws alone, crisp-fried tempeh slices, even breakfast cereals. If you use breakfast cereals you should remember that they are quite sweet. Taste the mix very carefully before adding more sugar.

This sambal goes well with a party rice supper. Arrange molded white rice in the middle of a large tray lined with lettuce or banana leaves and surround the rice with a colorful salad such as Vegetables with Thick Peanut Sauce (p. 144) or Vegetables with Roasted Coconut (p. 147), some Marbled Eggs (p. 155), some Stir-fried Beef (p. 121) or Crisp-fried Beef (p. 152), some Javanese Fried Chicken (see p. 125) or Spicy Chicken in Coconut Milk (see p. 99) and some Chili-fried Crunchy Sambal. Put a bowl of *sayur* on the table as well if you want something liquid to moisten the rice.

REMPEYEK KACANG # PEANUT CRACKERS

½ cup (125 g) rice flour
¾–1 cup (175–250 ml) coconut milk
Salt and pepper to taste
½ cup (125 g) raw peanuts, skinned
Oil for deep-frying

Spice Paste

1 teaspoon freshly ground coriander
1 clove garlic
1 shallot, sliced

Grind the Spice Paste ingredients to a paste. Combine the rice flour and the coconut milk to make a smooth batter. Add the Spice Paste, salt and pepper to taste and mix well. Set aside for 1 hour.

After the batter has rested, add the peanuts and mix well. Heat the oil in a wok and when it is hot drop a spoonful of batter into it and reduce the heat a little. Fry the batter until brown and crisp, turning if you need to. Lift out, drain and repeat until all the batter is used up.

When cool and well-drained these crisps will keep in a sealed plastic bag.

KERUPUK UDANG ## SHRIMP CRACKERS

This dish is made from a batter of dried shrimp. Even in Indonesia, it is bought prepared and only needs to be deep-fried and drained just before serving. This method is best, but you can also cook the slices quickly and effortlessly in a microwave oven. Place three or four slices on a plate, leaving enough space between to allow them to swell up, and cook on high for 1 minute.

Be sure when you buy *kerupuk* to get the authentic large one, slightly brown in color and natural-looking, rather than the small pink and white "shrimp crackers" available in packets, as these are a poor substitute.

EMPING MELINJO ## BITTER NUT CRACKERS

Smaller, finer and more delicate than Shrimp Crackers, Bitter Nut Crackers come in thin, semi-transparent medallions about 1½ in (3 cm) in diameter. The batter for this cracker is made from the melinjo nut from the tree whose leaves and fruit are used in Tamarind Vegetable Soup (p. 75). Bitter Nut Crackers and other crackers, such as fish crackers (*kerupuk ikan*) or tapioca crackers, are available in Asian grocery stores. All are prepared in the same way as Shrimp Crackers.

Another favorite crunchy, Tempeh Cracker (*Kerupuk Tempeh*), is often available in packets in ready-to-eat form in some Asian food stores. It is made from slices of tempeh spiced with garlic and coriander, dried in the sun and then fried.

SPECIAL RICE, RICE MEALS AND NOODLES

LONTONG COMPRESSED RICE CAKES

Lontong and *ketupat* are plain rice cakes that are eaten with certain dishes such as saté and some *soto* in place of ordinary rice. *Ketupat* are made using palm-leaf packets cleverly woven by the cook on the spot—a trick that I have never been able to perform.

Lontong are much simpler to make and are a fine substitute for *ketupat*. They do, however, require access to banana leaves or cheesecloth. Assemble banana-leaf or cheesecloth pieces measuring about 10 x 7 in (24 x 18 cm). If you are using banana leaves, soften them over a hot stove or in hot water until they are pliable. Roll the packet material across the shorter length into a cylinder about 2 in (5 cm) in diameter. With banana leaves, fold one end like a package with the point upwards and secure with a toothpick. (If you use cloth tie the ends tightly with kitchen twine bon-bon style.)

Wash the rice well and then fill the packet half full with it, leaving plenty of room for the rice to expand. Then fold and secure the second end in the same way as the first.

Place the packets in a rice steamer or a saucepan filled with boiling water. Steam or boil gently until cooked. This will take about 2 hours or more and you should add more water if and when necessary. Cool and then take the rice rolls out of the packets, cut them in half lengthwise and then across into 1-in (2½-cm) pieces.

If you find this process too labor intensive, use the Malay Compressed Rice recipe (p. 206) instead as I often do.

Fancy Rice

On some special occasions such as weddings, significant times in the religious calendar or celebrations or *slametan* held to mark other events, Indo-nesians serve special rice. The presentation on these occasions usually follows a particular form—even when only white rice is used. First a platter or bamboo tray for each person is covered entirely with plain or braided banana leaves. The cooked rice is then pressed into a mold (traditionally a cone-shaped one but often, these days, simply a bowl that has been wet on the inside), and placed in the center of the tray. There it is garnished lightly and surrounded decoratively by portions of dry dishes cooked to go with it. Every occasion seems to have its own particular formula of associated dishes, depending, of course, on locality and level of wealth.

NASI GURIH   FRAGRANT COCONUT RICE

This is a basic rice dish that appears on many festive occasions, both family and religious ones, and is served with different accompaniments according to the occasion. At a wedding feast it would be accompanied by the traditional wedding side dishes of the area—in central Java perhaps some kind of spicy chicken in coconut milk or a colorful omelette rolled up and sliced, a chili-fried sambal with coconut milk, some Beef and Coconut Patties, Cucumber Pickle and Plow Sambal; in Sumatra, Potato Croquette with Peanut-coconut Garnish, Grilled Chicken, Mixed Vegetable Pickle, and one or two other substantial dishes according to the host's purse.

Certain Javanese calendrical festivals often feature Fragrant Coconut Rice served with accompanying dishes, which together make up a meal known as *Nasi Wuduk*. It consists of Fragrant Coconut Rice arranged in a wide circle around the edge of a plate with Mild Chicken Curry placed in the center. The whole dish is then decorated with basil leaves, chopped celery and cucumber slices and garnished with a crunchy such as Shrimp Crackers. It is accompanied by a separate plate of Chili-fried Shrimp with Coconut Milk, some sambal and a bowl of roasted peanuts.

1 lb (500 g) white rice (short grain is preferable because
   of its absorbent texture; including a handful of
   glutinous rice improves the absorbency even more)
4 cups (1 liter) coconut milk
1 pandan leaf, tied into a loose knot, or 1 or 2 drops of
   clear pandan essence
Salt

Thoroughly wash the rice in a strainer, stirring it as you rinse until the water that pours through runs nearly clear. Drain well and put into a heavy saucepan or a rice cooker together with the coconut milk, the pandan leaf or pandan essence and salt to taste (this is one way of cooking rice where adding salt does improve the flavor). Cook until the liquid has been absorbed. Take the saucepan off the stove and wrap it in a kitchen towel or put a teatowel under the lid of the rice cooker and set it to "keep warm" for a while until the rice is cooked and dry (about 30 minutes or more).

NASI KUNING FRAGRANT YELLOW RICE

The traditional foods served at the Javanese *Bruwah* (the Breaking of the Fast) include Fragrant Yellow Rice and an Indonesian omelette. Both may be combined in a special garnished dish for parties.

Cook the rice according to the instruction provided for Fragrant Coconut Rice (p. 166) but when you add the coconut milk add half a tablespoon of mashed fresh turmeric (or ½ teaspoon ground turmeric), mixing well to achieve an even color. Also add 1 kaffir lime leaf, a salam leaf and a bruised stalk of lemongrass in addition to the pandan leaf.

To serve, remove the leaves and the lemongrass, mold the yellow rice on to a flat plate and scatter some thin omelette sliced into strips, some lemon basil leaves and some sliced red chilies over the top. Arrange small separate heaps of Chili-fried Lamb (p. 117) or Chili-fried Crunchy Sambal (p. 162), Peanut-coconut Garnish (p. 153), some very small Beef and Coconut Patties (p. 157) or fine slices of roast chicken and perhaps Crisp-fried Beef with Hot and Tangy Sauce (p. 127) around the edge of the plate. Serve garnished with a shrimp cracker and sliced cucumber.

NASI KEBULI INDIAN RICE

1 small chicken
Oil for frying
1 stalk lemongrass, bruised
2-in (5-cm) piece cinnamon stick
2 cloves
Pinch of nutmeg
3 cups (750 ml) water
1 lb (500 g) long-grain rice
3 tablespoons oil or ghee (more if necessary)
Fried onion flakes and chopped Asian celery for
   garnish

Spice Paste
1 teaspoon coriander seed or 2 teaspoons ground
   coriander
½ teaspoon cumin seed or ¼ teaspoon ground cumin
1 slice fresh ginger root, peeled and sliced thin
3 small cloves garlic
6 shallots, coarsely chopped

Cut the chicken into serving pieces. If using whole coriander and cumin seeds, grind them to a powder in an electric grinder. Grind all of the Spice Paste ingredients to a paste. Heat the oil in a wok and fry the Spice Paste until it is fragrant. Add the lemongrass, cinnamon, cloves and nutmeg and the chicken and stir-fry until it has changed color. Add the water, bring to a boil, reduce the heat and simmer until the chicken is tender. Remove the chicken pieces, drain them on paper towel and set them aside to dry. Strain the cooking liquid and reserve.

Wash the rice and soak it in water for about 1 hour. Drain. Heat the oil or ghee in a saucepan and fry the rice until transparent and yellow. Add enough of the strained chicken broth to completely cover the rice and cook until all the liquid has evaporated. Reduce the heat to low, cover the saucepan, and steam the rice gently for another 20–30 minutes until it is dry but tender.

Heat more oil in the wok and fry the chicken pieces until they are golden brown. To serve, heap the rice on a plate and garnish it with fried onion flakes and Asian celery. Arrange the fried chicken around the edges.

NASI GORENG ## FRIED RICE

While this dish has epitomized Indonesian food in many people's eyes, it has no ritual status and is simply a local adaptation of Chinese fried rice enjoyed as a quick family meal on informal occasions. The beef that is used in this particular version makes the meal a rounded one.

For this one-dish meal, Fried Rice is served on individual plates, topped with a fried egg with a soft yolk, and garnished with sliced tomatoes and cucumber slices. For a party dish, garnish it with thin strips of omelette.

3 tablespoons or more oil
8 oz (250 g) rump steak or boneless chicken, cut into
  very thin strips
7 oz (200 g) shrimp, peeled and deveined (optional)
3 cups (750 g) steamed rice, cooled (leftover is best)
1 tablespoon Javanese soy sauce
1 tablespoon light soy sauce
Fried onion flakes, for garnish
1 egg per person
Shrimp Crackers

Spice Paste
4 medium-length red chilies, seeded and coarsely
  chopped
½ teaspoon shrimp paste (*terasi*)
2 cloves garlic
5 shallots, sliced

Grind the Spice Paste ingredients to a rough paste. Heat 2 tablespoons of oil in a wok or a pan and fry the Spice Paste until it is fragrant. Add the beef and shrimp and stir-fry until they are cooked. Add the rice and mix well. Add more oil, if necessary, and the soy sauces, and keep stirring until the rice grains are coated, everything is warm and the color is even. Set aside and keep warm.

In a separate pan, fry the eggs until they are cooked but the yolks are still soft. Serve the rice on individual plates, garnished with the fried onion flakes and a fried egg on top. Decorate the plates with the sliced tomatoes and cucumber. Serve with a dish of shrimp crackers.

NASI MI NOODLES, RICE AND SOUP

This combination of fried noodles, fried tofu and a bean sprout soup with white rice, sambal and a pickle makes a tasty and filling lunch.

7 oz (200 g) dry Chinese egg noodles (*mi*) or 1¼ lb
   (600 g) fresh yellow egg noodles (*bakmi*)
Oil for deep-frying
1 lb (500 g) firm tofu, cut into four
4 tablespoons oil
2 lb (1 kg) shrimp, peeled and deveined
4 tablespoons Javanese soy sauce
3 quarts (3 liters) chicken stock or equivalent chicken
   stock cubes mixed with water
5 stalks Asian celery, stems cut into bite-sized pieces,
   leaves chopped
Salt to taste
1 lb (500 g) bean sprouts, trimmed and washed
7 shallots, sliced
4 cloves garlic, chopped
½ teaspoon freshly ground white pepper
Fried onion flakes for garnish
2 tablespoons sliced green onion

Spice Paste
4 cloves garlic
½ teaspoon freshly ground white pepper
¼ teaspoon freshly ground nutmeg

Accompaniments

Steamed white rice
Three-Tone Pickle (p. 155)
Chili Shrimp-Sauce Sambal (p. 171) or other sambal

Soak the dry egg noodles in hot water 4–5 minutes, teasing them out as they soften. Drain, rinse and set aside.

Heat enough oil for deep-frying in a wok and deep-fry the tofu pieces, turning them frequently until they are golden brown. Remove them from the pan, drain them on paper towel and set aside.

Grind the Spice Paste ingredients to a fine paste. Remove the paste, add 2–3 tablespoons of water to the mortar or food processor, scraping the residual spices from the sides and mixing them with the water. Set aside.

Heat 2 tablespoons of oil in a pan and fry the Spice Paste until it is fragrant. Add 1 cup (250 g) of the shrimp and 2 tablespoons Javanese soy sauce and fry until cooked. In a large pot, bring the chicken stock to a boil, then reduce the heat to a simmer. Add the shrimp to the simmering stock, taking care to include all of the residual spices in the pan they were fried in. Add the celery stems, salt and the bean sprouts and turn off the heat.

Heat 2 tablespoons of vegetable oil in the wok and fry the sliced shallots and the garlic until fragrant. Add the remaining shrimp and ground pepper and 2 tablespoons of Javanese soy sauce and stir-fry until the shrimp are cooked. Add the chopped celery leaves, the soaked or fresh noodles and the water from the mortar or food processor used to grind the Spice Paste. Stir, taste and add more salt if necessary. Cook until the noodles are heated through.

To serve, place the noodles on one end of an oblong plate and garnish with fried onion flakes. Cut the fried tofu into thin slices and arrange on the other end of the plate.

Pour the soup into a tureen and garnish with sliced green onions. Serve with the plate of noodles and tofu, the rice, pickle and sambal. Diners take some rice, tofu and sambal and spoon soup over it, helping themselves separately to noodles and pickles.

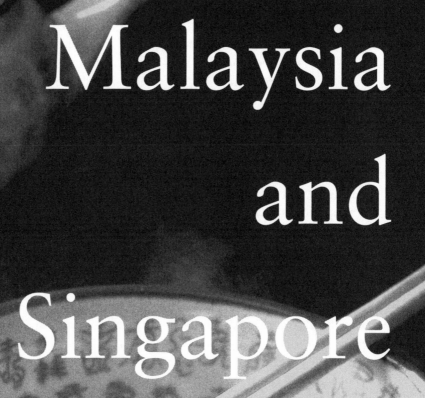

Malaysia

and

Singapore

All the flavors of Southeast Asia, social as well as culinary, are concentrated in Malaysia and Singapore. The population of Malaysia is composed of about 60 percent Malay, 26 percent Chinese and 7 percent Indian. One wonderful outcome of this dynamic mix is a vivid food scene consisting of conventional Malay, Chinese and Indian cuisines together with three that are quite unique: Nyonya, Eurasian and a vibrant and inventive body of street food.

Singapore had a population of about 3.5 million; about 76 per cent of them ethnic Chinese, 15 percent Malay and 6 percent Indian. In spite of the dominance of Chinese, however, Singapore's highly developed culinary culture embraces a similar range of cuisines to Malaysia, the result of a shared history prior to 1965 and of inheriting the same basic mix of communities and traditions, albeit in different proportions. Therefore I have dealt with Malaysia and Singapore together in this book although this is not a reflection on the sovereignty of either.

The rich culinary tapestry of Malaysia and Singapore comes from a particular mix of historical and geographic circumstances. The original population of the Malay Peninsula was not a large one, consisting of a forest-dwelling people, the *orang asli*, and small groups of "strand and sea people," the *orang laut*, whose skills and specialization lay with their ability to exploit the harvests of sea and coastal reef. But the country was rich in the kind of resources sought in the ancient world: resins and aromatic woods, gold and tin, palm products, shells and corals—the natural wealth of its jungles and oceans. It is located, too, on the convergence of two major monsoonal sea trade routes connecting the markets of India and China. From early times it was visited by Indian, Arab and Chinese traders, who rested there or operated overland portage routes as they waited for the monsoonal changes that would take them forward. *Orang asli* and *orang laut* groups combined their different skills to deliver jungle products to coastal collection points. Coastal populations and developing maritime settlements were infused with foreign cultural influences in the process, particularly from India.

Indian notions of statecraft and political organization saw some substantial ports and nascent states develop out of estuarine settlements in the first millenium AD, even at the times when Sumatran Srivijaya held sway in the area. The trend accelerated from the 12th to the 14th centuries as ports in Trengganu were able to guarantee their sea lanes in the face of an increase in piracy in the Malacca Straits, and as private

Chinese trade in the region took to circumventing Srivijaya and sailing directly into Malay ports. From this time on, Malay states of some substance began to develop on the peninsula.

However, it is to the kingdom of Malacca, founded around 1400 on the Straits of that name, that modern Malays attribute their direct cultural heritage. Said to have been established by a renegade prince from Palembang in Sumatra (the home of the now declined Srivijaya), Malacca quickly became a great trading center in the Srivijaya tradition and in the early 15th century embraced Islam. Its physical advantages, its rulers' ability to provide the security and order required by traders from the many countries who brought, stored and exchanged a huge variety of goods there, ensured both a brilliant prosperity and an unequalled position in Southeast Asian trade at the time. In terms of Malay culture the statecraft and lifestyle forged there became the model for all subsequent Malay kingdoms and is still recognized as expressing the essence of the Malay tradition. In culinary terms the most important legacy of Malacca derived from its involvement in the spice trade, its openness to the ingredients and culinary techniques introduced by the foreigners who lived there and its cultivation of a rich eclectic gastronomy. It is a legacy shared by much of north Sumatra.

Apart from its contribution to Malay cuisine, Malacca was also the catalyst for the development of two other rich and unique culinary cultures found in Malaysia and Singapore today—cuisines known respectively as Nyonya and Eurasian.

Malacca's status as a great trading entrepôt drew, among others, many Chinese merchants, who settled there and married Malay women. When the British established settlements in Penang and Singapore in the late 18th and early 19th centuries, some of the descendant families migrated to these two places as well, attracted by the new commercial opportunities there. A new wave of Chinese immigrants moved into mining and agriculture in the 18th century, some of these in turn marrying into the older families in the settlements.

These were the people known over time as Baba Chinese, Straits Chinese, or Peranakan (children of mixed blood). Though they lived and decorated their houses in conformance with the paternal culture, much of their domestic life was deeply influenced by the Malay side of their heritage. Their cuisine combined Chinese ingredients and flavorings with Malay ones and most dishes were cooked in a Malay manner. It became known as Nyonya cooking—Malay was the language of Baba house-holds and loosely translated "nyonya" is the Malay word for "Chinese married woman." A selection of Nyonya dishes appears on pp. 250–271.

Captured by the Portuguese in 1511 and then by the Dutch East India Company in 1641, Malacca also saw the creation of another distinct group, the Eurasians. Members of this group were the progeny of intermarriage and liaisons between the Portuguese or Dutch and members of the many Asian communities present in this thoroughly cosmopolitan place. The Eurasians, too, proudly uphold a distinct and exotic culinary tradition in Malaysia and Singapore today. I give a tiny sample of Eurasian dishes on pp. 317–325.

In the centuries before and after Malacca there were other non-Malay groups who were absorbed into Malay society and had varying degrees of influence on Malay food. Arabs, granted special trading privileges because they were of the same race as the prophet, penetrated Malay society extensively in the 18th century, and the Minangkabau from Sumatra had been filtering in and establishing settlements in the Negri Sembilan area over some centuries. Along with them, Bugis from south Sulawesi, and large groups of Javanese were absorbed at different times, aided by a similarity of lifestyles and a common religion. Some visible influences from these groups will be discussed in the Malay section on pp. 179–208. Then there were the British, whose culinary impact can only be described as slight.

However, it was not until the 19th and early 20th centuries that large and distinct streams of Chinese and Indian cuisine became entrenched there.

At this time the Chinese miners and agriculturalists who had estab-lished themselves earlier extended their wealth by importing slave labor from China to work in growing pepper and gambier plantations, tin mines and the urban centers that were developing to sustain them. They were encouraged in these endeavors by the British, who viewed Chinese enterprise and industriousness as a source of wealth and revenue for their territories. Migration continued steadily throughout the 19th century. By 1891 the Chinese comprised 79 percent of the population of Kuala Lumpur; at the beginning of the present century they were the most numerous community in Singapore and Penang, in large towns such as Perak and Selangor and in the tin-mining areas of western Malaya. With immigration came Chinese cooking in a huge variety of regional styles.

The crowded urban conditions that many of the immigrants lived in also gave rise to a brilliant and adaptive Chinese street cuisine.

A broad-based Indian community, though smaller in numbers, also grew dramatically at this time. In previous generations there had been a small trickle of Indian traders (largely Muslims from the Coromandel coast) settling in the Peninsula, some of whom became quite influential in Malay courts. Indian immigration skyrocketed under the British and its profile broadened. Some of the new arrivals were urban moneylenders and businessmen (Gujerati merchants, both Hindu and Muslim; south Indian Muslims; a few Sikh businessmen; and Chettiars from south India); some were minor bureaucrats familiar with British administration who had transferred from India and what was then Ceylon. The majority, however, were Tamils and Telugu people from south India, brought in as plantation workers and unskilled laborers.

There is no doubt that social and political developments in Malaysia and Singapore since independence have brought about a change from earlier times when the different communities lived very separate lives. Today there is a national consciousness and a growing degree of shared culture and cuisine. Many people now cook or experiment with dishes from the cuisines of other communities, prompted sometimes by intermarriage on the part of siblings and friends and subject to household religious taboos.

Government policies and health regulations are also forcing food vendors off the streets into indoor food halls, especially in Singapore. Many street dishes are acquiring a new kind of respectability as a result and are finding their way into the repertoires of home cooks. For this reason, I have included some dishes created on the street, despite the book's primary focus on home cooking.

When you plan to serve Malaysian food at home, two questions present themselves: first, how many dishes should you serve at one time and in what combination? The general practice at formal meals is more or less the same as with formal meals in other countries of Southeast Asia. A number of separate dishes are placed on the table, sometimes calculated as one dish for each person present, though half the quantity specified in these recipes is cooked of each dish. Rice and condiments are served with a combination of dishes based on different classes of ingredients and cooked in different ways: a seafood or fish dish, for example, and/or one containing meat or poultry, a vegetable dish, a salad and/or fresh pickle. One dish should be liquid (boiled, stewed or braised), one dish dry (fried, grilled or roasted), and another dish should be fresh or crunchy. All (with the exception of some soups) are served in central bowls or plates, and each person has an individual plate or bowl and appropriate implements (spoons and forks, chopsticks for Chinese) or uses their hands alone. Beside the main plate there may be a small soup bowl and individual dishes of sauces. Diners help themselves to whatever they want when they want it, or are directed to special dishes by the host. They do not pile their plates with a serving from every central dish at one time; this is considered rude and not gastronomically desirable. Soups, if they are served, are intended to cleanse the mouth and refresh the palate. Diners take a sip from their soup bowl in between other dishes. Main courses are usually followed by fresh fruit only. The more complex sweets and cakes are reserved for between-meal snacks.

On special occasions the Chinese meal becomes a banquet, where each dish is served separately after the one before it has been completely finished and with time for resting and toasting allowed. The Chinese banquet is a complicated matter with its own rituals, and I do not address it here.

For a Western family, and certainly for the beginner, I suggest serving only two dishes with rice and accompaniments, each one in a larger quantity than that which might be usual at a more heavily laden Asian table. Hence most of the recipes in this book have been calculated to serve three people generously when only one dish is served, and twelve or more if there are four or five dishes. Branch out only if you have guests and are intent on impressing them, for preparing an elaborate Asian meal is a time-consuming process. Even in urban households in Southeast Asia itself where once cooks, servants and extended family might have prepared a number of different dishes daily, busy parents—many of whom no longer have cooks—have reduced their efforts for a family meal to one or two dishes.

When you do have a dinner party and want to serve four or five dishes for variety, remember to recalculate the amounts given in each recipe here to fit the numbers if you need to.

The second question that comes to mind when serving Malaysian food at home is whether you should stick to the style of one community at each meal, or if you can combine Malay, Chinese and Indian dishes. While mixing is certainly done in modern Malaysian and Singaporean homes more than it used to be, it is a rather risky business unless and until you are very well acquainted with the flavors of the different cuisines. Feel free, however, to do so if you are confident.

MALAY

As discussed in the introduction to this chapter, a number of culinary influences have combined with the legacy of Malacca to contribute to the form and variety—particularly the regional variety—of Malay food today.

In the north there is a distinct Thai influence, due not only to southern migration of Thai people at various times but also to formal Siamese suzerainty over the northern Malay states from the 16th century until the establishment of British control there in the early 20th century. This is evident in the area's appreciation of tamarind sourness and an occasional combination of spices that is authentically Thai.

In the western coastal states Indian sailors and traders were frequent visitors at harbors in early times as they worked the sea trade route between China and India, some of them no doubt settling there. They also are known to have operated a portage route across the north of the peninsula to Pahang where ships would be carried across land to the Muar-Pahang waterway. By the 18th century there was also a substantial population of Muslim traders from the Coromandel coast there. Kedah, in particular, was renowned for its wealthy and powerful Indian commercial community, and it is not surprising that Malay food in the west and the northern areas shows a distinct Indian Muslim influence, similar to that of the ports of north Sumatra, their curries being thicker and richer than usual with a particularly heavy use of trade spices.

In the cities where they eventually settled, the influx of south Indian laborers brought in by the British to work on rubber estates in the early part of the twentieth century has had a noticeable influence on Malay food. South Indian ingredients and techniques are used frequently: okra and purple eggplants are favored vegetables, and brown mustard, fenugreek and curry leaves are often combined in tempering—the Indian technique that imparts extra flavor in a dish through the addition of spices fried in oil.

There is a direct Minangkabau influence in the food of Negri Sembilan. From at least the 14th century and probably well before, it was a normal feature of life for young Minangkabau men to seek economic and spiritual gain through *merantau*, a period spent trading goods beyond the borders of the Minangkabau kingdom in west Sumatra. Some moved across the Malacca Straits into the southern Malay Peninsula and remained to settle there. Momentum increased in the 17th and 18th centuries with Negri Sembilan eventually coming together as a Minangkabau confederation. Dishes from this area are rich with coconut milk and the common items of west Sumatran agriculture such as ox meat or beef, cultivated vegetables and fiery bird's eye chilies (known in Malay as *cili padi*).

In Johore there is a Malay heritage from Malacca with a strong Javanese element, introduced by immigrants in the 19th century who established some irrigation and paddy cultivation there.

Malay food in the eastern states is generally simple. This area, which was once part of the Javanese empire of Madjapahit, enjoys a coastal resource base with rich supplies of seafood, and much of its population is involved in fishing. It also produces an abundance of rice, herbs and vegetables on its coastal plains and river deltas. Generally speaking, the food is mildly spiced using the chilies, fresh roots and herbs typical of rural Southeast Asia. Grilled Coconut Chicken (p. 200) is a good example.

In the northeast there are again echoes of involvement with the historical spice trade and with Thai Ayutthaya, which reveal themselves in the occasional use of seed spices as well as fresh roots and herbs.

Predominantly rural, the southeast and its coast show strong pan-Malay and Javanese influences: fish and seafood are rubbed with turmeric and deep-fried; there are piquant fried or fresh sambal with lots of shrimp paste; and fresh vegetables or fruits made into tangy pickles or pungent salads. The liquid in these dishes is often a sour fish soup/stew (*ikan asam*) or a light coconut milk fish *gulai* more like the *masak lemak* style of Negri Sembilan than the *gulai* of the north.

Regional differences aside, an everyday Malay meal—as elsewhere in Southeast Asia—would consist of a plate of rice surrounded by a number of side dishes dictated by situation, season, region and supply. As usual the side dishes are best understood as compliments to the rice rather than dishes to be eaten in large quantities for their own sake. There may be a wet dish dependent on region: fish, meat or vegetable cooked with plenty of rich gravy (*masak lemak*, *gulai* or *kari*) or a thin sour stew (*masak asam*). There may be a sharp braised dish flavored with soy sauce (*masak kicup*). For contrast there could be some fish or seafood rubbed with turmeric or tamarind and deep-fried (*goreng, asam goreng*); fish, chicken or pieces of beef marinated and grilled (*panggang, percik* or *bakar*), or a strong-flavored accompaniment of spicy dry-fried shredded meat or fish with coconut (*serunding*). There may be small crisp salads of fresh vegetables, fruits or herbs with hot, sometimes sweet, or coconut dressings, sauces or dips (*rojak, ulam-ulaman, kerabu*); a vegetable fried with shrimp paste and spices (*goreng rempah*); and, as in Indonesia, a pickle of crisp vegetables in vinegar (*acar*); and a small but concentrated burst of sambal made from a base of chili, tamarind and shrimp paste.

As in Indonesia, meals on celebratory occasions will often include richer and heavier dishes, though in this case more like the ones found in Sumatra than those from Java—a *rendang*, or a rich, thick korma adopted from Muslim India.

Wet Dishes

Malays enjoy Spicy Chicken Soup (p. 83) as a meal on its own with compressed rice (*Nasi Impit*, p. 206), or a Vegetable Soup (p. 76) cooked with mixed vegetables such as carrots, beans or small Asian eggplant. Recipes for these dishes are given in the Indonesian section. For the Malay version of Vegetable Soup, however, do not prepare a meat stock but fry a couple of tablespoons of dried shrimp, soaked and ground, with the spice paste and simply add plain water.

IKAN ASAM PEDAS ## HOT SOUR FISH

This is a Malay version of the sour fish soup/stew found all over mainland Southeast Asia, sometimes rather misleadingly called "*Gulai Tumis*." Compare it with the Sumatran Sour Fish Stew, the Thai or Lao Sour Fish Curry or the southern Thai Yellow Sour Fish Soup, the Vietnamese Sour Fish Soup and Cambodian Sour Chicken Soup. The dish is also a popular one in Nyonya cooking.

2 tablespoons oil
A few okra or green beans, cut into bite-sized lengths

2 pieces dried tamarind or ½ cup (125 ml) tamarind
  water (p. 55)
2–3 cups (500–750 ml) water
Salt to taste
1 lb (500 g) fish fillets (sea perch, cod, freshwater trout,
  pike) or small whole fish, cleaned

Spice Paste
12 medium-size dried chilies, soaked in warm water until
  soft, then squeezed dry
2 stalks lemongrass, finely sliced
1½-in (4-cm) piece galangal, peeled and coarsely
  chopped
1-in (2½ cm) piece turmeric root, peeled and coarsely
  chopped, or ⅛ teaspoon ground turmeric
1 teaspoon shrimp paste (*belacan*)
3 cloves garlic
10 shallots, sliced

Grind the Spice Paste ingredients to a fine paste. Heat the oil in a wok or
a saucepan and fry the Spice Paste until it is fragrant and no longer sticks
to the pan. Add the okra or green beans and stir-fry for a few minutes
until they are coated with the spices. Add the tamarind water (if using)
and mix well. Add the water, salt to taste and dried tamarind slices (if
using). Bring to a boil, reduce the heat and simmer until the vegetable is
nearly cooked. Add the fish and simmer gently until cooked.

**IKAN ATAU UDANG
LEMAK**
FISH IN COCONUT MILK

The style of cooking known as *masak lemak* in Malaysia comes from Negri Sembilan, whose people were
originally Minangkabau from Sumatra who settled
there some centuries ago. Note the close similarity
between this recipe and the one for Padang-style Fish
Curry (p. 93) in the Indonesian section. This dish is
often called a *gulai*—a simmered dish with lots of
gravy. It should, however, be distinguished from the
dishes in Curries and Rich Coconut Milk Dishes on
pp. 186–191 as these employ the dry trade spices and
are often called curries in English. This recipe is good
made with either fish or shrimp.

1½ cups (375 ml) thin coconut milk
1 stalk lemongrass, bruised
2 thick slices galangal, bruised
3 dried tamarind pieces
1 lb (500 g) fish fillets (Spanish mackerel, salmon, ling, barramundi) or shrimp, peeled, deveined, rubbed with salt and rinsed
1 cup (250 ml) thick coconut milk
Salt to taste

Spice Paste
4–5 medium-length red chilies, sliced
1-in (2½-cm) piece turmeric root, peeled and coarsely chopped or ¼ teaspoon ground turmeric
½-in (1½-cm) piece fresh ginger root, peeled and coarsely chopped
2 cloves garlic
8 shallots, sliced

Grind the Spice Paste ingredients to a fine paste. Combine the thin coconut milk, the Spice Paste, the lemongrass, galangal and tamarind pieces in a saucepan or a wok, mix well and bring to a boil. Add the fish or shrimp, reduce the heat and simmer, stirring carefully from time to time, until the fish is cooked and the gravy thickens. Add the thick coconut milk and salt to taste, stir again, return to almost a boil and remove from the heat.

KUBIS MASAK LEMAK ## CABBAGE IN COCONUT MILK

Southern Malays often cook vegetables in coconut milk. Although this recipe is for cabbage, it may be used for other vegetables such as sliced bamboo shoots, green beans or bean sprouts. With bean sprouts, however, put them in at the same time as the thick coconut milk so they will not become soggy.

1½–2 cups (375–500 ml) thin coconut milk
1 lb (500 g) cabbage or curly kale, shredded
4 oz (125 g) small shrimp, peeled and deveined
1 cup (250 ml) thick coconut milk

Spice Paste

2 medium-length chilies or more to taste

½ teaspoon shrimp paste, roasted in foil (p. 53)

2-in (5-cm) piece turmeric root, peeled and coarsely
   chopped or a pinch of ground turmeric

1 clove garlic

4 shallots, sliced

Grind the Spice Paste ingredients into a paste. Combine the thin coconut milk and the Spice Paste in a saucepan, stir well and bring to a boil. Add the cabbage and cook until it is tender. Add the shrimp and simmer until they are cooked then add the thick coconut milk and return to almost a boil before serving.

This dish is usually served with sour-cooked fish or grilled fish and a pickle.

EGGPLANT IN COCONUT MILK

TERUNG DYAK LEMAK

This is a recipe from Sarawak. *Dyak* eggplant is a variety of vegetable grown by farmers after they have burned their fields and before they plant rice. It is round and orange in color, the size of a small grapefruit, and more delicate than purple eggplant. Orange eggplant is sometimes available from specialty greengrocers. The dish is still good made with purple eggplant, however.

1 lb (500 g) orange or purple eggplant

1½–2 cups (375–500 ml) thin coconut milk

Salt to taste

1 cup (250 ml) thick coconut milk

Spice Paste

6 medium-length dried chilies, seeded, soaked in warm
   water until soft and squeezed dry

4 small cloves garlic

6 shallots, sliced

1 teaspoon shrimp paste, roasted in foil (p. 53)

2 tablespoons dried shimp, washed

1 stalk lemongrass, finely sliced

Peel the eggplant and cut it into wedges. Combine the eggplant and the thin coconut milk in a saucepan and simmer, uncovered, until the vegetable is nearly cooked.

Grind the Spice Paste ingredients to a rough paste. Add the Spice Paste to the simmering eggplant and salt to taste. Stir and cook gently until the vegetable is tender. Add the thick coconut milk and return to a boil, stirring constantly, then serve.

Curries and Rich Coconut Milk Dishes

The dishes included here predominantly contain both coconut milk and some dried trade spices such as coriander, cumin, fennel, cinnamon bark, cloves and cardamom. *Rendang*, though it contains no trade spices, is included because it is a rich and thick special occasion dish. While many people—even in Malaysia—use packet mixes of spice powder for these dishes, the recipes below denote the individual spices for the sake of freshness and variety.

GULAI IKAN ## FISH CURRY

This is the classic southern Malay version of fish curry.

3 tablespoons oil
2 cups (500 ml) thin coconut milk
2 slices dried tamarind or 1–2 tablespoons tamarind
    water (p. 55)
1 lb (500 g) thick fish fillets (salmon, Spanish mackerel,
    mullet, ling)
½–1 cup (125–250 ml) thick coconut milk
Salt to taste

Curry Paste
2 tablespoons coriander seed or 1½ tablespoons ground
    coriander
½ teaspoon cumin seed or ¾ teaspoon ground cumin
1 teaspoon fennel seed or anise
½ teaspoon black peppercorns or ⅓ teaspoon freshly
    ground black pepper
6–10 medium-sized dried chilies, soaked in hot water
    until soft then squeezed dry
1-in (2½-cm) piece turmeric root, peeled and coarsely
    chopped or ½ teaspoon ground turmeric
1 thick slice fresh ginger root, peeled and coarsely
    chopped
2 cloves garlic
6 shallots, sliced

If using whole dry spices for the Curry Paste, grind them to a powder in an electric grinder, add the remaining Curry Paste ingredients and grind to a fine paste. Alternatively, grind the garlic and shallots and add 3 tablespoons of commercial Malay fish curry powder (*rempah kari ikan*). Mix the ground spices or the commercial curry powder, adding as much water as necessary to make a paste.

Heat the oil in a saucepan. Add the Curry Paste and fry it until it smells fragrant, reducing the heat to prevent it from burning. Add the thin coconut milk and the tamarind and bring to a boil. Add the fish and simmer until it is cooked. Add the thick coconut milk and salt to taste and return to a boil before serving.

In the north, 4 oz (125 g) of okra or a couple of thin purple eggplant are sliced thickly on the diagonal and added. Add them after the Curry Paste has been fried until fragrant, and stir-fry until they are coated with oil and spices before adding the coconut milk. Simmer until the vegetable is nearly cooked and then add the fish.

For a more modern pan-Malaysian touch prepare the following tempering from the Indian-influenced north to add at the end.

Tempering
3 shallots, sliced
1 clove garlic, sliced finely lengthwise
½ teaspoon fenugreek seed
½ teaspoon brown mustard seed
10 curry leaves

Heat a little oil in a pan and fry all the ingredients together until the shallots are golden brown. Pour over the curry before serving.

GULAI DAGING LEMBU ## BEEF CURRY

This rich and hot curry comes from the north, and is very much like the Thai Muslim Curry (p. 206). Serve with plain rice or Roti (p. 354), and a fresh sweet and sour accompaniment such as Tomato Pickle (p. 203) or Green Mango and Soy Sauce Sambal (p. 205).

1½ lb (750 g) chuck steak, trimmed of fat and cubed
4 tablespoons oil

5 shallots, sliced

2 cloves garlic, sliced

Small piece stick cinnamon

2 points of star anise

2–3 cups (500–750 ml) very thin coconut milk or water

3 medium-sized potatoes, quartered (optional)

1 cup (250 ml) thick coconut milk

1–2 tablespoons tamarind water, or more to taste

Palm or dark brown sugar to taste (optional)

Salt to taste

Spice Paste

2 tablespoons coriander seed or 1½ tablespoon ground
    coriander

2 teaspoons fennel seed

2 teaspoons cumin seed or 1 teaspoon ground cumin

Small piece cinnamon stick or ¼ teaspoon ground
    cinnamon

6 cloves or ¼ teaspoon ground cloves

2 cardamom pods, broken open or ¼ teaspoon ground
    cardamom

2 points of star anise or ¼ teaspoon anise

Pinch of freshly ground black pepper

1 teaspoon ground turmeric

¼ teaspoon ground nutmeg

10 medium-sized dried chilies, soaked in warm water
    until soft and squeezed dry, or chili powder to taste

1-in (2½-cm) piece fresh ginger root, peeled and
    coarsely chopped

2 cloves garlic

10 shallots, sliced

If using whole spices for the Spice Paste, grind them to a powder in a mortar or an electric grinder. Add the remaining Spice Paste ingredients and grind together with a little water. Alternatively, substitute 4 tablespoons of Malay meat curry powder (*rempah daging*) for the ground dry spices and the chilies in the paste. Mix the meat and Spice Paste in a bowl and set aside.

Heat the oil in a saucepan and fry the garlic and shallots with the cinnamon and star anise until brown and fragrant. Add the meat and stir-fry for a few minutes. Add the thin coconut milk or water, cover, and simmer until the meat is tender, adding the potatoes (if using), halfway through. When the meat is cooked, reduce the heat to low, add the thick coconut milk and stir, then add the tamarind water, sugar and salt to taste and reheat but do not boil.

CLASSIC BEEF RENDANG

RENDANG NEGRI SEMBILAN

This dish was brought into Malaysia by the Minangkabau from west Sumatra who settled in Negri Sembilan, but it has since been adopted by the Malays and differs in style according to region. I have included a northern (Sumatran) version in the Indonesian section, but this version is the classic one, not dry like the former.

2 lb (1 kg) beef topside, cubed
3 cups (750 ml) coconut milk
1 stalk lemongrass, bruised
1 piece dried tamarind
4 tablespoons grated fresh coconut, roasted in a dry pan
    until brown then finely ground (p. 40)
Salt to taste

Spice Paste
15–20 medium-sized dried chilies, soaked in warm water
    until soft and quezzed dry or 4–5 teaspoons dried chili
    flakes
2 stalks lemongrass, fnely sliced
¾-in (2-cm) piece galangal, peeled and coarsely
    chopped
¾-in (2-cm) piece turmeric root, peeled and coarsely
    chopped or 1 turmeric leaf
¾-in (2-cm) piece fresh ginger root, peeled and coarsely
    chopped
6 cloves garlic
12 shallots, sliced

Grind the Spice Paste ingredients to a fine paste. Mix the beef with the Spice Paste and set aside for 15 minutes. Combine the beef, the coconut milk, lemongrass and dried tamarind in a wok and bring to a boil, stirring constanly. Reduce the heat and simmer, continuing to stir, until the gravy has thickened.

Add the roasted coconut, reduce the heat to low and cook gently, stirring occasionally, until the meat is tender and the gravy is very thick but not dry. This should take a little more than one hour and you may wish to use less coconut milk to bring the gravy to sufficient thickness in less time. Add salt to taste and serve.

KORMA INDIAN CURRY

Korma is a very rich but mild curry that is found in almost identical forms on the north and the west coast of Malaysia, in north Sumatra and in west Java—all areas heavily influenced by early Arab and Indian Muslim involvement in the spice trade. Its richness and opulence make it a favorite dish for serving at weddings, festivals and family gatherings.

While employing almost the same spices as the Muslim north Indian version of this dish, the Malay korma is cooked with coconut milk rather than yogurt. It clearly shares a heritage with the Thai Muslim Curry (p. 354).

1½ lb (750 g) lamb, lean beef, or chicken cut into bite-sized pieces
4–6 tablespoons oil
5 shallots, sliced
5 or 6 cloves garlic, chopped
3-in (8-cm) piece cinnamon stick, broken
10 cloves
3 points of star anise
2–3 cups (500–750 ml) thin coconut milk
Salt to taste
2 pieces dried tamarind or fresh lime juice to taste
2 potatoes, peeled and quartered
2 small onions, peeled and quartered
1 cup (250 ml) thick coconut milk

Spice Paste

1 tablespoon coriander seed or 2½ teaspoons ground
  coriander

1 teaspoon cumin seed or 2½ teaspoons ground cumin

1 teaspoon fennel seed or anise

1 teaspoon whole black peppercorns or ¾ teaspoon
  freshly ground black pepper

2 cardamom pods or ¼ teaspoon ground cardamom

1 teaspoon poppy seed (optional)

1 stalk lemongrass, finely sliced

1½-in (4-cm) piece fresh ginger root, peeled and
  coarsely chopped

2 cloves garlic

4 shallots, sliced

If using whole spices for the Spice Paste grind them to a powder in a mortar or electric grinder. Add the rest of the Spice Paste ingredients and grind together with a little water. Coat the meat with the Spice Paste and set aside for 30 minutes.

Heat the oil in a saucepan and fry the garlic, shallots, cinnamon stick, cloves and star anise until everything is fragrant and the shallots are light brown. Add the meat and stir-fry for a few minutes.

Add the thin coconut milk, salt and dried tamarind to the pan and simmer until the meat is about halfway cooked (about 30 minutes). Add the potatoes, stir, and simmer until both the meat and potatoes are almost done. Add the onions and the thick coconut milk and simmer for 5–10 minutes. Taste and adjust the seasonings and serve.

This dish is good with Roti (p. 206), as is any other curry cooked with dried trade spices.

Braised Dishes

AYAM MASAK KICAP ## SPICED CHICKEN IN SOY SAUCE

This recipe came to me from Che Hafsah Harun of Kuching in Sarawak. It is a dish for special occasions. It might be served, for instance, at the feast that precedes the fasting period. The recipe has been prepared in Che Hafsah Harun's family for three generations.

2 lb (1 kg) chicken
5 tablespoons oil
1 cup (250 ml) water
1 cup (250 ml) tamarind water
3 tablespoons dark soy sauce
2 tablespoons sugar
2 stalks lemongrass, bruised
Salt to taste

Spice Paste
20 medium-sized dried chilies, soaked in warm water
    until soft and squeezed dry
6 slices galangal, peeled and coarsely chopped
2-in (5-cm) piece fresh ginger root, peeled and coarsely
    chopped
1 clove garlic
12 shallots, sliced

Cut the chicken into curry pieces (p. 23). Heat the oil in a wok and fry the chicken pieces until they are brown. Drain and set aside.

Grind the Spice Paste ingredients to a paste. Drain all but 2–3 tablespoons of oil from the wok, reheat it and fry the Spice Paste until it is fragrant. Add the chicken pieces, and stir-fry for 2 minutes until the chicken is coated with the spices. Add the water, tamarind water, soy sauce, sugar, lemongrass and salt. Stir and simmer, uncovered, until the chicken is tender, stirring occasionally as it cooks. If the dish gets too dry before it is cooked, add more water and finish cooking. Adjust the seasonings and serve.

WILHELMINA'S PICKLED CHICKEN

This recipe was given to me by Mrs. Wilhelmina Sim of Kuching. It is a dish that has been cooked in her family for many years. It can also be prepared with beef instead of chicken.

2 lb (1 kg) chicken, cut into 3-in (8-cm) pieces
4 tablespoons oil
1 cup (250 ml) water
4 tablespoons white vinegar
4 tablespoons sugar
Salt to taste

Dry Spices
4 tablespoons roasted coriander seed or 3½ tablespoons
   ground coriander
1 tablespoon cloves or ½ tablespoon ground cloves
4 cardamom pods or ½ teaspoon ground cardamom
1 teaspoon cumin seed or ¾ teaspoon ground cumin
1 teaspoon ground turmeric
2-in (5-cm) piece cinnamon stick or ¼ teaspoon ground
   cinnamon
1 teaspoon ground nutmeg

Spice Paste
12 medium-sized dried hot chilies, seeded and soaked in
   warm water until soft and squeezed dry
1 stalk lemongrass, finely sliced
2-in (5-cm) piece fresh ginger root, peeled and coarsely
   chopped
4 cloves garlic
8 shallots, sliced

If using whole dry spices, grind them to a powder in an electric grinder. Mix all the Dry Spices together. Coat the pieces of chicken well with these spices and set aside for at least 15 minutes.

Grind the Spice Paste ingredients to a paste. Heat the oil in a pan and fry the paste until it is light brown and aromatic. Add the seasoned chicken and stir-fry for 5 minutes. Add 1 cup (250 ml) of water and simmer until the chicken is tender. Add the vinegar, sugar and salt to taste. Stir and cook until fairly dry.

Fried Dishes
Stir-fries

FRIED GREEN VEGETABLES WITH SPICE PASTE

2–3 tablespoons oil
8 oz (250 g) small shrimp, peeled and deveined
1 lb (500 g) okra, green beans or zucchini strips
4 tablespoons water
Salt to taste

Spice Paste
3–5 medium-length red chilies
4 roasted candlenuts or raw almonds and macadamia
   nuts, coarsely chopped
1 teaspoon shrimp paste
2 cloves garlic
8 shallots, sliced

Grind all the Spice Paste ingredients into a paste. Heat the oil in a wok and fry the Spice Paste until it smells fragrant and no longer sticks to the pan. Add the shrimp and stir-fry for a minute. Add the vegetable and stir-fry, mixing until it it is coated with oil and spices. Add the water and salt to taste, and stir-fry, uncovered, until the vegetable is tender-crisp and the water has evaporated.

If you want the vegetable to be softer, cover the pan and steam for 1 minute after adding the water, but be careful not to overcook the shrimp.

**TERUNG GORENG
BELACAN**
FRIED EGGPLANT WITH SPICE PASTE

¼ cup (125 ml) oil
1 lb (500 g) unpeeled long green eggplant and/or long
   purple eggplant, cut in half lengthwise and either left
   full length or cut into bite-sized pieces
Salt to taste

Spice Paste

3 or 4 medum-length red chilies, coarsely chopped

1½ teaspoons shrimp paste (*belacan*)

2 cloves garlic

6 shallots, sliced

Grind the Spice Paste ingredients to a paste. Heat the oil in a wok or a pan and fry the paste over medium heat until it is fragrant and no longer sticks to the pan. Add the eggplant and stir-fry until it is coated with the spices. Add a splash of water and salt to taste, cover and cook until the eggplant is done. Uncover, stir again and serve.

Chili-fries

These dishes are the equivalent of Indonesian *sambal goreng*. They are very rich and concentrated, and are best eaten as part of a garnished rice meal where an individual plate of rice is surrounded by small servings of one of them, plain sliced cucumber, hard-boiled egg, fried peanuts, etc. Rice garnished in this way makes an excellent breakfast or lunch and may be packed into separate lunch boxes to be taken on picnics. More sambal recipes appear in the Nyonya section.

SAMBAL UDANG ## SHRIMP SAMBAL

3 tablespoons oil

¾ cup (175 ml) coconut cream (*pati santan*)

1 lb (500 g) shrimp, peeled and deveined, rubbed with salt and rinsed

3 tablespoons tamarind water, or less to taste

1½ tablespoon palm or dark brown sugar, or less to taste

Salt to taste

Spice Paste

10 medium-length dried chilies, soaked in warm water until soft and squeezed dry

3 medium-length fresh red chilies, coarsely chopped

1 teaspoon shrimp paste

12 shallots, sliced

Grind the Spice Paste ingredients. Heat the oil in a wok or pan and fry the Spice Paste until it is fragrant and no longer sticks to the pan. Add the coconut cream and cook, stirring constantly, until the oil separates. Add the shrimp and simmer, continuing to stir, until they are partially cooked. Add the tamarind water, sugar and salt to taste and stir-fry until the shrimp are cooked and the gravy is very thick.

For a simple side dish version of a fried sambal with shrimp see Sambal Fried in Oil (p. 205).

SAMBAL IKAN FISH SAMBAL

1 lb (500 g) skinned fish fillets (sea perch, red snapper, red emperor), cut into 1-in (2½-cm) slices
½ teaspoon ground turmeric
3 tablespoons oil
1½ tablespoons palm or dark brown sugar, to taste
Salt to taste
3 tablespoons tamarind water

Spice Paste
10 medium-length dried chilies, soaked in warm water then squeezed dry
1 medium-length fresh red chili
1 teaspoon shrimp paste
10 shallots, sliced
2 cloves garlic

Coat the sliced fish with the ground turmeric and set aside. Grind the Spice Paste ingredients to a rough paste. Heat the oil in a wok or a pan and fry the Spice Paste until it is fragrant and no longer sticks to the pan. Add the fish and stir-fry gently until it is almost cooked. Add the sugar and salt to taste and tamarind water and stir-fry until there is a small amount of thick gravy.

SAMBAL IKAN BILIS — DRIED ANCHOVY SAMBAL

Packets of fried dried anchovies are often available in Asian grocery stores. If you can find them it will save you considerable time and the first step in this recipe.

1½ cups (375 g) dried anchovies (*ikan bilis*), without heads
Oil for deep-frying
½ cup (125 g) tamarind water, or to taste
Palm or dark brown sugar to taste
Salt to taste

Spice Paste
6 medium-length dried chilies, soaked in hot water until soft then squeezed dry
1 stalk lemongrass, finely sliced
2 slices galangal, peeled and coarsely chopped
3 roasted candlenuts or raw almonds or macadamia nuts
½ teaspoon shrimp paste
2 cloves garlic
5 shallots, sliced

Dust any debris off the dried anchovies, rinse them quickly and dry them thoroughly. Heat plenty of oil in a wok and deep-fry the anchovies until crisp. Drain well and set aside. If you are not satisfied with their level of crunchiness, try frying them again.

Grind the Spice Paste ingredients to a paste. In a clean wok, heat 2 tablespoons of fresh oil and fry the Spice Paste until it is fragrant and no longer sticks to the pan. Add the tamarind water, sugar and salt to taste, and cook until the sauce is thick and dark. Mix in the fried anchovies and serve with Indonesian Fragrant Coconut Rice (p. 166) or the Malaysian verion on (p. 266), hard-boiled egg, fried peanuts and sliced cucumber.

For a special side dish to serve with plain rice, try stirring in 1 tablespoon of coconut cream after the sauce has become thick and dark.

Pan-fry

TELOR DARDEH   ## MALAYAN OMELETTE

Oil
1 onion, chopped
2 medium-length red chilies, chopped
Fresh coriander leaves, chopped
3 eggs beaten with 1 tablespoon water
Salt and pepper to taste

Heat the oil until it is hot. Mix all the other ingredients, pour them into the pan and fry the omelette until it is cooked, folding it over.

Deep-fries

IKAN GORENG   ## FRIED FISH

The common preparation Malays use before frying fish, squid or cuttlefish is simply to soak it in diluted tamarind water to get rid of any fishy smell, and then rub it with turmeric, salt and sometimes garlic. Generally, you should cut larger fish into steaks or fillets, leave small fish whole and cut the bodies of small squid into thick rings, leaving the tentacles in a bunch. For every 8 oz (250 g) of fish or squid, use ½ teaspoon of ground turmeric mixed with salt to taste. Add crushed garlic if you wish.

Wash and dry the fish steaks or fillets, the whole small fish (which should be slashed) and cut the squid. Rub the fish thoroughly with the turmeric mixture and set aside for 10 minutes. Heat sufficient oil for deep-frying (use the Asian method for fish on p. 26), and fry until brown but still moist.

Grilled Dishes

IKAN BAKAR

Whole oily fish such as mackerel or sea mullet are rubbed with turmeric and salt and are grilled over low heat, brushing with oil if necessary, until the skin is lightly charred. (Try making a brush from a stalk of lemongrass, the thick end lightly crushed to become flexible.) Alternatively, the fish may be wrapped in banana leaves and grilled until the leaves are brown. Either way, the fish are traditionally suspended crosswise between two pieces of split bamboo secured together. A wire fish grill works just as well.

IKAN ATAU UDANG PERCIK

CHARCOAL-GRILLED COCONUT FISH (East Coast)

1 small fish (dart, mackerel, trevally, snapper) or 6 shrimp
    per person
Fresh lime juice
½ cup (125 ml) thick coconut milk

Spice Paste
2 medium-length red chilies
½-in (1½-cm) piece turmeric root, peeled and coarsely
    chopped or pinch of ground turmeric
1 clove garlic
4 shallots, sliced

Grind the Spice Paste ingredients to a paste. Combine the Spice Paste with the thick coconut milk and set aside.

Clean and scale the fish and make two slashes across each side. If you are using shrimp either peel and devein them leaving their tails intact, or devein them with their shells on (p. 25). Rub the fish or shrimp with lime juice then marinate in the coconut milk and Spice Paste mixture for at least an hour. Grill until the skin is lightly charred, basting frequently with the marinade. Garnish with fresh lime juice if you wish.

AYAM PERCIK # GRILLED COCONUT CHICKEN
(East Coast)

2 cups (500 ml) thick coconut milk
⅓ cup (100 ml) tamarind water
Sugar to taste
Salt to taste
1 chicken, quartered and pierced all over with a fork or
   the point of a sharp knife

Spice Paste
6–10 medium-length dried chilies, soaked in warm water
   until soft and squeezed dry
2 stalks lemongrass, finely sliced
1½-in (4-cm) piece turmeric root, peeled and coarsely
   chopped or ½ teaspoon ground turmeric
1½-in (4-cm) fresh ginger root, peeled and coarsely chopped
1–2 cloves garlic
8 shallots, sliced

Grind the Spice Paste ingredients to a fine paste. Mix the paste with the coconut milk, tamarind water, sugar and salt. Pour over the chicken, mix well and marinate for at least an hour. Remove the chicken pieces and grill them over low heat until brown, either dipping them occasionally into the marinade or basting them well with more marinade as they cook.

MALAY SATAY

Satay—quintessential street food in Malaysia—vividly reflects the Arab and Indian influences brought to bear on the area before modern times. If you make this recipe with chicken, omit the fennel and cumin from the Spice Paste.

1 lb (500 g) beef fillet or skirt steak or boneless chicken
   thighs, cubed
Oil for basting

Spice Paste
1 stalk lemongrass, finely sliced
2 cloves garlic

Pinch of ground turmeric
½ teaspoon ground fennel
½ teaspoon ground cumin

Satay Sauce
2 teaspoons coriander seed or 1¾ teaspoons ground
   coriander
1 teaspoon fennel seed or ¾ teaspoon ground
   fennel
1 teaspoon cumin or ¾ teaspoon ground cumin
6 medium-length dried chilies, seeded and soaked in
   warm water until soft then squeezed dry or 1–2
   teaspoons ground chili
½ teaspoon shrimp paste
6 shallots, sliced
1 clove garlic
2 tablespoons peanut oil
¾ cup (200 g) fried peanuts, coarsely ground
1 cup (250 ml) coconut milk
4 tablespoons tamarind water, made from 1 teaspoon
   tamarind
1 teaspoon palm or dark brown sugar
Salt to taste

Soak several satay sticks in water to prevent them from burning. Grind the Spice Paste ingredients to a paste. Coat the beef or chicken with the paste and set aside for 2–3 hours.

Thread the spiced meat on to about one-third of the length of the satay sticks and grill them, brushing them frequently with oil.

To make the Satay Sauce, grind all the dry spices in an electric grinder. Add the remaining Spice Paste ingredients and grind to a paste. Heat the oil in a saucepan and fry the Spice Paste until it is fragrant. Add the peanuts, coconut milk, tamarind water and sugar, mix well and simmer, stirring for 10 minutes. Taste and adjust the seasonings, adding water if you want a thinner sauce.

When cooked, arrange the skewers on a plate with pieces of rice cake (p. 165), wedges of unpeeled cucumber and fresh yellow or Spanish onion. Serve the sauce in a separate bowl to be spooned over the meat or dipped into. Use your satay sticks to spear chunks of rice cake, cucumber and onion.

Salads

Though they may have different names, many Malay salads are very similar to Indonesian ones: Vegetables with Thick Peanut Sauce (p. 144), Crisp Vegetable and Sambal Salad (called *Ulam-Ulaman* in Malaysia, p. 146), Pungent Fruit Salad (called *Rojak* in Malaysia, p. 149), and Fried Tofu with thick Peanut Sauce (p. 145) or Vegetables with Peanut and Coconut Milk Sauce (p. 143).

KERABU   BEANSPROUT SALAD
(North)

This salad is similar to the Indonesian Vegetables with Roasted Coconut (*Urap*), but is less well known. It is very refreshing and goes well with the dark, highly spiced dishes of the north. It is also an important part of a favorite and satisfying take-out meal. To assemble something like this yourself, serve plain rice on a plate, surrounded by a cup of Beansprout Salad, a couple of tablespoons of Peanut-coconut Garnish (p. 153) and a small Malaysian-style fried fish. Scatter some fried onion flakes and some Shrimp Paste Sambal or sambal ulek over the top and spoon a little leftover curry gravy on to the rice to moisten it. Eat with your hands, pulling small pieces off the fish and mixing together whatever you wish as you go.

1 lb (500 g) mixed crisp raw vegetables (trimmed bean sprouts; shredded cucumber; sliced green beans or very young snowpeas sliced on the diagonal; crisp cabbage or Chinese celery cabbage, finely sliced)

6 tablespoons fresh grated coconut or soaked dried coconut (p. 40)

2 tablespoons dried shrimp

5 green onions, finely sliced

2 stalks Vietnamese mint, finely sliced

6 medium-length red chilies, finely sliced, or to taste

2 tablespoons fresh lime juice, or more to taste

Sugar to taste

Salt to taste

Scald the bean sprouts, if you wish, by running boiling water through them in a sieve, but quickly follow with cold water to keep them crisp. Leave all the other vegetables raw. Roast the grated coconut in a dry pan until it is light brown and aromatic, then grind it finely to resemble brown sugar. Wash the dried shrimp, drain, dry and grind them coarsely. Combine the vegetables, coconut, shrimp, green onions, mint and chilies. Toss with the lime juice, sugar and salt to taste.

Accompaniments

At least one pickle and a sambal should accompany every Malay meal, adding sharpness, zing and textural interest.

ACAR TOMATO TOMATO PICKLE

½ cup (125 ml) vinegar
¼ cup (65 ml) water
1 tablespoon sugar
2 tomatoes, cubed
1 pickling cucumber, cut into four lengthwise, seeded and sliced
6 shallots or green onions, sliced, or 1 Spanish onion, halved across then thinly sliced lengthwise
Medium-length red chilies, chopped, to taste (optional)

Heat the vinegar, water and sugar until the sugar dissolves. Cool and pour over the vegetables and mix well.

ACAR TIMUN CUCUMBER PICKLE

Follow the instructions for the Tomato Pickle Recipe, omitting the tomatoes and shallots and using vinegar, water, sugar, cucumber and more chilies. Or omit the onion and toss the vinegar, water, sugar and cucumber in a bowl.

For other pickle recipes, refer to the Indonesian section.

SAMBAL BELACAN SHRIMP PASTE SAMBAL

This is the most common Malay side dish, eaten with virtually everything. Only a tiny quantity is placed on the edge of the plate, to be dipped into cautiously.

2 kaffir lime leaves (optional)
8 medium-length red chilies, coarsely chopped
Salt to taste
1 teaspoon shrimp paste, or more, roasted (p. 53)—up to
   3 or 4 times this amount may be used depending on
   personal taste
Fresh lime juice to taste

Remove the spines from the lime leaves (if using) and shred them finely. Grind the chilies, the lime leaves and the shrimp paste to a fine paste. Add lime juice to taste and to moisten. Serve in a small dish.

SAMBAL RAMPAI MIXED SAMBAL

3 medium-length red chilies, finely sliced
1 teaspoon shrimp paste, roasted in foil (p. 53)
1 tablespoon dried shrimp, soaked in water for a few
   minutes
1 small tomato
4 shallots, chopped
Salt to taste
2 teaspoons fresh lime juice
2 teaspoons tamarind water

Grind everything to a rough paste, adding the lime juice and tamarind water to taste at the end. Serve in a small dish.

SAMBAL ASAM SOUR SAMBAL

The crunchiness of the green mango in this and the following recipe is often as refreshing as a salad.

1 green mango, peeled and shredded
6 medium-length red chilies
Salt to taste

1 teaspoon shrimp paste, roasted in foil
1 teaspoon sugar or to taste
Water or lime juice

Peel and shred the mango the way you would shred green papaya (p. 47) or cut it into strips. Grind the chilies, salt, shrimp paste and sugar to a paste. Add the mango and a little water or lime juice to moisten (the mango should be sour enough), and toss together.

If you do not have green mango, you can make this sambal using ⅓–½ cup (100–125 ml) thick tamarind water instead.

SAMBAL KECAP MANGGA
GREEN MANGO AND SOY SAUCE SAMBAL

1 small green mango
2 tablespoons Javanese soy sauce
2 or more sliced green bird's eye chilies to taste, or
    medium-length red chilies, seeded and sliced
Salt to taste

Peel and shred the mango the way you would shred green papaya (p. 47) or cut it into strips. Toss everything together and serve in a small dish or bowl as a fresh accompaniment to Deep-fried Fish and a light vegetable cooked with coconut milk.

SAMBAL TUMIS
SAMBAL FRIED IN OIL

Serve this as a tasty side with rice and other more substantial dishes.

3–4 tablespoons oil
2 teaspoons tamarind water or fresh lime juice
1–2 teaspoons palm or dark brown sugar to taste
Salt to taste
1 tablespoon small raw shrimp, peeled

Spice Paste
3 medium-length dried chilies, seeded, soaked in warm
    water until soft and squeezed dry
¼ teaspoon shrimp paste (optional)
5 shallots, sliced

Grind the chilies, shrimp paste and shallots to a paste. Heat the oil in a pan, and fry the paste until it no longer sticks to the pan. Add the tamarind water, sugar and salt and let it bubble, then add the shrimp and stir-fry until they are lightly cooked.

ROTI JALA

Roti Jala is a lightly cooked pancake with holes that is often served with rich Malay curries.

2 cups (500 g) flour
Salt to taste
3 eggs, lightly beaten
Thin coconut milk or water

Grease a frying pan and heat it over medium heat. Sift the flour and salt together, then add the eggs and enough coconut milk or water to make a thin batter.

The traditional way of proceeding is to dip all five fingers of one hand deep into the bowl of batter and let the mixture run from your hand into the pan in a lacy pattern. In Malaysia you can buy a special metal cup with four small funnels at its base. You pour enough batter for one pancake into this, letting it flow out through the four funnels as you move the cup in a circular motion over the hot greased pan or griddle. Alternatively, fill a plastic sauce bottle with a single pouring spout at the top with batter and squeeze it out very quickly in a lacy pattern. Turn the pancake over before it is brown and lightly cook the other side. Remove and stack in a pile one by one, folding them over into two when they cool.

Rice, Noodles and One-Dish Meals

NASI IMPIT COMPRESSED RICE

Cubes of compressed rice are eaten with Satay and also, by Malays, with Vegetable Soup (p. 76). This recipe is an easy substitute for Compressed Rice Cakes (p. 165) whenever they are called for in Malay or Indonesian food.

To compress the rice, use two rectangular tins or dishes, one of which fits inside the other.

2 cups (500 g) short-grain rice
6 cups (1½ liters) water
Salt to taste

Wash the rice and place it in a rice cooker or a saucepan with the water. Bring to a boil, reduce the heat and simmer. As the water reduces stir vigorously from time to time to break up the rice grains, especially toward the end of this stage as the rice becomes sticky. Cook the rice dry (over very low heat if you are cooking in a saucepan), then spread it out evenly in the larger tin. Put a layer of plastic wrap on top of the rice and place the second tin on top of this. Place a heavy weight on top to compress the rice. Refrigerate overnight and the next day remove the plastic wrap and cut into cubes, wetting the knife as you go to prevent it from sticking. Serve the cubes piled up on a plate.

STIR-FRIED BEEHOON

STIR-FRIED RICE VERMICELLI

This is a dish the Malays have taken over from the Chinese and made their own, adding chilies and using less soy sauce than the Chinese. It is a favorite afternoon snack.

8 oz (250 g) dried rice vermicelli
4 tablespoons oil
8 oz (250 g) small shrimp, peeled and deveined
7 oz (200 g) chicken or beef, finely sliced
Light soy sauce, to taste
7 oz (200 g) bean sprouts, washed and trimmed
A few leaves of young mustard greens, cut into 2-in
  (5-cm) lengths
Salt to taste
½ cup (125 ml) water

Spice Paste

4–5 medium-length red chilies

4–6 cloves garlic

5 shallots, sliced

Garnish

2 eggs

1 pickling cucumber, cut in half lengthwise, seeded and
  cut into strips

2 medium-length chilies, finely sliced

Fried onion flakes

Fresh coriander leaves

Soak the rice vermicelli in cold water until soft, drain, and set aside. To prepare the eggs for the Garnish, beat them and then fry them into a thin omelette. Cool, slice into fine strips and set aside.

Grind the Spice Paste ingredients to a fine paste. Heat the oil in a wok or a frying pan, and fry the paste until it is light brown and fragrant. Add the shrimp and then the chicken or beef, stir-frying until they change color. Add the soy sauce, bean sprouts and the mustard leaves and stir. Add the vermicelli and salt to taste and stir-fry to mix well and coat all the ingredients with the spices. Add the water and continue stirring and tossing until everything is cooked and mixed well. Serve garnished with the sliced omelette, cucumber, chilies, fried onion flakes and coriander leaves.

CHINESE

Chinese settlement in Malaysia and Singapore has produced three distinct streams in modern Malaysian and Singaporean cuisine: mainstream Chinese food, Nyonya cooking and Chinese street food. Nyonya cooking is recognized as a cuisine in its own right and will be dealt with in a separate section.

Similar though the two other streams in contemporary Malaysian and Singaporean Chinese cooking are compared to Nyonya cuisine, Chinese street cooking must also be singled out.

By the time the late 19th century wave of Chinese laborers began to settle in the Straits settlements and the Malay states, it was rare for Muslim Malay women to marry non-Muslim Chinese men. Many of the latter had to live with the social consequences of a severely unbalanced sex ratio until well into the 20th century.

Among the lucky ones who had families and access to cooking facilities, domestic cuisine was generally mainstream Chinese carried over directly from the communities they had left behind in China. For the single men who made up the majority, however, and for the many families who lived in cramped and overcrowded conditions in the towns, cooking at home was not a possibility. Chinese street food developed to cater to them.

In the beginning, Chinese street food was probably modelled on the cheap food once provided by employers to laborers on the job; it may also have been approached as a way for individuals to make a living by providing inexpensive but wholesome homestyle cooking to people who could not produce their own. Whatever its beginnings, its evolution over time has produced many dishes unique to Malaysia and Singapore—ones that you would never find in China itself.

Such dishes are well known on the streets or in the food halls of both Malaysia and Singapore today. Since this book focuses primarily on home cooking, I do not provide a separate section devoted to them here. Some of them, however, have found their way into home cooking and entertaining— especially in Singapore, where hawker food has been tidied into modern food halls and food complexes and has assumed a more mainstream status in the process. You will find a few favorite street food recipes embedded in this section. Where this occurs their origins are noted.

Most of the recipes here, however, directly follow the cooking styles of the various regions in mainland China that the waves of Chinese immigrants to Malaysia and their families came from. Local flavors are represented in the sauces placed on the table with them (dishes of light soy sauce with chili or of sambal); sometimes, too, a familiar dish will be given a Malaysian twist through the addition of some chili in the cooking.

Soups

There is never any doubt about the large role that soups play in a mainstream Chinese meal. Most Chinese soups consist of highly-flavored broth with small amounts of meat and vegetable. At a family meal a large bowl of soup is put on the table with all the other dishes. Soup is ladled into individual bowls for diners to dip in to to refresh their palates between mouthfuls of rice and other foods. At banquets a bowl of soup often marks a pause after a series of rich single dish courses and a soup is always served as a palate cleanser at the end.

ABALONE SOUP

1 tablespoon oil
5 slices fresh ginger root, chopped
Pork bones
6 cups (1½ liters) water
1 tablespoon soy sauce
1 teaspoon cornstarch
Salt and pepper to taste
½ teaspoon sugar (optional)
1¾ oz (50 g) dried Chinese mushrooms, soaked, stems
    discarded and caps sliced
3½ oz (100 g) lean pork, finely sliced
1 small bunch of Asian celery, cut into 1-in (2-cm)
    lengths or ¼ stick celery cut into long matchsticks
1 can abalone, drained and sliced
Sliced green onions and watercress for garnish

Heat the oil in a saucepan and fry the ginger until it is light brown. Add the pork bones and water and simmer for 1½ hours. Combine the soy sauce, cornstarch, salt, pepper and sugar in a bowl. Add the pork, mix well and set aside to marinate.

When the stock is ready, remove and discard the bones, add the mushrooms and the meat in its marinade. Simmer for 10 minutes. Add the celery and simmer another 5 minutes. Add the abalone and simmer gently to heat it through. Serve the soup in a large bowl garnished with green onions and watercress.

FISH BALL SOUP

1 lb (500 g) fine-fleshed fish (garfish, whiting, bream, flounder)
Salt to taste
4 tablespoons water
Small amount of rice flour or cornstarch
3½ oz (100 g) Chinese or mung-bean vermicelli
5 cups (1¼ liters) fish stock or light chicken stock
Salt to taste
Light soy sauce to taste
1 cup (250 g) Chinese mustard greens or celery cabbage, finely sliced

Garnish
Fried onion flakes
1 green shallot or green onion with leaves, chopped
1 small bunch of Asian celery, cut into ¾-in (2-cm) lengths or 1 stick celery, cut into matchsticks
1 medium-length fresh red chili, seeded and sliced diagonally

Flake the fish and grind it into a fine paste with salt to taste Add the water and enough rice or cornstarch to make a smooth paste. Wet your hand, take a handful of the mixture and squeeze it out through a clenched fist between thumb and forefinger in small balls.

Soak the vermicelli in cold water until it is soft. Bring the stock to a boil and season with salt and light soy sauce to taste. Add the drained vermicelli and fish balls and simmer until cooked. Add the mustard greens or celery cabbage and return to a boil. Pour the soup into a large bowl and garnish with fried onion flakes, chopped green shallot, celery and sliced chili before serving.

CHICKEN SOUP

This recipe can be made with pork or shrimp, substituting 8 oz (250 g) of finely sliced pork or peeled raw shrimp for the chicken and using coarsely chopped Chinese cabbage instead.

1 tablespoon oil
2 cloves garlic, chopped
1 whole boneless chicken breast, sliced across the grain
2 cups (1 liter) light chicken stock
2 thin slices fresh ginger root, chopped
6 dried Chinese mushrooms, soaked, stems discarded
   and caps halved
6 oz (170 g) shredded bamboo shoots
3 oz (80 g) snowpeas (optional)
Salt and pepper to taste
Fried onion flakes, sliced green onion or coriander leaves

Heat the oil in a saucepan and fry the garlic until it is brown. Add the chicken, stir-frying until it changes color completely. Add the stock, ginger and vegetables and simmer until the vegetables are tender crisp.

Serve the soup in a deep bowl, garnished with fried onion flakes or, if you have not used snowpeas, with chopped green onion or fresh coriander leaves.

PORK SOUP

This soup can also be made without the vermicelli or potatoes, using sliced cucumbers, diced zucchini or summer squash or up to 1 lb (500 g) of watercress shoots instead.

4 cups (1 liter) water or pork stock
2 cloves (optional)
2 waxy potatoes, peeled and diced
5 oz (150 g) lean pork, finely sliced across the grain

1¾ oz (50 g) Chinese or mung-bean vermicelli, soaked in
    cold water and cut into 2-in (5-cm) lengths
Salt to taste
Pepper to taste
Light soy sauce to taste

Bring the water or stock and the cloves to a boil. Add the potatoes and the pork and simmer gently until cooked. Add salt and the drained vermicelli and return to a boil. Sprinkle with a dash of freshly ground pepper, add soy sauce to taste and serve.

EGG-DROP SOUP

1½ tablespoons oil
1 clove garlic, chopped
4 oz (125 g) chicken, beef or pork, thinly sliced
4 cups (1 liter) chicken stock
1 egg, lightly beaten
2 green onions, finely sliced

Heat the oil in a saucepan and fry the garlic until it is light brown. Add the meat and stir-fry until it changes color. Add the chicken stock, bring to a boil, cover and simmer for 5 minutes. Remove the pan from the heat and slowly stir in the lightly beaten egg. The egg should not completely mix with the soup, but should float in it in shreds. Finally add the green onions, stir and serve.

SHARK FIN SOUP

In this recipe I have used a packet of prepared shark fin. This is by far the simplest way and I recommend it.

Roe from 4 crabs and 1 egg, or 2 eggs
3 tablespoons water
4 cups (1 liter) chicken stock
1 tablespoon light soy sauce
1 teaspoon salt
Pinch of pepper
Sugar to taste (optional)

1 teaspoon sesame oil

4 tablespoons cornstarch

5 tablespoons water

1 tablespoon oil

1 slice fresh ginger root, peeled and chopped

1 packet fully prepared shark fin, soaked in warm water
for 20 minutes to 1 hour and then drained—about 2
cups (500 g)

3½ oz (100 g) cooked chicken breast, finely sliced
(optional)

6 oz (175 g) crab meat

In a large bowl, mash the crab roe. Add 1 egg and add 3 tablespoons water and beat the mixture lightly. If you are not using crab roe, beat the 2 eggs with 3 tablespoons water. Set aside.

Combine the stock, soy sauce, salt, pepper, sugar and sesame oil and set aside. Mix the cornstarch with 5 tablespoons of water for thickening the soup and set aside.

Heat the oil in a pan and stir-fry the ginger for a minute. Add the shark fin, the stock mixture and a little extra water and simmer for 30 minutes. Add the chicken and crab meat and slowly add the cornstarch slurry and stir gently until thick. Remove the pan from the heat and stir in the crab roe and egg mixture. Return the pan to the stove and reheat, stirring constantly, until the soup just begins to boil. Pour into a bowl and serve.

Steamed and Poached Dishes

(Makes 6 rolls) ## EGG ROLLS

Egg Wrappers
Oil for greasing the pan
6 eggs, beaten but not frothy

Filling
8 oz (250 g) ground chicken or lean beef
2 teaspoons light soy sauce

1 teaspoon cornstarch

Salt and pepper to taste

Peanut oil

1 thick slice fresh ginger root, peeled and chopped

1 small onion, finely chopped

A few green beans or a stick of celery, finely sliced, or a
  small wedge of young cabbage, finely shredded

1 small carrot, cut into very thin matchsticks or strips

3 or 4 green onions, finely sliced

1 medium-length red chili, thinly sliced

To make the Egg Wrappers, grease a frying pan and set it on the stove over high heat. Make 6 very thin omelettes, one at a time, and pile them as they are cooked on to the back of a plate, as in the recipe for Popiah (p. 269).

To make the Filling, mix the chicken or beef with the soy sauce, cornstarch, salt and pepper. Heat a little peanut oil in a pan. Fry the ginger and onion until golden, add the beans, carrot and the meat, and stir-fry until the meat changes color and the vegetables are tender-crisp. Add the green onions and chili, stirring once more. Remove from the pan and set aside to cool.

When the Filling is cool, split it between the 6 Egg Wrappers. Roll each wrapper up, tucking in the ends, and seal the edges with a thick flour and water paste or with beaten egg. The rolls can be steamed for a few minutes on a rack over boiling water in a covered pan or deep-fried until brown in plenty of hot oil. Serve with salad, whole or sliced in rounds.

STEAMED TOFU WITH STIR-FRIED VEGETABLES

2 cups (500 g) soft tofu, drained and coarsely chopped

1 egg white, beaten

Pinch of salt

4 oz (125 g) ground chicken, pork or beef

1 egg yolk, lightly beaten

1 green onion, sliced

1 teaspoon ginger juice

½ teaspoon dry sherry

1 tablespoon sesame oil

3½ oz (100 g) snowpeas, washed and trimmed
3½ oz (100 g) carrots, peeled and cut into fine
  matchsticks
Light soy sauce, to taste (optional)
1 teaspoon cornstarch
½ cup (125 ml) water
Pinch each of salt and pepper
Fresh coriander leaves for garnish

Mix the tofu, egg white and salt in a bowl. In another bowl, thoroughly mix the chicken or other meat, egg yolk, green onion, ginger juice, sherry and a little salt.

Grease the inside of some small ramekins or an ovenproof dish, fill with alternate layers of the tofu and the meat mixture, and steam on a rack in a covered pan of boiling water for 15 minutes, or stand in a tray of warm water and bake in a moderately hot oven until set in the center. When set, turn out of the dish on to a plate or plates and keep warm.

Heat the oil in a pan and stir-fry the snowpeas and carrots for a few minutes. Add a splash of light soy sauce and stir again. Mix the cornstarch, water, salt and pepper. Add this slurry to the pan and, stirring everything to mix, let it simmer until the snowpeas and carrots are tender-crisp and the sauce has thickened. To serve, surround the steamed tofu with this mixture, and serve hot, garnished with coriander leaves.

STEAMED WHOLE FISH

1 lb–1¾ lb (500–800 g) whole flat fish (pomfret,
  snapper, bream, flounder)
4-cm (1½-in) piece fresh ginger root, peeled and grated
6 green onions, cut into 1-in (2½-cm) lengths
1½ tablespoons light soy sauce
2 teaspoons sesame oil
1 cup Asian celery, washed and cut into 1-in (2½-cm)
  lengths or chopped coriander leaves

Wash the fish and slash it 3 times across each side. Arrange the fish on a serving plate, stuffing the cavity with the ginger and green onions and scattering some on top of the fish. Sprinkle soy sauce over, put the plate on a rack in a steamer over rapidly boiling water and steam until just cooked. Remove, sprinkle with the sesame oil, garnish with Asian celery or chopped coriander. Serve with a dipping sauce of light soy sauce with sliced red chilies.

STEEPED CHICKEN

The chicken you use for this dish must be very fresh—do not attempt this recipe with a thawed frozen bird.

1 teaspoon salt
1 teaspoon pepper
1 tablespoon dry sherry
3 slices fresh ginger root
1 fresh chicken
Coriander leaves or green onion

Sauce
6 slices fresh ginger root, peeled and coarsely chopped
Salt and pepper to taste
1 tablespoon sesame oil

Set a pot with enough water to cover the chicken on the stove and bring to a boil. Add salt, pepper, sherry and ginger. Add the whole chicken and boil for 2–3 minutes, skimming the foam that forms on top of stock. Remove the pan from the heat and cover it, steeping the chicken for about 30 minutes. Return the pan to the heat and bring to a boil again and repeat the steeping process for another 30 minutes, by which time the chicken should be lightly cooked though still faintly pink near the bone. This is the way devotees prefer this dish, but if you prefer a more thoroughly cooked bird you can leave the chicken simmering in the pot for the first 15 minutes.

Remove the bird from the pot, drain it, and chop it into small frying pieces (p. 23), leaving the wings and drumsticks whole. Serve the chicken with individual dishes of sauce made by combining the slices of ginger, lots of salt and pepper and the sesame oil. This is a good lunch when served with rice.

The favorite way to serve a whole chopped chicken is to arrange all the pieces spread on a plate to resemble a chicken more or less in flight. It takes a practiced hand to serve this dish successfully—here is how you do it if you care to try: Cut the wings into two pieces each—the tip and its adjoining joint in one piece, the upper pieces in the other. Sit the chicken's head at one end of an oval plate. Arrange the upper wing pieces below the head on each side then place the lower joint and wingtip so that the tips reach beyond the edge on each side and look like spread wings. Place any neck pieces down the middle of the plate with the back sections down each side of them. Cover them with the strips of breast, skin side up, arranged crosswise neatly and evenly. Arrange the thigh pieces on the sides of the plate in the bottom half where the thighs look as if they should be, covering any uncovered back pieces in the process. Place the pope's nose at the center bottom of the plate and arrange the drumstick on each side below the thighs either with their "ankles" crossed or splayed out over the edges. Serve the plate ungarnished for dramatic effect if you have succeeded in this arrangement. Otherwise garnish the chicken plate with coriander leaves or green onion tassles (p. 22).

DRUNKEN CHICKEN

This dish makes a good hors d'oeuvre in a meal of separate courses.

1 small chicken
4 tablespoons dark soy sauce
½ cup (125 ml) Chinese wine or a pale, not too dry sherry
Vegetables for garnish (green onions, unpeeled cucumbers, fresh red chilies)

Put the chicken in a pot with enough water to cover it and bring to a boil. Cover and simmer for 30 minutes. Drain the cooked chicken and place it in a bowl. Combine the soy sauce and wine and pour it over the cooked chicken, setting it aside to marinate for several hours, turning the bird over and spooning the marinade over it every 30 minutes. For the best results, refrigerate the marinated bird overnight.

When it is marinated, chop the bird as described for frying pieces (p. 23) and arrange the pieces on a dish with the breast strips on top. Pour over the marinade and garnish as elaborately or as simply as you like with the vegetables.

Serve with a side dish consisting of an equal amount of garlic, ginger and finely chopped fresh red chilies, mixed together with salt then moistened with rice or coconut vinegar.

Braised Dishes

CHICKEN, BAMBOO SHOOTS AND MUSHROOMS

This dish can also be prepared using a small can of straw mushrooms instead of the dried ones.

8 dried Chinese mushrooms, soaked, stems discarded, hard stalks removed
1½ lb (750 g) chicken thighs and drumsticks, cut into 3-in (8-cm) pieces
¼ cup (65 g) flour
2 tablespoons oil
3 cloves garlic, chopped
2 thin slices fresh ginger root, peeled and cut into strips
3 oz (75 g) sliced bamboo shoots, drained
1 cup (250 ml) water
1–2 tablespoons dark soy sauce
½ teaspoon sugar, or to taste
Salt and pepper to taste

Leave the mushroom caps whole if they are small or halve them if they are large. Roll the chicken pieces in flour. Heat the oil and fry the garlic and ginger until they are light brown. Add the mushrooms and stir-fry for a few minutes. Add the chicken and fry until browned on all sides. Add the bamboo shoots and just enough water to cover the chicken (no more than 1 cup [250 g] and preferably less). Add the soy sauce, sugar and seasonings, and cook until the chicken is tender and the gravy has thickened.

BRAISED PORK IN SOY SAUCE

This dish is found all over Southeast Asia and is a favorite lunch in supermarket and airport canteens in Bangkok.

2 tablespoons oil
2 cloves garlic, chopped
2 slices fresh ginger root
1 lb (500 g) belly pork, cubed
2 teaspoons sugar, or more to taste
Pinch of freshly ground black pepper
2 tablespoons dark soy sauce
2 onions, finely sliced lengthwise
Salt to taste
1 medium-sized potato, cubed (optional)

Heat the oil in a heavy pot and fry the garlic and ginger until light brown. Add the pork and fry until it is browned on all sides. Add the sugar and pepper, reduce the heat and cook, stirring constantly, until the meat is coated with oil and spices. Add the soy sauce and enough water to cover, the onions and salt to taste and cook until the meat is half-cooked (about 30 minutes). Add the potatoes and continue cooking until the meat and potatoes are cooked and the sauce has thickened.

A richer version of this recipe uses pork hocks and hard-boiled eggs instead of the potatoes. Cut 1 lb (500 g) of boned pork hock complete with skin into fairly large pieces (or you could use belly pork again). Chop 3 cloves of garlic and 5 slices of peeled ginger and fry them. Add the pork and stir-fry until the meat is seared on all sides. Add 2 star anise and a small piece of cinnamon stick, salt, pepper, 4 tablespoons of dark soy sauce, sugar to taste (up to 2 tablespoons) and 4 cups (1 liter) of water, cover and simmer gently for about an hour. Note that onions are omitted in this version. Add 4 shelled hard-boiled eggs and cook uncovered for another 20 minutes, by which time the eggs should have turned brown in the gravy. Garnish with thinly sliced red chili and chopped green onions. The recipe also works with shin beef.

CLAYPOT VEGETABLES

3 tablespoons oil
1 onion, quartered
2 cloves garlic
½-in (1½-cm) piece fresh ginger root, bruised
1 red bell pepper, chopped
1 medium-sized carrot, cut in half across and then into strips

1 zucchini, cut in half across and then into strips
A few green beans, cut into bite-sized pieces
1 small head of bok choy or a wedge of European
   cabbage, cut into 1-in (2½-cm) lengths or cubes
1 tomato, quartered (optional)
2 tablespoons oyster sauce
Dash sesame oil
2 tablespoons light soy sauce
2 tablespoons water
2 dried Chinese mushrooms, soaked and stems removed
3½ oz (100 g) fried tofu, cubed
Chinese celery, cut into bite-sized lengths
Freshly ground white pepper

Heat the oil in a Chinese claypot on a gas or electric hotplate. Add the onion, garlic and ginger and stir-fry. Add all the other vegetables and stir-fry for about 2 minutes. Mix the oyster sauce, sesame oil and light soy sauce together and add to the pot. Wash the mixing bowl with about 2 tablespoons of water and add it together with the Chinese mushrooms and the tofu. Stir to mix, cover and cook for 5 minutes. Stir, replace the lid and cook for 15 minutes more. Finally remove the lid, stir in the Chinese celery, add a sprinkling of white pepper and serve in the pot.

Fried Dishes
Stir-fries

SHARK FIN WITH SCRAMBLED EGG

3 tablespoons oil
2 teaspoons grated fresh ginger root
½ small onion, chopped
3 oz (80 g) lean ham or Chinese roast pork (*cha siew*),
  shredded
4½ oz (125 g) crab meat
4½ oz (125 g) shredded bamboo shoots
4½ oz (125 g) prepared shark fin, soaked in water for 20
  minutes then drained
4 eggs, lightly beaten
Sliced green onions or coriander leaves for garnish

Heat the oil in a frying pan. Fry the ginger and onion until light brown. Add the pork, crab meat, bamboo shoots and shark fin, and stir-fry until mixed well. Add the beaten eggs and, when they start to set, scramble them gently until mixed but not dry. Garnish with chopped green onion or coriander leaves.

FLOWERING CRAB

1 lb (500 g) crabs
4 tablespoons oil
1-in (2½-cm) piece fresh ginger root, peeled and grated
  or finely chopped
2 cloves garlic, chopped
1 tablespoon brown fermented soy bean paste—if the
  beans are only available whole, wash and mash them
  into a paste
½ cup (125 ml) water
1 egg, beaten
Sliced green onions or coriander leaves for garnish

Wash the crabs, remove the bottom plate, clean out the spongy material then cut them into quarters complete with legs, or into two if they are small. Crack the claws. Heat the oil in a wok and stir-fry the ginger and garlic until fragrant, then add the bean paste and stir-fry again until fragrant. Add the crabs and stir until pink and coated. Add the water, cover and steam until cooked. Remove the lid, then add the beaten egg and continue stirring until the sauce is thick. Garnish with sliced green onions or coriander leaves.

PEPPER CRAB

Pepper Crab is a popular modern recipe in Malaysia, made with black pepper and chilies.

When cooking whole crabs, especially large ones such as mud crabs, buy them still alive if you can. Put them in the freezer for half an hour, then wash them, remove the bottom plate of the shell and clean out the spongy material. Cut into quarters with legs attached and crack the claws lightly before cooking to allow the sauces to penetrate.

1½ tablespoons black peppercorns
3 tablespoons oil
5 cloves garlic, chopped
2 medium-length red chilies
3 medium-sized mud crabs, cut into four

Chili Sauce
3 medium-length red chilies
1 clove garlic
Juice of 1 lime
½ teaspoon sugar

Grind the peppercorns coarsely and set aside. Heat the oil in a wok, add the garlic, chili and pepper and fry until the garlic starts to turn brown (be careful not to burn it). Add the crabs and stir-fry until they are coated with the spices. Add a splash of water, cover and cook over high heat for about 10 minutes, lifting the lid and turning them from time to time to make sure they do not dry out.

To make the Chili Sauce, mash the chilies and garlic to a paste. Add the lime juice and the sugar and mix. Serve the crab with individual sauce dishes.

SHRIMP IN SOY SAUCE

3 tablespoons oil
1-in (2½-cm) piece fresh ginger root, peeled and
    chopped
3 cloves garlic, chopped
1½ lb (750 g) large shrimp, shells left on
4 tablespoons dark soy sauce
Sliced green onions and coriander leaves for garnish

Heat the oil in a wok and fry the ginger and garlic until they are light brown. Add the shrimp and stir-fry until they turn red. Add the dark soy sauce and continue to stir-fry until cooked and well-coated, adding about ¼ cup (125 ml) of water if necessary. Serve garnished with sliced green onions and coriander leaves.

CHICKEN AND ALMONDS

1 whole chicken breast, sliced
1 tablespoon light soy sauce
½ teaspoon cornstarch
Pepper to taste
1¾ oz (50 g) blanched almonds
Peanut oil
A few water chestnuts, sliced or diced
1¾ oz (50 g) dried Chinese mushrooms, soaked, stems
    discarded, caps sliced
3 cloves garlic, chopped
2 small carrots, peeled and sliced
½ zucchini or summer squash or 1¾ oz (50 g) celery,
    sliced
1¾ oz (50 g) bamboo shoots, sliced
3 tablespoons water

Marinate the chicken breast in a mixture of the soy sauce, cornstarch and pepper for a few minutes. Deep-fry the blanched almonds in plenty of hot peanut oil until light brown. Drain and set aside. Drain the pan of all but 2 tablespoons of oil and lightly fry the water chestnuts. Remove, and set them aside. Slice and fry the mushrooms, and set aside. Fry the garlic until it is brown, add the chicken and stir-fry until the meat is cooked. Add all the other vegetables, including the water chestnuts, and stir-fry until seasoned. Add about 3 tablespoons of water and simmer uncovered for 1 minute. Serve on a large plate garnished with the fried almonds.

SEASONED SHREDDED PORK

1 lb (500 g) lean pork, shredded
2 tablespoons soy sauce
1–2 teaspoons sugar
Pinch of freshly ground white pepper
1 teaspoon cornstarch
1–2 tablespoons oil
4 cloves garlic, chopped

Mix the meat with the soy sauce, sugar, pepper and cornstarch. Heat the oil and lightly fry the garlic until fragrant. Add the seasoned meat, and stir-fry until it is cooked. Add a dash of water to moisten, stir to mix and serve.

This dish may be made with sliced onion instead of garlic for a change. Slice a large onion, fry the slices lightly in the hot oil first, then add the seasoned meat and cook according to the instructions above.

KIDNEY FLOWER

This recipe gets its name from the preparation of the meat—it is cut into cubes with a floral design.

1 pork kidney
Pinch each of salt and pepper
Pinch of sugar
1 tablespoon light soy sauce
Juice squeezed from 2-in (5-cm) piece of fresh ginger
   root
4 oz (125 g) shrimp, peeled and deveined
1 tablespoon oil
3 cloves garlic
½ small cauliflower, cut into florets and parboiled

Clean the kidney and cut it in half lengthwise, removing the central core of tubes. Place each half on a cutting board with the outside facing up.

With a sharp knife, cut crisscross diagonal lines halfway through each half kidney, and then cut the kidneys through and across into 1-in (2½-cm) cubes. Season the meat with salt, pepper, sugar, 2 teaspoons of light soy sauce, and ginger juice. Rub the shrimp with salt and rinse. Mix them in with the seasoned kidneys. Heat the oil in a pan. Flatten the garlic cloves with a knife, and fry them in the oil until they are brown and have released their aroma, then remove and discard them. Add the shrimp and kidneys into the pan and fry them lightly. Add the cauliflower and stir-fry for a few minutes. Add 2 more teaspoons of soy sauce and a little water if necessary, and stir until everything is mixed and heated through.

GINGER BEEF

1 lb (500 g) rump steak, thinly sliced across the grain
2 tablespoons dark soy sauce
1 teaspoon cornstarch
Sugar to taste
1 teaspoon oil
3½-oz (100-g) piece fresh ginger root, finely shredded
5 oz (150 g) sliced bamboo shoots (optional)
1 teaspoon sesame oil

Mix the beef with the soy sauce, cornstarch and sugar in a bowl. Set aside to marinate.

Heat the oil in a pan, add the ginger and fry until it is brown and crisp. Add the seasoned meat and bamboo shoots and stir-fry until the meat is cooked. Remove the pan from the heat and just before serving, stir in the sesame oil. Serve with rice and other dishes.

SHREDDED BEEF AND VEGETABLES

8 oz (250 g) fillet or skirt steak, thinly sliced
1 teaspoon cornstarch
½ teaspoon sugar, or to taste
3 teaspoons soy sauce
4 tablespoons oil
4 cloves garlic, chopped
1 cup (250 g) small cauliflower florets
1 cup (250 g) sliced bell pepper

1 cup (250 g) flower-shaped or roll-cut carrot slices
½ cup (125 g) sliced bamboo shoots
½ cup (125 g) sliced button mushrooms or canned straw
  mushrooms
4 thin slices fresh ginger root
½ –1 cup (125–250 ml) water
Salt and pepper to taste

Combine the steak with the cornstarch, ¼ teaspoon of sugar, 2 teaspoons of soy sauce and set aside. Heat 3 tablespoons of oil and fry half of the garlic until golden. Add the cauliflower, bell pepper and carrots and stir-fry until they are tender-crisp. Add the bamboo shoots and mushrooms and stir-fry one minute more. Remove the vegetables and set aside.

Add one tablespoon of oil to the pan and fry the ginger and remaining garlic. Add the meat and fry until it is just cooked. Mix together the water, salt and pepper, ¼ teaspoon sugar and a little more soy sauce. Add this to the meat and stir. Add the vegetables, heat through and serve immediately.

ZUCCHINI, EGG AND SHRIMP

This recipe is also good made with shredded cabbage or green beans that have been sliced on the diagonal. In both these cases the minute of steaming should be omitted so that the vegetables remain crisp.

2 tablespoons peanut oil
2 cloves garlic, chopped
8 oz (250 g) shrimp, peeled and deveined
12 oz (350 g) zucchini or cucumber, seeded and cut into
  matchsticks
Salt to taste
1 egg

Heat the oil and stir-fry the garlic until golden and remove it from the pan. Stir-fry the shrimp, remove them from the pan and then stir-fry the zucchini. Cover the pan and cook for a minute. Remove the lid, add salt to taste, break the egg into the center and break the yolk with the edge of the spatula. Return everything to the pan and stir-fry until all the ingredients are mixed and the egg is lightly scrambled.

STIR-FRIED GREEN BEANS

Almost any vegetable may be cooked this way—bean sprouts, Chinese cabbage, spinach, snowpeas or zucchini, to name only a few—and you can use peeled and deveined shrimp instead of pork.

2 tablespoons oil
2 cloves garlic, chopped
15 oz (50 g) pork, finely sliced
10½ oz (300 g) green beans, cut into 1-in (2½-cm)
   lengths
Salt to taste

Heat the oil in a wok or frying pan. Fry the garlic until it is light brown, then add the pork, stirring until it changes color. Add the beans and salt and stir until the beans are tender-crisp.

MALAYSIAN CABBAGE

This recipe is a good example of a local adaptation of a mainland Chinese recipe.

1 tablespoon oil
4 shallots, finely sliced
1 or more hot chilies, to taste, seeded then finely sliced
A few shrimp, peeled and deveined (optional)
3½ oz (100 g) ground pork
12 oz (350 g) cabbage, finely shredded
Salt to taste
Light soy sauce to taste

Heat the oil in a wok. Fry the shallots and chili until they are soft. Add the shrimp and pork and stir-fry until they change color. Add the cabbage, season with salt and stir-fry until it is wilted but still slightly crisp. Add soy sauce to taste.

STIR-FRIED TOMATOES WITH BLACK BEANS

This dish is also good using sliced silverbeet instead of tomatoes. It goes well with Ginger Beef (p. 226).

1 tablespoon Chinese black beans
1 tablespoon oil
1 lb (500 g) tomatoes, coarsely chopped
Sliced green onions for garnish

Wash the black beans, drain and mash them slightly. Heat the oil in a wok, add the beans and fry for 1 minute. Add the tomatoes and stir-fry until cooked but not too soft. Serve garnished with sliced green onions.

CHAP-CHYE

(Makes 3 as a single dish)

1 oz (25 g) dried lily buds
1 oz (25 g) dried tofu skin, soaked in warm water for 15 minutes or 1 oz (25 g) dried tofu twists, soaked overnight
½ cup (125 ml) water
½ teaspoon cornstarch
1 teaspoon Chinese wine or sherry
Salt and pepper to taste
4 tablespoons oil
6 very thin slices fresh ginger root, peeled and chopped
2 tablespoons brown or yellow soy bean paste or 1 tablespoon soy sauce
8 oz (250 g) pork or beef, sliced or peeled shrimp
8 oz (250 g) cabbage, roughly cut
1 oz (25 g) dried Chinese mushrooms, soaked, stems discarded and caps sliced
½ oz (15 g) cloud-ear mushrooms
3½ oz (100 g) bamboo shoots, sliced
1¾ oz (50 g) Chinese vermicelli, soaked then cut into 1½-in (4-cm) lengths
3 green onions, sliced
1 teaspoon sesame oil

If you have the patience, tie a knot in the middle of each lily bud. This will stop the vegetable from breaking up as it cooks, and retain its texture. Cut the soaked tofu skin into 1 x 1½-in (3 x 4-cm) pieces. Combine the water, cornstarch, wine or sherry, and salt and pepper and set aside.

Heat the oil in a wok or a large frying pan. Add the ginger and fry until light brown, then the bean paste and stir-fry a little. If you have used meat or twisted tofu add it now and stir-fry until the meat changes color. Add the cabbage and mushrooms and stir-fry. Add the lily buds and bamboo shoots and stir until everything is lightly cooked (the cabbage should be tender-crisp). Add the tofu skin and the vermicelli last as these both tend to stick to the pan. Add the seasoning mixture and stir until everything is done, adding more water if you need to.

Sprinkle the green onions on top. Remove from the heat, stir in the sesame oil, and serve.

A vegetarian version of Chap-chye can be made more substantial by serving it with a "coin-purse" egg on top of each portion or some cubes of the spiced tofu. To make "coin-purse" eggs, break a whole egg into hot oil in a frying pan and fry until fluffy and cooked to the degree desired.

Pan-fries

STUFFED BITTER CHINESE CABBAGE

Bitter Chinese cabbage (*kai choy*) is also known as mustard green. It is not to be confused with sweet Chinese cabbage (*pak choy*), which is too soft for this dish. Large stalks of celery could perhaps be used as a substitute.

500 g (1 lb) bitter Chinese cabbage
A little cornstarch
Oil for frying

Shrimp Paste
8 oz (250 g) shrimp, peeled, deveined and chopped
½ oz (15 g) pork or chicken fat, chopped
¼ teaspoon sugar
¼ teaspoon salt
⅛ teaspoon pepper
½ oz (15 g) bamboo shoots, chopped and squeezed dry

Sauce
1½ cups (375 ml) chicken stock
½ teaspoon sesame oil
½ teaspoon sugar
Pinch each of salt and pepper
1 tablespoon cornstarch mixed with 1 tablespoon water
8 oz (250 g) crab meat
2 tablespoons beaten egg

Cut the leaves from the cabbage and set them aside, leaving only those parts of the stalks that are suitable for stuffing. Cook them, uncovered, in boiling water for 5 minutes or until just soft. Drain, and leave them to soak in cold water. When cool, drain again, and cut into 3-in (7½-cm) lengths.

To make the Shrimp Paste, grind the shrimp with the pork fat, sugar, salt and pepper to a very fine paste, then stir in the bamboo shoots.

Sprinkle the cabbage stalks with a little cornstarch to make them dry, and stuff each with Shrimp Paste. Heat a little oil in a pan and fry the stuffed cabbage with the shrimp paste side down until it is cooked, then lift it out and drain off the excess oil carefully. Keep warm.

Bring the stock to a boil in a pan and simmer until it reduces by half. In another pan, blend the sesame oil, sugar, salt, pepper and the cornstarch slurry. Slowly add the stock to the sauce ingredients, stirring constantly, until the sauce comes to a boil and thickens. Add the crab and when it returns to a boil, remove from the heat and stir in the beaten egg. Return the saucepan to the stove, stirring again without letting it come to a boil. Pour the sauce over the stuffed cabbage and serve.

STUFFED SQUASH RINGS

For a healthier version of this recipe, cut the squash in two lengthwise, stuff it and steam it over boiling water in a covered pan.

2 medium-sized summer squash or large zucchini
8 oz (250 g) pork or peeled shrimp or a mixture of both,
    finely chopped or ground to a paste
1 teaspoon light soy sauce
2 cloves garlic, chopped
2 teaspoons cornstarch
2–3 tablespoons oil
Sliced green onions or fresh coriander leaves for
    garnishing

Peel the squash or zucchini and cut into ¾-in (1½-cm) slices and scoop out the seeds. Cook the rings in a little boiling water for a few minutes only until they are just starting to get soft. Drain and set aside.

Mix the meat, soy sauce, garlic and cornstarch together. Stuff the squash rings with this mixture and smooth it flat across the top. Heat the oil in a pan and fry the stuffed squash, meat side down, until the meat is cooked. Turn once, taking care not to dislodge any stuffing. Serve immediately, sprinkling sliced green onion or coriander leaves over the top.

If you like, you can make a sauce to accompany the stuffed squash. Fry a little crushed garlic in the oil left in the pan, lower the heat and add a splash of soy sauce and a pinch of sugar and mix well. Combine 1 teaspoon of cornstarch mixed with 1 tablespoon of water and about ¼–½ cup (75–125 ml) of chicken stock. Add this mixture to the pan, taste and adjust the flavors and cook until the sauce thickens. Pour over the stuffed squash before serving.

EGG FOO YONG

2 tablespoons oil
2 slices fresh ginger root, peeled and chopped, plus a
    little extra
3 green onions, finely sliced
4 oz (125 g) button mushrooms
8 oz (250 g) ground chicken, beef, smoked ham, shrimp
    or lobster (or a combination of two)
½ cup (125 g) cooked green peas
Pinch each of salt and pepper
1–2 tablespoons light soy sauce
6 eggs, lightly beaten

Heat the oil in a wok or pan. Fry the ginger until it is brown. Add the other ingredients except the eggs and stir-fry until cooked. Add the beaten eggs, let sit until they are half-set, then stir gently and cook like an omelette so that the eggs are set and brown on the bottom. Garnish with finely sliced green onions.

PORK AND BAMBOO ROLLS

Pinch each of salt and pepper
1 tablespoon soy sauce
1 teaspoon sugar
2 teaspoons dry sherry
1 teaspoon ginger juice
1 teaspoon cornstarch
1 lb (500 g) pork or beef, sliced thin across the grain
2 oz (60 g) bacon, cut into strips of similar size to the
    meat
4 oz (125 g) pork liver, lightly steamed or poached and
    thinly sliced
4 oz (125 g) shredded bamboo shoots

Mix together the salt and pepper, soy sauce, sugar, sherry, ginger juice, and cornstarch. Add the pork or beef and set aside to marinate for 30 minutes.

Spread each meat slice flat, place strips of bacon, liver and bamboo shoots over them, roll up and skewer with a toothpick. Heat a little oil in a pan and fry the rolls until they are brown and the meat is cooked. Serve with chili sauce.

Deep-fries

SWEET AND SOUR WHOLE FISH

1 medium-sized fish for steaming or frying (dart, snapper, bream, blackfish)
1 tablespoon flour
Oil for deep-frying
1 lime or lemon
1 cup (250 ml) water
1 tablespoon white vinegar
4 tablespoons sugar, or to taste
2 teaspoons light soy sauce
1 tablespoon cornstarch, more if you want a thicker sauce
Pinch each of salt and pepper
2 slices fresh ginger root, peeled and grated
2 cloves garlic, chopped
2 green onions, cut diagonally into 1-in (2½-cm) lengths
1 medium-sized tomato, cut into wedges
½ cucumber, unpeeled but halved, seeded and cut into fine strips
1 red chili, seeded and cut into fine strips
1 lemon, sliced
Fresh coriander leaves for garnishing

Clean, scale and dry the fish. Make 2–3 slashes through to the bone across each side and dust with flour. Deep-fry the fish in hot oil in a wok until brown and crisp. Take out, drain and keep warm on a serving plate.

Cut 3 thin slices off the lime and squeeze the rest. Mix the juice with the water, vinegar, sugar, soy sauce, cornstarch, salt and pepper.

Drain all but 1 or 2 tablespoons of oil from the wok and fry the ginger and garlic until they are light brown. Add the green onions and toss them in the oil until coated. Add the tomato, the cucumber and the sauce and bring to a boil, stirring as it thickens. Pour the sauce over the fish immediately, garnish with chili strips, lemon slices and fresh coriander leaves and serve.

FRIED FISH WITH SOY BEAN PASTE

The technique in this recipe is also a popular way of cooking mussels in their shells. Add the sliced chili and the mussels to the pan and stir-fry until they open, then add sugar and soy sauce to taste, stir and serve.

1 lb (500 g) fish (bream, snapper, dart, morwong), for frying
1 tablespoon flour
Oil for deep-frying
2 cloves garlic, sliced
3 slices fresh ginger root, peeled and cut into strips
1¾ oz (50 g) yellow soy beans, mashed
2 tablespoons water
Sugar to taste
Light soy sauce to taste (optional—the dish may be salty enough)
1–2 fresh red chilies, sliced diagonally

Clean, scale and dry the fish. Make 2–3 slashes through to the bone on each side, and dust with flour.

Heat plenty of oil in a wok and fry the fish until it is cooked and crisp on the outside. Drain and set aside, keeping the fish warm. Drain all but 2 tablespoons of oil from the wok and fry the garlic and ginger until they are light brown. Add the mashed soy beans and stir-fry until brown and cooked. Add 2 tablespoons of water and the sugar and soy sauce to taste, stirring together to produce a sauce. Pour this over the fish and serve garnished with sliced fresh red chili.

SHRIMP IN BATTER

1 lb (500 g) large shrimp, peeled and deveined
1¾ oz (50 g) cornstarch
Pinch each of salt and pepper

1 egg, separated
2 tablespoons water
Oil for deep-frying
Sliced cucumber and tomato for garnishing

Rub the shrimp with salt, rinse and dry. Sift the cornstarch, salt and pepper into a bowl. Make a well in the center and add the egg yolk and water. Beat slowly and lightly until smooth, and set aside for 15 minutes. Whisk the egg white until it is stiff and fold it into the flour mixture, making a thick batter.

Heat sufficient oil in a wok or frying pan to deep-fry the shrimp. Dip each shrimp into the batter by the tail and deep-fry until golden brown. To serve, arrange on a plate surrounded by sliced cucumber and tomatoes.

HONEY CHICKEN WINGS

2 teaspoons honey
1 teaspoon boiling water
3 cloves garlic, chopped
1 teaspoon soy sauce
Pinch each of salt and pepper
1½ lb (750 g) chicken wings and drumsticks
Oil for deep-frying

Mix the honey with the boiling water. Mix the honey and water, garlic, soy sauce and salt and pepper together. Rub the chicken with this mixture and refrigerate to marinate for at least an hour. Heat the oil and deep-fry the chicken pieces until they are golden brown. Drain and serve.

CHICKEN ROLLS

1 lb (500 g) cooked chicken, thinly sliced
2 teaspoons sesame oil
4½ oz (125 g) pig's caul
½ oz (15 g) ham, cut into fine strips
1 tablespoon finely shredded fresh ginger root
3 green onions, sliced
2 tablespoons beaten egg
3 tablespoons cornstarch
Oil for deep-frying

Seasoning

½ teaspoon salt

½ teaspoon sugar

Pinch of pepper

2 teaspoons oyster sauce

½ teaspoon sherry

2 teaspoons cornstarch

2 teaspoons light soy sauce

Combine the Seasoning ingredients in a bowl, add the chicken and mix well. Add the sesame oil and mix again. Set aside for at least 15 minutes.

Clean the pig's caul and wipe it dry. Cut into circular pieces about 6 in (15 cm) in diameter (you should get about 10 pieces). Spread each piece of caul flat and stuff each piece with some chicken, ham, ginger and green onion. Fold in the sides and roll up like a sausage. Seal with beaten egg and roll lightly in cornstarch.

Heat the oil in a wok or frying pan until very hot and remove from the heat. Deep-fry the rolls for 1 minute then return the pan to the heat and fry for 3 minutes. Drain and serve with bowls of soy sauce or chili sauce.

FRIED CHICKEN IN PAPER

1 small chicken (3 lb/1½ kg)

Oil for deep-frying

Seasoning

½ teaspoon salt

1 teaspoon sugar

1 teaspoon sesame oil

1 tablespoon light soy sauce

1 tablespoon ginger juice

1 tablespoon sherry

2 tablespoons oyster sauce

2 tablespoons oil

1 tablespoon cornstarch

Pinch of white pepper

Cut the chicken into curry pieces (p. 23). Mix all the Seasoning ingredients together and marinate the chicken in this mixture for at least 2 hours. When fully marinated, wrap each piece of chicken in a square of parchment paper, folding it like an envelope. Fold over and tuck in the corner last to prevent the package from falling apart. Deep-fry in plenty of hot oil until the paper is light brown. Lift out, remove the paper, arrange the chicken pieces on a plate and serve.

SLICED CHICKEN IN PAPER

1 lb (500 g) boneless chicken breast, thinly sliced across the grain
2 tablespoons oyster sauce
2 teaspoons sesame oil
Pinch of pepper
2 teaspoons medium sweet sherry
½-in (1½-cm) piece fresh ginger root, peeled, thinly sliced and then cut into shreds
1 small package frozen peas
8 dried Chinese mushroons, soaked, stems discarded and caps sliced
Oil for deep-frying

Season the chicken with the oyster sauce, sesame oil, pepper and sherry, then mix it with the ginger. Cut parchment paper into 6-in (15-cm) squares, put a teaspoon of peas, a slice of chicken and 2 or 3 slices of mushroom on to each square, and wrap it up as described in the recipe for Fried Chicken in Paper (above). Deep-fry the packets in hot oil for 10–15 minutes, turning occasionally. Serve the chicken in its paper packets.

SWEET AND SOUR PORK

1½ lb (750 g) pork (top loin is best, but belly will do if it is skinned), cubed
2 tablespoons light soy sauce
Pinch each of salt and pepper
Oil for deep-frying
Sprigs of fresh coriander and fresh red chilies, sliced diagonally

Batter
10 heaping tablespoons flour
1 cup (250 ml) water
Dash of dark soy sauce
Pinch each of salt and pepper

Sweet and Sour Sauce

3 tablespoons white vinegar

1 tablespoon light soy sauce

2 cups (500 ml) water

½ cup (125 g) sugar, or to taste

1 tablespoon cornstarch

Pinch each of salt and pepper

1 small carrot, sliced thin, ½ green bell pepper, chopped
and ½ cup (125 g) pineapple chunks (optional) or 1
small can Chinese pickled vegetables

Season the pork with the light soy sauce, salt and pepper and set aside. Mix all the ingredients for the Batter together in a bowl. Mix all the Sweet and Sour Sauce ingredients together in another bowl and set aside.

Heat plenty of oil until very hot in a wok. Coat the seasoned pieces of meat with the batter and drop them one by one into the oil. Reduce the heat to medium and fry the pork pieces until they are dark brown. This will take about 20 minutes.

Heat the Sweet and Sour Sauce in a pan, stirring well until it boils. Add the fresh vegetables or pickled vegetables and the pineapple. Add the drained pieces of fried pork to the sauce, mix well and serve, garnishing with coriander and chilies.

Grills, Barbecues and Roasts

GRILLED KING SHRIMP

3 tablespoons light soy sauce

1½ teaspoons ginger juice

1½ tablespoons sherry

1 tablespoon sugar

18 large shrimp, deveined

Oil

Sliced green onion

Soak 6 wooden satay sticks in water to prevent them from burning and set aside. Mix the soy sauce, ginger juice, sherry and sugar in a large bowl and marinate the shrimp in this mixture for 1 hour.

Thread 3 shrimp on to each satay stick, brush well with oil and grill or cook under the broiler, brushing with more oil if they look dry as they cook. Serve garnished with sliced green onion.

ROAST CRISPY CHICKEN

1 fresh chicken
2 teaspoons five-spice powder
1 teaspoon salt
2 teaspoons chopped red chili
2 points star anise
1 cinnamon stick
4 cups (1 liter) water
3 green onions, sliced
1 stalk coriander leaves
1 tablespoon honey
2 slices lime
1 cup (250 ml) hot water
Oil for deep-frying (optional)

Wash the chicken inside and out and dry it. Mix the five-spice powder with the salt and rub it all over the chicken including the cavity and then set aside.

Simmer the chili, star anise and cinnamon stick in 4 cups (1 liter) of water for 5 minutes. Remove the spices and stuff them inside the chicken with the green onions and coriander, closing it up with poultry pins. Tie a string around the neck of the bird if you can. Bring the spiced water to a boil. Holding the chicken over the pan, ladle the boiling spiced water over it several times to tighten up the skin. Set aside to dry.

In the meantime boil the honey, hot water and the lime slices. Ladle or brush this mixture over the chicken several times to thoroughly coat it. Use a hair dryer to thoroughly dry the bird then roast it in a medium-hot oven or deep-fry it whole, starting with very hot oil and then turning it down to medium.

Cut the cooked chicken into serving pieces and serve with individual dishes of spiced salt made from table salt and five-spice powder in the proportion 12:1.

PEKING DUCK

Never use a thawed frozen duck for this princely dish!

1 fat fresh duck (about 4 lb/2 kg), cleaned but with its
    neck still attached if possible
½ teaspoon five-spice powder
2 teaspoons salt
2–3 tablespoons oyster sauce
1 lb (500 g) fresh bean sprouts

Syrup
2 tablespoons honey
½ cup (125 ml) water
2 teaspoons white vinegar
1 teaspoon light dry sherry

Pancake Wrappers (Makes 18)
1¾ cup (400 g) flour
8 oz (250 ml) boiling water
1¼ cups (310 ml) oil

Plum Sauce
3 tablespoons plum jam
1½ tablespoons white vinegar

For the Packets
Green onions, cut into 2-in (5-cm) pieces
1 pickling cucumber, unpeeled, cut into 2-in (5-cm)
    lengths

Soup
Pinch of salt
1 green onion, sliced
Green onion tops, chopped
A few leaves Chinese celery cabbage, cut into thin strips
    or thin slices winter melon or zucchini

Place all the Syrup ingredients together in a pan and bring to a boil. Cook and stir until the honey is dissolved. Set aside.

Wash the duck and dry it with paper towels. Combine the five-spice powder and salt, and rub the inside of the duck well with this mixture. Tie a string around the neck of the bird if you can and hold it over a basin. Otherwise place it in a large strainer or colander. Pour boiling water over the duck at least six times, allowing the bird to dry thoroughly between each washing. Brush it with the Syrup and use a hair dryer or a fan as suggested in the recipe for Roast Crispy Chicken.

Heat an oven to 375–400°F (190–200°C). Place the duck on a rack in a baking dish, breast-side down, and roast for about 20 minutes, then turn it breast up and roast until the breast is crisp and brown and the meat is cooked—about another 20–30 minutes. The meat should remain quite pink since all but the skin and the very top layer will be cooked a second time.

To make the Pancake Wrappers, sift the flour into a bowl, make a well in the center, add the boiling water and mix with a wooden spoon until the dough is just soft enough to handle without being sticky. Knead the dough for about 5 minutes, cover the ball with a damp cloth and set aside for half an hour. Knead again, then form it into a long roll about 1½ in (4 cm) in diameter and cut it into 18 pieces. On a floured surface roll each piece out to a circle about 3 in (8 cm) in diameter. Brush one side lightly with oil and lay another circle on top. Roll out the double wrappers until very thin.

Cook on a dry hot griddle or heavy frying pan over a low heat for half a minute until flecked with brown spots. Turn over and cook the other side. Remove from the pan and pull apart into two wrappers. Fold each one loosely into a triangular shape. Arrange the folded triangles on a serving plate and cover with a dry cloth until needed.

To prepare the Plum Sauce, heat the jam and white vinegar in a small pan. Add water to taste and to achieve a suitable consistency. Provide a small side dish of sauce for each diner.

Peking Duck is classically served as three separate courses. Carve off the entire crisp skin in pieces with only very little meat attached. Serve the skin on a plate with side dishes of the Plum Sauce, Pancake Wrappers, the green onions and strips of cucumber. Each diner puts a pancake wrapper on their plate and places on it a couple of slices of duck skin, a piece of onion and one of cucumber, tops them with the homemade Plum Sauce, and folds everything loosely into an oblong packet.

For the second course, cut the meat off the carcass in strips, season with the oyster sauce and stir-fry it in a little oil with the bean sprouts. Serve this with two or three other dishes and rice.

Finally, to make the Soup, chop up the carcass, cover it with water, add a little salt and bring to a boil. Add one green onion, some chopped green onion tops and green leafy vegetable such as young spinach or Chinese cabbage and serve the resulting soup last in a large bowl.

OVEN BARBECUED PORK

Pork belly or pork loin
Pinch of salt
Oil

Marinade
For each 2 lb (1 kg) of pork use:
½ teaspoon five-spice powder
1 tablespoon dark soy sauce
1 teaspoon sugar
¼ teaspoon coarsely ground pepper
3 cloves garlic, crushed
Salt to taste
1 tablespoon honey

Score the meat lightly then turn it skin-side down and cut between the bones as far as necessary to separate them but without reaching through the fat to the skin.

Combine the Marinade ingredients in a dish. Add the pork and marinate for a few hours or overnight, turning it occasionally.

Remove the meat from the marinade and dry it with a fan or a hair dryer. Rub the skin with salt and brush it lightly with oil. Heat the oven to 400°F (200°C). Place the meat on a rack in a roasting dish, skin side up (or spear it on a rotisserie if you have one). Cook until the skin has a good crackling but the meat is still moist (about 30 minutes), taking care not to burn it—it may be best to turn the oven down after about 20 minutes. Remove the pork from the oven and let it rest before cutting it into strips and serving.

BAKED TOFU

4 oz (125 g) lean ground pork or chopped shrimp
2 cloves garlic, chopped
1 teaspoon soy sauce

1 tablespoon oil
1 lb (500 g) soft tofu, drained and coarsely chopped
2 eggs, lightly beaten
2 green onions, sliced
1 small stick celery, chopped
Salt and pepper to taste

Season the pork with the chopped garlic and soy sauce and set it aside. Heat the oil in a pan, and when it is hot, stir-fry the seasoned pork until it is cooked. Drain and transfer to a mixing bowl. Stir in the tofu, adding eggs, green onions and celery. Mix well, add salt and pepper to taste and place in a medium-hot oven for 45 minutes. The mixture is cooked when it resembles a scrambled egg custard.

Rice, Noodles and One-dish Meals

HAINANESE CHICKEN RICE
(Street Food)

Hainanese Chicken Rice is a favorite hawker lunch in Malaysia and Singapore, and a Chinese dish found in related forms all over Southeast Asia (see Thai Chicken Rice p. 417).

1 fresh chicken, cleaned but with the pads of fat found
    inside the body cavity intact
¼ onion
2 cloves garlic
1-in (2½-cm) piece fresh ginger root, bruised
2 tablespoons sesame oil
2 tablespoons soy sauce
Fresh coriander leaves or sliced green onion or a mixture
    of both for garnish
1 tablespoon oil
4 cups (1 kg) long-grain rice, washed and drained
Salt to taste

Pinch of ground white pepper
Cucumber, zucchini or celery cabbage, sliced (optional)
Sliced tomato and cucumber

Chili-Ginger Sauce
6 fresh red chilies, chopped
2-in (5-cm) piece fresh ginger root, peeled and chopped
3 cloves garlic, chopped
Salt to taste
Dash of white vinegar to taste

Remove the pads of fat from the chicken and set aside. Bring a saucepan of water large enough to cover the chicken to a boil and add the chicken together with the onion, garlic and ginger. Cook the chicken according to the technique in the recipe for Steeped Chicken (p. 217). When it is done, take it out, rinse it under cold water and set aside to drain. Reserve the stock. Chop and reassemble the chicken on a plate. Pour the sesame oil and soy sauce over the top, garnish with coriander and green onions and set aside.

To prepare the Chili-Ginger Sauce, grind the chilies, ginger and garlic to a rough paste. Add salt and vinegar to taste and moisten if necessary with a little of the stock. Place in sauce bowls.

Meanwhile, heat the oil in a saucepan and fry the pads of chicken fat to produce liquid chicken fat. Remove the residue. Add the rice and stir-fry for 2–3 minutes until the rice is transparent and coated in oil. Add 6 cups (1½ liters) of stock and a little salt if you wish. Boil until the stock is absorbed then proceed as usual when cooking rice.

Heat the remaining stock and add salt and pepper to taste. Add sliced cucumber, zucchini or sliced celery cabbage to the stock if you wish, or leave it clear. Pour into a serving bowl and garnish with coriander leaf and chopped green onion.

Serve the rice on a plate surrounded by slices of cucumber and tomato alongside the plate of chicken, bowls of the sauce and the hot soup.

FRIED RICE

Fried rice, rice porridge or noodle dishes are the traditional Chinese breakfast, but are rapidly being displaced by Western toast or cereal. However they also make great lunches.

2 tablespoons oil
2 eggs, beaten with a pinch of salt
1 onion, chopped
8 oz (250 g) shrimp, peeled and cooked
Dash of light soy sauce
4 oz (125 g) Chinese sausages (optional)
4 oz (125 g) Chinese barbecued pork (*cha siew*)
1 large plate cold cooked rice
2 tablespoons light soy sauce
3 green onions, sliced

Heat ½ tablespoon of oil in a pan or a wok and fry the beaten eggs, stirring them into separate pieces as they cook. Remove and set aside. Heat another ½ tablespoon of oil and fry the onion, adding the shrimp and a dash of light soy sauce. Remove and set aside. Fry the sausages, lift them out and cut them up. Fry the barbecued pork, remove and slice.

Add 1 tablespoon of oil to the pan and fry the rice, stirring until each grain is well coated. Add the soy sauce and continue to stir until it is absorbed. Add the barbecued pork, the shrimp, sausages, eggs and the green onions, continuing to stir and toss everything together.

These quantities are intended for fried rice served on its own. To serve it as a side dish, don't use as much meat as is suggested here. Use either Chinese barbecued pork or Chinese sausages, but not both.

RICE PORRIDGE

Rice porridge was brought by the Chinese to every country in Southeast Asia.

Two variations exist—one in which the rice grains remain separate, which is the Teochew version, and one which is cooked long enough for the grains to be no longer visible (the version favored by the Cantonese and Hainanese).

For 1 lb (500 g) of short-grain rice use about 3 quarts (3½ liters) of water. You will probably need to increase the amount of water to a little more than 5¼ quarts (5 liters) as the rice cooks in order to achieve the desired consistency (up to 12 times the ratio of water to rice is sometimes used). Simmer over very low heat for at least 1½ hours, stirring frequently.

Another approach is to start cooking the rice in the usual way with a normal amount of water, then as water evaporates stir the rice and slowly add more boiling water until you end up with a porridge of the consistency you want. This will also take a long time, and if you proceed this way you will have to keep an eye on the contents of the saucepan so that the porridge does not get too thick.

Plain rice porridge has an extremely comforting blandness and sweet taste. Try adding fish, sliced thin and marinated in soy sauce and ginger then stir-fried, to a bowl of rice porridge, with a garnish of sliced green onion or fresh coriander leaves. Break an egg into a piping hot bowl of rice porridge and let it set, stir in light soy sauce to taste and garnish with fresh coriander leaves or fried garlic and Chinese celery. Serve with bowls of soaked and chopped dried shrimp, slices of Chinese sausage, some fried or roasted peanuts (small ones with red skins preferably), and slices of Chinese pickled radish.

No matter what else you serve with rice porridge, always include a small side dish of fermented soy beans and Chinese pickled vegetables for each person.

The choice of side dishes is endless and each country seems to have its favorites. Thai and Vietnamese versions of rice porridge are given on p. 416 and p. 538, respectively.

FRIED KWAY TEOW
(Street Food)

Kway teow are rice noodles about ½-in (1-cm) wide and cut from a rolled-up slab of fresh rice-noodle sheets. Slabs of this kind are usually available in the refrigerators of Southeast Asian food stores.

1 lb (500 g) cockles or baby clams
1 lb (500 g) wide rice flat noodles (*kway teow*, p. 50)
3–4 red chilies, sliced, or to taste
3 cloves garlic, sliced
2–3 tablespoons oil
4 oz (125 g) skirt steak, sliced thin or shredded pork
  (optional)
7 oz (200 g) shrimp, peeled and deveined
Pinch of sugar (optional)
1–2 tablespoons light soy sauce
7 oz (200 g) bean sprouts, washed and trimmed

½ bunch of Chinese leeks or garlic chives, cut into bite-sized
   pieces
1 tablespoon dark soy sauce, or Javanese soy sauce
Salt and pepper to taste

Pour boiling water over the cockles until they open, then drain them immediately. Remove the meat from the shells and set it aside. Unravel the noodles. Grind the chilies and garlic to a rough paste. Heat the oil in a wok and fry the paste until it is fragrant. Add the meat and stir-fry until it is cooked, then add the shrimp and stir-fry until they change color. Add a pinch of sugar and the light soy sauce and mix well. Add the noodles and stir-fry until mixed and coated with oil. Add the bean sprouts, Chinese leeks and the dark soy sauce and toss well, until the noodles are heated and everything is cooked and mixed. If you wish, add more dark soy sauce and/or a splash of water. Add the cockles last and stir-fry for about half a minute. Serve immediately.

FRIED HOKKIEN NOODLES

Long strands of noodles are a symbol of longevity to the Chinese and are often eaten on birthdays. These yellow Hokkien wheat noodles are favorites for frying.

14 oz (400 g) pork or chicken, finely sliced
2 cloves garlic, chopped
1 teaspoon sherry
1 tablespoon soy sauce
1 teaspoon cornstarch
15 oz (450 g) package fresh Hokkien noodles
7 tablespoons oil
2 eggs, lightly beaten
3 slices fresh ginger root, peeled and chopped
8 oz (250 g) shrimp, peeled and deveined
6 dried Chinese mushrooms, soaked, stems discarded,
   caps sliced
3 stalks celery, sliced diagonally, or 2 small cucumbers,
   peeled, seeded, cut in two lengthwise and sliced or
   some green beans, sliced diagonally
8 oz (250 g) bean sprouts, washed and trimmed

5 oz (150 g) shredded bamboo shoots, drained
   (optional)
Salt to taste
Sliced green onions or fresh coriander leaves, chopped

Mix the meat with the garlic, sherry, soy sauce and cornstarch and set it aside.

Rinse the noodles in boiling water to untangle and soften them. Drain and set them aside.

Heat 1 tablespoon of oil in a pan and make a thin omelette with the 2 lightly beaten eggs. Roll up, slice into fine strips and set aside.

Heat 2 tablespoons of oil in a wok and stir-fry the seasoned meat then set aside.

In a clean wok, heat 1 tablespoon of oil and fry the ginger until it is light brown. Add the shrimp and stir-fry, then the sliced mushrooms, celery, bean sprouts and bamboo shoots. Stir-fry until cooked then set aside.

Heat 3 more tablespoons of oil in the wok. Add the noodles and stir until they are heated through. Add the meat, shrimp, vegetables and salt to taste and toss to mix thoroughly until everything is hot. Add a splash of stock or water if you wish. Serve on a large plate, garnished with sliced green onions or coriander leaves and the sliced omelette.

NYONYA

Nyonya cuisine developed in the families known as Baba Chinese, Straits Chinese or Peranakan. These were the descendants of early Chinese settlers in Malacca who, faced with restrictions on the immigration of Chinese women, had married Malays. Most of these families prospered with economic development in the Straits settlements in the 18th and 19th centuries.

Baba families stood apart from the Chinese immigrants who came to Malaya later as laborers—they were wealthy and established, they held British citizenship, and they possessed a distinct Malay-influenced domestic culture and cuisine. Caught up in business and increasingly wealthy as time went on, the households lived well and entertained lavishly. No matter how wealthy the family, however, daughters were thoroughly trained in the kitchen as part of their education as future Peranakan wives. In this way the distinctive cuisine was preserved and developed.

Confined as it was to the domestic sphere of a small and elite social group, Nyonya food was not widely known and appreciated until after independence. It is the many social changes that have occurred in Malaysia and Singapore in recent times—a more widespread affluence, freer and more open lifestyles and new roles for women—that have made it so. Nyonya restaurants now exist where there were none before and Straits Chinese women—though still too few of them—teach and write books about their culinary heritage.

Ironically the same dynamic also poses quite serious threats to the cuisine's future. In her book *Goodbye Culinary Cringe*, Cherry Ripe notes how modernization and affluence are favoring the adoption of Western food habits among the new generations in the Nyonya community as in others. Social traditions have changed too. No longer do the Peranakan form a distinct community that trains its daughters as custodians of a unique domestic culture. Nyonya cuisine now depends on deliberate commercial, personal and professional promotion to preserve it, and time alone will tell whether this will prove sufficient.

A slight difference of emphasis exists between the Nyonya cooking of the south and that of Penang in the north. Southern Nyonya food is more influenced by the southern Malays, using creamy coconut milk gravies, and by the Javanese of Johore and Malacca. Northern Nyonya food reflects the sour tastes of Thailand and favors thinner gravies and sauces. The difference is clearly visible in the southern and the Penang versions of the unique noodle dish *laksa*. In both areas, however, the range of tastes represented in a single meal will be similarly wide. On the table with rice, sour and hot dishes such as Hot Sour Fish (p. 181), stews (*gulai*) or vegetables cooked with coconut milk Malay-style, something deep-fried, stir-fried or braised Chinese-style, a Malay salad, some specialty Nyonya sambal and a pickle will appear. The combined heritage of two such vital culinary traditions as Malay and Chinese makes for an especially rich, different and interesting cuisine, only a small sample of which I am able to give here.

Wet Dishes

The dishes that fall into this category have been taken over from either Malay or Chinese cuisine and are to be found in those sections of this chapter. They include Chinese soups and Malay hot and sour fish dishes such as Hot Sour Fish (p. 181) or vegetables cooked in coconut milk (*Masak Lemak*). The recipe for Cabbage in Coconut Milk (p. 183) is also nice cooked with water spinach or eggplant instead of cabbage, or any combination of beans, carrots, cabbage, zucchini, squash or pumpkin.

Steamed Dishes

OTAK-OTAK SPICED FISH

This dish is related to both the Indonesian dishes cooked in banana leaf packets and the Thai steamed fish curry mousse and its predecessors. Like them it is sometimes steamed and sometimes grilled. After cooking, the packets or covered dish may be opened and their contents eaten hot, or they may be stored for a day or two in the refrigerator and sent out on summer picnics. For a simpler approach, steam the Spiced Fish in a large covered dish or individual ramekins, or bake it in a pan of water in the oven and serve it with salad or rice. When cooled, it makes an excellent sandwich or canapé spread.

1 lb (500 g) fish (mackerel, salmon, ling, barramundi)

1 cup (250 ml) thick coconut milk

2 small eggs

Salt to taste

Pinch of sugar, or to taste

4 kaffir lime leaves, spines removed and leaves finely sliced

Banana leaves, heavy aluminum foil, ramekins or an oven-safe dish

20 betel leaves or young spinach leaves

Freshly ground white pepper to taste

Spice Paste

5 fresh chilies, sliced, or dried chilies, seeded, soaked in warm water until soft and squeezed dry

1 stalk lemongrass, finely sliced

2 slices galangal, peeled and coarsely chopped

1-in (2½-cm) piece turmeric root, peeled and coarsely chopped or 1 teaspoon ground turmeric

5 roasted candlenuts or raw almonds or macadamia nuts

½ teaspoon shrimp paste

2 cloves garlic

5 shallots, sliced

Clean and skin the fish and flake the flesh. Grind the Spice Paste ingredients to a paste.

Combine the fish, Spice Paste, coconut milk, egg, salt, sugar and lime leaves in a bowl and mix together gently by hand until they are thoroughly mixed (see the technique used for Steamed Shrimp or Fish Curry Mousse, p. 366).

Cut the banana leaves into pieces (about 7 x 8 in/18 x 20 cm). Hold them over a gas flame or heated electric element until softened. Place three betel leaves overlapping in the center of the banana leaf, spooning 2–3 tablespoons of the fish mixture on top (when the packet is folded, there should be room left for expansion). Pleat in the sides. Fold one side of the pleat to the front and one side to the back. Repeat on the other side to firmly encase the contents. Secure the top with a toothpick. Alternatively, grease an oven dish or individual ramekins lightly, line the bottom with betel leaves and fill with the fish mixture. Place on a rack in a steamer for about 20 minutes or until cooked and set. For grilling make closed banana-leaf packets as described on p. 114. Place betel leaves in the center before the fish mixture is spooned on, fold up and secure, then grill over low heat. Serve each helping in its banana-leaf wrapper or container.

Curries and Braised Dishes

GULAI AYAM NYONYA CHICKEN CURRY

This dish illustrates the fastidious elaboration of spices often employed in Nyonya cooking. Like all curries, it is good if prepared a few hours ahead and left to sit before serving.

1 chicken or 2–3 lb (1–1½ kg) chicken pieces
5 tablespoons oil
2 cups (500 ml) thin coconut milk
Salt to taste
Sugar to taste
1 cup (250 ml) thick coconut milk

Spice Paste
2 tablespoons coriander seed or 1½ tablespoons ground
   coriander
1 teaspoon cumin
1 teaspoon fennel seed or 1 teaspoon anise
1-in (2½-cm) piece of cinnamon stick
2 cloves or ¼ teaspoon ground cloves
10 dried chilies, seeded and soaked in warm water until
   soft and squeezed dry
1 teaspoon peppercorns or ½ teaspoon freshly ground
   pepper
½ teaspoon shrimp paste
1 stalk lemongrass, finely sliced
1-in (2½-cm) piece galangal, peeled and coarsely
   chopped
1-in (2½-cm) piece turmeric root, peeled and coarsel
   chopped or ½ teaspoon ground turmeric

4 candlenuts, coarsely chopped
3 cloves garlic
10 shallots, sliced

Chop the chicken into curry pieces (p. 23). If using whole spices for the Spice Paste, grind them to a powder in an electric grinder. Add the remaining Spice Paste ingredients and grind to a paste. Heat the oil in a claypot or a saucepan and when it is hot add the Spice Paste and fry until fragrant. Add the chicken pieces and stir until they are coated with the curry mixture. Add the thin coconut milk, salt and sugar, mix well and simmer gently until the chicken is tender. Add the thick coconut milk. Remove the pan from the heat and let it stand for a while before serving.

CURRY KAPITAN

Broadly influenced in its spicing, Curry Kapitan conjures up some of the cosmopolitan atmosphere of old Malacca and recalls the traditional role of the Kapitan in China as the functionary who stood between Malay rulers and Chinese communities. The Kapitan was a man of standing among both Malays and his own Chinese people and had considerable social mobility. Curry Kapitan reflects this in culinary terms.

3 lb (1½ kg) chicken, or about 1½ lb (600 g) thigh fillets cut the Thai way (p. 24)
½ fresh coconut, grated or 1 cup (250 g) steamed dried coconut
5 tablespoons oil
3 cups (750 ml) coconut milk
½ cup (125 ml) tamarind water (p. 55)
1-in (2½-cm) piece of cinnamon stick
Salt to taste

Spice Paste
1 teaspoon nutmeg
2 tablespoons coriander seed or 1½ tablespoons ground coriander
2 teaspoons cumin seed or 1½ teaspoons ground cumin

¼ teaspoon fenugreek seed

2 cardamom pods or ⅛ teaspoon ground cardamom

1 whole star anise or ½ teaspoon anise

10 dried chilies, seeded and soaked in warm water until soft and squeezed dry

1-in (2½-cm) piece turmeric root, peeled and coarsely chopped, or ½ teaspoon ground turmeric

1-in (2½-cm) piece fresh ginger root, peeled and coarsely chopped

½ teaspoon shrimp paste

4 cloves garlic

10 shallots, sliced

Cut the chicken into frying pieces (p. 23). To prepare the Spice Paste, grind all the dry spices to a powder. Mash the wet spices to a paste, adding the dry ingredients last. Heat a heavy frying pan and dry roast the grated coconut until it is brown. Grind the roasted coconut until it is the color and consistency of brown sugar.

Heat the oil in a saucepan or a claypot. Add a little water to the Spice Paste to prevent it from burning and fry until it is fragrant. Add the chicken pieces and mix to coat them with the spices. Add the coconut milk, tamarind water and cinnamon stick and simmer, uncovered, until the chicken is tender. Add the ground coconut and salt to taste and then cook until the gravy is thick. Serve in a large bowl, garnished with fried onion flakes and chili slices.

AYAM TEMPERAH CHICKEN IN HOT SAUCE

This style of braising works well with chicken or pork.

5 tablespoons oil

2 large onions, chopped

3 red chilies, sliced

3 cloves garlic, chopped

1-in (2½-cm) piece fresh ginger root, sliced

2 lb (1 kg) chicken, cut into curry pieces (p. 23)

3 tablespoons dark soy sauce

1–2 teaspoons sugar, or to taste

2 tablespoons coconut vinegar, or to taste
1 cup (250 ml) water
Salt to taste

Heat the oil in a wok or a pan, add the chopped onions, chilies, garlic and ginger and fry until they are soft. Add the chicken pieces and brown them. Combine the rest of the ingredients, add them to the pan and bring to a boil, simmering until the chicken is tender. Keep the pan covered until the meat is half-cooked. Remove the lid to reduce the sauce as the chicken finishes cooking. Adjust the seasonings and serve.

Fried Dishes
Stir-fry

KANGKUNG GORENG BELACAN ### FRIED WATER SPINACH WITH SHRIMP PASTE

2–3 tablespoons oil
10–16 oz (300–500 g) water spinach, washed, tough
  ends discarded, leaves cut into 2-in (5-cm) lengths

Spice Paste
3–4 red chilies, sliced
2 teaspoons shrimp paste (*belacan*)
6 shallots, sliced
3 cloves garlic

Grind the Spice Paste ingredients to a paste. Heat the oil in a wok and fry the Spice Paste until fragrant. Add the water spinach and stir-fry until it is coated with oil and spices and tender-crisp. Serve with rice.

This dish may also be cooked using 1 oz (25 g) of dried shrimp instead of or as well as the shrimp paste. Wash the dried shrimp and soak them in warm water for a while. Grind them coarsely and fry with the Spice Paste until everything is fragrant before adding the vegetable.

Chili-fry

Essentially Javanese–Malay dishes, Nyonya fried sambal are tamarind-sour.

SAMBAL SOTONG ## CUTTLEFISH FRIED SAMBAL

This recipe also works well using peeled and deveined shrimp instead of cuttlefish. For a variation try adding 2 small peeled and chopped tomatoes to the pan once the spice paste is fragrant. Cook them to a thick purée before adding the tamarind water and the shrimp, then stir-fry until the shrimp are opaque.

4 tablespoons oil
1 small stalk lemongrass, finely sliced (optional)
1 lb (500 g) small cuttlefish or squid, cleaned and
    skinned, ink sac, quill or cuttlebone, eyes and beak
    removed, body and tentacles cut into two or four
¼ cup (65 ml) tamarind water or more to taste
1 tablespoon brown sugar, or to taste
Salt to taste

Spice Paste
6–10 dried chilies, seeded, soaked in warm water until
    soft and squeezed dry
½ teaspoon shrimp paste
4 candlenuts or raw almonds or macadamia nuts,
    smashed
10 shallots, sliced

Grind the Spice Paste ingredients to a paste. Heat the oil in a wok or a frying pan and fry the lemongrass and the Spice Paste until it is fragrant. Add the cuttlefish and stir-fry until it is coated with the spices. Reduce the heat, add the tamarind water, sugar and salt to taste and stir-fry until the gravy is thick and oily and the cuttlefish is cooked.

Serve with rice, a mildy-spiced dish and a crisp salad.

Deep-fries

UDANG GORENG ASAM ## FRIED TAMARIND SHRIMP

The marinade in this recipe is a favorite for seafood in both Nyonya and Malay cooking. Fish or squid sliced into thick rings also works well in this dish.

1 cup (250 ml) tamarind water
½ teaspoon sugar, or more to taste (optional)
Pinch each of salt and pepper
1 lb (500 g) large shrimp, deveined
½ cup (125 ml) oil
Cucumber and tomato slices
Coriander sprigs

Combine the tamarind water, sugar, salt and pepper in a bowl. Add the shrimp, mix well, and set aside for 30 minutes.

Heat the oil in a wok until hot. Drain the shrimp, add them to the pan, and fry them over medium heat until they are cooked (about 5 minutes). Drain and serve garnished with sliced cucumber and tomato and a sprig of coriander.

Malaysians enjoy eating both the body and the tail of the shrimp. They chew the shrimp shells and all to extract the greatest amount of flavor, spitting out pieces of shell as they go. If you plan to do this just make sure you remove the stomach pouch before cooking. Cut into the shell behind the mouth and pop out the black sac.

SAMBAL IKAN ## FISH SAMBAL

In Nyonya cooking seafood is often combined with rich and thick Malay-style fried sambal. This recipe uses a fried sambal sauce to punch up the flavor of Chinese fried fish. Serve with white rice or Nyonya Coconut Rice (p. 265).

1¼ lb (600 g) fish, cleaned and scaled
Oil for deep-frying fish the Asian way (p. 26)
⅓ cup (75 ml) tamarind water

1 teaspoon sugar, or more to taste

Salt to taste

½ cup (125 ml) water

3 lime leaves, shredded

Spice Paste

5 dried chilies, seeded, soaked in hot water until soft and
   squeezed dry

5 fresh medium-length red chilies, sliced

1 stalk lemongrass, sliced finely

1 teaspoon shrimp paste (*belacan*)

3 cloves garlic

10 shallots, sliced

Dry the fish and make 3 slashes across each side. Grind the Spice Paste ingredients to a fine paste.

Heat the oil in a wok and fry the fish until it is brown, turning to cook the other side. Lift out, drain and keep warm. Drain the wok of all but 3 tablespoons of oil and fry the paste until it is fragrant. Add the tamarind water, sugar and salt to taste, stir in the water, and cook until the sauce bubbles and thickens. Place the fish on a serving dish, pour the sambal over it and garnish with shredded lime leaves.

DEEP-FRIED CHICKEN IN CURRY POWDER

ENCHE KEBIN CHICKEN

This recipe from Penang presents a thoroughly hybrid deep-fried chicken, combining both Malay and Chinese flavors.

3 lb (1½ kg) chicken

1 tablespoon commercial Malaysian meat curry powder

2 teaspoons ginger juice

1 teaspoon dark soy sauce

1 teaspoon light soy sauce

1 teaspoon sugar

¼ cup (65 ml) thick coconut milk

Salt to taste

Oil for deep-frying

Cucumber slices for garnishing

Cut the chicken into curry pieces (p. 23). Mix all the other ingredients except the oil together in a bowl or zip top bag and marinate the chicken in this sauce for at least two hours. Remove the chicken from the marinade and set it aside to drain.

Heat the oil in a wok and deep-fry the chicken pieces until they are golden brown. Lift out, drain and chop each piece into bite-sized pieces. Arrange on a plate surrounded by cucumber slices.

Grilled Dishes

SATAY BABI PORK SATAY

This Nyonya satay uses pork, which would never be eaten by the Muslim Malays. Its inspiration, however, is Malay.

1¾ oz (50 g) pork shoulder or other cut with a little fat attached, cubed
4 tablespoons oil
Pinch each of salt and pepper
1 stalk lemongrass with its end crushed (to be used as a brush)
Oil
Cucumber slices

Marinade

2 teaspoons coriander seed or 1½ teaspoons ground coriander
1 teaspoon cumin seed or ½ teaspoon ground cumin
1 teaspoon fennel seeds or ½ teaspoon ground fennel
1-in (2½-cm) piece turmeric root, or ½ teaspoon ground turmeric
1 teaspoon tamarind purée
1 teaspoon sugar
2–3 tablespoons thick coconut cream

Peanut Sauce

8 dried chilies, seeds removed, soaked and squeezed dry
1 thick slice galangal root, peeled and coarsely chopped

1 stalk lemongrass, sliced thinly
1 teaspoon shrimp paste (*belacan*)
1 clove garlic, chopped
10 shallots, sliced
Oil for frying
1 cup (250 g) roasted peanuts, coarsely chopped
1½ cups (375 ml) coconut milk
½ cup (125 ml) tamarind water
1 teaspoon sugar
Salt to taste

If using whole dry spices for the Marinade, roast them in a dry pan until brown, then grind them to a powder. Grind the turmeric, the spices, the tamarind purée and the coconut cream to a paste. Marinate the pork in the paste for at least an hour. Soak some wooden satay sticks in water.

To make the Peanut Sauce, grind the chilies, galangal, lemongrass, shrimp paste, garlic and the shallots to a paste. Heat the oil in a wok or a pan and fry the paste until it is fragrant. Add the peanuts, coconut milk, tamarind water, sugar and salt. Mix well, bring to a boil and cook and stir until the oil floats on top.

Thread the pork on to the top one-third of the satay sticks, leaving two-thirds free for holding. Grill or cook under the broiler, basting them frequently with oil, using the lemongrass brush. Arrange on a plate with cucumber slices and serve with a bowl of Peanut Sauce for dipping and compressed rice or serve at a barbecue with other meats and a salad.

Accompaniments

Tart pickles, hot or sharp sambal, and fried crunchies are important accompaniments to every Nyonya meal. Nyonya pickles, in particular, are quite elaborate—much more so than their Malay cousins.

ACAR AWAK OR PENANG ACAR ## MIXED VEGETABLE RELISH

This relish exemplifies the degree of extra attention and refinement that became the mark of the Nyonya kitchen. It makes a good vegetable dish for a party and keeps well in the refrigerator. You can halve the quantity to make it a side dish for a family meal.

1 English cucumber or 3 pickling cucumbers, cut into
   four lengthwise, seeded and cut into strips
Salt to taste
7 oz (200 g) carrot, cut into strips
7 oz (200 g) green beans, cut into bite-sized pieces
7 oz (200 g) cigar-shaped eggplant, cut into strips
7 oz (200 g) cauliflower or cabbage, cut into florets or
   shredded
3 medium-length red chilies, cut into four lengthwise,
   seeds removed
¼ cup (65 g) unsalted peanuts, roasted
¼ cup (65 g) sesame seed, roasted in a dry pan
3 tablespoons oil
6 shallots, sliced
5 cloves garlic, sliced
¼ cup (65 ml) white vinegar
1½–2 tablespoons sugar
¼ cup (65 ml) water

Spice Paste
10 dried chilies, seeded, soaked in warm water until soft
   and squeezed dry
1 teaspoon shrimp paste, roasted in foil (optional)
4 roasted candlenuts, or raw almonds or macadamia
   nuts, coarsely chopped
1½-in (4-cm) piece turmeric root, peeled and coarsely
   chopped or 1 teaspoon ground turmeric
1½-in (4-cm) piece galangal root, peeled and coarsely
   chopped

Put the cucumber strips into a strainer, salt them, place a weight on top and set them aside to drain for 30 minutes. Heat a saucepan of salted water to boiling point and blanch, in separate batches, the carrot, beans, eggplant and cauliflower for about a minute. Drain each batch thoroughly, then spread them along with the chilies on a clean kitchen towel to dry further while the cucumbers are draining. Rinse the salt off cucumbers and thoroughly dry them with paper towels.

Grind the Spice Paste ingredients to a paste. Heat a little oil in a wok and fry the shallots and the garlic until golden brown. Remove, drain and set aside. Fry the Spice Paste until it is light brown and fragrant. Add the vinegar, sugar and salt to taste and bring to a boil. Add the shallots, the garlic and all the vegetables and stir until everything is mixed and the vegetables are tender-crisp. Set aside. When cool, mix in the peanuts and sprinkle with sesame seeds before serving.

The relish will keep in a covered dish in the refrigerator for a few days.

CUCUMBER SAMBAL
SAMBAL TIMUN

2 tablespoons dried shrimp
4 medium-length red chilies, sliced
1 teaspoon shrimp paste, roasted in foil
2 pickling cucumbers or 1 large cucumber, cut into two or four lengthwise, seeded and sliced diagonally into thick strips
Juice of 2 limes, or to taste
Sugar to taste

Soak the dried shrimp in warm water for 10 minutes and drain. Grind the shrimp, chilies and shrimp paste to a fine paste. Toss this with the cucumber, add lime juice and sugar to taste and mix well.

FRIED DRIED ANCHOVIES
IKAN BILIS GORENG

Serve as an accompaniment to Nyonya Coconut Rice or as a delicious nibble with drinks.

Oil for deep-frying
1½ cups (375 g) small raw peanuts (skin on preferably)
1½ cups (375 g) dried anchovies (*ikan bilis*)
2 tablespoons sugar
¼ cup (65 ml) tamarind water, or to taste

Spice Paste
3 shallots, sliced
2 cloves garlic
5 dried chilies, or more to taste, soaked in warm water and squeezed dry

Grind the Spice Paste ingredients to a rough paste. Heat sufficient oil for deep-frying in a wok until hot. Add the peanuts, reduce the heat and deep-fry until they start to brown. Lift out and drain on paper towel, setting them aside to cool.

Remove the heads from the dried anchovies and dust them of debris. Wash them quickly, drain and dry well. Put them into the hot oil and fry until brown and crisp. Lift out and drain.

Drain the wok of all but 2 tablespoons of oil. Stir-fry the Spice Paste until it is light brown and fragrant. Add the sugar, anchovies and peanuts and stir-fry, adding a dash of tamarind water to taste.

Store in a sealed container with a tight lid and salt just before using. If you want very crisp anchovies fry them a second time after draining and cooling. Drain and cool again and mix as above.

Rice, Noodles and One-Dish Meals

NASI LEMAK NYONYA

NYONYA COCONUT RICE

This is a one-dish meal of Malay-Indonesian origin and is a favorite of the Singapore Peranakan. The meal consists of fragrant rice cooked with coconut milk and served with a number of side dishes on a single plate. For the rice use the recipe for Indonesian Fragrant Coconut Rice (p. 166). Make a mold of the rice by filling a Chinese rice bowl or soup bowl then inverting it on to the middle of a dinner plate. Surround the rice with small servings of dried anchovies or Dried Anchovy Sambal together with some fried peanuts; Fried Tamarind Shrimp or Cuttlefish Fried Sambal; halves of hard-boiled egg; sliced fresh cucumber with a spoonful of Shrimp Paste Sambal next to it; and perhaps a little Mixed Vegetable Relish.

LAKSA LEMAK

NOODLES IN COCONUT MILK SOUP

This recipe has its origins in Malacca and is a very rich dish of noodles combined with coconut milk, Malay curry spices and shrimp or chicken. It is famous as a mid-morning snack in Singapore, southern Malaysia and Sarawak. Smooth and spicy, Noodles in Coconut Milk Soup is quite different from the Sour Noodle Soup (p. 267) of the north. It is particularly good as a pick-me-up the morning after it is made.

1½ lb (750 g) shrimp, deveined (4 large ones—the rest small)
4 tablespoons oil

1½ lb (750 g) fresh thick, round, rice noodles (*laksa*) or 1
   packet dried coarse rice vermicelli
6 cups (1½ liters) thin coconut milk and 1 cup (250 ml)
   thick coconut milk
8 oz (250 g) cuttlefish balls (available in Asian food
   stores), deep-fried until brown then sliced (optional)
Salt to taste
Crushed fresh chili or sambal ulek

Spice Paste

8–15 dried chilies, seeded, soaked in warm water until
   soft and squeezed dry
2 stalks lemongrass, finely sliced
1-in (2½-cm) piece galangal root, peeled and coarsely
   chopped
1½-in (3-cm) piece turmeric root, peeled and coarsely
   chopped, or ½ teaspoon ground turmeric
4 candlenuts or almonds or macadamia nuts, coarsely
   chopped
1¼ teaspoons shrimp paste
1 clove garlic
15 shallots, sliced
1½ tablespoons coriander seed, freshly ground

Garnish

3½ oz (100 g) deep-fried tofu, sliced
8 oz (250 g) bean sprouts, washed and trimmed
1 pickling cucumber cut in 4 lengthwise then sliced
   across
Leaves of 8 sprigs knotweed or Vietnamese mint,
   coriander, or purple mint, roughly sliced, or sliced green
   onions
Fried onion flakes

Put the Garnishes in separate bowls and place them on the table with
serving spoons alongside. Grind the Spice Paste ingredients to a paste.
Wash and peel the small shrimp, leaving the large ones in their shells.
Heat 2 tablespoons of oil in a wok, add the large shrimp in their shells
and stir-fry for 2–3 minutes until cooked. Drain and set aside.

If you are using fresh noodles, rinse them under cold water to
separate. Bring a large saucepan of water to a boil and dip the noodles

into the water briefly to scald them and heat them through. Drain, rinse to separate and place in a large bowl. If using dried vermicelli, add the noodles to the boiling water, return to a boil, then remove the pan from the heat, cover it and set aside for 8 minutes or more until the noodles are soft. Drain, rinse the noodles in cold water and place them in a large bowl.

Add the rest of the oil to the wok and when it is hot fry the Spice Paste until it is fragrant. Stir in the thin coconut milk and bring to a boil. Add the sliced cuttlefish balls if you are using them, add the peeled shrimp and return to a boil. Reduce the heat and simmer until the shrimp are cooked. Add the thick coconut milk, return to a boil, stirring constantly, and serve very hot, together with the bowl of noodles and the Garnishes.

Put a good serving of noodles in the bottom of a deep soup bowl for each person. Place a selection of Garnishes and a shrimp in its shell on top and pour lots of hot shrimp gravy over to create a thick soup. Serve with a side dish of crushed fresh red chili or sambal ulek to which guests help themselves if they need more heat.

I have had this dish with baby clams in their shells or a few small shelled raw oysters added with the garnishes before the gravy (which in this case must be still boiling) is poured over. To make this dish with chicken, first poach skinned chicken breasts in 2–3 cups (500–750 ml) of water until cooked. Remove the meat, shred it and set it aside. Make the spiced gravy with 3 cups (750 ml) of thin coconut milk and 3 cups (750 ml) of chicken stock. Add the chicken, stir to mix, and add the thick coconut milk and proceed as above. For variety, you can add a few baby clams or small shrimp at the end.

SOUR NOODLE SOUP

PENANG ASAM LAKSA

For this scented northern noodle soup you really need access to wild ginger flower (*bunga kantan*). Though the dish will still taste good without it there is no substitute for its distinctive scent.

1 lb (500 g) fine-fleshed fish (short-bodied mackerel, tommy ruff, garfish, sand whiting)
4 cups (1 liter) water
3–4 dried tamarind slices or 1–1½ cups (250–375 ml) tamarind water (if you use this alternative reduce the plain water component to 3 cups [750 ml])

1 wild ginger flower (*bunga kantan*), sliced

8 stalks knotweed or Vietnamese mint (*daun kesum*)

1–2 teaspoons sugar to taste

Salt and pepper to taste

1 lb (500 g) fresh thick, round, rice noodles (*laksa*) or 1 packet dried coarse rice vermicelli

Spice Paste

6–10 dried chilies, seeded, soaked in warm water until soft and squeezed dry

2 stalks lemongrass, finely sliced

2 slices galangal root, peeled and coarsely chopped (optional)

½-in (1½-cm) piece turmeric root, peeled and coarsely chopped or ⅛ teaspoon ground turmeric

2 teaspoons shrimp paste, roasted in foil

15 shallots, sliced

Garnish

1 small handful mint sprigs or leaves

½ small pineapple, cut into strips 2 x ¼ in (5 x ½ cm)

1 pickling cucumber, cut in four lengthwise then sliced across, or into short julienne strips

2 Spanish onions, sliced into rings

4 medium-length red chilies, sliced into rounds

Wash and scale the fish and poach it in 2 cups (500 ml) of water until cooked. Remove, cool, and flake off the flesh. Discard the bones, head, fins, etc., and set the stock and the flaked flesh aside.

Grind all the Spice Paste ingredients to a paste. Add 1 cup (250 ml) of water and process until well mixed. Pour this water into a saucepan, add the remaining plain water, the dried tamarind slices or tamarind water, the wild ginger flower, and the knotweed. Simmer gently until fragrant. Add the fish stock, sugar and salt and pepper to taste and simmer for 30 minutes. Remove the knotweed, add the flaked fish and return to a boil.

Prepare the noodles according to the instructions in Noodles in Coconut Milk Soup (p. 265). Put servings of noodles in individual bowls, place Garnishes on top (except for the chili) and pour the soup over. Serve the chili rounds on the table for diners to help themselves.

POPIAH STUFFED PANCAKE ROLLS

These are Nyonya spring rolls that incorporate Chinese and Southeast Asian ingredients. One roll makes an interesting snack or entrée; two or three a satisfying lunch. Stuffed Pancake Rolls are prepared and eaten in two different ways: most commonly as a kind of crêpe, or sealed and deep-fried in the manner of a mainstream Chinese spring roll.

The only dish elsewhere in Southeast Asia resembling the crêpe version—so far as I know—is the Vietnamese rice paper roll.

Try to buy true *popiah* skins at a Malaysian food store if you can, otherwise make your own with the following instructions.

Pancake Roll Skins (makes about 30–32)
1¼ cups (290 g) flour and 1½ oz (60 g) tapioca flour (for a lighter mix), or 1½ cups (350 g) flour
8 large eggs
4 cups (1 liter) water
Pinch of salt

Filling
3 tablespoons oil
4 cloves garlic, finely chopped
3 tablespoons fermented soy beans (*tauco*), mashed into a paste (optional)
8 oz (250 g) small shrimp, peeled, deveined and coarsely chopped
8 oz (250 g) ground pork
1¼ lb (600 g) shredded bamboo shoots (2 large cans), drained
2 yambeans, peeled and shredded
8 oz (250 g) firm tofu, cut into shreds and deep-fried until brown
1 teaspoon dark soy sauce, or to taste
Pinch of sugar to taste (optional)
Salt to taste

Garnish

Asian lettuce leaves, washed and drained

Chinese sweet black sauce (*tim cheong*) or substitute a
  little Indonesian *kecap manis* or hoisin sauce

Fresh medium-length red chilies, pounded to a paste or
  sambal ulek

12 cloves garlic, mashed to a paste

8 oz (250 g) bean sprouts, washed and trimmed

1 pickling cucumber, shredded

2 or 3 tablespoons Chinese leeks, Chinese chives or
  coriander leaves, coarsely chopped

8 oz (250 g) small shrimp, peeled, deveined and cooked

8 oz (250 g) crab meat

3 eggs, cooked into thin omelettes then rolled up and
  finely sliced

½–1 cup (125–250 g) fried onion flakes or freshly fried
  or roasted peanuts, coarsely chopped

To make the Pancake Roll Skins sift the flour into a bowl. Make a well in the center, add the eggs, and mix lightly, adding the water and salt to produce a batter. Stir until there are no lumps and set the batter aside for at least one hour.

Brush a frying pan lightly with oil. Heat the pan over low heat, and when it is hot pour in enough batter to just cover the bottom of the pan. Cook until the pancake lifts around the edges and is cooked. Cool on top of an upturned plate. If the batter is too thick add a little more water and mix before proceeding. Cook the pancakes one at a time until all the batter is used up, piling each successive pancake on top of the last.

To make the Filling, heat the oil in a wok, add the garlic and fry until golden. Add the soy bean paste and stir-fry until fragrant. Add the shrimp and the pork and stir-fry until they change color. Add the bamboo shoots, yambeans and a splash of water, cover the pan and steam until the vegetables wilt. Uncover and cook until any remaining water evaporates, add the tofu, soy sauce, sugar and salt, and continue stir-frying over high heat until the vegetables are cooked. Serve in a bowl alongside the Garnishes and the stack of Pancake Roll Skins. Diners place a skin flat on their plate and position some lettuce leaf near one edge. They spread a little sweet dark sauce, chili and garlic paste on the lettuce leaf, with some bean sprouts, cucumber and a little fresh herb. About 2 tablespoons of the Filling (drained of any liquid) are added, along with a few shrimp, a little crab meat and shredded omelette. Top with fried onion flakes, fold in the sides and roll up into a spring roll. The roll can be cut into 4 pieces on the plate if you find this easier to handle.

For the fried version (*popiah goreng*) buy prepared Malaysian *popiah* skins or large spring roll skins in an Asian grocery store.

INDIAN

As I mentioned in the introduction to this chapter, the Indian community in Malaysia and Singapore is much smaller than the Malay or Chinese. And although a large proportion of that community owes its heritage to the south of India, a wide variety of styles of cooking from all the regions of India are represented. Where possible I have noted the locality of the dishes so that readers may identify the subtle differences in flavor and food habit associated with the different areas.

A regular family meal in Indian households in Malaysia is likely to consist of rice with a vegetable dish, a meat or fish dish if the family is not vegetarian (otherwise two vegetable dishes) and some lentils (*dal*)—sometimes served on their own, sometimes combined with vegetables or meat. Also served would be small crunchy salads or yogurt to cool the palate, and some complimentary side dishes to contribute to the five flavors (sweet, sour, salty, hot and bitter) make the meal complete.

Basic cooking styles are familiar: there are dishes containing a lot of thin liquid; wet and dry curries with rich and spicy gravy; fried dishes; vegetables in sauces and tasty side dishes or accompaniments of various kinds. One technique found in modern Malaysian Indian cooking but not in other Southeast Asian cuisines is tandoori cooking, a method which in its classic form uses a high heat from a charcoal fire inside a clay oven to sear and cook food. It is a technique that was developed among the bread and meat-eating populations of India's north and not among the vegetarians and rice-eaters of the south, from whom the majority of Malaysia's Indian families inherit their cultural and culinary heritage.

Forty years ago I was not aware of tandoori cooking at all in Malaysia or Singapore; the Indian restaurants that were prolific then were the famous banana-leaf ones which served simple home-style vegetarian meals to an Indian community, many of whom still suffered the social consequences of gender imbalance and crowded living conditions in urban areas.

Today there are many restaurants that serve tandoori dishes. These dishes have been widely adapted to modern Indian home cooking there, though in this case they are usually cooked in electric or gas ovens. Elsewhere in Southeast Asia oven cooking is still a rarity.

Curry powders

For a long time Westerners entertained a picture of an Indian dish called curry made with a ground, standardized mixture known as a curry powder. In fact there is no such dish in Indian cuisine, the word having been adopted by the British to denote any spicy dish of a stew-like consistency they encountered on the subcontinent. The name probably derives from the Tamil word *kari*, meaning something like "sauce."

Many different combinations of spices (masala) go into individual Indian dishes, and each cook will make up his or her own appropriate blend using separate spices ground on the curry stone in the household at the beginning of that day. The most trustworthy Indian recipes will name every separate spice involved. Amounts expressed as measures are intended as suggestions only since they would normally be added in conformity with the cook's or the family's taste.

The occasional recipe will, however, include a measure of one or another ambiguous spice mixture, and I sometimes call for a standard "meat" or a "fish" curry powder in this chapter. The instructions for making these mixes follow but please note that they comprise only a part of the complete spicing of the few dishes in which they are used. They would never be sufficient or satisfactory as a curry base on their own. Remember, too, if you make up a batch you should use it quickly before it becomes stale.

Indian home cooking is still largely inclined to echo the traditions of India itself, and more particularly of southern India. Habits are changing, though. Just as north Indian cooking is increasing in popularity among modern Malaysian Indians, so too are tastes and practices changing in other ways. Commercial curry powder is now often used to save time, some street dishes are reproduced at home, and it is also fashionable among today's home cooks to experiment with the dishes of other communities. Shortcut curry powders are a sign of the times.

MEAT CURRY POWDER

3½ oz (100 g) coriander seed
1 oz (25 g) cumin seed
1 oz (25 g) fennel seed
1½ tablespoons ground turmeric
1 tablespoon peppercorns
35–70 medium-length dried chilies

FISH CURRY POWDER

3½ oz (100 g) coriander seed
1 oz (25 g) cumin seed
1½ tablespoons fennel seed
1½ tablespoons turmeric
1 tablespoon peppercorns
35–70 medium-length dried chilies

The technique is the same for both varieties: Roast the seeds lightly in a dry pan then grind all the ingredients together to a powder. Store in an airtight jar.

If fresh or dried chilies are called for in a recipe, be sure to adjust the amount according to the amount of heat you desire.

Commercial Malaysian Indian curry powders for meat, chicken and fish are available in Asian food stores with a Southeast Asian bias. These are more universal than the recipes I give and while it may be useful to occasionally use them for a quick curry, I do not recommend them for everyday use. They represent only one set of flavors in the wide spectrum of possibilities, and they almost always include rice flour as an extender, something that is never used in homemade curries. In particular, do not use them when one of my basic curry powders is called for in these recipes as this could result in a duplication of ingredients or underflavoring as a result of the rice-flour padding. Moreover, when buying commercial curry powders for Indian curries, make sure you get a Malaysian Indian one and not a Malaysian Malay curry powder.

TEMPERING

Tempering is a practice that is often used to increase flavor in south Indian curries (much as adding a garam masala at the last minute is done in the north). The technique involves frying onions, brown mustard seed or sometimes fenugreek seeds and curry leaves in oil until they are brown and aromatic. Tempering can be done either at the beginning of cooking or at the end, when the oil and its contents are poured on to the finished dish. Both of these approaches are used in many of the following recipes.

Wet Dishes

RASAM PEPPER WATER

This is the traditional dish used to moisten the rice when a dry curry is served. This recipe is for the vegetarian version, often served in a glass to accompany rice, lentils and vegetable dishes.

1 teaspoon peppercorns
1 teaspoon cumin seed or ¾ teaspoon ground cumin
2 cloves garlic, chopped
1 tablespoon oil
½ medium-sized onion, cut in half across and then finely sliced lengthwise
1 teaspoon brown mustard seed
2–4 medium-length dried chilies, each broken into two
½ teaspoon ground turmeric
⅓ cup (75 ml) tamarind water or fresh lime juice
2 cups (500 ml) water, or more to desired strength
Salt to taste

Grind the peppercorns and cumin seeds together coarsely and mix with the garlic. Heat the oil in a pot and fry the onion, mustard seed and chilies until the mustard seed sputters and everything is light brown. Add the garlic, pepper and cumin mixture, turmeric and tamarind water and mix well. Add the water with salt to taste and bring to a boil. Taste for sourness (it should be sour and hot), adding more water or tamarind juice if required.

Serve hot in a bowl as a refreshing soup with rice and a dry curry or strain and chill for a sustaining drink.

SOP KAMBING (Street Food) — INDIAN MUTTON SOUP

This is a popular dish developed in Malaysia by Indian hawkers—one you would not find in India itself. Originally made with goat, today it is almost always cooked with lamb. Serve with crusty bread or rice.

1 tablespoon coriander seed or 1¾ tablespoons ground coriander
¾ teaspoon cumin seed or ½ teaspoon ground cumin
¾ teaspoon fennel seed or ¾ teaspoon anise
1 teaspoon peppercorns
1½-in (3-cm) piece fresh ginger root, peeled and chopped
6 cloves garlic, sliced
Up to 2 lb (1 kg) leg or lean loin lamb chops, meat trimmed of fat and cubed, bones reserved
1 tablespoon oil
1 large onion, chopped
1 cinnamon stick, about 3-in (7-cm) long
4 cloves
3 cardamom pods, broken open
1 star anise
1 medium-length green chili, seeded and cut into 4 lengthwise
10 cups (2½ liters) water
Salt to taste
Fried onion flakes and sliced green onions

Grind the coriander, cumin, fennel and peppercorns to a powder, add the ginger and garlic and grind to a paste. Mix the spice paste with the meat and bones and set aside.

Heat the oil, add the onion, cinnamon, cloves, cardamom and star anise and stir-fry until the onion is soft and golden. Add the meat, bones, spice paste and chili and stir-fry until the meat is seared on all sides and the spices are fragrant. Add the water and salt to taste, bring to a boil and simmer gently for about 2 hours.

Remove the bones and whole spices, pour into a bowl and garnish with fried onion flakes and sliced green onions before serving.

For a complete one-dish family meal add some diced vegetables such as carrots, beans, summer squash or zucchini, or potatoes during the last half hour of cooking.

MULLIGATAWNY WITH BEEF STOCK

As far as I can tell, mulligatawny is an anglicized version of Pepper Water, invented in India for Europeans and Anglo-Indians. This version, brought to Malaysia via Sri Lanka, seems to me a likely source of inspiration for Indian Mutton Soup.

1 lb (500 g) stewing beef with bones
8–10 cups (2–2½ liters) water
Pinch of salt
10 whole peppercorns
1 cinnamon stick
6 cloves garlic, peeled
8 thin slices fresh ginger root
2 tablespoons oil
2 medum-sized onions, finely sliced lengthwise
1 tablespoon Meat Curry Powder (p. 273) or commercial
  curry powder
Leaves from 2 fresh stalks of curry
1 stalk lemongrass, bruised (optional)
3 large ripe tomatoes, peeled and chopped
3 potatoes, peeled and diced
2 plants Asian celery or 2 small sticks celery with leaves
1 cup (250 ml) thick coconut milk
Juice of 1 lime

Cut the beef into cubes and simmer in the water with the bones for 2 hours with salt, peppercorns and the cinnamon stick. Mash the garlic and ginger to a rough paste.

Heat 1 tablespoon of oil in a large saucepan. Add half the onions, the curry powder, garlic, ginger, some of the curry leaves and the lemongrass and fry until the onions are golden. Add the chopped tomatoes, potatoes, celery and the beef with its stock. Simmer gently for another 2 hours or until the water has reduced by half. Strain the broth into another pan, pressing the potatoes through the strainer and squeezing all the liquid out of the meat and then discarding the solids. Add the coconut milk to the broth and stir well. In a small skillet, heat 1 tablespoon of oil and sauté the remaining onion and curry leaves until light brown and add this to the pot of broth. Add lime juice and serve hot as a soup or with rice and dry dishes.

Curries

Curries, for the purposes of this section, are spiced dishes cooked on top of the stove, either in a saucepan or in the traditional way in a round, wide-mouthed claypot known as a *chatti* in Tamil or *belanga* in Malay. Some curries are wet, others are dry; some are heavily spiced, others lightly so; all have liquid added: sometimes water, sometimes coconut milk and sometimes yogurt. They constitute the largest category in Indian food so I have subdivided the recipes into groups according to the nature of the main ingredient.

Seafood

FISH CURRY WITH COCONUT MILK (South India)

Fish curry is very good the next day. An Indian friend of mine describes day-old fish curry as "heaven on earth" when eaten with "Old" Rice and yogurt.

3 tablespoons oil
2 cups (500 ml) coconut milk
¼–½ cup (65–125 ml) tamarind water
Salt to taste
1 lb (500 g) large fish fillets (ling, Spanish mackerel, snapper or salmon), cut into chunks

Tempering

1 teaspoon brown mustard seed

1 stalk fresh curry leaves or 6 dried curry leaves

½ teaspoon fenugreek seed

2 medium-sized onions, cut in half across and then finely sliced lengthwise

Spice Paste

2 tablespoons coriander seed or 1¾ tablespoon ground coriander

1 teaspoon cumin seed or ¾ teaspoon ground cumin

1 teaspoon ground turmeric

½ teaspoon peppercorns or ¼ teaspoon freshly ground pepper

10–20 medium-length dried chilies, seeded, soaked in warm water until soft and squeezed dry

2-in (5-cm) piece fresh ginger root, peeled and coarsely chopped

2 cloves garlic

If using whole spices for the Spice Paste, grind them to a powder, then add the remaining Spice Paste ingredients and grind to a paste, adding a little water if necessary.

To prepare the Tempering ingredients, heat the oil in a pan. Add the mustard seed, curry leaves, fenugreek and onions and fry until the seeds pop and the onions are golden. Add the Spice Paste and fry until fragrant. Add the coconut milk, tamarind water and salt to taste. Stir well and simmer for a minute or two, then add the fish. Cover the pan and simmer gently for 5 minutes. Uncover the pan and keep simmering until the fish is cooked and the gravy has reduced and thickened a little, its oil floating on top.

FISH HEAD CURRY
(Singapore Street Food)

Curry made from giant fish heads alone is a very popular version of fish curry offered in curry shops and food stalls in Singapore today, although it is not a dish you would find in India itself. According to Margaret Chan's *Foodstops*, it was first created by two Indian cooks in Singapore in 1964, though I do not remember it figuring prominently there in 1965 when I went to research the first edition of this book.

3 tablespoons commercial Malaysian fish curry powder

3 tablespoons oil

2 small red chilies, seeded and sliced in two lengthwise

6 okra, cut diagonally in two

2 small tomatoes, peeled and quartered

3 cups (750 ml) coconut milk

¼–½ cup (65–125 ml) tamarind water

Salt to taste

1 large fish head (2 lb/1 kg), or 2 smaller ones

Tempering

½ teaspoon whole brown mustard seed

½ teaspoon whole cumin seed

½ teaspoon whole fennel seed

¼ teaspoon whole fenugreek seed

1 stalk fresh curry leaves

1 medium-sized onion, cut in half across and then finely sliced lengthwise

Spice Paste

1-in (2½-cm) piece of fresh ginger root, peeled and coarsely chopped

2 cloves garlic

5 shallots, sliced

Grind the Spice Paste ingredients together. Add the curry powder and mix well, adding a little water to achieve a paste.

Heat the oil in a pan. Add the tempering ingredients and fry for a minute, then add the chilies, okra and the Spice Paste and stir-fry until everything is fragrant. Add the tomatoes and mix, then add the coconut milk, tamarind water and salt to taste. Bring to a simmer, stirring constantly, and cook for a few minutes. Add the fish head and simmer gently until it and the okra are nearly cooked. Turn the head over and continue simmering until done.

SOUR FISH CURRY

4 tablespoons oil

2 medium-sized onions, cut in two across and finely sliced lengthwise

1 teaspoon brown mustard seed

1 stalk fresh curry leaves or 6 dried curry leaves

Salt to taste

½ cup (125 ml) tamarind water

1 lb (500 g) fish fillets (ling, Spanish mackerel, snapper or salmon), cut into chunks

Spice Paste

2 tablespoons coriander seed or 1¾ tablespoons ground coriander

1 tablespoon cumin seed or ¾ tablespoon ground cumin

½ teaspoon ground turmeric

1 teaspoon peppercorns or ½ teaspoon freshly ground pepper

12 medum-length dried chilies, seeded, soaked in warm water until soft and squeezed dry

½-in (1-cm) piece fresh ginger root, peeled and coarsely chopped

2 cloves garlic

If using whole spices for the Spice Paste, grind them to a powder and then grind all of the Spice Paste ingredients to a paste. Heat the oil in a wok or skillet. Fry the onions, mustard seed and curry leaves until the seeds sputter and the onions are golden brown. Add the Spice Paste and fry until it is fragrant. Add salt and tamarind water, stir well and bring to a boil. Add the fish, reduce the heat to medium, cover the pan and simmer gently for 5 minutes. Remove the lid and shake gently until the fish is cooked and the gravy is thick. Add extra water if you would like the dish to be more moist.

FISH MOLEE

The *molee* style of cooking uses coconut milk and fresh flavorings and comes from south India.

1 lb (500 g) fish fillets (mackerel, Spanish mackerel, salmon)

Salt to taste

Oil for frying

1 medium-sized onion, finely sliced

1 clove garlic, chopped

6 thin slices fresh ginger root, peeled and cut into strips

3 medium-length red chilies, seeded and cut lengthwise into strips

½ teaspoon ground turmeric
1½ cups (375 ml) thick coconut milk

Rub the fish fillets with salt, then wash and dry them. Heat sufficient oil in a pan and lightly fry the fish turning once until it is golden on both sides. Remove and set aside.

Drain the pan of all but 1 tablespoon of oil and fry the onion and garlic until golden. Add the ginger, red chilies and turmeric and stir-fry until everything smells fragrant. Add the coconut milk and salt to taste and mix, then return the fish to the pan and simmer gently for 5 minutes, spooning the sauce over it. Serve with rice and other dishes.

DRY SHRIMP CURRY

4 tablespoons oil
5 shallots or 1 medium-sized onion, finely sliced
    lengthwise
¾-in (2-cm) piece of cinnamon stick
A few curry leaves
1 lb (500 g) large shrimp, peeled and deveined
2 medium waxy potatoes, parboiled, peeled and diced
¾ cup (200 ml) thick coconut milk
1 tablespoon tamarind water, or to taste
Salt to taste
Pinch of fennel seed

Spice Paste
3 cloves garlic
¾-in (2-cm) piece fresh ginger root, peeled and coarsely
    chopped
1 teaspoon ground chili
½ teaspoon ground turmeric

Grind the Spice Paste ingredients together with a little water to form a thick paste. Heat the oil in a wok and fry the shallots, cinnamon and curry leaves until the shallots are golden. Add the Spice Paste and stir-fry until fragrant. Add the shrimp and stir-fry until they are almost cooked. Add the potatoes, the coconut milk, tamarind water and salt to taste and boil hard, stirring constantly, until the gravy is dry and the shrimp and potatoes fry in the remaining oil. Add a pinch of fennel seed and serve when everything is crusty and fragrant.

Chicken

CHICKEN CURRY WITH COCONUT MILK

This dish is best reheated and eaten at least 24 hours after it is cooked.

1 chicken, skin removed, cut into curry pieces (p. 23)
2 cloves garlic, chopped
2-in (5-cm) piece fresh ginger root, peeled and chopped
2 tablespoons oil
2 medium-sized onions, halved and finely sliced lengthwise
¼ teaspoon fenugreek seed
2-in (5-cm) piece of cinnamon stick
1 stalk curry leaves
1½–2 cups (375–500 ml) thin coconut milk
½ cup (125 ml) tamarind water made from 1 teaspoon
   tamarind pulp
Salt to taste
1 cup (250 ml) thick coconut milk

Spice Paste
1 tablespoon coriander seed or ¾ tablespoon ground
   coriander
½ teaspoon cumin seed or ½ teaspoon ground cumin
½ teaspoon fennel seed (optional)
½ teaspoon peppercorns or ¼ teaspoon freshly ground pepper
1 teaspoon ground turmeric
8–12 dried chilies, seeded, soaked in warm water until
   soft and squeezed dry or 2–3 teaspoons ground chili

Dry roast all the Spice Paste ingredients lightly in a pan then grind them to a powder, adding the soaked chilies last (if using). Add sufficient water to blend to a thick paste. Cool the paste and mix it thoroughly with the chicken pieces. Set aside for an hour or two.

Grind the garlic and ginger into a paste. Heat the oil and fry the onions, fenugreek, cinnamon and curry leaves until the onions are transparent. Add the garlic and ginger and fry until fragrant. Add the thin coconut milk and stir as it comes to a boil. Add the spiced chicken, tamarind and salt to taste, mix well, reduce the heat, and simmer uncovered until the chicken is nearly cooked. Add the thick coconut milk and cook until the chicken is tender.

DRY CHICKEN CURRY

1 chicken, skin removed, cut into curry pieces (p. 23)
2 tablespoons oil
½ medium-sized onion, finely sliced
1 stalk curry leaves
1 cup (250 ml) water
Salt to taste
2 small potatoes, quartered

Spice Paste
2 tablespoons ground coriander
2 teaspoons cumin seed
1 teaspoon fennel seed
½ teaspoon ground turmeric
½ teaspoon ground chili (or more to taste)
3 cloves or ¼ teaspoon ground cloves
1 cinnamon stick or ½ teaspoon ground cinnamon
3 cardamom pods or ¼ teaspoon ground cardamom
1-in (2½-cm) piece fresh ginger root, peeled and
  coarsely chopped
3 cloves garlic
6 shallots, sliced

If using whole spices for the Spice Paste, grind them to a powder then combine with the remaining Spice Paste ingredients and grind to a paste. Mix with the chicken pieces and set aside for 2 hours.

Heat the oil in a pan and fry the onion and the curry leaves until the onion is golden. Add the chicken and any remaining Spice Paste and fry until fragrant. Add the water, salt and potatoes and cook, stirring until the chicken is tender, the potatoes are done and the gravy is almost dry.

Meat

MRS. NAIR'S DRY LAMB CURRY
(Malabar style)

This curry is originally from Malabar on the southwest coast of India. There the use of fresh grated coconut is a common practice.

1 lb (500 g) boned leg of lamb, cubed
1 teaspoon ground hot chili
2 medium-sized onions, chopped
3 cloves garlic, chopped
2 thick slices fresh ginger root, peeled and chopped
1 tablespoon oil or ghee
1 heaping tablespoon coriander seed or 2 heaping
    teaspoons ground coriander
¼ teaspoon freshly ground pepper
½ fresh coconut, grated
5 curry leaves
Salt to taste

Mix the meat with the chili and set it aside. Fry three-quarters of the onions, the garlic and ginger in the oil or ghee until soft. Add the meat and chili and a little water and cook uncovered over medium heat until the meat is tender and the curry is dry.

In the meantime, roast the coriander seeds (if using) in a dry frying pan and grind them. Add the coriander and the pepper to the cooked meat mixture and stir. Mix the grated coconut, the remaining finely chopped onion and the curry leaves together and add these to the curry, with salt to taste. Stir well, and cook for a few minutes more before serving.

SIMPLE MEAT CURRY

3 cardamom pods or ¼ teaspoon ground cardamom
3 cloves or ¼ teaspoon ground cloves
1-in (2½-cm) piece cinnamon stick
2–3 medium-sized onions, chopped
2 tablespoons oil or ghee

4 cloves garlic, chopped
4 thin slices fresh ginger root, peeled and chopped
1 lb (500 g) lamb, cubed
1½ tablespoons Meat Curry Powder (p. 273)
Salt to taste
1 tomato, peeled and chopped

If using whole dry spices, grind them coarsely. Fry the chopped onions in hot oil or ghee until they are soft. Add the garlic and ginger and fry until fragrant. Add the meat and brown it, then the curry powder and dry spices. Mix well, add salt and a little water and cook for a few minutes over high heat. Reduce the heat and simmer, covered, until the meat is nearly cooked (about 30 minutes). Add the tomato, cook a few minutes more and serve.

LAMB KORMA

Korma is a rich yogurt-braised, spicy but not necessarily hot dish from the Mogul courts. The Malay korma replaces yogurt with coconut milk. For the best flavor korma should be cooked the day before it is eaten.

½-in (1-cm) slice fresh ginger root, peeled and chopped
1 cup yogurt
1½ lb (750 g) lamb from the leg (2 or 3 thick slices with
    the bone left in), cubed
1 teaspoon coriander seed or ¾ teaspoon ground
    coriander
1 teaspoon ground chili, or to taste
½ teaspoon ground turmeric
5 cardamom pods, broken open
6 whole cloves or ½ teaspoon ground cloves
3-in (7-cm) piece cinnamon stick or ½ teaspoon ground
    cinnamon
4 cloves garlic, chopped
4 tablespoons butter or ghee
2 medium-sized onions, chopped
Salt to taste

Mash the ginger with 1 tablespoon of the yogurt to a paste. Marinate the meat in this mixture for at least 2 hours. Grind the dry seeds (if using) and spices to a powder. Add the garlic and a little water and grind to a paste. Heat the butter in a saucepan and fry the onions until they are light brown. Add the garlic and spice paste, stirring and frying until fragrant. Add the meat, the rest of the yogurt and salt to taste and mix well. Cover the saucepan and simmer until the meat is tender, adding a little water if necessary so the dish does not cook dry.

KHEEMA GROUND BEEF CURRY
(North Indian Muslim)

For a complete meal, serve with Kitchree, raita, chutney and a crispy salad.

2-in (5-cm) piece cinnamon stick or ¼ teaspoon ground cinnamon
6 cloves or ½ teaspoon ground cloves
6 cardamom pods or ½ teaspoon ground cardamom
4 cloves garlic
2-in (5-cm) piece fresh ginger root, peeled and coarsely chopped
Pinch of ground turmeric
2–3 tablespoons oil
2 medium-sized onions, chopped
2 green chilies, chopped
1 lb (500 g) lean ground beef or lamb
Salt to taste
2 large ripe tomatoes, peeled and chopped
1 small waxy potato, parboiled and cubed, or peas (optional)
Chopped fresh coriander leaves for garnish

Grind the cinnamon, cloves and cardamom pods to a powder to make garam masala. Mash the garlic and ginger together and mix with the turmeric to form a paste. Heat the oil in a heavy pan and fry the onions, the garlic paste and the chilies until the onions are golden and everything is fragrant. Add the meat and fry until it changes color. Add salt and garam masala and cover. Reduce the heat to low and cook for 15–30 minutes until dry and oily. Add the chopped tomatoes and potatoes or peas if you wish and cook a little longer. Garnish with chopped coriander leaves.

LAMB AND SPINACH

2 tablespoons oil or ghee
1 large onion, cut in half across and finely sliced
   lengthwise
1 cardamom pod, broken open
1 stick cinnamon
2 cloves garlic, chopped
1 tablespoon Meat Curry Powder (p. 273)
1 lb (500 g) lean lamb, cubed
2 tomatoes, peeled and chopped or 2 tablespoons
   yogurt
Salt to taste
1 package frozen spinach or 1 lb (500 g) fresh spinach,
   washed, cooked and puréed
Fresh chopped mint (optional)
Pinch of ground cumin
1 teaspoon garam masala, or to taste (p. 46)

Heat the oil or ghee in a pan. Add the onion, cardamom and cinnamon stick and fry until the onion is browned.

Mix the garlic and curry powder together, adding a little water to make the mixture moist enough not to burn. Add this and the meat to the pan, mix well and sauté until the meat changes color and the spices smell cooked and fragrant. Add the tomatoes or yogurt and mix. Add salt and spinach, a little water (if necessary) and mint. Simmer gently until the meat is cooked. Add cumin and garam masala to taste and serve.

PORK VINDALOO
(Goa)

4 tablespoons vinegar
3 tablespoons oil
1 medium onion, cut in half across and thinly sliced
½ teaspoon brown mustard seed, coarsely ground
1 lb (500 g) pork, cubed
Water
Salt to taste

Spice Paste

2 teaspoons chili powder

½ teaspoon black peppercorns or ¼ teaspoon freshly ground black pepper

1 teaspoon cumin seed or 1 teaspoon ground cumin

½ teaspoon fennel seed or ½ teaspoon anise

4 cloves garlic

1-in (2½-cm) piece fresh ginger root, peeled and coarsely chopped

Grind the Spice Paste ingredients with a little vinegar to form a paste. Heat the oil in a pan and fry the onion and the mustard seeds until they are lightly browned. Add the Spice Paste and fry until fragrant. Add the meat and stir-fry until the meat is seared on all sides, then add the rest of the vinegar, the water and salt to taste and mix well. Reduce the heat, cover and simmer gently until the meat is tender. Stir occasionally, adding more water if necessary to prevent the dish from drying out.

Vegetable

BRINJAL CURRY
(Sri Lanka)

1 lb (500 g) long purple eggplant, sliced or cubed

Pinch of ground turmeric

Salt to taste

Oil for frying

1½ medium-sized onions, cut in half across and finely sliced lengthwise

2 cloves garlic, finely sliced

1 tablespoon Fish Curry Powder (p. 273) or Ceylon Curry Powder

2–4 fresh green chilies, sliced lengthwise, or to taste

1 cup (250 ml) thick coconut milk

Salt

2 teaspoons tamarind water (p. 55), white vinegar or
  fresh lime juice

Tempering
Oil
½ teaspoon brown mustard seed
½ teaspoon fenugreek seed
2 sprigs fresh curry leaves

Sprinkle each slice of eggplant with a little ground turmeric and salt and set aside. Heat the oil in a wok or a pan. Dry the moisture off the egg-plant slices with a paper towel and fry the slices until they are light brown. Drain and set them aside.

In another pan, fry the onion and garlic in a little oil until they are soft. Add curry powder and green chilies and mix well. Add the coconut milk, salt and tamarind water and boil until thick. Add the eggplant and cook over low heat until the gravy is thick and the oil floats on top. Heat the Tempering oil and fry the mustard seeds, fenugreek and curry leaves, then pour this over the curry.

FRESH VEGETABLE CURRY

This dish can also be made with grated carrot or broccoli cut into small florets.

2 tablespoons oil
3 chilies, sliced
12 pearl onions or 3 medium-sized onions, quartered
6 small zucchini, sliced into rounds or cubed
2 teaspoons Fish Curry Powder (p. 273)
1 cup (250 ml) thick coconut milk
Tamarind water or fresh lime juice to taste
Salt to taste

Heat the oil in a pan and sauté the sliced chilies and the onions until light brown. Add all the other ingredients and bring to a boil, stirring. Simmer until cooked and thick but not dry.

WHITE CURRY

Omit the shrimp for a vegetarian variation on this dish.

4 medium-length green chilies, sliced in rounds
2 medium-sized onions, chopped
1 clove garlic, chopped
¼ teaspoon ground turmeric
½ teaspoon fenugreek, coarsely ground
A few shrimp, peeled and deveined (optional)
1 large purple eggplant (about 1 lb/500 g), chopped or
   mixed Indian vegetables (waxy potatoes; pumpkin;
   winter squash; carrot; green beans)
2 tablespoons grated green mango or fresh lime juice to
   taste
1 cup (250 ml) thin coconut milk
1 cup (250 ml) thick coconut milk
Salt to taste

Place the chilies, onions, garlic, turmeric, fenugreek and shrimp (if using) in the bottom of a saucepan. Add the eggplant (or mixed vegetables) and the grated green mango (if using). Pour the thin coconut milk over the top, without stirring, and cook over low heat. Stir the pot when the vegetable is half-cooked, add the thick coconut milk and salt to taste and cook, stirring gently, until everything is tender.

If you're using lime juice, add it to taste at the end.

AVIAL WHITE CURRY WITH CABBAGE OR SPINACH

Green beans or other green vegetables can be used in place of the cabbage or spinach in this recipe.

1 lb (500 g) cabbage or spinach, finely shredded
1 tablespoon grated fresh coconut
1 clove garlic, chopped (optional)
Pinch of fresh grated ginger or ground ginger (if using
   cabbage only)
5 medium-length green chilies, sliced diagonally
¼ teaspoon ground turmeric

Salt to taste

2 tablespoons oil

2 small onions, finely sliced lengthwise

A few curry leaves

½ teaspoon brown mustard seed

½ –1 cup (125–250 ml) thick coconut milk or water

Mix the vegetable with the coconut, garlic, ginger, green chilies, turmeric and salt. Heat the oil in a pan and fry the onions, curry leaves and mustard seed until the seeds sputter. Add the vegetable mixture and fry for 1 minute, stirring constantly. Add the coconut milk or water and cook the cabbage or other vegetable until it is tender-crisp and there is a small amount of gravy.

VEGETABLES IN THICK COCONUT SAUCE
(Malabar)

This special dish from Southwest India calls for a large amount of vegetables. Include as many Indian-style ones as you can—pumpkin, potatoes, winter squash, yam, purple eggplant and carrots—but not leafy vegetables. It is usually prepared in large quantities for special occasions and is best left to sit and then served at room temperature.

2 lb (1 kg) mixed vegetables, peeled, washed and cut
   into thin strips

8–10 medium-length green chilies, sliced in half

Salt to taste

Pinch of ground turmeric

4 stalks fresh curry leaves or equivalent dried ones

1½ cups (375 ml) grated fresh coconut or 1 cup (250 g)
   dried coconut, steamed (p. 40)

2 cups (500 g) thick yogurt

2 tablespoons oil

Mix the vegetables and chilies together, adding salt to taste and a little turmeric for color. Add just enough boiling water to cook the vegetables (about ½ cup/125 ml). Add the curry leaves, cover and steam gently until just cooked.

Process the coconut until it is finely ground and mix with the yogurt. Add this mixture to the saucepan then stir carefully to mix without breaking up the vegetables. Bring everything to a boil and remove the saucepan from the heat.

Spoon 2 tablespoons of oil over the top (coconut oil is traditionally used).

BITTER MELON CURRY

This dry curry recipe is one instance where commercial Indian fish curry powder from Malaysia is acceptable. Sliced okra also works well for the vegetable.

1 bitter melon or 3 green bell peppers, chopped
1 heaping tablespoon Fish Curry Powder (p. 273)
2–3 tablespoons oil
Salt to taste
Fresh lime juice to taste

Cut the bitter melon (if using) in half lengthwise then slice each half across into fine slices. Soak the slices in salted water to remove the bitter taste. Mix with the curry powder.

Heat the oil in a pan and fry the bitter melon or chopped green bell pepper and curry powder until the vegetable is cooked and dry. Add salt and a squeeze of lime juice to taste and serve.

EGGPLANT SALAD
BRINJAL PUTCHREE

This dish is good with Lamb Biryani, Pilau or Yellow Rice.

1 lb (500 g) cigar-shaped eggplant or large purple eggplant
2 tablespoons oil
1½ teaspoons fenugreek seed
1 medium-sized onion, cut in half across and finely sliced lengthwise
2 tablespoons Fish Curry Powder (p. 273)

1 cup (250 ml) tamarind water made from ½ tablespoon
    tamarind pulp
1 teaspoon sugar, or to taste
Salt to taste

Slice the eggplant and prepare and fry them according to the directions in the recipe for White Curry (p. 290). Remove and drain. In another pan heat 1 tablespoon of oil and fry the fenugreek and onion until the onion is soft and transparent. Add the curry powder and and the eggplant and stir-fry for 2 minutes. Add the tamarind water, sugar and salt to taste and cook until the eggplant is soft and the gravy is thick.

Lentils

Lentil (*dal*) dishes form a regular part of Indian family meals in Malaysia. Historically such dishes have been an important source of protein for south Indian vegetarians from whom the majority of Malaysian Indians trace their origins. Lentil-based dishes may be thick or thin, complimenting the other dishes on the table. They may be plain and spiced or may include vegetables or meat to become the focus of a meal.

LENTIL I

1–2 tablespoons oil or ghee
1 large onion, sliced
2–3 cloves garlic, chopped
2 thick slices fresh ginger root, peeled chopped
2 cloves
2 cardamom pods
1 teaspoon Fish Curry Powder (p. 273)
½ teaspoon ground turmeric
1 cup (250 g) split green lentils (*mung dal*), washed,
    soaked for 15 minutes and drained
2 medium-length green chilies, seeded and cut
    lengthwise
Salt to taste

Heat the oil or ghee in a saucepan and fry the onion, garlic, ginger, cloves and cardamom until the onion is translucent and the mixture is fragrant.

Add the curry powder and turmeric and mix, frying for 1 more minute. Add the lentils, sliced chilies and water to a level 1½-in (3-cm) above the surface (or more if you want a thinner consistency), add salt to taste and cook gently for about 30–45 minutes until the lentils are soft but still whole.

SAMBHAR

Plain lentils may be turned into Sambhar by adding 1 lb (500 g) of Indian vegetables (cubed winter squash, potatoes, yam or eggplant, sliced carrots, pumpkin or green beans) to the recipe above when the lentils are almost cooked. Sometimes thick coconut milk is added toward the end but health conscious Indians tend to substitute chopped tomatoes at this stage if anything at all.

LENTIL II

1½ –2 tablespoons ghee
1 medium-sized onion, cut in half across and thinly sliced lengthwise
1-in (2½-cm) piece fresh ginger root, peeled and chopped
1 teaspoon fenugreek seed
2–3 dried chilies, broken into two
½ cup (125 g) split green lentils (*mung dal*), washed, soaked for 15 minutes and drained
Salt to taste
1 teaspoon garam masala

Heat the ghee in a pan and when it is hot fry the onion, ginger, fenugreek seed and chilies until the onion is brown and crisp. Add the lentils and water to a level about 1½-in (3-cm) above the surface (or more if you want a thinner consistency). Add salt to taste and cook until the lentils are soft. Just before serving stir in 1 teaspoon of garam masala (p. 46).

DHALCHA LENTILS WITH MEAT

This dish may be served as one of a number of dishes in a full Indian meal but is also satisfying on its own with rice and raita for lunch or for an informal family meal.

The final tempering in this recipe is nice but optional as the spices are fragrant from frying them early on.

2–3 tablespoons oil
8 shallots, finely sliced or 2 medium-sized onions, chopped
3 cloves garlic, chopped
8 oz (250 g) lamb, cut into small pieces or cubed
½ cup (125 g) yellow lentils (*toor dal*)
2 cups (500 ml) water
2 medium-sized potatoes, cut into quarters
Tamarind water made from 1 tablespoon tamarind pulp soaked in 1 cup (250 ml) hot water
3 cigar-shaped purple eggplant, cubed
3 medium-sized tomatoes, peeled and diced
3 fresh medium-length green chilies, seeded and cut in half lengthwise
Salt to taste

Spice Paste

1 tablespoon coriander seed or 2 heaping teaspoons ground coriander
1 teaspoon cumin seed or ¾ teaspoon ground cumin
½ teaspoon fennel seed or ½ teaspoon anise
¾ teaspoon ground turmeric
6–8 dried chilies, seeded, soaked in warm water until soft then squeezed dry
Salt to taste
¾-in (2-cm) piece fresh ginger root, peeled and chopped

Tempering (optional)

2 tablespoons oil
1 tablespoon brown mustard seed
4 shallots, finely sliced lengthwise
10 curry leaves, preferably fresh ones

If using whole seeds for the Spice Paste, grind them to a powder. Add the remaining Spice Paste ingredients and grind to a fine paste. Heat 2–3 tablespoons of oil in a saucepan and fry the shallots and garlic until soft.

Add the Spice Paste and fry until fragrant. Add the meat, lentils and 2 cups (500 ml) of water. Bring to a boil and simmer until the lentils are soft but not mushy. Add the potatoes, and when the potatoes are half-cooked add the tamarind water, the rest of the vegetables and salt to taste and simmer until the meat and vegetables are cooked.

If you want to add the Tempering, heat 2 tablespoons of oil in a small pan and fry the Tempering ingredients until golden brown. Pour over the lentils and serve.

ABGOOSHTH

A Muslim version of Lentils with Meat. It too can be served with rice and other dishes but makes a good informal meal on its own accompanied by thick chunks of crusty bread and salad.

1 lb (500 g) lamb, cut into 8 big pieces, and 4 good
    marrow bones if you have them
3 medium-sized onions, chopped
1 cup (250 g) yellow split lentils (*channa dal*), washed
    and soaked in water for 15 minutes
4 large ripe tomatoes, peeled and chopped
1 cinnamon stick
4–5 cardamom pods, broken open
4–5 cloves
A few whole peppercorns
Pinch of salt
Chopped fresh mint to taste
Chopped fresh coriander to taste
Fresh lime juice to taste
2 medium-sized round purple eggplant, sliced thin
Oil for frying
Lime wedges

Put the pieces of meat, bones and all the other ingredients except the egg-plant, lime juice, mint and coriander into a large saucepan. Add 4–6 cups (1–1½ liters) of water (more for a soup-style main dish or less for an accompaniment). Bring to a boil, reduce the heat and add salt to taste. Cover and simmer until the meat and the lentils are soft and cooked. Remove the bones, take the saucepan off the stove and stir in most of the chopped mint and coriander and some lime juice to taste. Meanwhile, fry the eggplant in oil until brown, then drain.

Pour the contents of the saucepan into a large tureen. Arrange the browned eggplant slices on top and garnish with the remaining chopped mint and coriander. Serve with a plate of lime wedges.

Oven-Cooked Meats

FRIED LAMB

This recipe can also be prepared Western-style: dip the meat in egg and breadcrumbs before deep-frying. Serve with rice, potatoes or fries and salad.

2 cloves garlic, chopped
2 tablespoons dark soy sauce
1 tablespoon sugar
1–2 teaspoons vinegar
1 teaspoon ground black pepper
Salt to taste
1 lb (500 g) lamb steaks or escalopes cut from the leg
 or loin of lamb
Oil for deep-frying

Combine all the ingredients except the meat. Marinate the meat in this mixture for several hours. Heat the oil in a wok, drain the meat from the marinade and then deep-fry it until crispy. Serve with rice.

SHAMI KEBABS
(Muslim)

4½ oz (125 g) yellow split lentils (*channa dal*)
1½ teaspoons cumin seed or 1½ teaspoons ground
 cumin
4 cardamom pods or ⅛ teaspoon ground cardamom
5 cloves or ⅛ teaspoon ground cloves
1-in (2½-cm) piece cinnamon stick or ¼ teaspoon ground
 cinnamon

2 medium-sized onions, chopped

4 cloves garlic, chopped

¾-in (2-cm) piece fresh ginger root

1 lb (500 g) lean ground lamb

Salt and pepper to taste

1 egg

¼ cup (65 g) finely chopped mint leaves and fresh
coriander leaves

Oil for deep-frying

Rinse the lentils and soak them in water for 2 hours. Drain and place them in a saucepan. Cover with water and boil until they are soft—about 45 minutes to 1 hour. Drain well. Grind the dried spices to a powder and set it aside. Mash the onions, garlic and ginger to a paste. Add the ground lamb, the spice paste and the dried spices to the lentils, stir together and cook without adding any water or oil until the meat is cooked and the mixture is fairly dry.

When cool, grind the mixture to a fine paste, adding salt and pepper to taste. Beat the egg and mix it with the mint and coriander and the ground lentils and lamb. Heat the oil in a skillet. Shape the mixture into cutlets and deep-fry them in the oil until golden brown. Serve with chutney, lemon twists and salad.

TANDOORI CHICKEN
(North India)

2 lb (1 kg) chicken legs and thighs, skinned

Juice of ½ a lime or lemon

¼ cup (65 g) melted ghee for basting

Marinade

2 teaspoons coriander seed or 1¾ teaspoons ground
coriander

1 teaspoon cumin seed or ¾ teaspoon ground cumin

8 dried chilies, seeded, soaked in warm water until soft
then squeezed dry or 1–2 tablespoons sambal ulek

6 cloves garlic

1-in (2½-cm) piece fresh ginger root, peeled and finely
chopped

½ cup (125 g) yogurt

½ teaspoon mild paprika (for color—optional)

2 teaspoons oil
1 teaspoon vinegar
½ teaspoon Garam Masala (p. 46), plus a little extra for
   garnishing
Salt to taste

Prick the chicken all over with a fork or the point of a sharp knife. Rub the chicken with lime juice and set it aside for 30 minutes.

To prepare the Marinade, grind the coriander and cumin seeds (if using) to a powder. Grind all of the Marinade ingredients together and rub the mixture over the chicken and marinate in the refrigerator for at least two hours, preferably overnight.

Cook the chicken either on a rack in a roasting pan in a moderately hot oven for 40 minutes or so, or on the grill over indirect heat. Turn the pieces frequently, basting with ghee, and sprinkle finely with garam masala.

RAAN ROAST SPICED LEG OF LAMB

6 cloves garlic
1½-in (3-cm) piece fresh ginger root, peeled and finely
   chopped
1–2 teaspoons chili powder, to taste
½ teaspoon ground turmeric
2 tablespoons Garam Masala (p. 46)
1 cup (250 g) yogurt
2 tablespoons ground almonds
3 tablespoons chopped fresh mint
Salt to taste
4 lb (2 kg) leg of lamb, with bone

Mash the garlic and ginger to a fine paste. Mix the paste with the chili powder, turmeric, garam masala, yogurt, almonds, mint and salt to taste. Trim the lamb of all fat and membrane and make deep cuts all over it with a sharp knife. Place the lamb in a shallow cast iron casserole or baking dish and spread the yogurt mixture all over and around it, rubbing it well into the slits. Cover the dish with foil or a lid (or both, if possible) and put it into the refrigerator to marinate for at least 24 hours and preferably for 2 days.

Remove the lamb from the refrigerator and let it come to room temperature (keep it covered). In the meantime, heat the oven to 300°F

(150°C). Put the dish in the oven and cook for 2 hours or until very soft and tender. Raise the temperature to 375°F (190°C), remove the covers and roast the leg for another hour, turning it from time to time and basting it with the marinade juices.

Transfer the meat to a serving plate and let it rest in a warm place for 10 minutes. Meanwhile tilt the oven dish and pour the oil off the top of the spicy sauce. If the sauce is very thick, put the dish over low heat and add sufficient water, stirring constantly, to produce a sauce with thick pouring consistency. Slice the meat at the table and serve the sauce on the side. Serve with Pilau or Yellow Rice, Pepper Water, Eggplant Salad or sautéed vegetables and side dishes.

Sautéed Vegetables

These vegetable dishes are good with hot wet curries, rice and accompaniments and provide variety in vegetarian meals.

SAUTÉED SPINACH

This is good served with lentils.

2–3 tablespoons oil
1 onion, halved and finely sliced lengthwise
1 teaspoon brown mustard seed
1 stalk curry leaves
2 medium-length red chilies, sliced diagonally
1lb (500 g) fresh spinach, washed (not dried) and
    shredded
¼ teaspoon ground turmeric
Salt to taste
3 tablespoons grated fresh or dried unsweetened
    coconut

Heat the oil in a wok. Add the onion, mustard seed and curry leaves and fry until the onion is light brown and the mustard seed sputters. Add the chili and stir to soften a little, then add the spinach, turmeric and salt. Stir well to mix and coat the spinach with oil and spices. Cover and cook until the spinach has wilted and is tender. Uncover and stir until the liquid has evaporated. Sprinkle with grated coconut, stir-fry for another minute and serve.

SAUTÉED OR STEAMED CABBAGE

To sauté cabbage follow the instructions provided in the preceeding recipe for Sautéed Spinach but add a little chopped ginger and garlic and use green chilies instead of red.

To steam the cabbage, select only the green outer leaves of a head of savoy cabbage. Shred the leaves finely and mix with 1 small sliced onion, 3 green chilies, finely sliced, and a pinch of turmeric. Put the mixture in a covered saucepan without any added water and cook over high heat. Be certain that the heat is high enough or the cabbage will release its water and will lose its vivid green color. When it is almost tender-crisp, add 2 tablespoons of grated coconut that has been mixed with a pinch of turmeric. Toss well and continue cooking, stirring constantly. The dish is ready when the coconut is fragrant.

SAUTÉED CAULIFLOWER

The cardamom used in this recipe makes for an interesting departure from mustard seed.

3 tablespoons oil
1 stalk curry leaves
1 cardamom pod
1 onion, chopped
1 clove garlic, chopped
3 green chilies, chopped
½ head of cauliflower, cut into florets
¼ teaspoon ground turmeric
Salt to taste
½ cup (125 ml) water
3 tablespoons grated fresh or dried unsweetened
    coconut

Heat the oil in a wok and fry the curry leaves and the cardamom until the curry leaves are brown. Add the onion, the garlic and the chilies and stir-fry until fragrant. Add the cauliflower, turmeric and salt. Stir to mix and coat the cauliflower with oil and spices. Add the water, cover and cook until the cauliflower is tender. Remove the lid and cook until any remaining water evaporates. Add the grated coconut and stir-fry for another minute before serving.

SAUTÉED PUMPKIN

2 tablespoons oil
1 teaspoon brown mustard seed
1 stalk curry leaves
1 onion, chopped
1 clove garlic (optional)
3–4 medium-length green chilies
1 lb (500 g) pumpkin, peeled and cubed
½ teaspoon ground turmeric
Salt to taste
½ cup (125 ml) water (or a little more)
3 tablespoons grated fresh or dried unsweetened
   coconut

Heat the oil in a wok. Add the mustard seed and curry leaves and fry until the mustard seed sputters and the curry leaves are brown. Add the onion, garlic and green chilies and stir-fry until the onion is transparent. Add the pumpkin and stir to coat with oil and spices. Add the turmeric, salt and water, stir, cover and simmer until the pumpkin is cooked but not soft and the water has evaporated (remove the lid at the end if necessary to achieve this). Sprinkle with the coconut, mix well and stir-fry for another minute before serving.

SAUTÉED POTATOES

Sautéed Potatoes go very well with coconut milk curries.

3 tablespoons oil
1 teaspoon brown mustard seed
1 stalk curry leaves
1 onion, halved across and thickly sliced lengthwise
1 medium-length green chili, sliced diagonally
1 teaspoon ground red chili (for color), or more to taste
1 lb (500 g) small potatoes, peeled and quartered
Juice of ½ lime

Heat the oil in a pan. Add the mustard seed and curry leaves and fry until the seeds sputter. Add onion and green chili and stir-fry until the onion is transparent. Add the ground chili and the potatoes and stir to mix and coat the potatoes with the oil and spices. Continue to cook until the potatoes are a little crusty. Just before serving squeeze fresh lime juice over the top to taste.

Accompaniments

The ideal Indian meal should include five tastes: sweet, sour, hot, salty and bitter. Cool and crisp dishes should also be included. Accompaniments and side dishes help to add the missing tastes that the main dishes leave out.

Salads

CUCUMBER SALAD

1 cucumber, about 8 in (20 cm) long
1 green chili, finely sliced
3 shallots, finely sliced
Splash of thin coconut milk
Salt to taste
Fresh lime juice to taste (optional)

Cut a small slice off one end of the cucumber and rub the two cut surfaces together in a circular motion for about 30 seconds, to remove any bitterness. Peel the cucumber, slice it in half lengthwise and remove the seeds, then score the outside with a fork and slice it finely.

Toss the cucumber, chili and shallots together and place them in a serving dish. Pour a small amount of thin coconut milk (enough for the salad to sit in) over the cucumber and refrigerate it until you are ready to serve it. Add salt and a squeeze of fresh lime juice (if desired) just before serving.

ONION AND COCONUT SALAD

This salad is a perfect accompaniment to Lamb Biryani.

Slice small Spanish onions very thin, lengthwise. Mix with grated fresh or dried unsweetened coconut that has been finely ground, adding salt and lime juice to taste.

TOMATO AND ONION SALAD

This is a good everyday dish. Diced cucumber can also be added.

Peel and mix an equal amount of diced tomatoes and finely chopped onions. Toss with sliced green chilies, chopped fresh coriander leaves, salt, black pepper and lime juice to taste.

Alternatively, if you want a sweet flavor, combine 3 large chopped tomatoes and 3 chopped onions in a bowl. Mix 3 tablespoons of white vinegar with 1½ tablespoons of sugar and cook over medium heat until the sugar dissolves. Cool, add a little water to dilute and pour over the tomato and onion mixture. Add chopped fresh coriander leaves and toss. Refrigerate until you are ready to serve.

CRISP SALAD PLATE

Peel Spanish onions and daikon and slice them into thin rings. Combine the onions and daikon with chopped unpeeled cucumber and arrange on a plate with or without the addition of lime juice and salt.

Coolers

CUCUMBER RAITA
(North India)

1 medium-sized cucumber, peeled and cut into four
   lengthwise, seeds removed
1 onion, finely chopped
1 clove garlic, chopped
Freshly ground black pepper
1 cup (250 g) thick yogurt
Salt to taste
¼ teaspoon chili powder
Chopped fresh coriander leaves or ground cumin

Slice the cucumber thin or, if you prefer, grate it. Mix the cucumber, onion, garlic, black pepper and yogurt together and refrigerate for a few hours. Add the salt just before serving in order to avoid drawing water out of the cucumber. Garnish with a sprinkle of the chili powder and finely chopped fresh coriander leaves or ground cumin.

ZUCCHINI RAITA

Grate some small zucchini into a bowl and toss with thin sour cream and a dash of pepper to produce a dish with the consistency of coleslaw. Chill in the refrigerator and add salt just before serving.

POTATO PACHADI
(South India)

Pachadi is the southern counterpart of raita. Though it is cooked, it provides a smooth and cooling effect when paired with a meal of hot, spicy southern food.

4 potatoes, boiled, drained and coarsely mashed
3–4 medium-length green chilies, seeded and finely
    chopped
6 shallots or 1 large onion, finely chopped
1 thin slice fresh ginger root, peeled and mashed to a
    paste
Fresh grated or dried unsweetened coconut
Salt to taste
½ –1 cup (125–250 g) yogurt, beaten

Mix the potatoes, chilies, shallots and ginger together. Add sufficient grated coconut, stirring, to produce the consistency of thick porridge. Add salt to taste and the yogurt and mix well. May be served as is or reheated.

For a variation, add a tempering of 2 stems of fresh curry leaves (or the equivalent dried ones), 1 teaspoon of brown mustard seed and 2 broken dried chilies, fried in a little oil. Pour over the Potato Pachadi, heat and serve.

MARROW OR WINTER MELON PACHADI
(Malabar)

This is another cooling vegetable dish similar to Potato Pachadi.

6 medium-length green chilies, finely chopped or 1
    teaspoon ground chili

3-in (8-cm) slice of large marrow or winter melon, peeled
and diced
Salt to taste
A few curry leaves
1 cup (250 g) thick, sour yogurt (at least 3 days old)
2 teaspoons brown mustard seed, coarsely ground
½ of a fresh coconut, ground fine or 1 cup (250 g) dried
unsweetened coconut, steamed (p. 52) and then finely
ground
¼ teaspoon mustard seed
Dried chili, chopped or coarsely ground
3–4 stems of fresh curry leaves or a handful of dried,
chopped curry leaves
Oil

Mix the chilies with the melon and salt to taste in a saucepan and add just enough boiling water to cook the melon. When the melon is lightly cooked, add the curry leaves, remove the saucepan from the stove, cover, and set aside. Mix the yogurt, mustard seed and all but a handful of the coconut together. Pour this over the vegetable and mix well. Reheat or leave at room temperature.

Take another handful of coconut, mix it with ½ teaspoon of mustard seed, chopped dried chili and curry leaves. Fry this mixture in a little oil and add to the vegetable before serving.

Sambol and Chutneys

There are many kinds of Indian sambol and fresh chutneys that are served as an accompaniment to a main dish. A wide variety of fruit, vegetables or herbs lend themselves to treatment in these ways.

COCONUT SAMBOL

1 cup (250 g) finely grated fresh coconut or steamed
dried coconut (p. 52)
3–6 medium-length green chilies, chopped
1 medium-sized onion, chopped
Salt to taste
½ –1 tablespoon fresh lime juice, to taste

Grind all the ingredients together, adding the lime juice last and a little water if necessary to keep everything turning.

COCONUT CHUTNEY

3–4 medium-length green chilies, chopped
½-in (1-cm) piece fresh ginger root, peeled and chopped
2 cloves garlic, sliced
1 cup (250 g) grated fresh coconut or steamed dried
  coconut (p. 52)
3 tablespoons finely chopped fresh coriander leaves
1–2 teaspoons fresh lime juice
Salt to taste

Grind the chilies, ginger and garlic to a paste. Add the coconut, coriander leaves and lime juice and blend well. Add water to moisten and salt to taste.

GREEN MANGO SAMBOL

½ cup (125 g) or more grated fresh coconut to taste or
  steamed dried coconut (p. 52)
½ cup (125 g) chopped green mango
2 medium-length red or green chilies
6 fresh curry leaves
Salt to taste

Grind all the ingredients to a fine paste. Serve with rice and other dishes.

TOMATO SAMBOL

Tomato Sambol is very good with Pilau, Kitchree or Yellow Rice.

4 large, ripe tomatoes, peeled and diced
4 medium-length green chilies, finely chopped
1 large onion, finely chopped
1 tablespoon finely grated fresh coconut or steamed
  dried coconut (p. 52)

Mix everything together and cook to a pulp.

MINT OR MINT AND CORIANDER CHUTNEY

This fresh chutney frequently accompanies any Indian meal and is good served as a dip for fried appetizers as well.

1 bunch of mint leaves, or a small handful each of mint
   and coriander leaves, mixed
3–6 medium-length green chilies
2 cloves garlic (optional)
2–3 tablespoons fresh lime juice or tamarind water to taste
Salt to taste

Grind the leaves, chilies, garlic and lime juice or tamarind water to a smooth paste, adding a little water if necessary to keep everything moving. Add salt to taste.

TOMATO CHUTNEY

Tomato Chutney stores well. Other chutneys that keep, such as mango chutney, are readily available in jars. Keeping them on hand helps to provide variety to the dishes you serve. A sweet mango chutney goes particularly well with north Indian lamb dishes.

4 lb (2 kg) ripe tomatoes, peeled and quartered
3 cloves garlic, finely chopped
1-in (2½-cm) piece fresh ginger root, peeled and finely
   chopped
2–3 tablespoons ground chili
1 tablespoon salt
1 cup (250 g) golden raisins
1 lb (500 g) sugar
2½ cups (600 ml) malt vinegar

Put the tomatoes, garlic, ginger, chili and salt into a saucepan and cook the tomatoes almost to a pulp (they should still be chunky). Add the golden raisins, sugar and vinegar and cook until thick. Cool and bottle.

Pickles

The pickle recipes given here need to be enjoyed within a few days. You can purchase jarred pickles to have on hand to ensure variety. Lime pickle is particularly good.

PINEAPPLE PICKLE

This pickle should be served right away, and should not be kept for more than 2–3 days.

1 medium-sized sweet pineapple, peeled and diced
2 teaspoons ground chili
1 tablespoon brown mustard seed
1 clove garlic
2 slices fresh ginger root, peeled and coarsely chopped
Pinch of ground turmeric
¾ cup (200 ml) white vinegar (or vinegar diluted with a
    little water to taste if you wish)
Salt to taste

Grind all the spices together with a little vinegar. Add the remaining vinegar, the pineapple and salt and mix well.

EGGPLANT PICKLE
(Sri Lanka)

This pickle will keep for a week in the refrigerator.

½-in (1½-cm) piece fresh ginger root, peeled and
    coarsely chopped
3 cloves garlic, sliced
28 shallots—2 sliced, the rest peeled and left whole
½ cup mustard seed
Pinch of ground turmeric
5 medium-length red chilies
Oil for deep-frying
1¼ lb (600 g) long purple eggplant, cut 1½ x ¾-in
    (4 x 2-cm) pieces
10 medum-length green chilies

1 small onion, halved and finely sliced lengthwise
Ground chili to taste
Sugar to taste
Salt to taste
Up to 1 cup (250 ml) white vinegar

Grind the ginger, garlic, the two sliced shallots, the mustard seed, ground turmeric and the fresh red chilies to a fine paste then set it aside.

Heat the oil in a wok and deep-fry the eggplant pieces until they turn brown. Remove and drain. Fry the shallots until they are transparent, drain and set them aside. Fry the green chilies until they change color and are slightly cooked and drain them too. Remove all but 2 tablespoons of oil from the pan and fry the sliced onion and the chili paste until they are fragrant, adding ground chili to taste. Add a little water, sugar, salt and vinegar to taste. Simmer for 5 minutes, then add the fried eggplant, shallots and chilies. Mix and simmer until the liquid thickens a little.

Regular Fresh Accompaniments

Always serve the following accompaniments with a curry alongside a chutney, a pickle and a cooling salad.

- Slice some banana and mix it with grated fresh or dried coconut.
- Grate or mash some fresh ginger root into a small dish, add a little sugar and a squeeze of fresh lime juice to taste.
- Mash some fresh garlic with salt and place in a small dish.

Rice, One-dish Meals and Breads

Rice

Various savory and fancy rice dishes appear in Indian cuisine, sometimes as accompaniments to other dishes, sometimes substantial enough to be a meal on their own, accompanied by side dishes only. The recipes here appear in ascending order of richness.

"OLD" RICE
Yesterday's rice, treated this way, makes the perfect accompaniment to yesterday's curries, particularly Fish Curry with Coconut Milk (p. 277).

At the end of an evening rice meal, give the rice left in the pot a good stir to loosen it, cover it well with cold water and set is aside overnight. The next day drain it and reheat it.

PEA PILAU

Pretty and perfumed but not too rich, this is good with a special curry meal. You can omit the vegetable if you like.

1 onion cut across and finely sliced lengthwise, or packaged fried onion flakes
3 tablespoons ghee or 2 tablespoons oil and 1 tablespoon ghee, for flavor
4 cloves
2-in (5-cm) piece of cinnamon stick, splintered
4 cardamom pods, broken open
2 cups (500 g) Basmati rice, washed, soaked for 2 hours and drained
2¼ cups (565 ml) water
1 cup (250 g) shelled young or frozen peas or grated carrot
½ cup (125 g) slivered almonds

If you are using fresh onion, heat the combined ghee and oil in a pan or a wok and fry the slices until they are brown and crisp. Drain and set them aside.

Reheat the ghee and oil in a heavy saucepan and fry the spices for a minute. Add the rice and fry, stirring until the rice is translucent. Add water and cook covered until the water has evaporated. Reduce the heat to low, add the peas, cover, and cook for 10 minutes. Remove the pan from the stove, wrap in a kitchen towel and set aside to steam. Just before serving stir in the almonds and garnish with fried onion flakes.

KITCHREE

(Serves 8 as an accompaniment, 4 as a luncheon dish)

Kitchree usually goes with north Indian meat curries but is elegant enough to serve just with salad and side dishes for a simple lunch.

4 cloves garlic, crushed
1-in (2½-cm) piece fresh ginger root, peeled and
  chopped
½ cup (125 g) ghee or butter
2 medium-sized onions, cut in half across and thinly
  sliced lengthwise
4 cardamom pods, broken open
2-in (5-cm) piece cinnamon stick, splintered
6 cloves
¼ teaspoon peppercorns
3 cups (750 g) Basmati rice, washed and drained
Pinch of ground turmeric
6 cups (1½ liters) boiling water
1 cup lentils (*masoor dal*), washed, soaked in water for
  at least 1 hour and drained
2–3 tablespoons milk
Chopped fresh coriander leaves for garnish
2 hard-boiled eggs, sliced or coarsely chopped

Mash the garlic and ginger to a smooth paste.

Heat the ghee in a large heavy saucepan, and when it is hot fry the onions, ginger and garlic paste and the whole spices until the onions are soft. Add the drained rice and the turmeric and fry it, stirring constantly, until the grains are translucent. Add the boiling water and let it boil rapidly, uncovered. When the rice is half-cooked (about 5–10 minutes), add the drained lentils and continue to cook until the water has evaporated. Take the saucepan off the stove, cover it with a tight-fitting lid, wrap it in a kitchen towel and set it aside to steam for an hour or so.

Before serving, sprinkle the rice with the milk. Serve garnished with the chopped fresh coriander leaves and the hard-boiled eggs.

YELLOW RICE

Yellow Rice goes well with dry chicken curries, chutneys and sambols.

2 cups (500 g) Basmati rice, washed and drained
Coconut milk
½ teaspoon ground turmeric
1 cinnamon stick, splintered
4 cardamom pods, broken open
2–3 tablespoons ghee or butter
1 large onion, cut in half across then finely sliced
   lengthwise
¼ cup (65 g) raw cashew nuts
¼ cup (65 g) raisins

Put the rice in a saucepan with about 2 in (5 cm) of coconut milk. Add the turmeric, cinnamon stick and cardamom pods, stir, and cook according to the evaporation method (p. 14), stirring occasionally to prevent the rice from sticking to the bottom of the pan.

When the rice is cooked, heat the ghee or butter in a pan and fry the onion and the cashew nuts until they are golden brown, adding the raisins and frying them until they puff up. Sprinkle the nuts and raisins on top of the rice and serve.

(Serves 12) LAMB BIRYANI

2-in (5-cm) piece fresh ginger root
6 cloves garlic
Salt to taste
2 cups (500 g) yogurt
3½ lb (1¾ kg) lamb, cubed

1 tablespoon coriander seed or 2½ teaspoons ground coriander

1 teaspoon cumin seed or 1 teaspoon ground cumin

1 cup (250 g) ghee

4 onions, cut in half across and then finely sliced lengthwise

½ cup (125 g) blanched almonds, finely ground

Rice

2 onions, cut in half across and then finely sliced lengthwise

1 small piece of cinnamon stick, broken

8 whole cloves

1 teaspoon salt

5 cups (1¼ kg) Basmati rice, washed until clear and soaked for 1 hour

6 cardamom pods

2-in (5-cm) piece cinnamon stick

1 teaspoon black cumin seed

¼ teaspoon ground nutmeg

1 cup (250 ml) milk

Pinch of saffron or 1 teaspoon ground turmeric

Juice of 1 lime

6 medium-length green chilies, cut into two pieces

A handful of mint and fresh coriander leaves, coarsely chopped

Extra Garnishes (optional)

2 tablespoons raw cashew nuts

2 tablespoons golden raisins

3 tablespoons ghee

Mash or grind the ginger, garlic and salt to a fine paste. Mix with 2 tablespoons of yogurt to make a marinade. Mix this with the meat and marinate for 2 hours or more. In the meantime roast the coriander and cumin seeds (if using). Cool, grind them to a powder and set aside.

Heat the ghee in a pan and fry the 2 sliced onions to be used as garnish for the rice until brown and crisp. Remove, drain on paper towel and set aside, leaving the ghee in the pan. Reheat the ghee and fry the remaining onions until golden. Lift out with a slotted spoon and set aside.

Pour out all but 4 tablespoons of the remaining ghee. Reheat it and stir-fry the ground almonds, coriander and cumin and the marinated meat until the meat is seared on all sides and the spices are fragrant. Add the rest of the yogurt, mix everything well and cook, uncovered, until the meat is tender and the gravy is fairly dry. Add a little water if the dish becomes too dry before the meat is tender. Set aside (the flavor will mature if left overnight in the refrigerator before you prepare the rice).

To prepare the Rice, bring about three-quarters of a large saucepan of water to a boil. Tie the cinnamon stick and the cloves in a piece of cheesecloth and add it to the water with salt. Add the rice and parboil for about 8 minutes then drain well. Discard the spices and set the rice aside to cool.

Lightly grease a deep casserole dish. Spread half the rice in a layer on the bottom of the dish, spread the cooked meat on top of this, and the onions on top of the meat. Cover with the second half of the Rice.

Heat the oven to 400°F (200°C). Grind the cardamom pods, the cinnamon stick, the black cumin and the nutmeg to a powder. Warm the milk and add the saffron or turmeric, the ground spices and the lime juice. Pour this mixture over the rice in the casserole and scatter the chilies, fried onions, mint and coriander leaves over the top. Cover the pot with foil and a tight-fitting lid, making sure that it is tightly sealed. Put the casserole into the oven for 10–15 minutes. Remove, wrap in a kitchen towel and set aside for 30 minutes.

Alternatively, you may prefer to reserve the mint and coriander leaves and scatter them over the top just before serving, along with some cashew nuts and golden raisins fried in ghee.

Serve accompanied by an Onion and Coconut Salad (p. 303) and/or Tomato and Onion Salad (p. 304), Cucumber Raita (p. 304), a sambol, some pickles and chutneys, some banana and coconut.

Breads

I have not included the conventional Indian breads that go with north Indian food such as naan, chapati, paratha or puri as they are not often cooked at home, and recipes, if they are needed, can readily be found in almost any mainstream Indian cookbook. The following recipe, on the other hand, was specifically created by Indian hawkers in Malaysia. There is no exact counterpart in India and it has become a favorite in modern Malaysian and Singaporean cuisine.

ROTI CANAI
(Street Food)

1 lb (500 g) all-purpose flour
1 teaspoon salt
1 egg, beaten
3 tablespoons softened butter or ghee
Pinch of sugar, or to taste (optional)
¾ –1 cup (200–250 ml) warm water or milk

Sift the flour and salt together. Add the egg, butter, sugar and a little milk at a time, kneading until you have a soft dough. Gather up into a ball and put in a greased bowl and cover with plastic wrap to prevent it from drying out. Set aside for a few hours or overnight.

Divide the dough into 8 balls. Flatten and pat each one down with your fingers to a 5-in (12-cm) round, sprinkling or brushing with oil as you go.

At this point the cooks on the street stalls in Malaysia do some very showy lifting and tossing over their heads and back on to an oiled surface about a dozen times until the dough is stretched into a very thin membrane about 18 in (45 cm) in diameter. Without aspiring to perform this difficult feat, you should be able (if you oil your fingers well) to work the dough out as thinly as possible into a wide circle. Fold four pieces inwards around the circumference, pressing them down a little, then fold again at the four points you have created. You should end up with a round shape about 6 in (15 cm) in diameter. Bake, folded side down, in a greased heavy pan or on a griddle, brushing with a little ghee as you turn it to make the surface turn golden brown. The folds will give a layered quality that is an important part of this scone-like roti. Serve hot with a bowl of curry or lentils.

EURASIAN

Within the pluralist cultures of Malaysia and Singapore, the Eurasians are a social group that proudly expresses a distinct culinary tradition. The Eurasians trace their inheritance to Malacca in Portuguese and Dutch times. Eurasian food is a happy mixture of many cuisines, but especially of Indian, Malay, Chinese and European.

Celine de Souza of Singapore, who provided me with this small sample of Eurasian recipes, includes a mixture of Portuguese, Malay and Dutch in her ancestry.

EURASIAN MULLIGATAWNY SOUP

1 chicken
2–4 tablespoons Mulligatawny Soup Powder
1 thick slice fresh ginger root
2 cloves garlic, sliced
3 shallots, sliced
Fresh curry leaves
Salt
Juice of 2 limes, or more to taste
Croutons
Fried onion flakes

Mulligatawny Soup Powder
3 tablespoons coriander seed or 2½ tablespoons ground
    coriander
1 tablespoon cumin seed or ¾ tablespoon ground cumin
1 tablespoon fennel seed or anise
1 teaspoon whole black peppercorns or ½ teaspoon freshly
    ground black pepper
¼ teaspoon ground turmeric
2 cloves or ¼ teaspoon ground cloves
½-in (1-cm) piece cinnamon stick or ¼ teaspoon cinnamon
1 teaspoon brown mustard seed
6 dried chilies, seeded, soaked in warm water until soft
    and squeezed dry

Cover the chicken with water, bring to a boil and poach until tender.

Remove the chicken and shred the meat, setting it aside and returning the bones to the water. Simmer for 2 hours to make a concentrated stock.

To make the Mulligatawny Soup Powder, grind the ingredients together to a fine powder.

Strain the stock into a small saucepan, bring to a boil and add Mulligatawny Soup Powder to taste. Grind the ginger, garlic and shallots to a fine paste and add to the boiling soup with shredded chicken, a generous amount of curry leaves and salt to taste. Return to a boil and add enough lime juice to make the soup pleasantly sour. Serve the soup in individual bowls, garnished with croutons and fried onion flakes.

SEMUR STEW

Popular in Indonesia, this stew probably originates from Malacca. The cooking style for this recipe is European but its spicing is Asian.

1 lb (500 g) pork, diced
1 lb (500 g) beef, diced
1 tablespoon oil
1 large onion, cut into 8 wedges
1 small cinnamon stick
1 star anise
Pinch of ground nutmeg
3–4 potatoes, cut into chunks
1 tablespoon white vinegar, or to taste
Sugar to taste

Marinade
1 slice fresh ginger root
3 cloves garlic
1 tablespoon dark soy sauce
½ teaspoon cornstarch
Pepper to taste

To make the Marinade, crush the ginger and garlic to a paste and add the soy sauce, cornstarch and pepper. Add the meat and marinate for 1 hour.

Heat the oil in a saucepan and sauté the onion until golden. Add the cinnamon stick, star anise and nutmeg and continue frying until fragrant. Add the meat and the marinade and stir-fry until it changes color. Add water to cover and simmer, covered, until the meat is almost cooked. Add the potatoes (and more water if desired), the vinegar and sugar to taste and continue cooking over low heat until the potatoes are cooked. Serve with rice and Shrimp Paste Sambal.

DEVIL CURRY

1 chicken, cut into pieces
4–5 tablespoons oil
1 large onion, sliced
½-in (1¼-cm) piece fresh ginger root, peeled and sliced
3 cloves garlic, sliced
1–1½ cups (250–375 ml) water
1½ teaspoons brown mustard seed, ground and mixed with water
¼ cup (65 ml) white vinegar, or to taste
1–2 teaspoons sugar, to taste
3 potatoes, quartered
Salt to taste

Marinade
1 teaspoon light soy sauce
1 teaspoon dark soy sauce
Dash of Worcestershire sauce
Pepper to taste

Spice Paste
30 medium-sized dried chilies, seeded, soaked in warm water until soft and squeezed dry
10 shallots
3 cloves garlic
½-in (1¼-cm) piece fresh ginger root, peeled and coarsely chopped
½ teaspoon ground turmeric

Grind the Spice Paste ingredients to a paste.

Mix all the Marinade ingredients together, add the chicken pieces and mix thoroughly. Set aside for 30 minutes. Heat the oil in a wok and fry the onion, ginger and garlic until golden and fragrant, then add the Spice Paste and stir-fry until everything smells fragrant. Add the chicken and its marinade and fry for a few minutes. As it cooks dry, add water to cover (about 1–1½ cups/250–375 ml) and simmer until the chicken is nearly cooked. Add the mustard, the vinegar, the sugar to taste and the potatoes and continue cooking until the potatoes are tender. Add salt to taste.

CHICKEN KAPITAN

3 tablespoons oil
1 medium-sized onion, cut into 4 wedges
1 chicken, cut into bite-sized pieces or chicken thigh cut
  the Thai way (p. 24)
Salt to taste
1–2 teaspoons fresh lime juice
Pinch of sugar (optional)

Spice Paste
30 medium-sized dried chilies, or to taste, seeded,
  soaked in warm water and squeezed dry
15 shallots
6 candlenuts

Grind the Spice Paste ingredients to a fine paste. Heat the oil in a wok and fry the onion wedges until soft, then add the Spice Paste and fry until fragrant. Add the chicken and stir-fry until brown and coated with the spices. Add salt to taste, the lime juice, sugar (if using) and a splash of water if necessary. Continue cooking on low heat until the chicken is tender and the gravy is dry.

FENG CURRY

Feng is a special dish eaten at Christmas by Portuguese Eurasians. The authentic version uses offal, although I have substituted pork.

3 tablespoons oil
1½-in (3-cm) piece fresh ginger root, peeled and shredded
2 lb (1 kg) pork, cubed
1½ cups (375 ml) pork or vegetable stock
1½ tablespoons vinegar, or to taste
Salt to taste

Spice Paste
2 tablespoons coriander seed or 1¾ tablespoons ground coriander
2–3 teaspoons cumin seed or 2–3 teaspoons ground cumin
2–3 teaspoons fennel seed or anise
2 teaspoons white peppercorns or 1 teaspoon ground white pepper
½ teaspoon ground turmeric
3 cloves garlic
7 shallots, sliced

If using whole spices for the Spice Paste, grind them to a powder. Add the remaining Spice Paste ingredients and grind, adding a little water if necessary, to make a paste.

Heat the oil in a wok and fry the ginger until light brown. Remove, drain and set aside. Add the Spice Paste and fry until fragrant. Add the meat and mix well. Add enough stock to simmer and cook over low heat until the meat is tender and the gravy is thick. Add the fried ginger, the vinegar and salt to taste. Serve with white rice or Pilau.

SOME MIXED APPETIZERS

People who order appetizers before a meal in Malaysian or Singaporean restaurants are likely to be offered a choice which ranges across the cuisines of all the different communities. It is a pattern I have followed here in this small collection of classics.

SPRING ROLLS
(Chinese)

Chinese spring rolls from Singapore are usually bigger than the Vietnamese ones and contain ingredients that are still distinct rather than mixed as in the latter case.

Filling
4 tablespoons peanut oil
8 oz (250 g) pork, shredded or ground
8 oz (250 g) shrimp, peeled, deveined and chopped
8 oz (250 g) crab meat
5 Chinese mushrooms, soaked, stems discarded and
   caps chopped
8 oz (250 g) bamboo shoots, drained and shredded, or
   washed bean sprouts
1 teaspoon finely chopped fresh ginger root
1–2 teaspoons sugar to taste
2 tablespoons oyster sauce
1 tablespoon light soy sauce
10 green onions, sliced
Oil for deep-frying

Wrappers
1 packet large spring roll wrappers
2 tablespoons cornstarch mixed with 1 tablespoon water

Heat the peanut oil and stir-fry the pork until it changes color. Add the shrimp, crab, Chinese mushrooms and bamboo shoots, then the ginger, sugar and the sauces and stir-fry until everything is lightly cooked and fairly dry (you may add 1–2 teaspoons of cornstarch dissolved in water if you feel you need to). Add the sliced green onions and give the mixture a final stir before removing it from the pan. Set aside to cool.

Place sufficient filling toward the edge of large spring roll skins (commercially bought), tuck in the ends and roll up, sealing each roll with the cornstarch paste. Alternatively, use small spring roll skins if you wish. Roll these up diagonally, folding in the two sides then sealing the last end as before.

Heat the oil for deep-frying in a wok and fry the rolls until they are golden brown. Drain and serve immediately with dishes of soy sauce, chili sauce or plum sauce for dipping.

SHRIMP TOAST
(Chinese)

8 oz (250 g) shrimp, peeled and deveined
½ oz (15 g) pork fat or 1 tablespoon oil
½ oz (15 g) bamboo shoots, finely chopped
1 clove garlic
¼ teaspoon sugar
Pinch each of salt and pepper
2 tablespoons cornstarch
1 egg white
A few thin slices of white bread
Ham cut into short strips for garnish (optional)
Oil for deep-frying

Rub the shrimp with salt, rinse and dry. Cut the pork fat (if using) into very small cubes (the size of peppercorns). Using a food processor or two cleavers grind these to a fine paste. Add the bamboo shoots, garlic, sugar, salt, pepper, cornstarch and egg white and mix well.

Cut the bread either diagonally or into four rounds using a cookie cutter. Spread the shrimp paste on one side. Garnish with strips of ham pressed into the top if you wish.

Heat the oil and deep-fry, spread side down until golden brown. Turn over and brown the other side. Remove and drain.

VADAY
(Indian)

This is a particularly good appetizer to serve with drinks or at a cocktail party.

1 lb (500 g) black gram lentils (*ooloonthu dal*), soaked
   in water overnight and drained
2 medium-sized onions, finely chopped
2–3 medium-length green chilies, sliced
Small piece fresh ginger root, peeled and chopped
Salt to taste
Oil for deep-frying

Grind the soaked lentils and set aside for an hour or so. Add the onions, chilies, ginger and salt to taste. Form the mixture into 1½-in (3-cm) balls and flatten on an oiled surface, to prevent sticking. Heat the oil and deep-fry the balls until crisp. Drain on paper towel and serve with chutney.

For a special occasion, press a peeled whole shrimp into each savory before deep-frying.

FRIED CURRY PUFFS
(Indian)

The pastry for Fried Curry Puffs may be made with or without coconut cream.

Pastry
8 oz (250 g) all-purpose flour, sifted
¼ teaspoon salt
½ cup (125 g) coconut cream or 3 oz (75 g) soft butter
3 oz (100 ml) water

Curry filling
1 tablespoon oil
1 medium-sized onion, finely chopped
8 oz (250 g) lean lamb, beef or chicken, finely chopped
   or ground
2 tablespoons commercial Malaysian Indian meat curry
   powder
½ teaspoon coarsely ground black pepper

Salt to taste
1 large potato, boiled, peeled and diced
Oil for deep-frying

Sift the flour and salt together. Add the coconut cream or butter and then water, and lightly knead into a soft dough. Set aside to rest for 15 minutes or so. Roll out thinly and cut into circles about 3 in (8 cm) across.

Heat 1 tablespoon of oil in a pan and fry the onion until golden. Add the meat, curry powder and pepper. Stir until everything is well mixed and the meat has changed color. Add salt to taste and a little water. Cook for 5 minutes—until the meat is done and the curry is dry. Add the potatoes and stir thoroughly to mix. Set aside to cool.

Place a little filling on each pastry round, fold over into a semi-circle and crimp edges to seal. Deep-fry in plenty of hot oil until golden brown. Drain and serve hot or cool, accompanied by a bowl of mint chutney for dipping.

Frozen ready-made flaky or puff pastry may be used instead of the one given above, but in this case the curry puffs should be cooked in the oven.

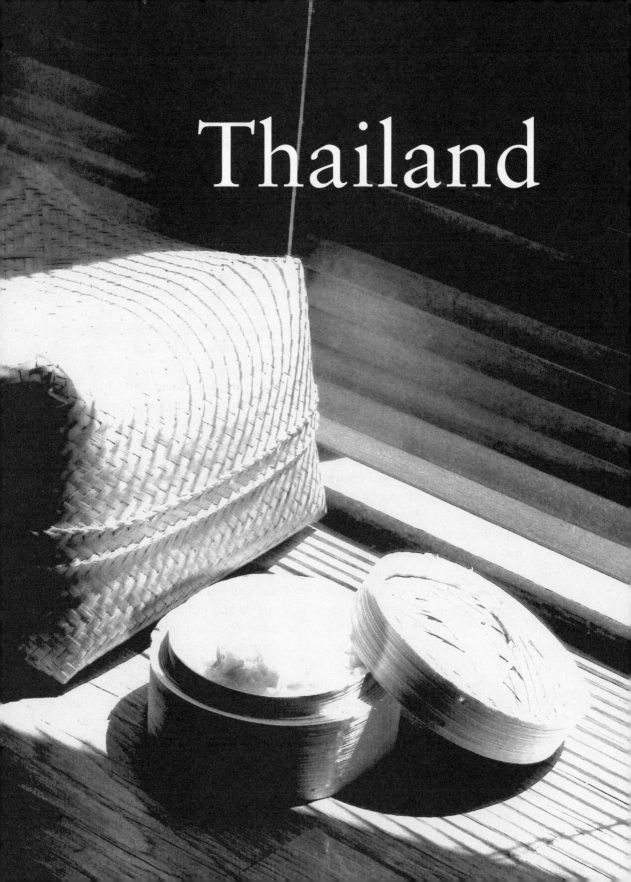

Thailand

Of all Southeast Asian cuisines, Thai is the one that most captures the Western imagination today. Thai food is generally perceived as a winner on a number of levels: its flavors are subtle and complex yet at the same time clean, vivid and distinct; it is visually enticing and delicately perfumed; it is light, healthy and well-balanced.

True though it may be in general terms, the prevailing perception is often a Bangkok-centered one. It is the impression you get when you eat in hotels in Thailand or in Thai restaurants throughout the rest of the world, where the cooks almost invariably come from Bangkok.

Unquestionably, Thai cuisine is unique. It offers a range of flavors across the country unmatched by any other single cuisine in Southeast Asia—indeed by few in the world. But the way you describe Thai food needs to vary significantly according to the part of the country you are considering. A broad general statement such as the one above fails to give proper credit to the variety and distinctiveness of Thailand's regional cuisines.

Cooking in the north, for example, emphasizes forest and upland foods. Meat and game (traditionally the harvest of hunting) are accompanied by uncultivated herbs and fresh raw leaves, often bitter ones from forest plants. Food here is generally meaty and robust, and may be mild or hot and salty. Coconut milk is not used at all and sugar only sparingly. Dishes are accompanied by sticky (glutinous) rice rather than plain rice.

The central plains have a very different cuisine from that of the north. Food in the central plains is built on the products of the paddy, the village, the waterways of the delta of the Chao Phraya River, the wet market and the permanent garden. This area is the country's rice bowl. Not only does it produce an abundance of fragrant rice but there are plenty of things to go with it: fish from the paddies and waterways, vegetables in huge variety from the village, fields and house plot—all existing in a setting of fecund growth. There are limes and other sour fruits, fresh rice noodles, spices and small amounts of meat bought in local markets when harvests are good and money is around, plenty of palms for palm sugar and some coconuts. This is the country of the aromatic soup, of eggplants, beans and all manner of fresh greens served with chili relishes, of cultivated vegetables stir-fried with small amounts of meat from the market, of eggs, small fish from the klongs and of coconut milk curries cooked for special occasions.

Cuisine in the northeast is different again. The northeast is dry, flat, chronically poor and unproductive country. The population is culturally Lao and the cuisine is closer to that of neighboring Laos than to "mainstream" Thai. Dryness and drought make crops unpredictable. Food is fiery with what sometimes seems like the only vegetable that is always available, the dried chili. The chili is unrelieved by coconut milk and is used in abundance to flavor whatever is available at the time. On top of a climate which makes vegetable foods unpredictable, large animals and meat sources are also in short supply. People here eat insects, frogs, bees—almost anything they can get hold of. An important source of protein is *pla ra*, made from freshwater fish, an inland equivalent of the shrimp paste used further south. The fish is packed in claypots with rice husk dust and left to ferment. Sometimes just the pieces of fish might be used in cooking, and sometimes only the liquid prepared by bringing the fish to a boil and straining it through a sieve. *Pla ra* is an important ingredient in the cuisine of the whole inland area in the north of Southeast Asia. It appears again under different names in the Lao and Cambodian sections, and as a sauce in North Vietnam. While the smell of *pla ra* is rather uncompromising, its taste in cooking is both pleasant and irreplaceable.

Around the Gulf of Thailand, the theme is fish, fish and still more fish as the produce of the sea is harvested for consumption in Bangkok and elsewhere. Harbors and fish markets are frenetic at nights and in the early morning. Later in the day restaurants beside the jetties do a roaring trade in seafood that is so fresh it practically jumps into the wok to be cooked. The cooking is usually done quite simply, with chilies, herbs, tamarind or lime juice, sugar and fish sauce. Old holiday haunts for Thai aristocrats face highrise beachfront strips that swarm with free-living tourists. Discerning travelers move on to quieter places even further south. Here the food is distinctly Malay-influenced, using much turmeric, coconut milk and lots of chilies.

Food in Bangkok, the epicenter, has the potential to reflect the country's huge variety. Bangkok probably harbors every possible kind of cooking in Thailand if you know where to look for it and have the time for the quest.

Much of Bangkok food is thoroughly influenced by Chinese cuisine, however. Bangkok is a city whose population is predominantly ethnically Chinese after large scale immigration from China in the 19th and early 20th centuries. Much of its cooking—even home cooking—places a great deal of emphasis on Chinese techniques such as stir-frying, deep-frying and steaming, with something from the favored Thai flavors of hot, salty, sour and sweet, and the inevitable garnish of fresh green coriander. Bangkok is also the home of classical Thai cuisine, in its highest and most refined form, often called—and for good reason as we shall see later—royal cuisine. Royal cuisine has been enriched by a thriving eclecticism at work at least in the last three centuries, and possibly a hundred years before that in the late Ayutthaya period.

According to the latest research the Thai-speaking people probably began their dispersal toward the part of Asia that is now modern Thailand from somewhere around present day North Vietnam. After many centuries of slow movement across country, the first independent Thai kingdom was established at Sukhothai in the 13th century.

We can only guess what Thai food would have been like at the time of Sukhothai. According to an inscription composed by Rama Khamhaeng, its third ruler, people there hunted wild game, fished and gathered wild fruits to supplement a cultivated diet. From the number of times it is mentioned, as well as the context, it is clear that rice was the staple while fish from the rivers was the major source of protein. Betel nuts were popular, and cultivated fruit trees included jackfruit, mangoes and tamarind. Sugar palm and coconut were present in groves.

In their history prior to Sukhothai the forebears of the modern Thai people would have been living alongside the Khmer, the Mon and the tribespeople of northern Thailand and the Menam Valley for many centuries. It may have been from the Mon that the Thai picked up tamarind and sugar palm as these were among vegetable items that were introduced into neighboring Pagan from India. From the Mons too the Thais are likely to have inherited pepper and ginger. It is possible, though, that they already possessed its relative, galangal, which to this day they prefer to ginger in their cooking. Though native to Indonesia, this rhizome could very well have been received from the Khmer, Cambodia having been under the suzerainty of Java in the 8th century and Java having also been the refuge from which the founder of the great Angkor Empire returned to reign in AD 802. Garlic was also used at Sukhothai, although its place of origin is not clear.

The techniques of cooking used were probably those common in both contemporary Indian and ancient Chinese cuisine: boiling and stewing, with some roasting over an open fire.

The Thai language makes it clear that at some stage the Thai had significant contact with ancient Chinese culture. This would suggest that the people in Sukhothai were already preserving fish by salting, drying or fermenting it into relishes, techniques dominant in the cuisine of ancient China and still used in modern Thailand.

There is no suggestion that stir-frying implements were present in Sukhothai, which is not surprising since sautéing does not turn up in Chinese gastronomic literature until the Sung period, and even then only in Chinese haute cuisine—the province, it seems, of "artists, scholars, priests, vulgarians and snobs" (Hsiang Ju Lin and Tsuifeng Lin, *Chinese Gastronomy*). Even if, as is often asserted, Rama Khamhaeng had brought in Chinese potters to teach the Thais their craft, these hard-working craftsmen would not have been of such a class.

I find it unlikely either that coconut milk was used in cooking at Sukhothai, though this is an unorthodox view and the evidence is circumstantial. Certainly coconut groves are mentioned in Rama Khamhaeng's inscription. But one cannot escape a general air of braggadocio in the inscription: it seems just as likely that these appear in order to highlight exotic aspects of the kingdom to demonstrate its wealth and reach than as a source of coconut milk used in cooking. The everyday food items mentioned in the inscription sound rather like the makings of Hot and Sour Soup (*tom som*) or of Chili-Hot Sour Soup without the chili paste. Both of these are basic country dishes common in Thailand that do not contain coconut milk. And while Rama Khamhaeng's conquests extended as far as northern Malaya, they read more like frontier exercises than periods of serious fraternization. There seems little reason to think that the cooking habits of the coast-dwelling, seaward-looking Malays would have been transported back into the everyday life of a classically agrarian kingdom like Sukhothai, with its focus and cultural heart in the inland. Nor does Sukhothai appear to have harbored the substantial foreign settlements that are the usual source of new techniques in a country's cuisine.

It was the succeeding kingdom of Ayutthaya, further downriver near the coast, that did that. Groups of foreigners involved in the spice trade settled there and among them were south Indians and Malays, both of whom used coconut milk in their cooking together with the exotic spices of their trade and also, after the Portuguese introduced it to Asia in the 16th century, the chili.

Even so, traditional Thai cuisine does not seem to have changed too drastically before the end of the 17th century. Simon de la Loubère, a French envoy at Ayutthaya, wrote of it in 1687:

> *their common Food is Rice and Fish...A Siamese makes a very good Meal with a pound of Rice a day...and with a little dry or salt Fish...Their Sauces are plain, a little Water with some Spices,*

Garlic, Chibols, or some Sweet Herb, as Baulm. They do very much esteem a liquid sauce, like Mustard, which is only Cray Fish corrupted, because they are ill-salted; they call it Capi...They have neither Nuts, nor Olives, nor any eating Oil, save that which they extract from the Fruit of Coco; which, tho always a little bitter, yet is good, when it is fresh drawn: but it presently becomes very strong, insomuch that it is not eatable by such that are not accustomed to eat bad Oil. (Simon de la Loubère, *A New Historical Relation of the Kingdom of Siam.*)

Foreign communities and their styles of cooking were well established in the capital by this time, however, as la Loubère attests. With the Thai kings themselves becoming more and more caught up in the trading community, exercising as they did an exclusive monopoly in the trade of Thai products and using foreigners as their employees, the conditions for culinary diffusion would have been ripe. The eclecticism in modern Thai cuisine would almost certainly have been evident in the court at this time.

It is not until the beginning of the Bangkok period in the early 19th century that we get our next recorded glimpse of Thai food. By this time eclecticism is well and truly evident. A record of a meal provided by the court of King Rama I to the monks who took part in the dedication of the Emerald Buddha in 1809 reads as follows:

food for the clergy to consist of cooked rice, accompanied by sausages, duck eggs, kai p'anaeng *(devilled capon) [a thick coconut milk curry, probably of Malay origin, see pp. 375–6—R.L.B.], fried prawns and pork, fried eggplant, omelettes, quenelles, prawn broth, bamboo shoots,* namprik, plahèng phad, *and watermelon with the following sweets,* Khanom foy, *crystallized rice,* khanom phing; *"chicken entrails" (fried batter dipped in molasses), banana chips,* sangkhya *(custard cooked in a coconut shell), golden shreds (a sort of oeufs filés) and* khanom talai. *Also, court attendants are to fetch from Her Excellency of the Inner Palace,* kèngron *(a soup of Chinese origin) and from the Moslem officials of the Harbour Department portions of Indian rice and curry, in supplement of the regular menu...(Quoted in Sibpan Sonakul,* Everyday Siamese Dishes.)

From this time on it's possible to broadly chart the adoption of new themes into Thai cuisine—first in Bangkok and then in the countryside.

One can see the evolution of an haute cuisine in which a meal is made up of rice, a traditional vegetable dish accompanied by a chili sauce (*nam phrik*) or an elegant coconut milk sauce (*lon*), a curry (*kaeng*), a piquant dressed dish of seafood or meat often called, in English, a Thai salad (*yam*), a stir-fried dish (*phat phet*), a deep-fried one (*thot*), and a highly flavored Thai broth (*tom yam*) or a light Chinese-style consommé (*kaeng jut*). Most of the recipes in this chapter are organized into sections under these headings. I will discuss the likely pathway to the adoption of new practices in my introduction to the section concerned. Other sections include dishes that would not normally form part of a main meal but would be served as snacks, one-dish meals or appetizers.

As Buddhists in the Theravada tradition, Thais have never liked to kill animals, especially large and warm blooded ones. Together with an agriculture that is predominantly water based, a cuisine heavily reliant on fish for protein evolved: fish from the sea in the southern isthmus, fish from the rivers, canals and paddies in the plains and in the north. Traditionally much of the fish used in cooking was dried, salted or fermented, as this was the only way it could be stored in a hot climate. Refrigeration has meant that much fish can be eaten fresh. More pork and other meats are eaten now too, especially in the cities, though Thais depend on Chinese butchers to kill it for them. Preserved fish and seafood products such as fish sauce (*nam pla*), shrimp paste (*kapi*) and country fish paste (*pla ra*) remain in use as desired flavors.

The most common flavors in Thai food come from a combination of the salty and fishy extracted in the traditional ways; a sourness contributed by tamarind, lime juice, vinegar, kaffir lime skin or a range of sour fruits; the hot of pepper or chili; and the sweetness of palm sugar. To these coconut milk is sometimes added for smoothness and depth, the sophistication of exotic spices such as cumin or coriander seed and, on occasion, cinnamon or cassia, the aromatic pungency of fresh herbs and leaves such as coriander, lemongrass, Asian and Thai basils and mint.

Nearly all of these ingredients are used individually in other parts of Southeast Asia, though nowhere else in quite the same combinations. Fish sauce, for example, is commonly used in Vietnam and shrimp paste in the southern lands of the region. Coriander leaf is used in some Malay dishes although it is by no means so universal a flavoring as it is in Thailand. Coriander root is limited to Thai cuisine and to a lesser extent to Khmer or Lao.

Chilies, coconut milk, garlic, sugar, tamarind, aromatics such as lemongrass and kaffir lime leaves, and most of the other herbs and spices used in Thai food are found throughout Southeast Asia. Their use tends to vary from region to region rather than country to country, reflecting each region's history and ecology, much as it does in Thailand itself.

While most Thais will reach for a balance of sour, sweet, salty and hot in their food, the balance that is favored will vary from region to region and from individual to individual. The combination of ingredients, too, extends from light to hearty and from elegant to earthy depending on where in the country you are and what is at hand. Cooking methods employed also vary. In the pages that follow I have tried to reflect these variations by giving the origins of recipes by region wherever I can.

The focus of a Thai meal is the plate or basket of cooked white rice. Other dishes are referred to as side dishes even though they are often substantial ones. Calling them side dishes asserts the primacy of rice in a meal, and most Thais will acknowledge this by eating a spoonful of plain rice (or a ball of sticky rice) before helping themselves to the side dishes. Diners then proceed to take only a spoonful from the dish of their choice, spread it over a patch of rice on their plate then spoon it to their mouths with the rice. They repeat the process from dish to dish until they have had enough.

Today when southern Thais eat ordinary rice they use a spoon and fork. In the north, however, people eat sticky rice. The rice is brought to the table in individual baskets and eaten with the fingers. To eat sticky rice, take a small clump, roll it into a ball about 1–1½ in (2–3 cm) in diameter, dip the ball into the dish of your choice then put it into your mouth.

In this chapter and in the Lao one I have used the officially accepted Thai Royal Institute system of transliteration for the names of dishes. Pronunciation is not phonetic but conforms to the following rules.

Consonants are pronounced as in English except that:
Initial **k**, **p** and **t** are unaspirated as in English **g**, **b** and **d**
Final **k**, **p** and **t** are unexplosive and unaspirated as in English **g**, **b** and **d**
kh = k aspirated as in English **k**
ph = p aspirated as in English **p**, *not* English **ph**

th = **t** aspirated as in English **t**, *not* English **th**
j = as in English **j**
ch = as in English **ch**
ng = as in English "si*ng*er"
Vowels are pronounced as follows:
a = **h** as in father
e = **eh** as in re
i = **ee** as in me
o = **oh** as in rope
u = **oo** as in boot
ae = **ea** as in bear
o = **aw** as in dawn
oe = **ur** as in surname
u = **ü** as in German ü

WET DISHES

As is the case everywhere in Southeast Asia, Thai soups are not served on their own as a separate course but are eaten among other dishes with rice. Indeed it is a foreign imposition to use the term "soup" at all: what we are talking about more accurately are wet (usually boiled) main dishes without the addition of a ground spice or curry paste.

Two sub-groups of this kind of dish—*tom yam* and *kaeng jut*—are presented a little differently from others. Diners are given an individual bowl next to their main plate into which their own serving is ladled.

A *tom yam* is a robust, grand and uniquely Thai dish. It consists of seafood, meat or vegetable cooked in a tasty broth flavored with lime juice and lime leaf, lemongrass, chili, fish sauce and galangal. It clearly presents the classic scale of flavors—hot, sour, salty and sometimes sweet—from which the particular music of every truly Thai dish is created, in this case the emphasis is on hot, sour and salty as background to a fragrant melody carried by seafood or meat and fresh Thai herbs. Its clear, sharp flavors make a wonderful counterpoint to sweeter, rich dishes such as coconut milk curries. Diners dip in to their bowl, transfer the broth to their plate, moisten some rice with this and then eat. A *tom yam* often comes to the table in a special Thai claypot sitting on a small charcoal stove or in a Chinese steamboat from which it is ladled into individual bowls. It adds to the drama to see the soup bubbling away gently in front of your eyes.

A *kaeng jut* is of Chinese derivation, and is thinner in flavor, serving as a palate cleanser during a meal of rich dishes. It is made without many spices and usually consists of a little meat, some vegetable and a lot of stock. The permutations are endless, with the addition of coriander root, fish sauce, garlic and pepper creating a uniquely Thai taste and smell. You may, of course, leave the coriander root out, as Sino-Thais often do, if you want a milder soup.

Other *tom* of interest ("*tom*" meaning "boiled") include *Tom Som* or *tom khlong* (a similar dish using dried or freshwater fish which is not included here). These are Thai versions of the sour soup that features regularly in everyday food right across this part of Southeast Asia, particularly in Cambodia, Laos and Vietnam.

A final group of dishes that I have placed in the wet category use a spice paste to provide their basic flavoring. Because their name in Thai includes "*kaeng*" they are sometimes listed among the curries in recipe books. The amount of liquid they contain and the way of serving them suggest, however, that they belong here.

Thai Soups

TOM YAM KUNG   HOT AND SPICY SHRIMP SOUP

For an elegant meal and in keeping with their grandeur, *tom yam*-style dishes may be brought to the table in a steamboat or a Thai charcoal claypot. There is nothing more enticing than the fragrance of bubbling *tom yam* before your eyes.

5 cups (1¼ liters) light chicken stock or water
3 stalks lemongrass, brusied and cut into 2-in (5-cm)
   pieces
7 thick slices fresh galangal root
7 kaffir lime leaves
½ can straw mushrooms, drained and halved (optional)

2 small cherry tomatoes, quartered (optional)

8 small red chilies, bruised

1¼ lb (600 g) large shrimp, peeled and deveined

1–2 tablespoons chili jam (*Nam Phrik Phao*, p. 412), more or less to taste

2–3 tablespoons fish sauce, or to taste

3–4 tablespoons fresh lime juice, or to taste

Fresh coriander leaves for garnish

In a soup pot, bring the water or stock, lemongrass, galangal and lime leaves to a boil and simmer gently until fragrant and flavorful. Add the mushrooms and tomatoes (if using), and the chilies and simmer a little longer. Add the shrimp, and when they have turned pink, remove the pan from the stove and add the chili jam, stirring until it dissolves, the fish sauce and the lime juice.

Pour the soup into individual bowls and scatter the fresh coriander leaves over the top. Serve with rice and extra fish sauce and lemon or lime juice so that diners may adjust the flavor to suit themselves.

TOM YAM PLA FISH TOM YAM

As a variation try this recipe using whole cleaned baby squid or mixed seafood. You can also make a vegetarian *tom yam* using a mixture of mushrooms cooked in water or vegetable stock with light soy sauce instead of the fish sauce.

5 cups (1¼ liters) light chicken stock or water

7 slices galangal root

2 stalks lemongrass, bruised and cut into 2-in (5-cm) pieces

6 kaffir lime leaves

1½ lb (700 g) fish fillets (ling, large Spanish mackerel, sea perch, barramundi)

3½ oz (100 g) straw or oyster mushrooms

8 small red chilies, bruised

2–3 tablespoons fish sauce, or to taste

3–4 tablespoons lime juice

1–2 tablespoons chili jam (*Nam Phrik Phao*), or to taste

Fresh coriander leaves and sliced shallots for garnish

Bring the stock or water to a boil with the galangal, lemongrass and lime leaves. Add the fish pieces and simmer gently until cooked. Add the mushrooms and chilies, fish sauce and lime juice. Remove the pot from the heat and stir in the chili jam. Serve garnished with fresh coriander leaves and sliced shallots.

PLA TOM SOM ## SOUR FISH SOUP

This is a southern Thai version of a classic sour fish soup found in slightly different forms all over Southeast Asia. It uses a mild coconut vinegar. In central or northern Thailand the sourness might well come from another source such as green tamarind or tamarind leaves. Khammaan Khonkhai in his novel *The Teachers of Mad Dog Swamp* (translated into English by Gehan Wijeyewardene) describes a northeastern version:

> *An aroma specially designed to get the gastric juices working arose with the steam from the catfish soup. The medium-sized catfish, caught in the rice fields, were cooked with lemongrass and young tamarind shoots.*

3 stalks lemongrass, finely sliced
3 cloves garlic, sliced
3 shallots, sliced
2 tablespoons chopped turmeric root or 1 teaspoon ground turmeric
Pinch of sea salt
1¼ lb (600 g) sea bass or cod fillets
4 cups (1 liter) water
4–6 tablespoons mild coconut vinegar
2 tablespoons fish sauce, or to taste
Fresh coriander leaves, sliced green onions, and finely sliced chili (optional) for garnish

In a mortar or a food processor grind the lemongrass, garlic, shallots, turmeric and a little salt to a fine paste. Rub the fish fillets with this mixture and marinate for 1 hour. Bring the water to a boil, add the coconut vinegar and fish sauce and add the fish piece by piece, returning the liquid to a boil in between. Add any leftover marinade and simmer until the fish is cooked. Taste and adjust the seasonings—it should be sour and fragrant. Garnish with any combination of coriander, green onions and chili.

TOM KHA KAI CHICKEN WITH GALANGAL IN COCONUT MILK

To make a vegetarian version of this dish use sliced pumpkin and/or button or other mushrooms and baby corn instead of chicken.

1 cup (250 ml) thick coconut milk and 3 cups (750 ml) all-purpose coconut milk or 1 can (14 oz/400 ml) canned coconut milk plus 1 can of water

1 lb (500 g) boneless chicken thighs, cut the Thai way (p. 24)

1½-in (4-cm) piece galangal root, peeled and cut into thick slices

2 stalks lemongrass, bruised with the side of a cleaver, cut into 5-cm (2-in) lengths

1 coriander root, bruised

6 kaffir lime leaves, torn

2 tablespoons fish sauce, or more to taste

3–6 fresh small red chilies, bruised

2 tablespoons fresh lime juice, or more to taste

Fresh coriander leaves for garnish

If you are using canned coconut milk do not shake the can before opening. Skim off 1 cup (250 ml) of the thick part at the top and set it aside. Put the chicken pieces into a wok or a saucepan, add the all-purpose coconut milk (and water, if using canned coconut milk), the galangal slices, lemongrass, coriander root, lime leaves, and 1 tablespoon of fish sauce, stir and bring to a boil. Simmer until the chicken is tender and add the thick coconut milk. Just before the liquid boils again remove the saucepan from the heat, and add the chilies, lime juice and more fish sauce to taste. Serve garnished with fresh coriander leaves, a small bowl of fish sauce and some decorative lime wedges (p. 49).

KAENG SOM CHILI-HOT SOUR SOUP

This soup is a more substantial and spiced version of the region-wide sour fish or vegetable soup. Traditionally it has stood alongside the various versions of Chili Jam (*Nam Phrik Phao*) as the most regular food of the Thai countryside along with rice. Both of these dishes utilize wild leaves and fruits gathered around the village and on the edges of river banks, foods which used to be the mainstay of country people in between seasons and in times of crop failure. Chili Jam (p. 412) adds flavor through a dipping sauce. This soup combines fish and local vegetables in a broth flavored with the ripe fruit and sometimes the leaves of the tamarind tree, which grows everywhere in villages and around paddy fields.

With increasing prosperity, a more scientific agriculture and a huge movement of people from the country to Bangkok in recent years, Chili-Hot Sour Soup sometimes includes farmed seafood and lots of market vegetables. This version is a country one, using a mixture of freshwater fish, the water spinach that still grows wild in unpolluted waterways, and the produce of house gardens. Note, however, that the recipe may be adapted to seafood of all kinds with more exotic vegetables.

4 cups (1 liter) water, or more if you wish

½ –1 teaspoon palm or dark brown sugar (optional)

3–4 tablespoons tamarind water (p. 67), to taste

2–3 cups (500–750 g) mixed green vegetables (water spinach, tough ends removed and the rest cut into 1½-in [4-cm] lengths; green beans cut into 1½-in [3-cm] pieces; Chinese cabbage sliced into strips)

2–3 tablespoons fish sauce, to taste

1¼–1¾ lb (600–800 g) freshwater fish fillets (catfish, pike, redfin, perch, barramundi, trout)

Spice Paste

5 dried red chilies, seeded, soaked in water until soft and
squeezed dry

1 tablespoon chopped galangal root

1 teaspoon shrimp paste, roasted (p. 53)

3 cloves garlic

6 shallots, sliced

Grind the Spice Paste ingredients to a fine paste. Bring the water, sugar and tamarind water to a boil. Add the Spice Paste and stir until it is mixed with the liquid then add the vegetables and simmer for a minute or two. Add the fish sauce and adjust the seasoning so that the dish is sufficiently sour and salty. Add the fish one piece at a time and simmer without stirring until done. Serve with rice and stir-fried curry or egg dishes or with deep-fried or grilled meat.

KAENG LUANG YELLOW SOUR FISH SOUP (South)

This soup is the far south equivalent of Chili-Hot Sour Soup. It uses turmeric, a universal ingredient in the cooking of this part of the south, and is strongly flavored. Compare this soup with the Malay Hot Sour Fish to which it is very similar (p. 181).

4 cups (1 liter) water

1 small pineapple, peeled and cut into fine wedge-
shaped slices or 2 cups (500 g) vegetables (green
beans; sliced fresh or pickled bamboo shoots; squash
of any kind; water spinach)

1 cup (250 ml) tamarind water, or to taste—less if you
use pineapple

1–2 tablespoons palm or dark brown sugar, or more to
taste

3–4 tablespoons fish sauce, or to taste

1 lb (500 g) fish fillets (ling, barramundi), cut into 2-in
(5-cm) pieces or large peeled shrimp

Spice Paste

10–20 dried or fresh small red chilies, chopped
1 tablespoon turmeric root, peeled and coarsely chopped
  or 1 teaspoon ground turmeric
1 tablespoon shrimp paste, roasted (p. 53)
3 cloves garlic
2 shallots, sliced

Grind the Spice Paste ingredients to a fine paste. Heat the water in a saucepan and dissolve the Spice Paste in it completely. Bring to a boil and add the vegetables, cooking until the liquid returns to a boil. Add the tamarind water, sugar and fish sauce until the broth tastes sour-sweet. Add the fish pieces or the shrimp one at a time so that the water stays boiling. Reduce the heat and simmer briefly until the fish is cooked. Serve with rice.

KAENG LIANG THAI VEGETABLE SOUP

4 cups (1 liter) light soup stock or water
1 cup (250 g) cubed pumpkin
½ cup (125 g) diced squash or zucchini
½ cup (125 g) chopped baby corn
Small handful of chopped spinach or any green leafy
  vegetable
½ cup (125 g) green beans, cut into 1-in (2½-cm) pieces
4 oz (125 g) small shrimp, peeled and deveined
½ –1 tablespoon fish sauce or salt to taste
1 small handful of lemon basil leaves or 1–2 kaffir lime leaves

Spice Paste

1½ tablespoons dried shrimp, soaked in water for 5
  minutes and drained
¼ teaspoon ground white pepper
1 teaspoon Chinese keys (*krachai*), chopped (optional)
1 teaspoon shrimp paste, roasted (p. 53)
5 shallots, sliced

Grind the Spice Paste ingredients to a paste. Bring the stock or water to a boil, add the Spice Paste and stir. Bring to a boil again, add the vegetables and cook for a few minutes, then add the shrimp and fish sauce to taste (use salt if everything seems fishy enough already).

When everything is cooked, add the lemon basil leaves or finely sliced kaffir lime leaves and serve.

Soups of Chinese Origin

KAENG JUT MU TAO HU

PORK AND TOFU CONSOMMÉ

3 cloves garlic, sliced

2 coriander roots, chopped

⅛ teaspoon ground white pepper

7 oz (200 g) lean ground pork

5 cups (1¼ liters) stock

8 oz (250 g) soft tofu, cubed

4 leaves Chinese celery cabbage, cut into strips or 2 small cucumbers, cut in half lengthwise and thinly sliced

1 plant Asian celery, cut into 1½-in (3-cm) lengths or 1 small stalk celery, cut into 1½-in (3-cm) strips

1–3 tablespoons fish sauce, or to taste

Fresh coriander leaves and sliced green onion for garnish

In a mortar or a food processor, grind the garlic, coriander root and pepper to a paste and mix with the ground pork. Form the meat into small balls about ¾ in (2 cm) in diameter and set aside.

Bring the stock to a boil in a saucepan and add the meat. Stir, return to a boil and skim the foam off the top. Add the tofu and simmer gently until the pork is cooked, add the Chinese cabbage or cucumber and simmer for a minute or two until the cabbage is tender-crisp. Add the celery and the fish sauce to taste and serve garnished with fresh coriander leaves and sliced green onions.

KAENG JUT MU CHOKO

PORK AND SQUASH CONSOMMÉ

4 cloves garlic, sliced

2 coriander roots, chopped

⅛ teaspoon ground white pepper

8 oz (250 g) lean pork, thinly sliced

1 tablespoon oil

5 cups (1¼ liters) light chicken stock

8 oz (250 g) squash, zucchini or cucumber, peeled, and cubed

2 tablespoons fish sauce, or to taste

Sliced green onion for garnish

Grind the garlic, the coriander root and pepper to a paste. Mix with the sliced pork and set aside for 10 minutes. Heat the oil in a saucepan, add the meat and stir-fry until it changes color and the spices are fragrant. Add the stock and bring to a boil. Add the squash and fish sauce to taste and simmer until the vegetable is cooked. Serve garnished with sliced green onion.

KAENG JUT PLA FISH BALL CONSOMMÉ

4 cloves garlic

⅛ teaspoon ground white pepper

8 oz (250 g) raw flaked fish

5 cups (1¼ liters) thin stock made with the fish bones

5 or 6 dried Chinese mushrooms, soaked in water until soft, stems discarded and caps quartered

4 oz (125 g) lean ground pork, rolled into small balls ¾-in (2-cm) in diameter

8 oz (250 g) soft tofu, cubed (optional)

1–2 tablespoons fish sauce, or to taste

4 green onions, sliced into 1½-in (4-cm) lengths

Chopped fresh coriander leaves for garnish

In a mortar or a food processor, grind the garlic and pepper together to a fine paste. Add the flaked fish and blend until everything is mixed and forms a smooth paste. Form the mixture into small balls according to the instructions on p. 211.

Bring the stock to a boil in a saucepan. Add the mushrooms, pork, tofu and fish balls and simmer gently, covered, until the pork balls are cooked and the fish balls float on top. Add fish sauce and green onions and stir. Remove from the heat, garnish with fresh coriander leaves and serve.

KAENG JUT KAI KAP HET

CHICKEN AND MUSHROOM CONSOMMÉ

1 small chicken
Salt to taste
2 green onions, tied into a loose knot
3 cloves garlic
2 coriander roots, chopped
⅛ teaspoon ground white pepper
Oil for frying
2 tablespoons fish sauce, or to taste
5 dried Chinese mushrooms, soaked in water until soft,
    stems discarded and caps halved or ½ can straw
    mushrooms, halved
Sliced green onion for garnish

Put the chicken into a saucepan and cover with water. Add salt and green onions, cover and simmer for 2 hours or until the chicken is tender. Lift the chicken from the stock, remove the flesh from the bones and cut it into small pieces. Set aside. Strain the chicken stock and set it aside.

In a mortar or a food processor grind the garlic, coriander root and pepper to a paste. Heat a little oil in a pan and fry the paste for a minute or two. Add the chicken and mix well. Add the stock and the fish sauce and bring to a boil. Add the mushrooms, cover the pan and simmer gently for a few minutes. Serve garnished with sliced green onion.

KAENG JUT TAENG KWA YAT SAI

STUFFED CUCUMBER CONSOMMÉ

Thais in Bangkok often enjoy this soup using Chinese bitter melon instead of cucumber. I find this vegetable too bitter and prefer cucumber, but if you soak the melon in salted water the bitterness will dissipate.

2 coriander roots
3 cloves garlic, sliced
⅛ teaspoon ground white pepper
8 oz (250 g) ground pork
3 medium-sized cucumbers, peeled, cored and seeded
4 cups (1 liter) pork bone stock

2 tablespoons fish sauce, or to taste
Fresh coriander leaves and/or sliced green onions for
    garnish

Grind the coriander roots, garlic and the pepper to a fine paste in a mortar or a food processor. Combine the paste with the ground pork and stuff the cucumbers with this mixture.

Bring the stock to a boil, add the stuffed cucumbers and simmer until the pork filling is cooked. Remove the cucumbers and slice them across into 1½-in (3-cm) rounds.

Arrange the slices in a serving dish, add fish sauce to taste to the stock and pour it over. Garnish with a few coriander leaves and/or sliced green onions.

CURRIES AND BRAISED DISHES

The word *kaeng* in Thai is usually translated into English as "curry." It is important not to be misled by this term, however. The stereotypical picture of a Thai curry is of a complex, highly flavored dish containing coconut milk, but this is only one type of *kaeng*. The real meaning of *kaeng* is more like "a dish with gravy." Coconut milk curries, though universal in the south, have been associated historically elsewhere in Thailand only with elegant cuisine or food for special occasions—and only then in central Thailand. It seems likely they were first introduced into the kingdom of Ayutthaya through communities of foreigners involved in the spice trade and that they penetrated central Thai cuisine only after being taken up by Thai royalty. There they became the special dishes served at the communal feasts which accompany temple festivals, ordinations, weddings, funerals, house blessings and so on. Even today, though coconut milk curries show up in restaurants almost anywhere in the country and in the regular repertoire of a growing middle class, they are not part of the everyday food of country people outside the south.

Most of the *kaeng* of the north and northeast, like the original ones of the central plains countryside, do not contain coconut milk and rely on the fresh herbs that grow in house gardens, paddies, fields or forests nearby rather than on widely traded dry spices. In the past this made them difficult to recreate in the West. Now, however, almost all of the ingredients required are available everywhere—at least in dried form.

The *kaeng* that appear in this section go through a braising process where the spices and usually the meat or flesh are first fried in oil released from thick coconut milk (or, if they do not contain coconut milk, another kind of oil) until the spices are fragrant and the meat seared. These dishes are therefore richer and more complex than those in the last section.

Thais, not being fond of food that is too oily, employ a technique that is different from that of the Indonesians or Malays when they cook curries with coconut milk. The curry paste is not fried in oil alone first but is cooked until fragrant in the oil that is released from thick coconut milk as it boils, evaporates and thickens. The following is a description of this technique.

Thick coconut milk from the first squeeze (p. 16) is brought to a rapid boil and evaporated sufficiently for the oil to visibly separate out. The curry paste is then added and stirred until it takes up the coconut and absorbs the separated oil. When everything smells fragrant, add the meat, vegetables and, a little at a time, the thin second-squeeze coconut milk until a smooth blended gravy forms. Add seasonings and simmer, uncovered, until the ingredients are cooked and the curry has thickened.

Curry Pastes

It is easy in Thailand to avoid making your own curry pastes. There are whole stalls in markets devoted to providing pastes and different mixes made every day—magnificent mounds of them, curry and chili pastes of every variety, various grades of shrimp paste, dried and roasted chilies and chili mixes—all wonderfully colorful and totally fresh. The same may seem true these days in other countries, with imported Thai curry pastes available in cans, packets and jars in Asian food stores and increasingly in supermarkets. Useful though these may be for busy people (and for Thai restaurants who almost universally rely on them), devotees of Thai food quickly tire of their sameness, preferring to make their own (pp. 348–349). Red and green curry pastes are the most common ones and I include general recipes for these for storage, although the best Thai cooks use a separately tailored paste for every separate curry. Leftover pastes made freshly from these recipes may be transferred into small covered containers and stored in the refrigerator for up to one month.

RED CURRY PASTE I

This curry paste may be used with chicken, quail, duck, pork or beef, although green curry is better for beef. The standard amount to use is about 3 tablespoons of curry paste for 1 lb (500 g) of meat but always feel free to use less if you prefer.

1 tablespoon coriander seed
1 teaspoon cumin seed
1 teaspoon peppercorns
6–9 large dried chilies, seeded, soaked in warm water
    for 30 minutes and squeezed dry
Salt to taste
1 tablespoon chopped coriander root
2 stalks lemongrass, finely sliced
1 tablespoon chopped galangal root
1 teaspoon kaffir lime skin
1 level tablespoon shrimp paste
8 cloves garlic, sliced
6 shallots, sliced

Roast the coriander and cumin seed in a hot dry pan for 1 minute or until they smell fragrant. Using a stone mortar and pestle or an electric grinder, grind all the ingredients to a fine paste.

This recipe yields 5–6 tablespoons of curry paste.

RED CURRY PASTE II

4 large dried chilies, seeded, soaked in warm water for
    30 minutes then squeezed dry
1 stalk lemongrass, finely sliced
2 slices galangal root, chopped
3 coriander roots, chopped
½ teaspoon kaffir lime skin, chopped
1 teaspoon shrimp paste
4 cloves garlic, finely sliced
3 shallots, finely sliced
⅛ teaspoon freshly ground pepper

Grind all the ingredients to a fine paste.

GREEN CURRY PASTE

Follow the recipe for Red Curry Paste but use 20 fresh green chilies instead of the dried red ones.

As with all curries, the dishes that follow are best eaten the next day when their flavors have had time to meld and develop.

KAENG PHET KAI   RED CHICKEN CURRY

1 cup (250 ml) thick coconut milk
3 tablespoons Red Curry Paste I (p. 348)
1 lb (500 g) boneless chicken thighs, cut the Thai way
   (p. 24)
2½ cups (625 ml) thin coconut milk
5 kaffir lime leaves, torn
8–10 hard green or white golf-ball eggplant, halved and
   immersed in salted water to prevent them from turning
   brown, or 7 oz (200 g) canned shredded bamboo
   shoots, drained
1 tablespoon palm or dark brown sugar
2 tablespoons fish sauce
A few fresh small red chilies, sliced diagonally
A handful of Asian sweet basil leaves

Put the thick coconut milk into a saucepan over high heat and boil it hard, stirring constantly until it has reduced and released its oil. Add the Red Curry Paste, stirring continuously as the oil separates out and the spices "fry." Continue stirring and "frying" until the spices are fragrant, then add the chicken and continue cooking until everything is mixed and the meat has changed color. Add the thin coconut milk little by little, stirring constantly. Add the lime leaves, eggplant or bamboo shoots, sugar and the fish sauce. Simmer, uncovered, until the chicken and vegetable are done and the gravy has thickened slightly. Taste and adjust the seasonings if necessary, and serve garnished with sliced chilies and basil leaves.

KAENG PHET PET YANG   RED DUCK CURRY WITH LYCHEES

1 roasted Chinese duck (available from a Chinese or
   Thai food store)
2 cups (500 ml) thick coconut milk

3–4 tablespoons Red Curry Paste I (p. 348; use
  3 tablespoons per 1 lb/500 g of meat)
2 cups (500 ml) thin coconut milk
8 kaffir lime leaves
3 tablespoons fish sauce
1 cup (250 g) canned lychees, drained
Sugar or palm sugar
4 red chilies, sliced diagonally
Small handful of sweet basil leaves

Cut the duck meat from the bones in bite-sized pieces and set it aside.
Put 1 cup (250 ml) of thick coconut milk into a saucepan and boil hard,
stirring constantly, until it has reduced and the oil has released. Add the
curry paste, continuing to stir and "fry" until it is fragrant, then add the
duck pieces and mix well.

    Add the thin coconut milk. Stir thoroughly, tear and add the lime leaves,
add the fish sauce and the lychees. Bring to a boil and simmer, stirring, for a
few minutes, uncovered. Taste and adjust the seasonings, adding sugar if
necessary. Add the remaining thick coconut milk, bring back to a boil and
serve garnished with chilies and basil.

KAENG KHIAO
WAN NUA

GREEN BEEF CURRY

Substitute boneless chicken thighs for the beef to
make Green Chicken Curry or fish fillets to make
Green Fish Curry. The addition of 2 teaspoons of
chopped Chinese keys (*krachai*) to Green Fish Curry
at the end is very good, though not essential.

1 cup (250 ml) thick coconut milk
2–3 tablespoons Green Curry Paste (p. 349)
1 lb (500 g) lean beef, cut the Thai way (p. 24)
2 cups (500 ml) thin coconut milk
2–3 tablespoons fish sauce
1 tablespoon palm or dark brown sugar
4 kaffir lime leaves
½ cup (125 g) diced eggplant
A handful of Asian sweet basil leaves
2–3 whole small red chilies

Put the thick coconut milk into a saucepan and bring to a rapid boil. When it has released its oil add the Green Curry Paste and mix, stirring constantly until the spices are "frying" and smell fragrant. Add the meat and mix well, stirring until it changes color. Add the thin coconut milk to the saucepan gradually and bring to a boil. Add the fish sauce, sugar and lime leaves. Simmer, uncovered, until the meat is tender, then add the eggplant. Add most of the Asian sweet basil and return to a boil. Serve garnished with the whole chilies and the remaining fresh basil leaves.

KAENG CHUCHI PLA — FISH "CHUCHI"

Chuchi is a thick seafood dish that uses a light red curry paste that contains no dry spices. Any of the following seafood suggestions work well: Fillets or steaks cut from large fish with solid flesh, such as large mackerel, kingfish or tuna; fillets of ling, barramundi, snapper; shrimp or scallops.

1 cup (250 ml) thick coconut milk
2–3 tablespoons Red Curry Paste II (p. 348)
1 cup (250 ml) thin coconut milk
1 tablespoon fish sauce
1 teaspoon palm or dark brown sugar
1 lb (500 g) fish steaks, shrimp or scallops
A few finely sliced kaffir lime leaves or fresh coriander
    leaves, and red chili sliced diagonally, for garnish

Bring the thick coconut milk to a rapid boil and stir constantly until the oil has come out. Add 2–3 tablespoons of Red Curry Paste and "fry" until it is completely incorporated and thick. Add the thin coconut milk little by little, stirring after each addition. Season to taste with fish sauce and sugar and cook until thick and oily, then add the fish, shrimp or scallops. Adjust the seasonings, return to a simmer and cook lightly. Serve scattered with finely sliced kaffir lime leaves or fresh coriander leaves and sliced red chili.

KAENG KHUA MU SAPPAROT

PORK AND PINEAPPLE CURRY
(Central)

This dish is the type of red curry of the central plains that traditionally appeared only on special occasions such as the feasts accompanying temple ceremonies, the ordination of monks and weddings. It contains as much vegetable as meat which is indicative of the farming lifestyle. "*Khua*" refers to the roasting of the dry spices.

2 cups (500 ml) thick coconut milk
2 cups (500 ml) thin coconut milk
8 oz (250 g) pork shoulder, cut the Thai way (p. 24)
½ –1 cup (125–250 ml) water
1 chicken stock cube (optional)
1 small fresh pineapple, peeled, cored and diced or 1 large can crushed or diced pineapple, drained
2 tablespoons fish sauce

Spice Paste
1 tablespoon coriander seed
½ tablespoon cumin seed
6 large dried chilies, soaked in warm water for 30 minutes and squeezed dry
1 stalk lemongrass, finely sliced
2 teaspoons kaffir lime skin, chopped
2 teaspoons shrimp paste
6 cloves garlic, sliced
4 tablespoons shallots, sliced

To make the Spice Paste, roast the coriander and cumin seeds in a dry pan until they are brown and aromatic. Grind them to a powder. Then grind all of the Spice Paste ingredients to a fine paste and set it aside.

Put 1 cup (250 ml) of thick and 1 cup (250 ml) of thin coconut milk into a saucepan and bring to a rapid boil. Cook and stir occasionally until the milk has evaporated considerably and the oil begins to float on top (about 10–15 minutes), then add the Spice Paste and mix thoroughly. Reduce the heat and stir as the oil continues to release until the spices smell cooked and aromatic. Add the meat and mix well. Add a little water or stock, made from water with a chicken stock cube dissolved in it. Stir well and simmer until the meat is half cooked.

Add the pineapple to the curry then the rest of the thin coconut milk and the water. Simmer, uncovered, until everything is blended then stir in the fish sauce to taste (the fish sauce should counteract the sweetness). Simmer gently on the stove for 1 hour or until the meat is tender, then add the remaining thick coconut milk, return to a boil and serve.

PORK AND PUMPKIN CURRY

KAENG KHUA MU FAK THONG

Red curry is also good made with equal amounts of pork and cubed pumpkin. Proceed according to the instructions provided in the recipe for Red Chicken Curry, using 10 oz (300 g) each of pork and pumpkin in place of chicken and eggplant and only 1–2 tablespoons of curry paste for a lighter curry. Garnish with finely sliced kaffir lime leaves.

Other common combinations are pork or chicken with either plain or sour pickled bamboo shoots, and chicken with tomatoes as in the recipe that follows.

CHICKEN AND TOMATO CURRY

KAENG KHUA KAI MAKHUA THET

Kaeng khua is a bit more sophisticated than the common *Kaeng Som*—it often features sour vegetables and the more accessible rural meats such as chicken, freshwater fish, shellfish and snails. The following recipe is an example of a sour variety. Other common versions include fish and sour bamboo shoots (no tamarind water) or dried salt fish and water spinach. Mussels in their shell and diced pineapple are another good combination, but in this case do not use tamarind water or tomatoes, as the pineapple is acidic enough. Add the pineapple and the flavoring ingredients with the mussels and cook only until the mussels open, about 1–2 minutes.

1 cup (250 ml) thick coconut milk and 2 cups (500 ml)
thin coconut milk or 14 oz (400 ml) can coconut milk
and 1 cup (250 ml) water

1 lb (500 g) boneless chicken thighs, cut the Thai way (p. 24)

2 tablespoons fish sauce, or to taste

2 teaspoons palm or dark brown sugar, or to taste

A few kaffir lime leaves

4 firm cherry tomatoes, peeled

2–3 tablespoons tamarind water, or fresh lime juice to taste

Spice Paste

½ teaspoon coriander seed

¼ teaspoon cumin seed

¼ teaspoon peppercorns

5 dried chilies, seeded and soaked in warm water for 30 minutes and squeezed dry

1 stalk lemongrass, finely sliced

2 slices galangal root, chopped

1 coriander root, chopped

½ teaspoon shrimp paste

4 cloves garlic, sliced

3 shallots, sliced

To make the Spice Paste, roast the coriander and cumin seeds in a dry pan until they are brown. Grind the roasted seeds and the peppercorns to a powder. Grind all of the Spice Paste ingredients to a fine paste.

Bring the thick coconut milk to a rapid boil in a saucepan and continue to boil it until it evaporates a little and the oil floats on top. Add the Spice Paste and stir until it "fries" and smells fragrant. Add the chicken and mix well, then add the thin coconut milk or water, fish sauce and sugar. Simmer until the meat is cooked and the surface is oily. Add the lime leaves, the tomatoes and the tamarind water, stir and cook the tomatoes for a few minutes, then serve.

KAENG MATSAMAN MUSLIM CURRY

This curry is of Indian Muslim origin, making notable use of the dry trade spices and using meat that is cut differently from the normal Thai way. It is an important dish in Thai royal cuisine, with the added spices producing a richer and less fiery curry than the previous recipes in this section. It is believed that this curry was introduced at the time of Rama I, when a new economic and cultural vibrancy was apparent in Bangkok after the Burmese wars and the sacking of Ayutthaya.

2 cups (500 ml) thick coconut milk
3 cups (750 ml) thin coconut milk
2 lb (1 kg) topside or round steak, sliced
4 tablespoons roasted peanuts
1 medium-sized onion, peeled and cut lengthwise into
    8 wedges
4 small potatoes, peeled and quartered
2–3 tablespoons palm or dark brown sugar
½ cup (125 ml) tamarind water (p. 55)
1½–2 tablespoons fish sauce

Spice Paste
7 large dried red chilies, seeded and roasted in a dry pan
    until brown
½ teaspoon peppercorns
1 tablespoon coriander seed
1 teaspoon cumin seed
5 cloves
Pinch of mace (optional)
½ teaspoon ground nutmeg
5 cardamom pods, broken open
¾-in (2-cm) piece of cinnamon stick
8 shallots, unpeeled
9 cloves garlic, unpeeled
¾-in (2-cm) piece fresh ginger root
½ teaspoon shrimp paste
1 stalk lemongrass, finely sliced

To make the Spice Paste, roast all of the dry spices (except the chilies) until they are fragrant. Grind all of the dry spices (including the chilies) to a powder and set it aside.

Grill the unpeeled shallots and garlic, the ginger and the shrimp paste (wrapped in foil) under the broiler turning them until they are browned on the outside. Set aside to cool, then peel and chop them. Alternatively, slice the shallots and the garlic, fry them in a little oil and drain. Grind all of the Spice Paste ingredients, adding a little water if necessary, to produce a smooth paste.

Combine 1 cup (250 ml) of the thick and all of the thin coconut milk and bring to a boil in a large saucepan. Add the beef and peanuts and simmer, uncovered, until the beef is half-cooked and the coconut milk has reduced somewhat.

Put the remaining 1 cup (250 ml) of thick coconut milk into a wok or a pan and boil hard until the oil releases and floats on top. Add the curry paste and "fry," stirring constantly until everything smells fragrant. Slowly add gravy from the beef pot to blend everything together then pour the spiced coconut milk back in to the pan with the beef and peanuts and mix well. Add the onion, potatoes and sugar to taste, tamarind water and fish sauce to achieve a rich, sour, sweet and slightly salty taste. Simmer until everything is cooked. Taste, adjust the seasonings and serve.

You can make this curry with chicken by substituting skinned chicken legs and thighs (bone-in) cut into curry pieces (p. 23) for the beef.

PHANAENG KAI I CHICKEN PHANAENG

Phanaeng is a very thick Thai curry that probably originated in Malaysia since the curry paste is first fried in oil. The grilled version of this dish echoes a style of grilling chicken that is Malay/Indonesian.

2 cups (500 ml) thick coconut milk or 14 oz (400 ml) can
    of coconut milk
1 lb (500 g) chicken breasts or thighs, whole or cut the
    Thai way (p. 24)
2 tablespoons oil
2 teaspoons palm or dark brown sugar
1 tablespoon fish sauce
Fresh coriander leaves and red chilies, sliced diagonally, for
    garnish

Spice Paste
1 teaspoon coriander seed
1 teaspoon cumin seed
8–10 dried red chilies, seeded, soaked in water until soft
    and squeezed dry

2 stalks lemongrass, finely sliced
1 tablespoon chopped galangal root
1 teaspoon chopped kaffir lime skin
1 teaspoon shrimp paste
4 cloves garlic
1 shallot, sliced
2 tablespoons ground roasted peanuts

To make the Spice Paste, grind the coriander and cumin to a powder then grind all of the Spice Paste ingredients to a fine paste and set aside.

Bring the coconut milk to a boil in a saucepan, stirring constantly. Add the chicken and simmer gently until it is cooked. Remove and set aside. Heat 2 tablespoons of oil in a pan and fry the Spice Paste until it is fragrant. Add the coconut milk, a little at a time, mixing until it is incorporated after each addition, add the sugar and the fish sauce and cook, stirring constantly until the mixture is thick and its oil is floating on top. Taste and adjust the seasonings if necessary, return the chicken to the pan, and cook completely. Garnish with coriander leaves and sliced red chilies and serve.

Pork or beef may also be cooked this way.

PHANAENG KAI II CHICKEN WITH THICK CURRY SAUCE

This dish is a variation on the preceeding recipe whereby the chicken is grilled and served with a curry sauce.

Cut 1 chicken or 2 small Cornish hens down the breastbone, remove the fat and flatten them out. Pour the coconut milk over, prick the chicken with a fork to let the liquid penetrate and marinate it for some hours or overnight. Remove the chicken and grill, still flattened out, either over low heat on the grill or under the broiler.

Heat 2 tablespoons of oil in a pan. Fry the Spice Paste until fragrant, then add the coconut milk, a little at a time, the sugar and the fish sauce, stirring constantly until the sauce is thick and its oil is floating on top. Taste and adjust the seasonings then pour the sauce over the chicken and garnish with fresh coriander leaves and sliced chilies.

KAENG PA JUNGLE CURRY

This is a modern version of a traditional country curry from the north–central region. The chicken and cultivated eggplant substitute for wild boar and gathered bamboo shoots. You could, of course, use the original items or substitute domesticated pork and store bought bamboo shoots if you wish or even try other game meat.

10 green or white golf-ball eggplant
2–3 tablespoons oil
1 lb (500 g) boneless chicken thighs, cut the Thai way (p. 24)
2 cups (500 ml) water
1 tablespoon fish sauce

Spice Paste
10–20 small red chilies
10 white peppercorns
1 stalk lemongrass, finely sliced
2 thick slices galangal root, peeled and coarsely chopped
1 teaspoon chopped kaffir lime skin
1 teaspoon shrimp paste
6 cloves garlic, sliced
3 shallots, sliced

Garnish
2 clusters fresh green peppercorns (optional)
2 medium-length red chilies, seeded and sliced into strips
A handful of holy basil leaves

Trim the eggplant and cut them into 4 wedges. Soak them in salted water to prevent their browning and set aside.

Grind the Spice Paste ingredients to a paste. Heat the oil in a wok or a pan and fry the Spice Paste until fragrant. Add the chicken and stir-fry until it changes color. Add the water and fish sauce to taste and when it boils, drain and add the eggplant. Simmer until it is cooked but not soft. Taste and adjust the seasonings and serve garnished with fresh peppercorns, red chili strips and holy basil and with rice.

HANGLÉ ROBUST CURRY
(North)

Found only in Chiangmai and the north, this curry comes from Burma. Note that the meat is cut in chunks, differently from the refined southern Thai strips. This curry has an intense flavor and is definitely one for the garlic lover. The recipe here comes from Khun Tuanjit Kannang, as do most of my northern Thai recipes.

1 lb (500 g) belly pork complete with skin and fat, cubed
1 lb (500 g) boneless pork neck, cubed
3 tablespoons fish sauce and more to taste
1½ tablespoons dark soy sauce
2 tablespoons *Hanglé* powder (a yellow curry powder
    consisting of milder spices such as coriander, cumin and
    turmeric) or 2 tablespoons mild Indian curry powder
4-in (10-cm) piece fresh ginger root, peeled, thinly sliced
    and shredded
1 teaspoon salt
4 cups (1 liter) water
3 tablespoons oil
1 chicken stock cube (optional)
1½ tablespoons dark brown sugar
15–20 small cloves garlic, peeled
Thick tamarind water made from 3 tablespoons tamarind
    pulp soaked in 1 cup (250 ml) water

Spice Paste
7 large dried chilies, seeded, soaked in warm water for 30
    minutes then squeezed dry
2 stalks lemongrass, sliced
2 teaspoons shrimp paste
¾-in (2-cm) piece turmeric root, peeled and coarsely chopped
12 small or 8 medium-sized cloves garlic, sliced
6 shallots, sliced

Grind the Spice Paste ingredients to a rough paste. Add 1 cup (250 ml) of water to the mortar or food processor bowl, stir to get every last bit of the Spice Paste and set it aside.

Put the meat in a bowl. Add 3 tablespoons of fish sauce, the dark soy sauce and the Spice Paste and mix. Add the *Hanglé* or curry powder and mix again. Set aside for at least 10 minutes.

Soak the shredded ginger in a bowl of water with 1 teaspoon of salt, stir, and set aside. Add 4 cups (1 liter) of water to a saucepan on the stove over medium heat.

Heat the oil in a wok. Add the meat and stir-fry over medium heat until it has changed color and the spices are fragrant. Transfer the water from the mortar to the meat bowl to take up any spices and flavors left there. Transfer the meat mixture from the wok to the saucepan, pour the spice water into the wok to scrape up the residue of flavors there and add this to the saucepan too. Add the chicken stock cube, cover and simmer over low heat until the pork is almost cooked (about 20 minutes). Add the sugar and stir.

Strain and wash the shredded ginger and add it to the saucepan together with 15–20 whole peeled garlic cloves. Simmer for about 1 hour, by which time the liquid should have reduced considerably. Add the tamarind pulp and more fish sauce to taste if necessary (it should be sweet, sour and salty), stir and continue to cook until the liquid is thick and just covers the meat.

This dish is good with fresh vegetables and a dip like Pounded Eggplant (p. 403). It keeps well and leftovers are delicious when reheated. It is the base for Northern Hash, the recipe for which follows.

KAENG HO NORTHERN HASH

This hash uses up what remains in the pots after feeding guests from three to five times a day on special occasions such as weddings (one day), ordinations (up to seven days) or funerals (three days). Only one leftover curry is included, making this the "proper" version of Northern Hash, but often two or three kinds of curry go into it.

2-in (5-cm) wedge of cabbage, roughly chopped
2 whole plants long-leafed coriander (*eryngo*) or
     coriander leaf, cut into ½-in (1-cm) slices
2 winged beans, cut into ½-in (1-cm) pieces (optional)

Small handful of Asian sweet basil leaves
15 betel leaves roughly chopped (optional)
1 bunch of young spinach or *phak tamlung* leaves
2 cups (500 g) sour or pickled bamboo shoots (canned and already cooked), cut in strips
1½ cups (375 ml) water
1 large bowl leftover Robust Curry
15 green beans, cut into bite-sized pieces
10 medium-length red and green chilies
1–1½ oz (30–40 g) mung-bean vermicelli, soaked in warm water for 10 minutes until soft, drained and cut into 1½-in (4-cm) lengths
10 kaffir lime leaves, spines removed and torn into four
2 stalks lemongrass, finely sliced
5 tablespoons oil
20 small cloves garlic, peeled and coarsely chopped

Mix all the greens except the wingbeans together in a bowl, wash them and set them aside to drain. Drain the bamboo shoots and bring them to a boil in a saucepan with the water. Add the leftover Robust Curry, the beans and the chilies. Return to a boil and simmer, partially covered, for 5 minutes.

Squeeze the greens to drain them of any water still clinging to the leaves and add them to the pan, mixing well. Reduce the heat to low and simmer until the beans are tender. Add the mung-bean vermicelli and mix well. Remove the saucepan from the heat and set aside to absorb any remaining liquid. Add the lime leaves and the lemongrass.

Heat the oil in a wok and fry the garlic until golden. Add the contents of the saucepan, mixing for about 2 minutes. Remove and serve with sticky rice.

KAENG OM SLOW-COOKED CURRY
(North)

Northern curries contain neither coconut milk nor trade spices and in true country style are braised dishes more closely related to soups than the conventional idea of a curry. Here I use beef, but this dish is often made with pork and sometimes chicken. This is a great dish for the crockpot.

2–3 tablespoons oil

2 lb (1 kg) blade or round steak, cut into bite-sized pieces

About 3 cups (750 ml) water

1 beef stock cube (optional)

A few kaffir lime leaves, finely shredded

Fish sauce to taste

Fresh coriander leaves and sliced green onions, for garnish

Spice Paste

9–10 dried red chilies

2 stalks lemongrass

1 tablespoon peeled, chopped galangal

1 tablespoon shrimp paste or country fish paste (*pla ra*)

¼ teaspoon peeled chopped turmeric root or a pinch of
   ground turmeric

½ tablespoon kaffir lime peel, chopped

5 shallots, sliced

7–8 cloves garlic

Grind the Spice Paste ingredients to a fine paste.

Heat the oil in a wok, add the Spice Paste and stir-fry until fragrant. Add the beef and stir-fry until it has changed color and is coated with the spices. Add water to cover and simmer until the meat is cooked. Add a stock cube if you desire an extra rich flavor. Add the lime leaves and fish sauce and taste and adjust the seasonings so that the stew is both salty and hot. Serve garnished with coriander leaves and green onion.

PET TUN ## BRAISED DUCK WITH PICKLED LIMES

This recipe comes from Nan, near the Lao border. The Chinese influence is evident in the use of duck, soy sauce and dried lily flower. The lily flower combined with the pickled limes give the dish a very distinct flavor.

1 duck
½ teaspoon salt
6 cups (1½ liters) water
2 coriander roots
2 cloves garlic
Pinch of freshly ground white pepper
2 oz (60 g) Chinese dried lily buds
Oil for frying
4 shallots, sliced
1 tablespoon dark soy sauce
½ tablespoon fish sauce
2 pickled limes (*manao dong*), quartered and 2
   tablespoons pickled lime liquor

Remove as much fat as possible from the duck. Remove the neck, backbone and wingtips, put them into a saucepan with ½ teaspoon of salt and the water and boil for an hour to make stock. Drain and set the stock aside. Cut the rest of the duck into 10 pieces.

In a mortar or a food processor grind the coriander roots, garlic and pepper to a fine paste. Rub the duck pieces with the coriander mixture and set them aside for at least 30 minutes.

Soak the dried lily buds in water for 20 minutes and cut them into small pieces.

Heat the oil in a saucepan and fry the duck and the shallots until brown. Add the stock and bring to a boil. Reduce the heat, add the soy sauce and fish sauce and simmer for 1 hour, adding more water if necessary.

When the duck is tender, add the pickled limes and the lily flowers and simmer for 30 minutes more. Taste and add more fish or soy sauce if necessary. Serve with rice.

STEAMED DISHES

PLA NUNG NAM MANAO

STEAMED FISH WITH LIME, CHILI & GARLIC SAUCE
(South)

Tastes in the south favor sourness over sweetness so sugar is omitted from this recipe.

1 whole fish about 1¼–2 lb (600–800 g) (flathead, small barramundi, snapper, red emperor, perch, trout, cod, dory, morwong)
2 stalks lemongrass, cut into 2-in (5-cm) pieces, bruised
3 thin slices fresh ginger root
Fresh coriander leaves and sliced green onion for garnish

Lime, Chili & Garlic Sauce
4 tablespoons fresh lime juice
2 tablespoons fish sauce
4–6 small red and green chilies, coarsely chopped
4 cloves garlic, chopped
½ cup (125 ml) water or light chicken stock

Clean and scale the fish and slash it three times across each side. Place the fish on top of the lemongrass on a plate, and stuff the ginger slices in the cavity. Steam lightly on a rack over boiling water in a covered wok or steamer until cooked (about 10–15 minutes).

In the meantime make the Chili, Lime & Garlic Sauce. Mix together the lime juice, fish sauce, chilies, garlic and water to taste. Pour the sauce over the fish and garnish it with coriander and sliced green onions.

This recipe also works well with peeled, steamed tiger shrimp, dressed as above or grilled in their shells over low heat and served with the sauce.

HOI NUNG ## STEAMED SCALLOPS WITH LEMONGRASS AND BASIL

10 oz (300 g) scallops (about 30) with 8–10 scallop
shells, or small, flat saucer-scallops complete with
shells
3 stalks lemongrass, brusied and cut into bite-sized
pieces
6 kaffir lime leaves, torn (optional)
10 segments shallot, peeled, lightly bruised and cut in
half
1 tablespoon fish sauce
1 tablespoon fresh lime juice
2 medium-length chilies, sliced
About 30 Asian sweet basil leaves

Arrange the shells around a Chinese claypot or a small wok with a lid
and place the scallops in the center. Scatter the other ingredients on top,
basil last. Cover and steam until cooked (about 5 minutes). The scallops
should produce enough juices of their own but add a splash of water if
you like. Serve in the claypot or the wok.

HOI MALAENGPHU NUNG ## STEAMED MUSSELS WITH LEMONGRASS AND GINGER

4 lb (2 kg) mussels
2 cloves garlic, chopped
5 shallots, finely sliced or 1 medium-sized onion,
chopped
2-in (5-cm) piece fresh ginger root, peeled and finely
shredded
2–3 medium-length chilies, finely sliced
3 stalks lemongrass, bruised and cut into bite-sized
pieces
6 kaffir lime leaves, torn
½ cup (125 ml) water
1 tablespoon fish sauce
Fresh lime juice to taste
1 lime, cut into wedges

Scrub the mussels and remove the beards. Place them in a Chinese clay-pot, a wok or a saucepan with a lid and scatter the garlic, shallots, ginger, chilies, lemongrass and lime leaves over the top. Add water and fish sauce, cover and bring to a boil. Shake well to mix everything together and cook, shaking again from time to time, until the mussels are cooked and open (about 10 minutes). Add fresh lime juice to taste and stir. Pour the mussels and the liquor into bowls and serve with wedges of lime.

HO MOK STEAMED SHRIMP OR FISH CURRY MOUSSE

This is an ancient Thai/Khmer dish that reaches a pinnacle of refinement in Thai cuisine through the use of egg and coconut milk. Compare this version with the steamed fish or chicken in packets of Laos and the Steamed Spiced Chicken of Cambodia.

Banana leaves or small ramekins
3–4 kaffir lime leaves
1½ cups (375 ml) thick coconut milk and 1 cup (250 ml) thin or 2½ cups (625 ml) canned coconut milk
2–3 tablespoons Red Curry Paste II (p. 348) or prepared red curry paste
1 lb (500 g) shrimp, peeled or firm fish (ling, barramundi, orange roughy, warehou or freshwater fish), sliced
1 duck egg or 2 small hen eggs
2 tablespoons fish sauce
½ –1 teaspoon palm or dark brown sugar
1 bunch Asian sweet basil leaves
A handful of fresh coriander leaves
1 medium-sized red chili, seeded and sliced diagonally into fine strips

If banana leaves are available, cut circles from them using the top of a Chinese rice bowl as a guide. Put two circles together for strength and take in four ½-in (1½-cm) tucks about 1½-in (4-cm) deep at equal distance around the outside, pinning the tucks down with a stapler or with tooth-picks. Set the cups aside. If banana leaves are not available use ramekins.

Cut the lime leaves down each side of the spine then slice each half lengthwise into very fine shreds. Set three-quarters of the shreds aside for garnish. Set 1 cup (250 ml) of the thickest coconut milk aside as well.

Place 2 tablespoons of the Curry Paste in a deep bowl (Thais use an unglazed terracotta pot) and slowly add 1 cup (250 ml) of the coconut milk, stirring until it is mixed well. Add the shrimp or fish and mix again. Add the unbeaten egg and stir in one direction with a wooden spoon until mixed. Add the rest of the coconut milk, the fish sauce and sugar to taste. Then stir in (still in the same direction) additional curry paste to suit your taste. Continue stirring rhythmically, still in one direction, for at least 15 minutes.

Cover the bottom of each banana leaf cup or ramekin with basil leaves and pour the mousse mixture on top, leaving room for it to expand slightly. Bring water to a boil in a steamer. Put in the banana cups or ramekins inside, cover the steamer and steam until nearly cooked (about 15–20 minutes).

Remove the lid, spoon 1 tablespoon of the reserved thick coconut milk on to the top of each cup of mousse, replace the lid and steam until completely cooked. When a skewer inserted into the mousse comes out clean it is done.

Garnish each cup with a whole coriander leaf topped with a few strands of chili and lime leaf and serve with rice.

FAN TAENG STUFFED CUCUMBER

4 oz (125 g) crabmeat or a few small shrimp, peeled, deveined and cooked
7 oz (200 g) ground pork
2 cloves garlic, chopped
Pinch of freshly ground pepper
½ tablespoon fish sauce
1 cucumber or zucchini, about 8 in (20 cm) long, peeled, cored and seeded
Fresh coriander leaves for garnish

Set a little of the crabmeat or shrimp aside for garnish but grind the rest. Mix the ground crab or shrimp, the pork, chopped garlic, pepper and fish sauce, and stuff the cucumber with this mixture. Steam on a rack in a steamer until the filling is cooked. Serve sliced in rounds and garnished with the reserved crabmeat or shrimp and fresh coriander or use in Stuffed Cucumber Consommé (p. 345).

KHAI TUNG STEAMED EGGS

This simple, homestyle dish goes well with country stews that do not contain coconut milk, such as Jungle Curry (p. 358).

3 eggs
1 green onion, sliced
⅔ cup (150 ml) water
½–1 tablespoon fish sauce
3 oz (100 g) pork, finely sliced in square pieces
15–18 fresh coriander leaves

Beat the eggs, adding the green onion, water and fish sauce to taste. Put the mixture into small ramekins or into one casserole dish. Bring water to a boil in a steamer, put in the dishes on a rack above the water, reduce the heat and steam gently until cooked. Take the ramekins out of the steamer, arrange the pork slices on top of the egg with a few coriander leaves. Set aside—the pork slices should cook on top of the hot mixture. Serve when the the pork is cooked through.

FRIED DISHES

Even in China, the first evidence of the existence of the metal wok, that essential utensil for stir-frying, does not appear until the 17th century when a technical work of the time describes its casting and panel-beating.

It seems likely that frying was not adapted as a technique in Thai cooking until the latter part of the Ayutthaya period when the city of Ayutthaya became a focus of international trade in a sea-trading arc stretching from China to the Mediterranean via Southeast Asia. Many Chinese traders settled there at that time, where they occupied a dominant position among other foreign traders. By the end of the 17th century they had become the most significant of the king's employees and officials in Ayutthaya in the management and operation of a royal trading monopoly in Siamese products. After the fall of Ayutthaya, succeeding kings, in need of mercantile and commercial skills to revitalize the Thai economy and kingdom, actively encouraged Chinese immigration to the new capital at

Bangkok. In the first half of the 19th century Chinese people made up more than half of the city's total population.

When the royal trading monopoly was relaxed and finally abolished in the middle of the 19th century Chinese traders fanned out into the countryside. Trading from town to town, they often settled, establishing shops and dominating local business. They brought the wok with them, sold it as a trade item, and bred large animals for meat, a practice that adherence to Buddhism had not encouraged the Thais to do themselves. With the perfect piece of equipment on the scene, a food item that lent itself logically to this style of cooking and a plentiful supply of the fat needed for the task, frying and stir-frying began to spread extensively throughout the countryside.

Today the wok is an important piece of equipment in any Thai kitchen. Deep-frying has replaced roasting over charcoal in much modern Thai cooking, and one of the dishes served at a family's main meal will often be a stir-fry.

Regional variations exist, however. Bangkok, with a population estimated still to be about half ethnically Chinese and a sophisticated supply of raw materials, is still the place most committed to stir-frying. There one encounters both refined urban dishes of a wholly Chinese kind and locally-inspired stir-fries using Thai chili pastes or curry pastes for flavoring. Stir-frying is also popular in the central plains region with fish sauce added rather than soy sauce. The central plains are the country's main agricultural area, and stir-fried dishes from this region contain a preponderance of farmed or gathered vegetables (tomatoes, gourds, snakebeans, bamboo shoots, etc.) with only a little meat. In the south where seafood is abundant, fish is deep-fried whole and covered with a sauce, and in the north, meat (in particular, pork) tends to dominate. When it is stir-fried it is done simply with fresh chilies and soy sauce.

In this section I have included only the more distinctively Thai versions of stir-fries and deep-fries. Where possible, I have identified the dishes' region of origin.

Stir-fries

PLA PHAT BAI HORAPHA

STIR-FRIED FISH WITH ASIAN SWEET BASIL
(South)

Whole cleaned baby squid or baby clams in their shells could be substituted for fish in this recipe. First fry the garlic and chilies until fragrant. Add the shellfish, sauces and basil and stir-fry until the shellfish open.

This method is also good for stir-fried beef or chicken. Instead of fish, put the meat in the pan after the garlic and chili paste and stir-fry until it changes color, then proceed with adding the flavorings as instructed below.

4 cloves garlic, coarsely chopped
6 small red and green chilies, coarsely chopped
2 tablespoons oil
1 lb (500 g) deep-sea fish fillets (ling, orange roughy), dried with paper towel and sliced
½ –1 tablespoon fish sauce
½ –1 tablespoon Japanese light soy sauce
About 20 leaves Asian sweet basil, roughly chopped or torn

Mash the garlic and chilies to a paste. Heat the oil in a wok or a pan and fry the fish pieces until they are golden brown but still firm. Add the garlic and chili paste and stir-fry everything until the spices are fragrant taking care not to break up the fish. Add the fish sauce, soy sauce and basil, plus a little water if you need it, stir again to mix and serve.

PHAT PHET PLA

FISH FRIED WITH CHILI PASTE

This dish may also be cooked as a stir-fry using sliced chicken, beef, pork or shrimp. Add the meat or shrimp to the chili paste after it has fried in the pan and stir-fry until cooked. Then proceed with the last cooking step. Sliced zucchini can be substituted for meat for a vegetarian version, but use less chili paste.

3 tablespoons oil
10 kaffir lime leaves, finely shredded lengthwise
1 lb (500 g) small fish fillets (whiting, tommy ruff, herring, mackerel, mullet)
2–3 tablespoons Red Chili Paste (*Nam Phrik Daeng*) (p. 414)
1–2 tablespoons water
1 tablespoon fish sauce
2 medium-length red chilies, sliced

Heat the oil in a wok until hot and fry the kaffir lime leaves until they are crisp. Drain and set them aside. Add the fish to the pan and fry according to the instructions in the recipe for Kingfish with Green Mango (p. 385). Remove and drain. To the hot oil in the wok, add the Chili Paste and stir-fry until fragrant, making sure it does not burn. Add the fish steaks and turn carefully in the chili paste so that they are coated. Add a splash of water and the fish sauce and stir carefully to mix. Serve garnished with the lime leaves and chili slices.

MU PHAT PHRIK KHING — DRY CURRY PASTE STIR-FRY (Bangkok)

This stir-fry keeps well and is good cold on picnics. Peeled and deveined shrimp may be used instead of pork. You can also use this recipe without the meat or the beans but with a little water added to make a sauce for the lightly barbecued or grilled jumbo shrimp, on p. 389.

3 tablespoons Red Chili Paste (*Nam Phrik Daeng*) (p. 414)
2 tablespoons ground dried shrimp
5 tablespoons oil (depending on the fattiness of the meat)
7 oz (200 g) green beans, cut into bite-sized pieces
12 oz (350 g) cooked crispy barbecued pork belly, sliced (available in Asian food stores)

1–2 tablespoons fish sauce to taste
1 tablespoon palm or dark brown sugar
A few kaffir lime leaves, shredded
2 medium-length red chilies, shredded, for garnish

Combine the Red Chili Paste and the ground shrimp and mix well. Heat 1 tablespoon of oil in a wok. Add the beans and stir-fry until half-cooked. Remove the beans and set them aside. Heat 4 tablespoons of oil in the pan. Add the Chili Paste and ground shrimp mixture and stir-fry until fragrant. Add more oil if necessary, although barbecued pork should release its own fat when stir-fried and shouldn't require extra oil. Reduce the heat, add the pork and stir-fry until it changes color. Add the beans, fish sauce and sugar to taste, mix well and stir-fry until everything is cooked. Add the kaffir lime leaves, garnish with shredded red chilies and serve.

MU PHAT NAM PHRIK PHAO   PORK STIR-FRIED WITH CHILI JAM (Bangkok)

1–2 tablespoons oil
2 cloves garlic, chopped
1 lb (500 g) pork shoulder, sliced
2 tablespoons chili jam (*Nam Phrik Phao*, p. 412)
1 teaspoon sugar, or to taste
1 tablespoon fish sauce, or to taste
1 long red chili, shredded
Splash of stock or water
30 leaves Asian sweet basil

Heat the oil in a wok and stir-fry the garlic for a minute, adding the pork and stir-frying until it is slightly cooked. Add the chili jam, sugar, fish sauce and shredded chili and stir-fry until done. Add a splash of stock or water and mix in. Remove from the heat, add the basil and serve.

This recipe is one of those all-purpose ones that also work well with other main ingredients. Try it with shrimp or baby clams in their shells. If using baby clams, wash 2 lb (1 kg) well and drain them. Proceed as above, using the shellfish in place of pork, but after adding the clams and stir-frying for a minute, add the water, cover and and steam until the shells open. Remove the lid and finish as above.

KAI PHAT BAI KAPHRAO

STIR-FRIED CHICKEN WITH HOLY BASIL
(Bangkok)

Sliced or ground pork also works well in this dish.

6 tablespoons oil
Small handful of holy basil leaves
3 cloves garlic, coarsely chopped
1 red and 1 green small chili, crushed
1 lb (500 g) ground chicken
1–1½ tablespoons fish sauce, to taste
1 teaspoon palm or dark brown sugar, or to taste
Pinch of freshly ground pepper
1 medium-length red chili, seeded and sliced into 4
  lengthwise

Heat the oil in a wok and deep-fry a quarter of the holy basil leaves. Drain and set them aside.

Drain the wok of all but 2 tablespoons of the oil and fry the garlic until it is golden brown. Add the crushed chilies and the chicken and stir-fry until the chicken changes color. Add the fish sauce, sugar and pepper and stir-fry until the chicken is cooked. Add the sliced chilies and the raw basil leaves and continue to stir-fry until the basil leaves begin to wilt. Serve garnished with the deep-fried basil leaves.

PHAT PRIAO WAN TAENG KWA

SWEET AND SOUR STIR-FRY WITH CUCUMBER (Central)

The sweet chili sauce called for in this recipe is usually available in Asian food stores with a good Thai section—sometimes called Sweet Chili Sauce for Chicken.

2 tablespoons oil
3 cloves garlic, chopped
12 oz (350 g) sliced lean pork, chicken, rings of baby
  squid and peeled shrimp, alone or in combination
2 tablespoons sweet chili sauce

2 teaspoons vinegar, or more to taste
2 teaspoons fish sauce
5 pickling cucumbers (about 4 in/10 cm long), peeled,
cut in 4 lengthwise, seeded and sliced into 1-in (2½-
cm) pieces
2 small firm tomatoes, quartered
1 medium-sized onion, cut into strips lengthwise
Coarsely chopped fresh coriander leaves for garnish

Heat the oil in the pan and fry the garlic for a minute. Add the meat and stir-fry until it changes color. Add the sweet chili sauce, the vinegar and the fish sauce and mix well. Add the cucumber, tomatoes and onion and stir-fry until sufficiently cooked. Taste and adjust the seasonings to the right balance of sweetness and sourness, adding extra vinegar if you wish. Garnish with fresh coriander and serve.

PHAT MU STIR-FRIED PORK
(North)

In the far north where there is no access to the sea, the country is mountainous and the climate rather dry, a much more no-nonsense approach is taken to stir-frying than in Bangkok. Soy sauce is used instead of fish sauce; pork is often the focus.

2 tablespoons oil
3 cloves garlic, chopped
1 lb (500 g) pork, sliced
½ of a small onion, sliced lengthwise
4 medium-length red chilies, 2 sliced into shreds and 2
cut into four
1 tablespoon Maggi Seasoning Sauce
2 tablespoons soy sauce
Pinch of sugar (optional)
1 tablespoon water

Heat the oil in the wok. Add the garlic, pork, onion and chilies and stir-fry until cooked. Add seasoning sauce, soy sauce, sugar and water, toss well and serve with rice.

PHAT THUA FAK YAO ## STIR-FRIED GREEN BEANS

Adding sugar to every recipe, and often by the tea-spoonful, is characteristic of central Thai cooking. I prefer to omit it and have therefore made its addition optional in this recipe.

2 tablespoons oil
2 cloves garlic, chopped
4 oz (125 g) pork or chicken, finely sliced
1–1½ tablespoons fish sauce
Sugar to taste (optional)
3 cups (750 g) green beans, cut into 1-in (2½-cm)
    pieces
1 medium-sized onion, sliced lengthwise

Heat the oil in a wok. Stir-fry the garlic until it is golden, then add the pork until it changes color. Add the fish sauce, sugar, green beans and onion and mix. Cover the wok for a minute then remove the lid and stir-fry vigorously until everything is mixed well and cooked.

PHAT PHAK KUNG ## STIR-FRIED VEGETABLES WITH SHRIMP (Central)

2 tablespoons oil
2 cloves garlic, chopped
5 oz (150 g) small shrimp, peeled and deveined
1 medium-sized onion, sliced lengthwise into strips
3 cups (750 g) mixed vegetables (cauliflower or broccoli
    florets; baby corn; snowpeas; sliced red bell pepper;
    bean sprouts)
1 tablespoon fish sauce
Pinch of sugar (optional)

Heat the oil in a wok. Add the garlic and the shrimp and stir-fry until the shrimp are opaque. Add the onion and the longer-cooking vegetables first, stir-frying and adding the quick-cooking vegetables as you go. Add the fish sauce and sugar to taste and a splash of water if the dish seems dry.

PHAT PHAK   STIR-FRIED VEGETABLES (Central)

2 tablespoons oil
2 cloves garlic, chopped
1 large onion, sliced or ½ cup green onion, cut diagonally
    into 1-in (2½-cm) lengths
3 cups (750 g) mixed vegetables (snowpeas; cauliflower
    cut into florets with some stalk; sliced mushrooms;
    sliced zucchini)
1 tablespoon light soy sauce
2 tablespoons oyster sauce
Sugar to taste (optional)
Fresh coriander leaves, roughly chopped

Heat the oil in a wok or skillet and fry the garlic and onion until the onion is transparent. Add the rest of the vegetables and stir-fry until tender-crisp. Once the vegetables have been coated in oil, you may want to cover the pan to steam them for a minute. Do not steam for long, however, as the green vegetables will lose their vivid color.

Add the soy sauce, the oyster sauce and sugar (if desired), and stir-fry for about 1 minute. Garnish with fresh coriander leaves.

PHAT NO MAI   STIR-FRIED BAMBOO SHOOTS (Central)

3 tablespoons oil
4 cloves garlic, finely chopped
3 oz (100 g) pork, thinly sliced
1 tablespoon fish sauce
Pinch of sugar
1 lb (500 g) bamboo shoots, sliced
3 bell peppers, sliced
1 green onion, sliced
Fresh coriander, with stems chopped

Heat the oil in a wok. Fry the garlic for 1 minute, add the pork and stir-fry for 1 minute more. Add the fish sauce, sugar, bamboo shoots and bell pepper and stir-fry for 5 minutes, adding more oil if necessary. Taste and adjust the seasonings. Add the green onion and the fresh coriander and serve.

PHAT THUA NGOK # STIR-FRIED BEAN SPROUTS

8 oz (250 g) fresh bean sprouts
1 tablespoon oil
4 cloves garlic, chopped
2 oz (50 g) pork loin, finely sliced
3 oz (100 g) shrimp, peeled and deveined
1 tablespoon fish sauce
Pinch of sugar
¼ teaspoon freshly ground pepper

Clean and wash the bean sprouts. Heat the oil in a wok or pan and fry the garlic until it is golden. Add the pork and stir-fry until it changes color. Add the shrimp and stir-fry. Add seasonings to taste, then the bean sprouts and stir-fry until they are tender-crisp.

PHAT PHAK KHANA # STIR-FRIED CHINESE BROCCOLI

I learned a more traditional version of this dish in Chiangmai in the north using *pla khem* (a slab of moist salted fish sold in a packet in Asian food stores) instead of pork.

Remove the fish from its packaging, wash it and wipe it dry. Remove the bones and cut it into cubes. Proceed according to the instructions provided below but add the fish pieces to the wok after the garlic and cook them well. Add the broccoli and stir-fry. Stir in 1 tablespoon of light soy sauce instead of the oyster sauce and serve.

3 small Chinese broccoli (kale) plants, washed
2 tablespoons oil
4–6 cloves garlic, chopped
2 tablespoons oyster sauce, or more to taste
Salt to taste
Pepper to taste
Stock or water to moisten
3 2-in (8 x 5-cm) piece cooked belly pork with crisp
   skin (available in Asian food stores), sliced, or thick
   slices fat bacon, fried crisp

Cut the leaves off the stems of the Chinese broccoli at their base and peel the main stem at the bottom where it is tough and fibrous. Bunch the leaves together and cut them into 1-in (2½-cm) pieces. Bruise the main stems slightly at their base and slice them diagonally into 3-in (7-cm) pieces.

If the broccoli is young, proceed to stir-fry. If it is mature and tough, blanch it first. Put 2 cups (500 ml) of water in a pan and bring it to a boil. Add the stalks and cook for 5 minutes, adding the leaves for the last two. Drain and dry.

Heat the oil in a wok until it is hot. Add the garlic and stir-fry until it is golden brown. Add the broccoli and stir-fry until it is coated with oil but the stems are still crisp. Add the oyster sauce, salt and pepper and stock or water to moisten and stir to mix. Stir in the pork or bacon at the last minute to ensure it remains crisp and serve.

This dish may also be cooked using chicken or pork, or no meat at all, with oyster sauce.

PHAT SATO STIR-FRIED PUNGENT LOCUST BEANS (South)

Locust bean (in Thai *sato*), is a special kind of bean that grows in the south of Thailand, in Indonesia and in Malaysia. Locust beans have a strong and unique taste and smell—to me a bit like a cross between garlic and durian. You can often buy locust beans frozen or in brine in jars from Asian food stores. The frozen ones are better. If you must find a substitute use fresh lima beans—they look somewhat similar although, comparatively speaking, they contribute no taste.

4 shallots, sliced
2–4 small red chilies, chopped
1 tablespoon shrimp paste
2 tablespoons oil
10 oz (300 g) belly or shoulder pork, skinned and sliced
   or peeled shrimp or a mixture of both
1–2 tablespoons palm or dark brown sugar
3–4 tablespoons fish sauce
2 cups (500 g) locust beans, split in halves or slivered

1 tablespoon fresh lime juice

2 medium-sized chilies, sliced lengthwise into four

Grind the shallots, small chilies and the shrimp paste to a fine paste. Heat the oil in a wok and stir-fry the spice paste until fragrant. Add the pork and/or shrimp and stir-fry until cooked. Add the palm or dark brown sugar and the fish sauce to taste, mix, and reduce the heat. Add the locust beans and stir-fry for a few minutes. Add a splash of water or stock, lime juice to taste, and adjust the seasonings. Add the chili, mix and serve immediately.

PHAT NO MAI/THUA PHU KHAI — STIR-FRIED SHREDDED BAMBOO SHOOTS WITH EGG

Other vegetables can be cooked according to the instructions in this recipe—shredded cabbage, green beans cut into 1-in (2½-cm) lengths or sliced zucchini. If you use green beans, you might need to add a splash of water and cover the pan for a few minutes to steam them. Make sure, however, that all the water has evaporated before you add the egg.

2 tablespoons oil

2 cloves garlic, chopped

2 cups (500 g) shredded bamboo shoots or winged
   beans, thinly sliced across

1 large egg

2 teaspoons fish sauce

Up to 1 teaspoon sugar (optional)

Heat the oil in a wok, add the garlic and stir-fry until golden. Add the vegetable and stir-fry until tender-crisp. Add the egg and stir everything together until cooked, adding fish sauce and sugar (if desired) to taste.

PHAT NAEM — STIR-FRIED FERMENTED PORK SAUSAGE (North)

Naem is a specialty sausage of the north and north-east made from ground pork and pork skin wrapped in banana leaves and left for a few days to ferment. Manufactured under hygienic conditions, wrapped in banana leaves and then in plastic, it is usually available in small packets in Asian food stores with a Thai, Lao or Vietnamese bias. So too is blanched shredded pork skin, a favorite textural food across the north of Thailand, Laos and Vietnam.

3 oz (100 g) blanched finely shredded pork skin
2 tablespoons oil
4 cloves garlic, chopped
4 green onions, sliced diagonally
2 small onions, sliced lengthwise into thick slices
7 oz (200 g) fermented pork (*naem*), roughly chopped or sliced into strips
1 tablespoon fish sauce
1–1½ teaspoons sugar
1 large egg
Sliced green onion and torn mint for garnish

Rinse the pork skin, drain and dry it well. Heat the oil in a wok and fry the garlic until golden. Add the onions and the fermented pork and fry for a few minutes. Add the fish sauce and the sugar and mix well. Add the whole egg, stirring and cooking until the egg is slightly cooked with both yellow and white streaks in it. Take the pan off the stove and stir in the pork skin. Garnish with green onion and mint and serve with rice.

KHAI YAT SAI STUFFED OMELETTE

2 tablespoons oil
½ medium-sized onion, finely chopped
½ cup (125 g) ground pork or chicken
1 tomato, diced
6 snowpeas, cleaned and cut into 1-in (2½-cm) pieces
1 tablespoon tomato sauce or Maggi seasoning sauce
Sugar to taste (optional—in Thailand this dish is made quite sweet)
Salt and pepper to taste
Fresh coriander leaves, finely chopped
4 eggs
Fresh whole coriander sprigs for garnish

Heat 1 tablespoon of oil in a wok over medium heat. Add the onion and stir-fry until transparent, then add the meat and stir-fry until it is cooked. Add the tomato and cook until any liquid it releases is reduced, add the snowpeas and mix well. Add the tomato sauce or Maggi sauce, sugar, salt and pepper, mix well and place into a bowl. Stir in the chopped coriander leaves and set aside.

Rinse the wok and brush it clean (do not use soap). Wipe it completely dry then heat it over medium heat. Add the remaining tablespoon of oil and swirl it around over the entire surface of the wok. Lightly beat the eggs and pour them into the wok, reducing the heat a little. Swirl the egg around the wok surface, spreading it evenly around the sides to form a large crêpe omelette. When it is set, add the filling into the center and fold four sides of the omelette over to form a square package. Slide carefully out onto a serving plate and garnish with the coriander sprigs.

PHAT PHAK BUNG KHAI   WATER SPINACH TOPPED WITH EGG

This version of stir-fried water spinach from the north makes a delicious one dish meal. For each person you will need the following ingredients.

Oil for deep-frying
1 egg
1 small slice fresh ginger root, peeled and chopped
1 clove garlic, chopped
1 green onion, cut into 3 pieces
1–2 bird's eye chilies, finely chopped
1 tablespoon light soy sauce
Splash Maggi seasoning sauce (optional)
4 oz (125 g) water spinach, washed, dried, hard ends
    discarded and leaves chopped
Hot cooked rice

Heat the oil in a wok and carefully add the egg so that the yolk does not break. Fry the egg until it is puffy and brown around the edges but still soft in the middle. Lift out, drain and set it aside.

Leave 1 tablespoon of hot oil in the wok, add the ginger, garlic, green onion and chili and stir-fry until fragrant. Add the soy sauce, the seasoning sauce and the water spinach and stir-fry until the leaves are coated with the spices. Add a splash of water and continue stir-frying until the spinach is tender-crisp. Serve the spinach over hot rice and top with the egg.

Deep-fries

PLA RAT PHRIK   FRIED FISH WITH FRAGRANT SAUCE

Khai Rat Phrik is a dish of fried eggs served with the same sauce prepared for the following recipe. When the oil for deep-frying is hot break in an egg (or more than one if there is plenty of room), spooning a little hot oil over the edges until they have puffed up and are crisp. Remove and drain then proceed to cook the sauce, pouring the sauce over the eggs.

1 saltwater fish for frying, about 1¼–2 lb (600–800 g)
   (bream, mackerel, red snapper, emperor, blackfish, dart,
   sea perch, nannygai, trevally)
6 medium-length chilies, seeded
4 cloves garlic
6 shallots
Oil for deep-frying
1 tablespoon palm or dark brown sugar
2 tablespoons fish sauce
3 tablespoons tamarind water or vinegar
¼ cup (60 ml) water
Fresh coriander leaves for garnish

Clean and scale the fish, leaving the head and tail intact but removing the gills. Slash it across three times on each side and dry it thoroughly.

Coarsely chop the chilies together with the garlic and shallots.

Heat the oil in a wok until hot. Add the fish and reduce the heat to medium, frying one side of the fish until it is golden brown and crisp with the flesh coming off the bone easily. Turn and fry the other side. Remove, drain and plsce it on a serving plate.

Drain the wok of all but 2 tablespoons of oil and stir-fry the garlic, shallots and chilies together until fragrant. Add the sugar, the fish sauce and the tamarind water to taste and stir everything together as it comes to a boil. Add some water if the sauce looks too thick. Taste and adjust the seasonings, which should be hot, salty, sweet and sour in reasonable balance—add more sugar and/or fish sauce if you wish. Pour the sauce over the fish and serve. Garnish with fresh coriander leaves.

FRIED FISH WITH SWEET SAUCE

PLA THOT NAM PLA WAN

1 fish for frying, about 2 lb (800 g) (snapper, bream, mackerel, sea perch, emperor, blackfish, dart, dory)
Oil for deep-frying
2–3 tablespoons oil
6 small dried chilies
8 shallots, finely sliced lengthwise or equivalent fried red onion flakes
4 cloves garlic, finely sliced lengthwise
3 tablespoons palm or dark brown sugar
1 tablespoon fish sauce
½ tablespoon tamarind water
Fresh coriander leaves and red chilies soaked and cut into flower shapes (p. 21) for garnish

Clean, scale and slash the fish and dry it thoroughly. Fry the fish according to the instructions provided in the recipe for Fried Fish with Fragrant Sauce (p. 382) and place it on a serving plate. Drain the wok of the oil and wipe it clean.

Heat 2–3 tablespoons of fresh oil in the wok and add the bird's eye chilies, cooking them until crisp. Remove, drain and set them aside for garnish. Add the sliced shallots and fry them until brown and crisp without burning them. Remove, drain and set them aside, then add the sliced garlic and repeat the process. Leave a little flavored oil in the wok.

Mix together the sugar, fish sauce and tamarind water, pour it in the seasoned wok and bring it to a boil. Adjust the flavors if you wish (the emphasis should be on sweet), and simmer gently, stirring until the sauce has been thoroughly mixed and has thickened a little. Pour the sauce over the fish and top with the crisp-fried ingredients. Garnish with fresh coriander leaves and chili flowers.

PLA THOT THA SOUTHERN MARINATED FISH

The turmeric and lemongrass in this marinade are characteristic of the south.

1 whole fish, about 1¼–1¾ lb/600–800 g (dart, bream, mackerel, snapper, sea perch, emperor)
1 stalk lemongrass, finely sliced
¾-in (2-cm) piece fresh turmeric root, peeled and coarsely chopped or ½ teaspoon ground turmeric
4 cloves garlic, sliced
Pinch of salt
Oil for deep-frying
2 tablespoons Japanese soy sauce or light soy sauce
1 lime, thinly sliced into rounds

Clean, scale, slash and dry the fish according to the instructions in the recipe for Fried Fish with Fragrant Sauce (p. 382).

Grind the lemongrass, turmeric and garlic to a fine paste, adding a little salt. Rub this on to the fish, both inside and out and set it aside to marinate for an hour or two.

Heat the oil in a wok and fry the fish until it is cooked and the skin is crisp. Transfer the fish to a serving plate, pour the Japanese soy sauce over the top and garnish with slices of lime.

PLA THOT THA KRATHIAM PHRIK THAI DEEP FRIED FISH WITH GARLIC AND PEPPER

Coriander root, garlic and pepper are a classic Thai flavor combination that is used to transform essentially Chinese soups into distinctively Thai ones. It is also used to flavor deep-fried fish, poultry and meats or when grilling them over charcoal.

1¼ –1¾ lb (600–800 g) whole fine-fleshed fish for frying (whiting, garfish, mackerel, bream, emperor, sea perch, flounder, dart)
4 coriander roots
Pinch of salt
3 cloves garlic

½ teaspoon whole peppercorns, ground
Oil for deep-frying

Clean, scale, slash and dry the fish. Grind the coriander roots, salt, garlic and peppercorns to a fine paste. Rub this over the fish and set it aside to marinate for an hour.

Deep-fry the fish until it is crisp. Drain it and serve accompanied by Chili Fish Sauce (p. 414).

Oily or dry fish such as catfish, kingfish, small mackerel, mullet or trevally treated this way should be grilled over low heat or baked in the oven. Wrap the fish in banana leaves before cooking if you have access to them, otherwise put the fish in an oiled fish grill. Turn to cook both sides, then remove and serve with the dipping sauce. Firm-textured fish of low to medium fat content such as morwong or rock cod should be wrapped in foil.

PLA SAMLI DAET DIAO   KINGFISH WITH GREEN MANGO

1¼ –1¾ lb (600–800 g) thin kingfish fillets
Oil for deep-frying
2 cloves garlic, chopped
2 tablespoons finely sliced shallots
2 medium-length chilies, sliced into shreds
4 tablespoons shredded green mango (p. 47)
3 green onions, sliced diagonally
1–2 teaspoons palm or dark brown sugar
1–2 tablespoons fish sauce
Fresh lime juice to taste (only if the green mango is not
	sour enough)

Dry the fish fillets with paper towel. Heat a wok or a frying pan and add the oil. Add the fish and fry until brown on one side, then turn carefully and brown the other side. Remove the fillets and keep them warm. Drain the wok of all but 2 tablespoons of oil and add the garlic, the shallots and the chilies and stir-fry until they are soft, then add the green mango and the green onion, stirring briefly until they are coated with oil. Reduce the heat and add the sugar, fish sauce and just enough water to make a sauce. Taste and adjust the seasonings—it should be sour. Add fresh lime juice to taste if the sauce is not sufficiently sour. Bring the sauce to a boil, pour over the fish and serve.

DEEP FRIED CHICKEN WITH GARLIC AND PEPPER

KAI THOT KRATHIAM PHRIK THAI

Quail are very good cooked good this way too.

4 cloves garlic
½ teaspoon whole peppercorns, ground
3 coriander roots
1 lb (500 g) chicken breasts or chicken pieces
Oil for deep-frying

Grind the garlic, pepper and coriander roots to a paste. Rub the chicken with this paste and set it aside for an hour. Heat the oil in a wok or pan and add the chicken pieces. Fry until the chicken is brown and tender, reducing the heat if necessary to prevent it from burning. Drain the chicken pieces on paper towel and serve with rice and sweet chili sauce for chicken (available in bottles in Asian food stores).

DARLING CRAB

PU JA

4 blue swimmer crabs, washed
5 coriander roots, chopped
2 cloves garlic, chopped
¼ teaspoon ground white pepper
2 eggs
6 oz (170 g) ground pork
2 tablespoons fish sauce
Oil for deep-frying
4 coriander leaves
Chili shreds or flowers (p. 21) and fresh coriander leaves
    for garnish

Steam the crabs whole. Remove and discard the entrails then remove and flake all the meat, including the legs. Wash the body shells, dry them and set them aside.

Grind the coriander root, garlic and pepper to a fine paste. Lightly beat one egg. Mix the pork, crab meat and fish sauce with the spice paste, add the egg and mix well.

Stuff the mixture into the crab shells and steam them until the filling is cooked.

In the meantime beat the other egg and heat the oil for deep-frying. Place one coriander leaf on top of the stuffed portion of each crab, spoon beaten egg over it and deep-fry one at a time until the stuffed part of the crab is golden brown. Remove, drain and garnish with chili shreds or chili flowers and fresh coriander leaves and serve on a plate decorated with a row of overlapping sliced tomato around one edge. Serve with Cucumber Relish.

KHAI LUK KHOEI ## SON-IN-LAW EGGS

Anyone who knows the Thai language will recognize a secondary meaning in the name of this dish.

6 duck or hen eggs
Oil for deep-frying
8 tablespoons palm or dark brown sugar
4 tablespoons fish sauce, or more to taste
4 tablespoons tamarind water, or more to taste
Fried onion flakes (p. 20) or fresh coriander leaves, and
    shreds of fresh red chili for garnish

Boil the eggs until they are hard (about 6–8 minutes). The yolk should not be fluid but it should be tender. Cool the boiled eggs in cold water, then peel and cut them very carefully in half lengthwise. Heat sufficient oil in a wok to deep-fry the boiled eggs, with the flat side down, until golden. Lift, drain and keep warm on a plate with the yolk side facing up.

Drain the wok of all but 1 tablespoon of oil, add the palm or dark brown sugar and dissolve it. If its consistency is too thick, add a little water. Add the fish sauce and tamarind water and stir for about 5 minutes as the mixture bubbles or until you have a thick, brown sauce. Pour the sauce over the eggs and garnish with the fried onion flakes or fresh coriander leaves and the chili.

LUK CHIN NUA THAI MEAT BALLS

3 cloves garlic, chopped
2 coriander roots, chopped
½ teaspoon ground pepper
8 oz (250 g) ground pork
8 oz (250 g) ground beef
2 tablespoons finely chopped onion
1 tablespoon fish sauce
Oil for deep-frying
½–1 tablespoon chopped fresh coriander leaves for
    garnish

Grind the garlic, coriander roots and pepper to a paste. Combine all the ingredients, mix well and form into small meat balls or large hamburgers (the hamburger version is a Western adaptation). Small meat balls should be thinly coated with flour and deep-fried in plenty of hot oil until brown, then drained. Hamburgers should be cooked on both sides on a lightly greased griddle or in a frying pan. In either case, garnish with fresh coriander leaves and serve with Cucumber Relish or sweet chili sauce.

GRILLED DISHES

KUNG PHAO ## BARBECUED SHRIMP

Roasting over charcoal is an ancient method of cooking. For a long time it was largely replaced by frying in much of modern Thailand. Today it is making a comeback, especially in the fashionable coastal resorts of the south.

Select large saltwater shrimp, small lobsters or freshwater shrimp. Remove the feelers and legs but leave the top part of the body attached with its shell intact. Leave the shell on the tail as well initially, but split it down the back, remove the vein and push in a dot of butter or margarine to keep the flesh moist as it cooks. Cook the shellfish over a low charcoal fire. Split the lobsters in half and pour a little melted butter over them before grilling.

Do not overcook the shellfish, and when you take the shrimp off the fire, carefully pull the shell off the meaty part of the tail, leaving it on both the upper body and the tail "flipper." Arrange the shrimp on a plate and dress with lime, chili and garlic sauce (p. 364), or a fried curry paste sauce (*phat phrik khing*). Spoon the dressing over the tail-end of the grilled shrimp and serve.

PLA PHAO ## GRILLED FISH IN BANANA LEAF

1 catfish or firm-fleshed saltwater fish, or a large trout, about 1¼–1¾ lb (600–800 g)
1 teaspoon light soy sauce
3 garlic cloves, chopped
½ teaspoon ground pepper
Oiled banana leaf or aluminum foil

Clean and scale the fish, slash it three times on each side and rub it with soy sauce, garlic and pepper. Wrap it in an oiled banana leaf or a piece of aluminum foil and cook on the grill or in the oven for 20 minutes. An oily fish such as mackerel may not need to be wrapped.

Serve with Fish Sauce and Lime with Bird's Eye Chilies (p. 414).

KAI YANG I CHARCOAL-GRILLED CHICKEN (Central)

A traveling Thai is a snacking Thai. This dish is sold by hawkers in major train and bus stations throughout the country. The particular recipe or way of serving it varies, however, in different regions. Here is the first of three versions.

1 teaspoon freshly ground pepper
3 coriander roots
4 cloves garlic
½ tablespoon fish sauce
½ tablespoon light soy sauce
Pinch of sugar
1½ lb (750 g) small chicken quarters (leg and thigh; breast and wing)

Grind the pepper, coriander roots and the garlic to a paste and add the fish sauce, soy sauce and sugar to make a marinade. Marinate the chicken in this mixture for a few hours then grill or roast in the oven.

In Bangkok this dish would be eaten with Thai sweet chili sauce for chicken, available in bottles in Asian food shops.

KAI YANG II   CHARCOAL-GRILLED CHICKEN II (Northeast)

In the northeast the marinade would be the same as in the central version except that it would not contain coriander root. The sauce to accompany the chicken would be one made from fish sauce, lime juice and tomatoes as follows.

5 shallots
6 small fresh chilies, chopped
6 cherry tomatoes or 1 medium tomato, chopped
6 tablespoons fresh lime juice (juice of 3 limes)
3 tablespoons fish sauce
1 teaspoon palm or dark brown sugar (optional)

Thread the shallots on a skewer and roast them over the charcoal fire, turning until their skins turn dark brown all over. Remove the skins and slice the flesh.

Grind the chilies, shallots and tomatoes to a rough paste. Add the lime juice, fish sauce and the sugar (if using) and mix until the sugar dissolves and pour into a bowl.

KAI YANG III   CHARCOAL-GRILLED CHICKEN III (South)

2–4 dried red chilies, seeded, soaked in warm water until
   soft and squeezed dry
3 stalks lemongrass, thinly sliced
2 tablespoons chopped fresh turmeric root or 2
   teaspoons ground turmeric
3 coriander roots, chopped
6 cloves garlic, chopped
¼ teaspoon freshly ground pepper
1 cup (250 ml) thick coconut milk
2 tablespoons fish sauce
1½ lb (750 g) chicken, quartered or chicken pieces

Grind the chilies, lemongrass, turmeric (if using root), coriander roots, garlic and pepper to a fine paste. Mix this paste with the coconut milk, turmeric (if using ground) and fish sauce. Pour over the chicken and marinate for at least an hour, preferably more. Grill the chicken, brushing occasionally with the rest of the marinade as it cooks.

Serve with sweet chili sauce.

KADUK MU ## BARBECUED SPARERIBS
(North)

This recipe comes from the north where meat, especially pork and pork products are very popular and servings are more substantial than elsewhere.

4 cloves garlic, chopped
¼ cup (60 ml) soy sauce
2 tablespoons sherry (optional)
1 tablespoon sugar
¼ teaspoon freshly ground pepper
2 lb (1 kg) pork belly spareribs

Combine the garlic, soy sauce, sherry, sugar and pepper and marinate the spareribs for 2 hours in the mixture, turning them over from time to time. Grill the ribs, basting them occasionally with the marinade. If you intend to eat the spareribs with rice, chop them into smaller pieces, and arrange on a serving dish with lettuce, cucumber and tomato.

The spareribs may also be cooked under the broiler, or better still, roasted on a rack in a medium oven.

MU RU NUA YANG

SEASONED GRILLED PORK OR BEEF

Large pieces of meat like this are not common in Thailand. This recipe is an adaptation of a classic Thai flavoring for use on a Western-style grill. As a further adaptation, a whole piece of pork loin or beef fillet could be seasoned in the same way and then roasted in the oven.

1 tablespoon chopped coriander root
½ teaspoon freshly ground pepper
5 cloves garlic
1 tablespoon fish sauce
1 tablespoon soy sauce
Sugar to taste (optional)
1 lb (500 g) pork belly spareribs or pork chops or 1½-in
   (4-cm) thick steak for barbecuing

Grind the coriander roots, pepper and garlic to a paste. Mix with the fish sauce and soy sauce and a little sugar if you wish. Spoon this mixture over the meat and set it aside to marinate for at least an hour (if using beef, marinate in the refrigerator for a day). Grill the meat, preferably over a charcoal fire. Grill the whole piece of steak rare and then slice it on the diagonal thin. Serve with the sauce given in the recipe for Charcoal-Grilled Chicken II (p. 391).

DRESSED DISHES AND SALADS

This group of dishes more than any other reveals the layers of complexity and eclecticism of Thai food.

For all the shared "great tradition" of most of Southeast Asia in ancient times that I referred to in the Introduction, distinctly individual cultural patterns have also emerged within the countries of the region. Its close proximity to China and Vietnam and shared ancient geographical ties with both of these countries, and its shared borders with Burma, Laos, Cambodia and Malaya, Thailand must have been surrounded by a greater variety of potential influences than any other country in Southeast Asia even in pre-modern times. History shows that the Thais formed the habit of borrowing and absorbing useful practices and techniques from neighbors and other cultures very early, and this is clearly evident in Thai food.

We have seen how borrowing led to the introduction of complex curries using coconut milk after Ayutthaya, and how it led to the widespread adoption of frying and stir-frying as techniques not long after that.

In the 19th and early 20th centuries the status of Thailand's neighbors as colonies of European powers brought specific European culinary influences to bear on their cuisines. Thailand's position as the only independent kingdom in the region at the time did not isolate it from European influence. If anything it produced an even broader exposure as a variety of European nations sent emissaries to Bangkok and entertained Thai royalty in Europe in a quest for economic and political preferment.

Groups of recipes in this section track this varied cultural history.

The first group of dishes—the chili sauce or *nam phrik*—embrace what is probably an ancient culinary technique and a common one among Southeast Asian cultures. Wild herbs and fruits are combined with the only sources of protein that in the past were always available to rice farmers in tropical climates—ones that were preserved through salting or fermenting—to make dips or condiments which add zest to rice and substance to seasonally available foods. One of the most important ingredients included in chili sauce today—the chili—would only have been included after the Portuguese brought it to Asia in the 16th century.

The second group contains a miscellany of traditional dressed meat, fish and vegetable dishes of Lao origin from the north and northeast of Thailand. Here lime juice is used for dramatic effect and also, I suspect, as an agent for cleansing and helping to break down some tough foods. Lots of chili is used in these dishes to add aggressive flavor. Encountered in their classic form the *lap* and *tam* involved in this group can sometimes be a bit daunting. The recipes I include here are ones that appeal to more sensitive Western palates.

Lon, the third group of dishes, involve cooked sauces with a little chopped meat, fish or shellfish added, rather subtle flavorings, and coconut milk. They are known to have been very popular in court circles from at least the 19th century. I would not be surprised to discover that they were developed as a refined aristocratic alternative to *nam phrik* using more expensive ingredients and more European-inspired saucing techniques.

It is difficult to work out the provenance of the fourth group of dishes, the *yam*. "*Yam*" literally means something like "mixed together, assembled." *Yam* include lightly cooked seafood (the most common main ingredient), fresh or cooked vegetable, or sometimes even grilled rare meat. These are mixed with fresh herbs and chili, tossed in a delicately balanced dressing of lime juice, fish sauce and often palm sugar and served at room temperature. *Yam* are modern urban food. Until recently their place was among the nibbles and curtain-raisers that accompanied Thai whisky (*mekong*) sipped by men as they waited for the main meal. In present-day Thailand, however, especially in Bangkok, it is quite common to find *yam* served as part of the main meal.

The inspiration for *yam* would have to have come from the traditional *lap* and the *tam*, but they also have a tossed salad quality that probably owes a great deal to a fascination for things European in the 19th century. It is interesting that similar salad-style dishes appear in French-influenced Vietnamese cuisine.

As with most Thai dishes, getting the right balance between sweet, sour, salt and hot flavors is extremely important. This is very much an individual matter, however, so please be prepared to taste and adjust for yourself as you go.

Nam Phrik

Probably the most universal Thai dish of all would be one of the varieties of chili sauce (*nam phrik*) accompanied by vegetables, either raw, boiled, or fried in batter, alone or in combination. Most Thais eat these more often than anything else other than rice in ordinary family meals, and different versions of the basic sauce appear in all parts of the country.

I have mentioned before how in the countryside a dish of chili sauce would often be accompanied by wild leaves and fruits gathered around the village or on the edges of canals and riverbanks. In the past village girls would take turns foraging while men and boys fished in the streams in order to supplement the family's diet of rice and homegrown vegetables. A wonderful autobiography written by a country schoolgirl for her English homework (Prajaub Thirabatana, *Little Things*) mentions the following as some of her regular afternoon activities: going to find bamboo shoots, mushrooms and new shoots of young leaves; collecting fallen mangoes in the temple grounds at the beginning of the rainy season; catching crabs and snails and small fish in the paddies or shellfish in the streams at rice-planting time; finding bulbs and bamboo shoots in the woods; and picking ripened tamarind fruits around the village.

Foraging of this kind probably dates back to a time before food production was introduced. With increasing modernization, even in the countryside, it is practiced less and less. People still eat chili sauce, however, with a keen appreciation of the freshness of the vegetables and the pungency of the dip.

Many different vegetables are used, depending on what is available and what part of the country you are in, although there are some basic patterns. In these recipes I recommend the mixture of accompanying vegetables suggested to me by cooks in Thailand, but you should feel free to substitue whatever ones you like.

Most chili sauce mixtures are served with small fish that have been fried or steamed and fried. The favorite and most common fish used for this purpose is a small mackerel (*pla tu*). You see these regularly in the markets all over Thailand: three little fish, each 4–6 in (10–15 cm) long, already steamed and arranged on a small bamboo tray ready to be taken home for final frying. Any small fried fish would do as well as these.

NAM PHRIK KAPI CHILI SAUCE WITH SHRIMP PASTE
(Central)

In central Thailand a particular eggplant known as
ma-uk—the size of a golf ball, orange in color and
hairy—is used to ensure the sourness of this dish. The
hairs are scraped off first and the fruit sliced and
added to the mortar at the same time as the pea eggplant. You may need to add more lime juice if you
make this dish without the *ma-uk*.

10 cloves garlic, sliced
1 heaping tablespoon shrimp paste, roasted
15 pea eggplant (optional)
10 bird's eye chilies
Juice of 2 limes
1 tablespoon palm or dark brown sugar
1 tablespoon fish sauce

Grind the garlic and shrimp paste to a fine paste. Add the pea eggplant (if
using) and pulse the food processor a few times to process them roughly.
Add the chilies, the lime juice, sugar and fish sauce and mix lightly, taking
care not to completely break up the chilies or eggplant—both should
remain bruised but intact. Adjust the seasonings to taste—it should be
more sour than sweet or salty.

Served with rice, very small fried fish and vegetables prepared in any
one of the following ways.

Raw Vegetables
4 green golf-ball eggplant, cut through about ½ of the
    way down, turned 90 degrees and cut again
3–4 pickling cucumbers, quartered lengthwise and cut
    into 2-in (5-cm) pieces
10 green beans
A wedge of raw cabbage

Steamed Vegetables

1 cup (250 g) young jackfruit, cubed or 8–10 spears
    young asparagus
1 cup (250 g) young pumpkin leaf and stalk or snowpea
    shoots or young spinach leaves
½ cup (125 g) purple cigar-shaped eggplant, cut into
    large cubes with skin
½ –1 cup (125–250 g) fresh thick coconut milk

Lightly steam the vegetables separately and pour the coconut milk over them. Serve with fish and Chili Sauce with Shrimp Paste (p. 397).

Fried Vegetables

Beat 2 eggs. Peel some long green eggplant, purple cigar eggplant, pumpkin or zucchini and cut them into thin slices. Heat 1 cup (250 ml) of oil in a wok until hot. Dip each vegetable into the beaten egg and drop it into the hot oil. (Limit the contents of the wok to about 8 pieces at any one time in order to give each piece sufficient space.) Lift out each piece when cooked, drain well and arrange on a plate.

NAM PHRIK KUNG ## CHILI SAUCE WITH SHRIMP (Bangkok)

6 dried red chilies
4 cloves garlic
3 shallots
4–6 ripe but firm cherry tomatoes
½ teaspoon shrimp paste, roasted
3 oz (100 g) finely chopped grilled shrimp or flaked
    grilled fish
2–3 kaffir lime leaves, torn into small pieces
1 tablespoon fresh lime juice
1 tablespoon fish sauce
1 teaspoon or more of palm or dark brown sugar

Grill the chilies, garlic, shallots and tomatoes until they are brown. Seed the chilies and peel the garlic, shallots and tomatoes. Grind the chilies, garlic, shallots and shrimp paste to a paste. Add the tomatoes, the shrimp and the kaffir lime leaves and mix together. Add the lime juice, fish sauce and palm or dark brown sugar to taste and mix well, mashing together lightly. Taste and adjust the seasonings again if necessary and pour into a bowl. Serve with raw vegetables, as outlined in the recipe for Chili Sauce with Shrimp Paste (p. 397) and rice.

NAM PHRIK ONG ## COOKED CHILI SAUCE WITH PORK (Chiangmai)

This chili sauce is usually eaten with Thai fried pork skin (available in Asian food stores but a packet of pork cracklings will do) and the raw vegetables described on p. 397 or steamed ones such as pumpkin, long green eggplant, green beans and Chinese cabbage.

7 oz (200 g) lean ground pork
2 tablespoons oil
6 cloves garlic, chopped
1¼ cup (300 g) diced tomatoes
1 pork or chicken stock cube
Sliced green onions and chopped fresh coriander leaves
    for garnish

Spice Paste
7 medium dried red chilies, soaked in warm water until
    soft and squeezed dry
2 teaspoons shrimp paste
10 cloves garlic, sliced
6 shallots, sliced

Grind the Spice Paste ingredients to a fine paste. Add the ground pork and mix well.

Heat the oil in a wok, add the garlic and fry until fragrant. Add the pork and Spice Paste mixture, fill the mortar with water and set it aside. Stir-fry the pork and Spice Paste until the meat is cooked. Add the tomatoes and cook until soft. Add the water from the mortar and the stock cube, stir to mix and bring to a boil. Taste and adjust the seasonings, simmer for a minute or two then pour into a serving bowl and garnish with green onions and fresh coriander.

GREEN CHILI DIP
(North)

I first encountered this dish in Nan near the Laos border. I did not see it cooked until later in Chiangmai, where my friend Tuanjit Kannang walked me through this recipe, but I was surprised, in such a remote country town as Nan, to be taken to a very informal fresh food co-op where I could have bought all the necessary ingredients assembled in a plastic bag ready to cook. Who said the fast food revolution in Thailand was confined to Bangkok?

2–3 pieces of small mackerel (*pla ra*), finely chopped, in
    2–3 tablespoons *pla ra* liquor or 2–3 tablespoons
    Budo Sauce (p. 42) (optional)
12 shallots
8–10 cloves garlic
8 large dark green or banana chilies
6 cherry tomatoes, peeled and chopped
2 tablespoons fish sauce
3 green onions and a handful of fresh coriander leaves,
    chopped, for garnish

Vegetables
3 wedges of pumpkin (1½ in /3 cm thick), peeled and
    cut into chunks
1 bunch young green beans, cut into 4-in (10-cm)
    lengths
5 young cigar-shaped eggplant, sliced down the middle
    for ½ of their length but not peeled
3 wedges (1-in/2½-cm thick) cabbage
Handful of young spinach leaves

Double wrap the mackerel (if using) in aluminum foil and roast for a few minutes in a dry pan. Roast or grill the shallots, garlic and chilies until brown (p. 21) and peel the skins off. Chop the chilies. Grind the chilies, the mackerel (if using), the shallots and the garlic to a fine paste. Add the tomatoes and mix everything together without mashing the tomatoes completely. Add the fish and half of the green onions and coriander. Transfer to a bowl, garnish with the remaining green onions and coriander and set aside.

To prepare the vegetables, put the hard vegetables in separate piles in a large steamer and steam until they are almost cooked. Add the spinach leaves and finish steaming until everything is cooked.

Traditional Dressed Dishes

LAP ISAN NORTHEASTERN DRESSED BEEF

Lap is one of the favorite dishes of north Thailand as well as the northeast. Most foreigners and more than a few southern Thais find the classic country version unappetizing. Below is a description from *The Teachers of Mad Dog Swamp*, a novel by Khammaan Khonkai (translated into English by Gehan Wijeye- wardene) about a young teacher, trained in Bangkok, who returns to teach in a village in the northeast, the region of his childhood:

The headmaster took the meat out of the bamboo strips which held it together. He picked out the meat still on the bone and the pieces of stomach and put it in a pot with various vegetables which had already been chopped. The fillet and meat off the leg, of which there wasn't very much, he chopped very finely. He put some into a large dish and poured on it the phia—gastric fluids, in truth, digested food which the animal would have used to nourish its body. It was a green fluid from the small intestine. It was bitter to the taste. He mixed up the fluid with the minced meat. He put it in the dish, not yet putting anything else in except the entrails, which had also been finely chopped, and which he sprinkled over the meat. After that, he sprinkled various condiments into the dish. He added, in proper proportion, fermented fish (pla ra), finely chopped green chillies, rings of onions, shredded kaffir lime and lemon juice; what could not be omitted from the larp was the parched rice—rice parched until it was yellow—and the finely chopped onion.

When all the ingredients had been put in, he used a spoon to mix it all up together. Mint may be added with the other condiments, or it may be added later. The fresh blood is put in at the same time...

"It's very nice, but it's a bit bitter," the young man observed, not knowing that the more bitter the larp the better.

"Of course it's bitter. It's delicious. I especially asked for the di." Di was the green liquid which comes from a little sac adjacent to the liver...[i.e. the bile—R.B.]

The recipe that follows is a tame version by comparison, but it too is delicious.

> 1 heaping tablespoon rice
> 6 dried chilies
> 1 lb (500 g) lean beef, pork or chicken, ground or finely chopped
> Juice of 1½ limes (3 tablespoons)
> 1½ tablespoons fish sauce or more to taste
> 30 mint leaves
> 6 green and red chilies, sliced
> 3 stalks lemongrass, finely sliced
> 20 segments of shallot, finely sliced or 4 small Spanish onions, finely chopped
> 2–3 fresh small red chilies for garnish

Roast the rice in a dry pan on top of the stove until it is yellow in color, then grind it roughly until it is the consistency of coarse sand. Roast the dried chilies in the same pan, and grind them.

Boil about 2½ cups (625 ml) of water, add the ground beef, and stir gently until the meat changes color, then drain well, and reserve the stock for some other purpose. Transfer the meat to a serving dish, mix the lime juice with about 1½ tablespoons of fish sauce to start with and pour it over, mixing it in. Add half of the mint leaves, the 6 sliced chilies, lemongrass and shallots. Taste and season with more fish sauce if necessary, decorate the platter with the remaining mint leaves and the fresh chilies, and serve with sticky rice and a plate of salad greens, including some bitter lettuce and, if you have it, long-leafed coriander or Vietnamese mint.

TAM MAKHUA ## POUNDED EGGPLANT
(North)

Long green eggplant (*makhua yao*) are the best kind to use for this recipe as they are drier than the purple ones.

12 whole shallots
3 long green eggplant or 6 cigar-shaped purple eggplant
3–4 large mild green or banana chilies
12 small cloves garlic, peeled and chopped
Pinch of salt
2 eggs
3–4 tablespoons fish sauce
A handful of mint leaves
2 tablespoons of chopped fresh coriander leaves and
    ¼ cup (65 g) sliced green part of green onion mixed
    together

Grill the shallots, whole eggplant and chilies on skewers on a rack over low heat or under the broiler until their skin is blackened. Peel off the blackened skin. Put the eggplant on a board and chop and mash it with a knife or in a mortar until you have a rough paste (you can use a food processor but take care not to grind the eggplant too much) Seed the chilies and grind them with the shallots and garlic to a rough paste.

Combine the eggplant and the chili mixture in a mortar, add salt to taste and mix thoroughly with the pestle. Transfer to a bowl and refrigerate until needed (at least 2 hours).

Hard-boil the eggs. Cool, peel and chop one of them roughly. Put the chopped egg into the eggplant mixture and mix. Add the fish sauce to taste, the mint leaves and half of the coriander-green onion mixture, mix well and plate. Garnish with sliced hard-boiled egg and the remainder of the coriander-green onion mixture. Serve with fresh mint and 6–8 green onions on a separate plate.

SOM TAM MALAKO   POUNDED GREEN PAPAYA (Northeast)

4 medium-sized garlic cloves
6 small fresh chilies or 1½ teaspoons ground chili flakes
3 cups (750 g) finely shredded green papaya (p. 47)
¼ cup (65 g) ground dried shrimp
8 firm cherry tomatoes, halved, or 2 medium tomatoes
   cut into wedges

Dressing
3 tablespoons fresh lime juice
1–3 tablespoons fish sauce
1–2 tablespoons palm or dark brown sugar
Freshly ground pepper to taste

In a large earthenware mortar mash the garlic and, if you are using fresh chilies, bruise but do not crush them. Add the papaya, ground dried shrimp and tomatoes and mix them roughly with the pestle without mashing them further. Take special care not to break up the tomato too much.

To make the Dressing, mix the lime juice, fish sauce, sugar and chili flakes (if using), and pepper. Mix well, taste and adjust the flavors—it should be quite sweet, hot and sour. Pour the Dressing over the salad and mix everything lightly with the pestle. Serve with sticky rice.

Lon

LON KUNG COOKED COCONUT SHRIMP DIP

Crabmeat, ham, or a mixture of lean ground pork and shrimp can also be used in this recipe.

1 cup (250 ml) thick and 1 cup (250 ml) thin coconut
   milk or 14 oz (400 ml) can of coconut milk
1 lb (500 g) shrimp, ground
3 teaspoons palm or dark brown sugar
Salt to taste
9 shallots, sliced or 2 small Spanish onions, chopped
2–3 medium-sized or 4 small chilies, cut into bite-sized
   pieces
1½–2 tablespoons tamarind water (p. 67)
Chopped fresh coriander leaves for garnish

If you are using canned coconut milk open it without shaking it and skim 1 cup (250 g) of the thick coconut milk off the top. Put the thick coconut milk in a saucepan and bring it to a boil. Boil hard, stirring constantly until it has evaporated and the oil has come out. Add the shrimp and stir-fry until it changes color. Add the thin coconut milk and the sugar and salt. Stir to mix, reduce the heat and simmer until the sauce is creamy. Add the shallots and chili and cook for a few minutes more. Add tamarind water to taste and serve garnished with chopped coriander leaves.

Good accompaniments include crisp raw vegetables such as green beans cut into ½-in (1-cm) pieces, a wedge of cabbage, pickling cucumbers cut lengthwise into quarters, thick strips of bell pepper, celery or golf-ball eggplant.

Yam

The balance of flavors in a *yam* is unique to each dish and will vary according to the flavor of the main ingredient. It is more important than ever to taste as you go and adjust the seasonings given to suit yourself. A general guideline worth following is to start out with a more or less equal balance of lime juice and fish sauce but make the dressing with twice the amount of lime juice to fish sauce first. Mix this into the dish initially, taste it, then add however much more fish sauce you need. You should not be daunted by this approach—it is, after all, exactly what a lot of us do with a vinaigrette. The amounts given in the recipes generally suit me but I do not expect them to be right for everyone.

YAM HOI MALAENGPHU

DRESSED MUSSELS

2 lb (1 kg) mussels in the shell, bearded and scrubbed
4–6 small red chilies
1 small clove garlic (optional)
2 tablespoons fresh lime juice
1½ tablespoons fish sauce
4 shallots, finely sliced or 1 small Spanish onion, chopped
2 stalks lemongrass, finely sliced
Small handful of mint leaves
Pinch of sugar (optional)
Asian or frilly lettuce leaves for decoration

Steam the mussels in ½ cup (125 g) of water in a covered saucepan until they open. Take them out, remove the meat and discard the shells.

Seed two of the chilies and mash them with the garlic, the lime juice and the fish sauce. Scatter the shallots, lemongrass, the remaining chilies sliced diagonally and half the mint leaves, torn, over the mussels in a bowl. Pour the lime juice dressing over the mussels and toss gently. Check and adjust the flavors, tossing again if you add anything.

Line a plate with the lettuce leaves, spoon the mussels onto the center and garnish with the remaining mint leaves.

YAM KUNG DRESSED SHRIMP

To make Dressed Squid (*Yam Pla Muk*) proceed according to the instructions below but use 1 lb (500 g) of squid instead of the shrimp. Prepare the squid according to the instructions on p. 26. Put it in a strainer with 1 teaspoon of finely chopped fresh ginger root and set it over boiling water until lightly cooked. The squid will curl up into a flower-like shape. Lift out and drain, then proceed.

1 lb (500 g) shrimp, peeled and deveined or peeled
    cooked shrimp
3 tablespoons thinly sliced shallots or 1 small Spanish
    onion, chopped
2 stalks lemongrass, very finely sliced
2 tablespoons sliced green onions
3 tablespoons sliced mint leaves
1 tablespoon chopped fresh coriander leaves
Asian or frilly lettuce leaves and sliced lime for decoration
Mint sprigs for garnish

Dressing
3 tablespoons fresh lime juice
2 tablespoons fish sauce, or to taste
4–6 red chilies, finely chopped
Pinch of sugar (optional)

If using shrimp, bring a saucepan of water to a boil, place the shrimp in a strainer and set them in the water until they are cooked. Remove, drain and place the shrimp in a shallow dish.

To make the Dressing, combine the lime juice, fish sauce and chilies. Taste and adjust the flavors, adding more lime juice or fish sauce and/or a touch of sugar if you wish. Pour the Dressing over the shrimp and scatter the shallots, lemongrass, green onions, mint leaves and coriander leaves over the top. Toss and refrigerate for an hour or two.

Line a serving plate with lettuce leaves. Toss the shrimp again and pile them in the center of the plate. Garnish with mint sprigs and decorate the edges of the plate with slices of lime.

YAM NUA DRESSED BEEF

I like this dish with some "bite" but you should adjust the amount of chili to suit yourself.

1 lb (500 g) fillet, rump or sirloin steak, sliced thick
8 shallots, finely sliced or 1½ small Spanish onions, cut in
    two across and then thinly sliced lengthwise
2 tablespoons chopped mint
2 tablespoons chopped fresh coriander leaves
Asian or frilly lettuce leaves and diagonally sliced red
    chilies for decoration

Dressing
4 cloves garlic, chopped
6 small red chilies, sliced into strips or ½ tablespoon or
    more of dried chili flakes
3 tablespoons fresh lime juice
1 teaspoon sugar
2 tablespoons fish sauce

Grill the steak to medium-rare. When cool, slice it diagonally into thin slices. Put the sliced beef, shallots, mint and coriander into a shallow dish.

To make the Dressing, combine the garlic, chilies, lime juice, sugar and fish sauce and mix well. Taste and adjust the flavors—it should be tangy, salty and hot. Add more of any of the ingredients if you wish.

Pour the dressing over the beef and herbs and toss gently. Line a serving plate with lettuce leaves and arrange the beef on top in overlapping slices. Garnish with diagonally sliced fresh red chilies.

To make a larger quantity for a party, slice the meat more finely and mix everything together in a bowl first before heaping on to a lettuce-lined dish. Garnish with diagonally sliced fresh chilies.

YAM MAKHUA YAO DRESSED EGGPLANT

5 oz (150 g) lean ground pork
2 cloves garlic, chopped
Pinch of pepper to taste
2 tablespoons fish sauce
2 long green eggplant (*makhua yao*), depending on size
   or 4 cigar-shaped purple eggplant
1 tablespoon oil
2–3 tablespoons fresh lime juice
1 teaspoon sugar
5 shallots, finely sliced
4 small red and green chilies, finely sliced into strips
3 tablespoons ground dried shrimp
Chopped fresh coriander leaves, for garnish

Mix the pork with the garlic, pepper and 1 tablespoon of fish sauce and set aside. Grill or roast the eggplant under the broiler, turning it regularly until the skin is blistered and the flesh is soft but not mushy. When cool, peel off the skin, cut them in half lengthwise and then into 2-in (5-cm) pieces. Arrange on a plate.

Heat the oil in a pan or a wok and stir-fry the pork, breaking it up and cooking it until it changes color. Add the lime juice, sugar, the rest of the fish sauce or more to taste, sliced shallots and chilies and mix well. Taste and adjust the seasonings and spoon the meat and the sauce over the eggplant pieces on the plate. Top with dried shrimp then garnish with a little fresh coriander.

YAM MU YO DRESSED PORK ROLL, TOMATOES AND ONION

This is a very popular *yam* which makes use of a Vietnamese-style pork roll, *mu yo*. The pork is wrapped in banana leaves and then covered in clear plastic. It can be found in the refrigerator at any Asian food store with a Thai or Vietnamese bias. Pork roll adds an interesting texture to this dish.

3 oz (100 g) pork roll, sliced thin then quartered

2 small onions, peeled, cut in half and thinly sliced

8 small ripe tomatoes, sliced

1 tablespoon fish sauce

1 tablespoon fresh lime juice

1 teaspoon sugar

2 cloves garlic, chopped

2 small green chilies, thinly sliced

1 tablespoon roughly chopped fresh coriander leaves

Arrange the pork roll, onion and tomato slices carefully on a plate. Combine the fish sauce, lime juice, sugar, garlic, chilies and coriander leaves in a jar and shake. Pour the dressing over the sliced ingredients and serve.

YAM YAI GRAND SALAD

7 oz (200 g) lean pork loin or butterfly chops

½ chicken breast, skinned

7 oz (200 g) cooked shrimp, peeled and deveined

5 small round radishes, trimmed and sliced thick

2 oz (50 g) mung-bean vermicelli, soaked in warm water
until soft, drained and cut into bite-sized pieces

1 tablespoon chopped Chinese cloud-ear mushroom
(optional), soaked in warm water and drained

6 shallots, finely sliced or 1 small onion, finely chopped

3 pickling cucumbers, sliced

3 oz (100 g) bean sprouts, washed and trimmed

Leaves from 6 mint sprigs

Freshly ground black pepper

Dressing

3–4 tablespoons fresh lime juice

2 cloves garlic, chopped

2 teaspoons sugar

2 fresh red chilies, finely chopped

2 tablespoons fish sauce

Garnish

3 hard-boiled eggs, quartered

Chili flowers (p. 21)

Torn fresh coriander leaves

Bring a small pan of water to a boil and gently simmer the pork until cooked. Cool the meat in the water, remove it and slice into thin strips. Steam the chicken breast, cool and slice it into thin strips.

Combine the sliced pork, the chicken, shrimp, radishes, mung-bean vermicelli, cloud-ear mushroom, shallots, cucumber and bean sprouts into a serving bowl, add the mint leaves and season with freshly ground black pepper. To make the Dressing, combine the lime juice, the garlic, sugar, finely chopped fresh chili and fish sauce to taste, and pour over the ingredients in the bowl.

Garnish the salad with hard-boiled egg, chili flowers and torn coriander leaves.

YAM TAENG KWA · TOSSED DRESSED CUCUMBER OR CRISP SALAD

8 oz (250 g) cucumbers, seeded and sliced or 8 oz (250 g) mixed crisp vegetables (cucumber; water chestnuts; radishes), sliced
2 tablespoons sliced cooked shrimp, pork or crabmeat or ground dried shrimp
½ red Spanish onion, finely chopped

Dressing
1–2 tablespoons fresh lime juice
1–2 teaspoons sugar to taste
Salt to taste
1–1½ tablespoons fish sauce
Pinch of ground chili (optional)

Garnish
1 tablespoon fried garlic slices (p. 20)
Sprigs of fresh mint or coriander leaves
Chili flowers (p. 21)

Place the cucumber or vegetables, shrimp and onion in a salad bowl. To make the Dressing, mix the lime juice, sugar, salt, fish sauce and ground chili and toss with the salad ingredients. Garnish with fried garlic, mint or coriander sprigs and chili flowers.

NAM PHRIK DAENG RED CHILI PASTE

5 large dried chilies, seeded, soaked in water until soft
  and squeezed dry
2 stalks lemongrass, finely sliced
1 tablespoon chopped shallots
1 tablespoon chopped garlic
1 tablespoon chopped galangal
1 teaspoon chopped coriander root
¼ teaspoon shrimp paste
½ teaspoon chopped kaffir lime skin

In a mortar or a food processor, grind all the ingredients to a fine paste.
Use in recipes as directed.

NAM PLA PHRIK KHI NU FISH SAUCE AND LIME WITH BIRD'S EYE CHILIES

This sauce is always present on the Thai table for
dipping. It is good with rice, including fried rice,
and with grilled dishes or anything that needs a lift.

4 tablespoons fish sauce
1 tablespoon fresh lime juice
1 clove garlic, finely sliced lengthwise
3–4 bird's eye chilies, sliced into rings
Sugar to taste (optional)

Mix everything together and serve as a dipping sauce.

NAM PLA PHRIK FISH SAUCE WITH CHILI

4–6 small green or red bird's eye chilies, finely sliced
¼ cup (60 ml) fish sauce

Mix the chilies with the fish sauce. Serve in a bowl as an accompaniment
to noodle dishes.

PHRIK PON # THAI GROUND CHILI FLAKES

Dry-roast as many large whole dried chilies (with their seeds) as you like until brown and grind them into flakes. Serve in a bowl as an accompaniment to noodle dishes.

PHRIK NAM SOM # CHILIES IN VINEGAR

3–4 long red and green chilies
¼ cup (60 ml) white rice vinegar

Slice or roughly chop the chilies and mix them into the vinegar. Serve in a bowl as an accompaniment to noodle dishes.

RICE-BASED ONE-DISH MEALS AND NOODLES

The dishes in this section are Thai versions of the ones commonly eaten for breakfast and lunch and as snacks at any time of the day all over Southeast Asia.

KHAO TOM KAI CHICKEN RICE PORRIDGE

Rice porridge is the traditional breakfast dish throughout mainland Southeast Asia. Every country has its own version—the Thai one is always garnished with fried garlic. Compare it with the Chinese and Vietnamese versions. Like them, Chicken Rice Porridge is especially good when you are not feeling well.

5 cups (1¼ liters) light chicken stock or water
2 cups (500 g) cooked rice
8 oz (250 g) ground chicken
1½–2 tablespoons fish sauce
1 tablespoon Chinese pickled or salted vegetable
   (optional)
1 Asian celery plant, cut into 1½-in (3-cm) pieces, or
   1 stalk celery, cut into strips
2 tablespoons oil
2 tablespoons sliced or roughly chopped garlic
Freshly ground pepper to taste
3 green onions, finely sliced

Bring the stock to a boil. Add the rice and drop the ground chicken into the soup in teaspoonfuls. Add fish sauce to taste and salted vegetables (if using), simmering for about 10 minutes until the chicken is cooked. Add the celery at the last minute and stir.

In the meantime, heat the oil in a small pan and fry the garlic until it is golden brown. Remove the rice soup from the stove and serve in bowls garnished with fried garlic, pepper and sliced green onion.

KHAO MAN KAI CHICKEN RICE

A favorite lunch, Chicken Rice is another dish of Chinese origin found all over Southeast Asia. Com-pare it with Malaysian Hainanese Chicken Rice (p. 244).

1 lb (500 g) chicken breasts, skinned but not boned
5 cups (1¼ liters) water
2 coriander roots
Salt to taste
2 cups (500 g) rice
Sliced cucumber
Green onions
Sprig of coriander for garnish

Sauce
5 white peppercorns, ground
3 cloves garlic
2-in (5-cm) piece fresh ginger root, peeled
3 teaspoons fermented yellow soy bean paste, mashed
2 teaspoons soy sauce
1 tablespoon chicken stock
1 tablespoon fish sauce
1 tablespoon vinegar
Sugar to taste
3–4 small red chilies, sliced
Coriander leaves, roughly chopped

Put the chicken breasts in a saucepan with the water, coriander roots and salt and bring to a boil. Skim the foam that forms off the top and simmer gently until the chicken is tender but not overcooked. Remove the chicken and chop it into wide strips. Reserve the stock.

Steam the rice using the strained chicken stock instead of water.

To make the Sauce, grind the pepper, garlic and ginger to a fine paste in a mortar or a food processor. Add the fermented soy beans, soy sauce and chicken stock. Mix well. Add the fish sauce, vinegar and sugar to taste. Add the chilies and coriander leaves and mix well again.

Spoon a single serving of rice onto a plate beside some sliced cucumber and whole green onions. Arrange the chicken slices over the top of the rice and garnish with a sprig of coriander. Serve with a bowl of Sauce.

KHAO PHAT THAI THAI FRIED RICE

Lime juice gives this fried rice a special piquancy.

1 cucumber, peeled
8 green onions
2 limes, cut the Thai way (p. 48)
4 tablespoons oil
12 small cloves garlic, peeled
2 thick slices of fatty bacon, cut into strips
1½ small onions, sliced lengthwise
3 eggs
5 cups (1¼ kg) cooked rice
1 tablespoon fish sauce
1 teaspoon sweet dark soy sauce (*si yu dam*) or
  Javanese soy sauce
1 tablespoon light soy sauce
2 teaspoons chicken seasoning powder (optional)
3 cherry tomatoes, each cut into 8 wedges

Scrape a fork down the outside of the cucumber, cut it in half lengthwise and then cut each half into diagonal slices. Clean the green onions, trimming off most of the green tops. Cut the green tops into 1-in (2½-cm) lengths and set them aside. Arrange the cucumber, the lime pieces and the cleaned green onions on a serving plate.

Heat the oil in a wok or a pan over medium heat. Add the whole garlic cloves and fry until they are golden. Add the bacon and fry until both the bacon and garlic are brown. Add the onions and fry for 1 minute, then break in the eggs, piercing the yolks and mixing them until they are scrambled but retain flecks of white. Add the rice and mix everything together well. Mixing and stirring between each addition, add fish sauce to taste, the sweet soy sauce, the light soy sauce and the chicken seasoning powder. Add the tomato wedges and the green onions that have been set aside and serve. Diners help themselves to cucumber and green onions and use the lime pieces to squeeze juice onto the rice then mix it in.

KHAO SOI # CURRIED NOODLES
(North)

This rich curry noodle dish is reminiscent of Malaysia's noodle dish *Laksa* with a Burmese origin.

2 lb (1 kg) fresh egg noodles
2 cups (500 ml) oil
1 cup (250 ml) thin coconut milk and 1 cup (250 ml)
  thick or a 14 oz (400 ml) can coconut milk
1 lb (500 g) skinless chicken breast fillets, sliced into
  ½-in (1-cm) slices
2 tablespoons curry powder
2 tablespoons sweet dark soy sauce (*si yu dam*) or
  Javanese soy sauce
3 tablespoons fish sauce
2 large chicken stock cubes dissolved in 8 cups (2 liters)
  water

Spice Paste
7 large dried chilies, seeded, soaked in warm water until
  soft and squeezed dry
1 stalk lemongrass, finely sliced
1-in (2½-cm) piece turmeric root, peeled and coarsely
  chopped
1 teaspoon shrimp paste (optional)
8 cloves garlic, sliced
6 shallots, sliced

Accompaniments
Chili–Garlic Mix (p. 420)
Special Fish Sauce with Chilies (p. 421)
Thick Coconut Cream (p. 421)
½ jar of pickled mustard greens, sliced
3 limes, cut into wedges the Thai way (p. 48)
9 shallots, peeled and cut into quarters
Sweet dark soy sauce (*si yu dam*) or Javanese soy
  sauce
Chopped fresh coriander leaves and green onion tops,
  mixed

Assemble the Accompaniments first and place them on the table.

Grind the Spice Paste ingredients to a fine paste in a mortar or food processor.

Separate out about 12 oz (350 g) of the fresh noodles. Heat the oil in a wok and deep-fry the noodles (in four batches) until brown, and drain them well. Place in a bowl and set aside.

Put the thin coconut milk (or ½ a can) into a saucepan and bring it to a rapid boil. Boil hard until the milk reduces and the oil starts to come out. Add a little vegetable oil if this does not happen. Add the curry paste and stir constantly, letting it "fry" until it smells aromatic. Add curry powder and mix well, and then the chicken and stir-fry to mix and to seal the chicken. Add the sweet dark soy sauce, the fish sauce and the stock made from stock cubes and water. Bring to a boil, reduce the heat and simmer, uncovered, until the chicken is cooked. Take off the stove, stir in 1 cup (250 ml) of thick coconut milk (or the rest of the can) and pour it into a bowl.

Meanwhile bring plenty of water to a rapid boil. Add the rest of the noodles and boil for about 2 minutes. Drain and rinse thoroughly with hot water. Put the noodles in a bowl and mix in 1½ tablespoons of oil to prevent them from sticking.

Serve the boiled noodles, fried noodles and chicken curry with the Accompaniments. Serve about 1 cup (250 g) of boiled noodles into each individual plate, ladle lots of curry sauce over this and top with some fried noodles. Diners help themselves to the Accompaniments.

Chili–Garlic Mix
3 tablespoons oil
3 cloves garlic, peeled and coarsely chopped
20 medium-sized dried chilies

Heat 1 tablespoon of oil in a wok and fry the garlic until light brown. Remove, drain and set aside to cool. Fry the whole chilies until they are dark brown. Drain and cool. Coarsely grind the garlic and chilies in a mortar or a food processor. Mix with 2 tablespoons of oil and serve.

Special Fish Sauce with Chilies

3 tablespoons fish sauce
6 bird's eye chilies, sliced finely into rounds
7 cloves garlic, peeled and coarsely chopped
Juice of ½ lime

Mix all the ingredients together.

Thick Coconut Cream

Put 1 cup (250 ml) of thick coconut milk into a small saucepan, bring to a boil and cook, stirring constantly until it thickens. Pour into a bowl and serve.

KUAI TIAO RAT NA

FRESH NOODLES WITH GREENS AND SOY SAUCE

This is one of those dishes indicative of Southeast Asia. Introduced everywhere by overseas Chinese, it seems very much at home in the northern town of Nan, where this recipe comes from.

3 tablespoons oil
12 oz (350 g) fresh flat rice noodles (buy the folded
   slabs available in Asian food stores and slice into strips
   about ¾–1¼ in /2–3 cm wide, and then in two lengthwise)
2 teaspoons dark soy sauce
2 cloves garlic, chopped
8 oz (250 g) pork, finely sliced
8 oz (250 g) Chinese broccoli stalks or asparagus
   spears, peeled and sliced diagonally
1 teaspoon sugar
1 teaspoon yellow bean paste
2 tablespoons light soy sauce
½–⅔ cup (125–150 ml) stock or water
1 teaspoon sticky rice flour or cornstarch, mixed with a
   little water

Heat 1–2 tablespoons of oil in a wok, add the noodles and stir-fry for a minute. Add the dark soy sauce and stir-fry until they are coated with oil. Lift on to a serving plate and keep warm.

Heat the rest of the oil in the wok until hot, add the garlic and the pork and stir-fry until it changes color. Add the broccoli and stir-fry until it is coated with oil and then add the sugar, the bean paste, the light soy sauce and as much stock or water as required to make a light gravy. Add the flour-water mixture and stir thoroughly until the gravy has thickened slightly and everything is cooked.

Pour the contents of the wok over the noodles and serve with the following condiments in separate bowls for diners to adjust their own flavors: Fish Sauce with Bird's Eye Chilies (*Nam Pla Phrik*) and Thai Ground Chili Flakes (*Phrik Pon*) together with some chopped Chilies in Vinegar (*Phrik Nam Som*) and some white sugar.

THAI FRIED NOODLES

SEN CHAN PHAT THAI

Noodles in soup or fried are the standard lunch dish of urban Thailand. Most are close to the Chinese prototypes from which they are derived. Thai Fried Noodles (*Phat Thai*), however, contain flavors that are characteristically Thai. This particular version of the dish gets its name from the use of Chantaburi noodles, but use Thai *sen lek* noodles, available as "A grade Banh Pho imported from Thailand" in Asian food shops.

8 oz (250 g) narrow dried rice noodles
4 cloves garlic
5 tablespoons oil
4 large shrimp, peeled and deveined
3 shallots
1 teaspoon dried chili flakes (Thai ground chili)
3 oz (100 g) firm white tofu, diced
2 eggs
2 tablespoons fish sauce
1½–2 tablespoons sugar
4 tablespoons tamarind water (p. 67)
2 tablespoons dried shrimp, washed and ground
2 cups (500 g) bean sprouts, tailed and washed
½ cup (125 g) chopped Chinese leeks or garlic chives
½ cup (125 g) coarsely ground roasted peanuts

Garnish

20 leaves of Indian or Asian pennywort (*bua bok*) or 1–2
    leaves of Italian endive or other slightly bitter lettuce
½ cup (125 g) bean sprouts, washed and trimmed
3 green onion curls (p. 22)
½ cup (125 g) coarsely ground roasted peanuts
1 lime, cut into wedges the Thai way (p. 48)

Prepare all the ingredients first and place in separate bowls around the cooking area. Soak the noodles in cold water for 30 minutes, drain them thoroughly and cut them into manageable lengths with scissors (about 3 cuts across should be enough). Chop 1 clove of garlic, heat 1 tablespoon of oil in a wok over medium heat and fry the clove of garlic until it is yellow. Add the shrimp and stir-fry until they are cooked. Remove and keep warm. In a mortar or a food processor grind the rest of the garlic, the shallots and the chili flakes to a fine paste.

The balance of the cooking should be done in two batches in order to allow plenty of room in the wok or pan for tossing. Add 2 more tablespoons oil to the wok and when it is hot add half of the garlic, chili and shallot paste and stir-fry until fragrant. Add half of the noodles, a splash of water and stir-fry, turning constantly to prevent sticking and to ensure that everything is mixed and coated with oil. Push the noodles to one side of the wok. Add a little more oil if necessary, add half of the tofu and stir-fry for a minute. Push the tofu aside and break one egg into the wok and pierce its yolk. When the egg starts to set on the bottom, stir and scramble it lightly with the edge of the spatula. Return the noodles and the tofu to the middle of the pan and continue stirring until everything is mixed together. Reduce the heat a little, add half the fish sauce, sugar and tamarind water and toss everything together until the sugar has dissolved. Add half of the dried shrimp, half of the bean sprouts and half the Chinese leeks. Taste and adjust the flavors to your liking then turn off the heat and stir in ¼ cup (60 g) of the roasted peanuts.

Place the fried noodles in a bowl and set them aside while you cook a second batch. Add the first batch to the pan for a final stir and warming, then place all the fried noodles on one side of a serving platter. Arrange the shrimp on top or on the outside edge. Arrange the pennywort or bitter lettuce leaves, a handful of washed bean sprouts, a few green onion curls and the remainder of the peanuts decoratively in separate mounds on the other side of the dish. Add the lime wedges for individual diners to squeeze over the noodles to their taste and serve with a bowl of fish sauce with rounds of small red chilies (*Nam Pla Phrik*), one of chili flakes (*Phrik Pon*) and one of sugar so that each person may adjust the seasonings as desired.

MI KROP CRISP-FRIED NOODLES

This is another Chinese dish that the Thais have made their own. If a foreigner (*farang*) in Thailand will like only one Thai dish, it will almost certainly be this one. This is my adaptation of a modern version taught to cooking students at the Suan Dusit Teachers' College in Bangkok.

1 lb (500 g) fine rice vermicelli
Oil for deep-frying
2 eggs (duck eggs if you have them)
1½ cups (375 g) firm tofu, diced
2 cloves garlic, chopped
4 oz (125 g) each sliced pork, chicken and chopped
    shrimp or any combination thereof
6 tablespoons chopped garlic, set aside
6 tablespoons palm or dark brown sugar
1 tablespoon white sugar
2 tablespoons fish sauce
4 tablespoons fresh lime juice
2 tablespoons vinegar
1 tablespoon grated lime or mandarin zest (optional)

Garnish

1 bunch Chinese leeks, cut into 1-in (2½-cm) pieces
Fresh coriander leaves
Fresh red chilies, seeded and sliced diagonally
4 heads pickled garlic, sliced
Fresh bean sprouts, washed

Soak the rice vermicelli in cold water for about 30 minutes until it is soft, then drain it well and set it aside. Heat plenty of oil for deep-frying in a wok over medium-high heat. Place a small portion of the vermicelli into the hot oil and fry it until golden brown and crisp. Lift out and drain thoroughly on paper towel, repeating the process until all the vermicelli is fried.

Beat the eggs well. Reheat the oil for deep-frying and pour a third of the egg through a strainer into the oil. It will fluff up into a lacy nest. When it is golden brown remove and drain it thoroughly on paper towel. Repeat until all the egg is used up. Deep-fry the tofu until it is brown and crisp and set it aside to drain.

Drain the wok of all but 2 tablespoons of oil and fry the 2 cloves of chopped garlic. Add the meat and shrimp and stir-fry until cooked. Place on a dish and keep warm. Add 4 more tablespoons of oil and fry the 6 tablespoons of chopped garlic until golden brown. Drain off the excess oil and add the palm or dark brown sugar and the white sugar to the wok, stirring over low heat until the sugar has dissolved. Add the fish sauce, the lime juice and the vinegar and continue stirring until they have blended to form a thick brown syrup. Taste and adjust the flavors. Add the fried noodles a little at a time, breaking them up in the process. When everything is mixed carefully add the meat, the shrimp and the lime zest.

Serve on a large platter. Scatter the fried tofu, the leeks and the fried egg threads over the top and garnish with fresh coriander leaves, sliced chilies and slices of pickled garlic. Arrange the bean sprouts decoratively at the edge of the platter and serve immediately.

SNACKS AND APPETIZERS

Thais really enjoy eating strongly flavored, salty and crunchy snacks with the diluted Mekong whisky that men often drink with great gusto before a full meal. These are not the "internationalized" delicacies beloved of restaurants, but real thirst-provokers.

MU THOT, MU YANG GRILLED PORK, DEEP-FRIED PORK

Small pieces of pork are marinated as described in the recipe for Barbecued Spareribs (*Kaduk Mu*), but without the sugar, then either roasted over charcoal until crunchy or deep-fried until crisp. The favored cuts for this purpose are thinly sliced pieces of neck (particularly the skin at the back) or belly pork spareribs chopped into small pieces. Pig's ears also are used in the country.

MAMUANG HIMAPHAN THOT TANGY CASHEWS AND CHILIES

Oil for deep-frying
8 oz (250 g) raw cashew nuts
2 green and 1 red medium-sized chilies, sliced into rounds
2 green onions, cleaned and cut into ½-in (1-cm) pieces
Salt to taste (the mixture should be salty)

Heat the oil in a wok and fry the cashew nuts until they are brown. Drain well. When cool, toss with the chilies, green onions and salt and serve in a bowl.

THOT MAN PLA DEEP-FRIED FISH PATTIES

1 lb (500 g) fine-fleshed fish fillets (redfish or nannygai; carp or other freshwater fish), or 14 oz (400 g) fish fillets and 3 oz (100 g) shrimp, peeled and deveined
3 tablespoons Red Curry Paste II (p. 349)
3 oz (100 g) green beans, chopped
8 leaves Asian sweet basil, chopped (optional)
4 kaffir lime leaves, finely sliced (optional)
Oil for deep-frying

Cucumber Relish

2 pickling cucumbers
2 medium-sized chilies, seeded and sliced
1½ tablespoons sugar
3 tablespoons rice vinegar
1 tablespoon water
1 tablespoon coarsely ground roasted peanuts
Fresh coriander leaves for garnish

Flake the fish and chop the shrimp finely (if using) then grind them to a paste, adding the curry paste and mixing well. Beat the mixture with an electric mixer until it is smooth and elastic. Add the green beans, the basil and kaffir lime leaves and stir to mix. Refrigerate for an hour.

To make the Cucumber Relish, cut the cucumbers into four lengthwise and remove the seeds but do not peel them. Slice them across into thin slices and place in a bowl with the chilies. Combine the sugar, vinegar and water in a small pan and heat until the sugar has dissolved. Cool and pour over the cucumber. Spoon into small sauce bowls, scatter some roasted peanuts over the top and garnish with a coriander leaf.

Grease your hands and roll 1 tablespoon of the fish mixture into a ball and flatten each ball in your fingers into a disk-shape. Heat sufficient oil for deep-frying to medium hot and drop in the fish cakes a few at a time and deep-fry them until brown. Drain and serve with a small bowl of Cucumber Relish.

THOT MAN KUNG   DEEP-FRIED SHRIMP BALLS

4 cloves garlic
3 coriander roots
½ teaspoon whole peppercorns, ground
Salt to taste
1 lb (500 g) shrimp, peeled and deveined
Breadcrumbs (optional)
Oil for deep-frying

Grind the garlic, coriander roots, pepper and salt to a fine paste. Add the shrimp and mash into a smooth paste. Shape the mixture into small balls, which may be rolled in breadcrumbs if you prefer. Heat plenty of oil in a wok or a pan until very hot and deep-fry the shrimp balls until they are brown. Drain and serve.

These can be partially cooked and deep-fried again at the last minute. Serve with Cucumber Relish (p. 427) or Sweet Chili Sauce, which can be bought in Asian food stores.

RICE CRISPS WITH SWEET DIP
KHAO TANG NA TANG

Rice crisps are made from dried pieces of the layer of hard rice that adheres to the bottom of the pot when cooking rice by the evaporation method. They are usually available in packets in Asian food shops. You could substitute with pieces of rice cakes from any supermarket, though they are not so crunchy and delicious.

7 oz (200 g) lean ground pork
7 oz (200 g) shrimp, finely chopped
1 cup (250 ml) medium-thick coconut milk
3 tablespoons coarsely ground roasted peanuts
3 tablespoons chopped shallots
3 red chilies, bruised
Freshly ground pepper to taste
Salt or fish sauce to taste
2 teaspoons palm or dark brown sugar
Chopped fresh coriander leaves for garnish

Mix the pork and the shrimp together. Bring the coconut milk almost to a boil in a saucepan, stirring constantly. Add the pork and shrimp mixture and simmer until cooked. Add the peanuts, shallots and chilies, season with pepper, salt or fish sauce and sugar and stir. Simmer until the gravy thickens. Pour into a bowl and garnish with coriander leaves.

To make your own rice crisps, start by cooking rice in a saucepan without going as far as the last step where you wrap the saucepan in a kitchen towel (p. 14). Remove the rice and break the hard layer on the bottom of the pan into pieces and dry them completely. Deep-fry the pieces in oil, drain thoroughly and store in an airtight container.

MA HO GALLOPING HORSES

3 tablespoons oil
3 cloves garlic, chopped
2 red chilies, chopped
1 lb (500 g) ground pork
Fish sauce to taste
Palm or dark brown sugar to taste
Freshly ground pepper
2 oz (50 g) roasted peanuts, coarsely chopped
1–2 lb (½–1 kg) pineapple, peeled, cut lengthwise into
    four wedges, each wedge cored and sliced thick or 1–2
    lb (½–1 kg) rambutans, peeled, halved and stoned
Chopped fresh coriander leaves for garnish

Heat the oil and stir-fry the garlic until it is golden. Add the chilies, pork, fish sauce, sugar and pepper. Cook over medium heat, stirring frequently until the pork is cooked then add the peanuts. Spoon a little of the mixture on top of each pineapple slice or into each rambutan half. Garnish with fresh coriander.

SAKU SAI MU STUFFED SAGO BALLS

2 tablespoons oil
3 cloves garlic, chopped
3 tablespoons finely chopped shallots
1 lb (500 g) ground pork
2 tablespoons palm sugar
Freshly ground pepper
Fish sauce or salt to taste
2 oz (50 g) roasted peanuts, coarsely chopped
10 oz (300 g) sago or tapioca pearls
Chopped fresh coriander and chili strips for garnish

Heat the oil in a pan and fry the garlic until golden brown. Add shallots, pork, sugar, pepper, and fish sauce or salt. Cook over medium heat, stirring frequently for 10–15 minutes or until cooked and dry, then add the peanuts.

Wash the sago or tapioca well and soak it in 2 cups (500 ml) of hot water for 10–15 minutes until the pearls are dissolved. Once the mixture is cool, wet your hands and shape about 1 heaping tablespoon into a thin disk. Put a spoonful of the pork mixture into the middle and gather up the edges to form a sealed ball, rolling the ball smooth in your hands.

Fill a large saucepan with water and bring it to a boil. Drop in the sago balls one at a time so that the water remains boiling. Boil until the balls float on top and the sago or tapioca is transparent. Remove each ball with a slotted spoon, draining thoroughly. Alternatively, you could steam the balls in a steamer for 15 minutes. Cool slightly and serve on lettuce leaves, garnished with coriander and chili strips.

MIANG KAI KRATHONG KROP

THAI COCKTAIL CUPS

This is a sophisticated Bangkok adaptation of a country snack using the leaves of a wild creeper, *bai cha phlu* or betel leaf. For this adaptation you need a special brass mold for making cocktail cups. The wooden handle looks like the top of a ladle but it branches out into small fluted cups at the base. I have sometimes seen these molds in Asian food stores.

Batter
2 oz (50 g) rice flour
2 oz (50 g) all-purpose flour
3 cups (750 ml) thin coconut milk
Oil for deep-frying

Filling
1–2 teaspoons sugar
Pinch of salt
2 tablespoons fresh lime juice
½ tablespoon white rice that has been dry-roasted until golden brown, and ground (optional)
1 cup (250 g) steamed ground chicken
1 cup (250 g) skinned roasted peanuts
⅓ cup (75 g) peeled and chopped fresh ginger root
⅓ cup (75 g) chopped peeled shallots
⅓ cup (75 g) chopped pickled garlic (p. 46)
1½ tablespoons finely chopped or grated lime zest
Fresh chili sliced in rounds and chopped fresh coriander leaves for garnish

Sift and mix the two kinds of flour in a bowl, adding the coconut milk gradually, taking care to stir out all the lumps.

Heat sufficient oil in a wok or a saucepan for deep frying. Stand the mold in the oil as it heats. Remove the mold when hot, emptying it of any oil, then dip it into the batter, coating it with the mixture on the outside only. Return the coated mold to the pan of hot oil and cook the batter, easing the cup off the mold as it sets and finish cooking it in the oil as you repeat the process. Remove the cups when they are cooked and drain them thoroughly.

In a bowl combine the sugar, salt, lime juice, ground rice and chicken. Take a cup in one hand and add a little of each of the following ingredients: peanuts, ginger, shallots, pickled garlic and lime zest. Cover with a spoonful of chicken mixture and garnish the top with a slice of chili and some chopped coriander leaves. Repeat the process until all the cups are filled.

The country version of this dish uses young betel leaves served with small bowls of whole roasted or fried peanuts, fresh ginger root, shallots and young unpeeled limes—all chopped into cubes. Bowls of roasted mature coconut meat shaved into flakes, cut into cubes or grated, some chopped small chilies and some tiny dried shrimp, soaked in water and chopped are also added. Small amounts of the garnishes are placed on a leaf and topped with a spoonful of a sweet sauce made from equal quantities of grated fresh coconut and palm sugar mixed with a little shrimp paste to taste and blended to a smooth sauce with water. Wrap the leaf into a bite-sized package.

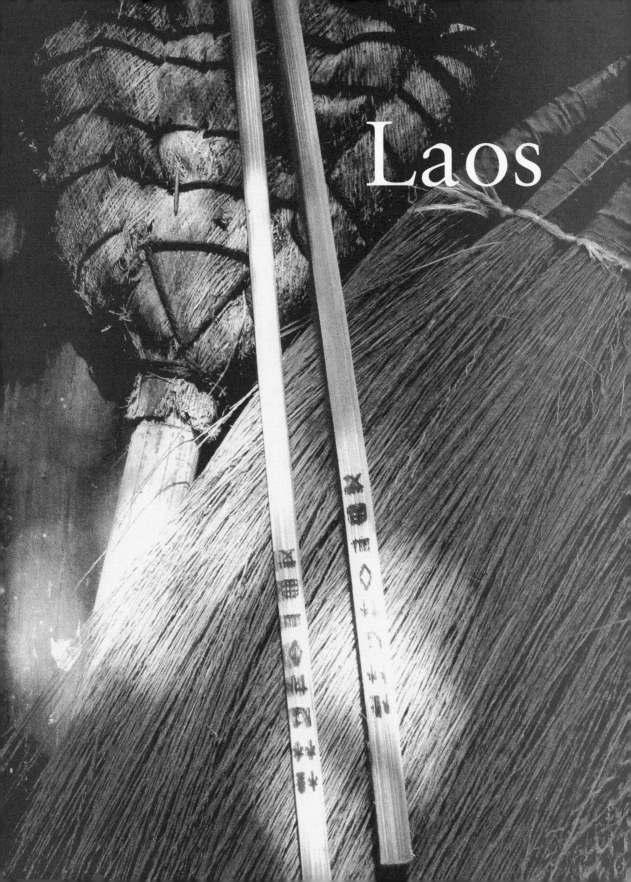

Laos

Like the food of northeast Thailand, whose heritage it shares, Lao food is magnificently earthy and robust. Laos is an inland country and here it is not common to find coconut milk used to enrich and smooth out flavors. The addition of coconut milk was probably borrowed from the Thai court by the cooks of the Lao royal household. Such dishes are certainly confined to food for special occasions among wealthier urban people.

Laos remains relatively undeveloped in the economic sense. For everyday food most people rely on what is at hand, though feasts and ceremonies accompanied by a great deal of gaiety are frequently held to mark life stages, changes of routine or special days. Hospitality is a deeply held value, and guests, whether expected or not, are given all the honor that the host can afford.

The verb "to eat" in the Lao language translates literally as "to eat rice," and the rice is generally of the sticky variety. Domestic animals such as pigs, chickens and ducks are kept by farming households but they are usually reserved for feasts or for serving honored guests. Although city people might eat a little meat more regularly, the most frequent source of daily protein is freshwater fish. As in northeastern Thailand and Cambodia the fish often appears on the table in a fermented form, called *padek* in Lao. (This is the same as the *pla ra* of northeastern Thailand and the *prahoc* of Cambodia.) Sometimes whole chunks or fillets of the fish from the *padek* pot are used, and sometimes only a liquid extracted from it. I have used only the liquid in the recipes that follow, calling it "country fish paste water" to distinguish it from the better-known fish sauce.

Like *pla ra* and *prahoc*, *padek* in its raw form has a smell that many people who have not grown up with it find unpleasant. Once cooked, however, its effect is seductive. There are few who know Lao food who could imagine it without this flavor.

Fruit and vegetables in Laos are cultivated around houses, in villages and on riverbanks. Among them are cucumbers, tomatoes, salad greens and cabbages, eggplant of various kinds, onions, snakebeans, winged beans, yam and water spinach; pineapple, mangoes, various gourds, pomelo, papaya and sugarcane. With fish they are the most common ingredients in Lao food. Herbs grown for flavoring include a variety of greater galangal that is larger than that used elsewhere, garlic, chilies, Asian basil, coriander, green onions and dill.

More evident here than in the areas of Southeast Asia that have better developed transport and marketing systems are animals and plants caught and gathered in the wild for food. As well as the usual fish, vegetables, chickens and ducks and the buffalo meat and pork that are butchered commercially, food items found in markets include frogs and snakes, insects, small birds and quail, a small deer known as mousedeer, wild herbs and gathered leaves of various kinds, edible canes, aromatic tree bark and a species of rat. The extent of this practice was perfectly illustrated recently when a Canadian teacher in Vientiane introduced the concept of animals that one might eat as a way of explaining the difference between wild and domesticated animals. It did not work because there was not one member of the Lao animal kingdom mentioned which someone in the class had not eaten at some time.

Being a landlocked country, Laos remained almost entirely unaffected by the culinary changes introduced into other Southeast Asian countries in the era of the spice trade. Lao cooking does not use dried curry spices such as cumin, coriander seed, anise, fennel or cinnamon. Nor, unlike Vietnam where most of the French officials lived at the time, was it significantly influenced by French cuisine in the colonial period.

As a result Lao cuisine has a very individual quality, one that has survived to the present time because of the country's isolation from international travel and an inward focus on the part of its government. Laos remains one of the few countries in Southeast Asia to have escaped pressures toward globalization in food.

All this may be in the process of changing, however. "Business" is the buzz word in Vientiane as companies from Hong Kong, Taiwan and Thailand set up garment factories there to employ cheap labor and offices spring up to service the ever increasing number of tourists coming into the country from Thailand and elsewhere. An overland bridge designed to carry heavy traffic over the Mekong River from north Thailand into Laos was completed in 1994. Laos is now permanently open to the outside world and, for better or for worse, its culinary influences.

In transliterating names from Lao script, for the sake of consistency I have employed the Thai Royal Institute system.

WET DISHES

KAENG SOM KALAMPI

SOUR CABBAGE SOUP

This soup is also a favorite in northern Vietnam and is good accompanied by Spicy Garlic Sauce (p. 452) and Dried Beef (p. 442) or Heavenly Beef (p. 443).

1 lb (500 g) pork bones, chicken bones and trimmings or
   1 lb (500 g) fish heads
6 cups (1½ liters) water
4 shallots or 1 small onion, peeled
2 stalks lemongrass, bruised
2 coriander roots
Fish sauce to taste
14 oz (400 g) cabbage, roughly chopped
2 plum tomatoes, cut into wedges
Fresh lime juice or tamarind water (p. 67), to taste
   (optional)
Green part of a green onion, sliced

Make a stock by covering the bones or fish heads with the water, add the shallots, lemongrass and coriander roots and boil for 1½ hours (less for fish). Skim any foam that forms off the top to keep it clear.

Strain the stock and bring it back to a boil. Add fish sauce and the cabbage and, when the cabbage is half-cooked, the tomatoes. Cook a little longer and taste, adding lime juice or tamarind water for sourness if necessary (the dish should be sour), together with more fish sauce if desired. Serve garnished with sliced green onion.

STEWS AND BRAISED DISHES

OLAM SIN NGUA RICH BRAISED BEEF

This is a famous dish in Lao court cuisine. Nothing quite like it exists in Thai cooking but it is similar to the Khmer stews. The calf's or pig's foot used in this recipe lends a rich glutinous quality to the stew and is a suitable replacement for the Lao dried buffalo skin.

2 lb (1 kg) shin beef
Beef tendon from the leg
1 calf's foot or 1 pig's foot, split
2 tablespoons country fish paste water (p. 42)
10–12 fresh young green golf-ball eggplant
6 long red chilies, grilled until brown
1 small packet pork cracklings, cut into ¼-in (1-cm)
    cubes
1 bunch of young spinach or young shoots and leaves of
    phak tamlung, cut into 1½-in (3-cm) lengths
1 dill plant, washed and cut into ¾-in (2-cm) lengths
6–8 green onions, cut into ¾-in (2-cm) lengths
A handful of Asian sweet basil leaves

Put the meat, the tendon and the calf's foot under the broiler or over a charcoal fire and grill over high heat until they are brown on the outside. Remove and cut the meat into cubes.

Place the tendon in about 4 cups (1 liter) of water and simmer it for an hour or so until it is soft, then add the other meats and the country fish paste water, the whole eggplants and the whole chilies and continue simmering. When the eggplant and chilies are soft, take them out, peel them and mash them to a paste in a mortar or food processor. Set the mash aside.

Add the pork cracklings to the stock. When they start to get soft add the spinach or *phak tamlung*, the dill and the green onions. Add the mashed eggplant mixture and the basil leaves. Taste and adjust the seasonings, adding salt if desired. Serve with Lao-style Salad (*Salat*, p. 450).

OLAM KAI RICH BRAISED CHICKEN

Like minestrone, this dish is even better the second day. It should be thick.

1 whole chicken, cut down the breastbone and flattened
    out
4–6 cups (1–1½ liters) water
2 tablespoons country fish paste water or fish sauce
10–12 young golf-ball eggplant
7 long red chilies, grilled until brown
2 lb (1 kg) mixed young green vegetables (green beans
    cut into small pieces; cigar-shaped eggplant sliced in
    chunks; small pea eggplants; cloud-ear mushroom
    soaked and sliced; lima beans; snowpeas; young pea
    shoots)
Cake of cooked sticky rice (*khao ti*), broken into small
    pieces (about 1½ in/4 cm in diameter and ¼–½ in/
    ½ –1 cm thick and grilled until brown, optional)
1 small packet pork cracklings, cubed
1 dill plant, washed and cut into ¾-in (2-cm) lengths
1 bunch young spinach or *phak tamlung*
A handful of Asian sweet basil leaves
6–8 green onions, sliced

Grill the chicken over a charcoal fire or under the broiler until brown on the outside. Chop it into bite-sized pieces complete with bone, Chinese-style (p. 22), and put it in a saucepan with water to cover. Add the country fish paste water, the golf-ball eggplant and the grilled chilies. When the eggplant and chilies are soft, remove and peel them. Mash them in a mortar or food processor and set them aside.

Add the vegetables to the saucepan in the order that they will take to cook—the pea eggplant, beans and the cloud-ear mushroom. Add the rice cake pieces and the pork crackling, dill, spinach or *phak tamlung*, basil and the green onions—but do not cook too long. Add more rice cake as desired to increase the thickness. Add the mashed eggplant and chilies, taste and adjust the seasonings and serve.

KAENG NO MAI GREEN BAMBOO STEW

3 stalks lemongrass, finely sliced

1–2 chilies, halved

2–3 tablespoons sticky rice flour, rice flour or tapioca flour

2 cups (500 ml) water

2 cans *yanang* leaf extract for green coloring (available in cans in Asian food shops)

1 lb (500 g) boneless fish fillets, cut into bite-sized pieces or 1 lb (500 g) belly pork, sliced

3 tablespoons country fish paste water

1 tablespoon fish sauce

1 lb (500 g) sliced bamboo shoot, cut into thin strips

3 oz (100 g) pumpkin, peeled and cut into small wedges

A few golf-ball eggplant, cut into wedges or cigar-shaped eggplant, cut into chunks

½ –1 cup (125–250 g) baby corn halved lengthwise

1 cup (250 g) fresh oyster mushrooms, sliced

3 cups (750 g) young pumpkin or choko leaves (p. 52) or any young green leafy vegetable, torn into pieces

4–5 whole stems Asian sweet basil

4 young green onions, sliced

In a mortar or a food processor grind the lemongrass and chilies to a fine paste. Add the rice or tapioca flour, mix and set aside. Add 2 cups (500 ml) of water to the *yanang* leaf extract and bring to a boil. Add the fish or pork, the country fish paste water, the fish sauce and the strips of bamboo shoot and simmer for about half an hour. Add the vegetables in the order they will take to cook, adding the pumpkin leaves last. Finally, add some of the stock to the flour mixture and stir until it is lump-free then add to the stew. Stir the pot and bring it back to a boil, stewing to thicken.

Remove the pan from the heat, garnish with basil leaves and chopped green onions and serve in a large bowl.

SUP NO MAI BAMBOO SHOOT "SUP"

The Lao "*sup*," in spite of its familiar-sounding name, does not denote anything like a Western soup. On the contrary, it is a dish of cooked vegetables with a sauce and is dry. In fact *sup* are drier than *kaeng* (Thai curries), many of which are quite liquid from the addition of stock, water or other liquid during cooking.

6 cloves garlic, peeled and sliced
¼ teaspoon ground chili (optional)
2 tablespoons oil
8 oz (250 g) lean ground pork
1 tablespoon fish sauce
2 tablespoons country fish paste water (optional)
Salt to taste (optional)
1 lb (500 g) shredded bamboo shoots, drained and
  rinsed in warm water
2–3 tablespoons sesame seed, roasted in a dry frying
  pan until brown and ground
A handful of fresh coriander, chopped

Grind the garlic with the ground chili to a fine paste. Heat the oil in a wok and fry the paste until it is brown then add the ground pork and stir-fry until it is lightly cooked. Add the fish sauce, the country fish paste water and/or salt if necessary and stir. Add the bamboo shoots and stir-fry until mixed and dry. Taste and adjust the seasonings if necessary. Serve garnished with the sesame seed and coriander.

For a richer, more mellow dish, try adding 1 cup (250 ml) of canned coconut milk to the pan before serving. Mix well and cook, stirring constantly, over high heat until everything is fairly dry.

SUP PHAK   MIXED VEGETABLE "SUP"

3–4 cups (2 lb /1 kg) vegetables (yellow-flowering
    Chinese cabbage [*choy sum*]; Chinese broccoli [kale];
    baby spinach; 7 oz [200 g] green beans, cut into bite-
    sized pieces; a handful of snowpeas, strings removed;
    a handful of oyster mushrooms; 3 oz [100 g] cloud-ear
    mushroom, soaked and cleaned; 6 round golf-ball
    eggplant; 7 oz [200 g] canned shredded bamboo
    shoots)
7 oz (200 g) fish fillets
10 cloves garlic
5 shallots
2-in (5-cm) piece fresh ginger root, sliced
1–2 dried chilies
3 tablespoons country fish paste water
1 tablespoon fish sauce
4 tablespoons sesame seed, roasted in a dry pan and
    ground
1 small bunch of coriander, coarsely chopped

Prepare the vegetables by cutting the green leafy ones into 1½-in (3-cm) pieces, slice the mushrooms and the eggplant into quarter wedges and drain and rinse the bamboo shoots. Put all the vegetables into a steamer in separate piles and lightly steam them. Place them in a bowl and mix them together. Steam or grill the fish. When cool, remove the skin and bones and lightly flake it. Set aside. Grill the unpeeled garlic and shallots, the ginger and the dried chilies until they are dark brown on the outside. Peel and crush them in a mortar or grind them in a food processor to a fine paste.

Mix the crushed paste, the flaked fish, the country fish paste water and the fish sauce into a thick sauce. Test for saltiness, adding more salt if necessary. Pour this over the vegetables in the bowl and mix everything thoroughly. Sprinkle the ground sesame seed over the top, toss again, garnish with chopped coriander and serve.

FRIED, GRILLED AND STEAMED DISHES

SIN HAENG DRIED BEEF

Traditionally the beef for this recipe is first dried on bamboo trays in the sun. The use of a food dehydrator or an oven makes it quicker and easier to prepare.

4 stalks lemongrass, finely sliced
3-in (8-cm) piece fresh ginger root, peeled and coarsely chopped
8 cloves garlic, peeled and coarsely chopped
3 tablespoons fish sauce
2 tablespoons dark soy sauce
2 lb (1 kg) topside beef or skirt steak, cut along the grain into thin strips

In a mortar or a food processor grind the lemongrass, the ginger and the garlic to a fine paste. Add the fish sauce and soy sauce and mix well. Pour this sauce over the meat, mix well and marinate overnight.

Spread the slices of meat flat and dry them in a food dehydrator or in the oven for about 4 hours at a low temperature (140–200°F/60–80°C) so there is no chance of cooking the meat. The dried meat does not have to be too dry. It may be wrapped in plastic and kept in the freezer.

Deep-fry the dried beef in plenty of hot oil for a few minutes and serve with a dipping sauce such as Fresh Green Chili Sauce (p. 453) and rice or without the rice as a snack.

SIN SAVANH HEAVENLY BEEF

The marinade for this recipe is the same as the one above, except that it has 4 tablespoons of sugar added to it. In this case the meat is sliced differently too—it is cut along the grain into strips then across the grain into fine slices. Dry in a food dehydrator or the oven. After drying, the slices will deep-fry very quickly so take care to remove them before they burn.

GRILLED PORK

SIN MU PING

6 cloves garlic, chopped
1 tablespoon fish sauce
1 tablespoon dark soy sauce
3 tablespoons oyster sauce (optional)
Pinch of ground pepper
2 lb (1 kg) pork

Combine the garlic, the sauces and the pepper. Add the pork and marinate, preferably for about 30 minutes. Grill over a charcoal fire or under the broiler.

GRILLED FISH

PING PA

Grilled pork, fish and other delicacies such as whole frogs balanced in split bamboo skewers are a common sight in markets in Laos and northeastern Thailand.

Use whole fish that are not too big. Clean and wash the fish, make three slashes across each side and rub with salt before grilling.

Serve the grilled meat or fish accompanied by a sauce such as Spicy Garlic Sauce (p. 452) or Fresh Green Chili Sauce (p. 453).

MOK PADEK COUNTRY FISH IN A BANANA LEAF
PACKET

To be truly authentic this dish should be made using
the fish from the *padek* or country fish paste pot.
Here I have attempted to reproduce the dish using
fresh fish combined with country fish paste water.
All banana-leaf stuffed packets may roasted or
grilled until the leaves are dark brown.

4 oz (125 g) small fine-fleshed boneless fish fillets, flesh
    flaked or chopped
4 tablespoons country fish paste water
½ tablespoon fish sauce
14 oz (400 g) lean ground pork
½ packet pork cracklings, cubed
5 slices galangal
3 stalks lemongrass, finely sliced
6 cloves garlic, halved
6 shallots, coarsely chopped
3 fresh chilies, seeded, cut across and sliced
3 kaffir lime leaves, torn
Leaves from 1 stem Asian sweet basil
3 eggs
6 banana leaves or pieces of aluminum foil
Sliced green onions or finely sliced lime leaves

Combine all the ingredients except the eggs, banana leaves and green
onions into a bowl and mix together. Break in the eggs and stir thoroughly in a clockwise direction until everything is blended together.
Divide the mixture among the six banana leaves or pieces of foil, sealing
carefully. Alternatively, divide the mixture among six ramekins. Place the
packets or ramekins on a rack in a steamer and steam for about 30 minutes. Unwrap, garnish with sliced green onions or finely sliced lime leaves
and serve with slices of cucumber and rice.

MOK PA FISH IN A PACKET

3 fresh chilies, seeded and chopped
3 stalks lemongrass, sliced
6 shallots, sliced
1 lb (500 g) boneless fish fillets, cut into pieces
  (3 x 1½ in/8 x 4 cm)
Fish sauce to taste
12 Asian sweet basil leaves
Banana leaves or aluminum foil
Sliced green onion for garnish

In a mortar or a food processor grind the chilies, lemongrass and shallots to a fine paste. Put the fish in a bowl, add the spice paste and fish sauce to taste and the basil and mix well. Wrap each piece of spiced fish in banana-leaf or foil packets, seal carefully and steam or grill over charcoal. Garnish with green onion before serving.

MOK KAI CHICKEN IN A PACKET

⅓ cup (75 g) sticky rice (optional)
3 dried chilies, seeded, soaked in warm water for 30
  minutes and squeezed dry
3 stalks lemongrass, sliced
1 lb (500 g) boneless chicken breasts, cut into small
  pieces
1 tablespoon fish sauce
2–3 tablespoons country fish paste water (optional)
6 green onions, sliced into bite-sized pieces
Leaves from 1 stem of Asian sweet basil, kaffir lime
  leaves or dill to taste
Salt to taste
Banana leaves or aluminum foil

If you plan to use the sticky rice, soak the rice in water overnight. The next day, dry it and grind it to the consistency of sand. In a mortar or a food processor grind the chilies and lemongrass to a fine paste. Put the chicken in a bowl and mix it with the spice paste, adding fish sauce and country fish paste water (if desired). Add the green onions and basil and mix thoroughly. Add the rice flour (if using). Divide the mixture among four banana leaves or pieces of foil and wrap each portion into a packet for steaming or grilling.

DRESSED DISHES AND SALADS

LAP PA DRESSED RAW FISH

3 tablespoons sticky rice
2 slices galangal, seared under the broiler until dry then finely chopped
Juice of 1½ limes
1¾ lb (800 g) fish fillets, skinned
2–3 tablespoons country fish paste water
1 tablespoon fish sauce
1 teaspoon dried chili powder or flakes
3 shallots, finely chopped or ½ of a large Spanish onion, finely chopped
Handful of mint, chopped
½ cup (125 g) chopped fresh coriander leaves
½ cup (125 g) sliced green onion
4 fresh chilies, sliced diagonally

First prepare the rice by roasting it until brown in a dry pan and then grinding it with the galangal to a consistency of fine sand and set it aside (ground rice that has been prepared in this way will keep in an airtight jar for up to a month).

Squeeze the lime juice over the fish fillets and set them aside for 20 minutes. Squeeze the marinade out of the fish, retaining the juice and leaving the fish dry. Put the juice in a saucepan, add the country fish paste water and the fish sauce and stir together. Bring the mixture to a boil then take off the stove and cool slightly.

Pour the sauce over the fish and mix, adding the dried chili and shallots. Add the ground rice and mix well. Taste and adjust the seasonings, adding more fish sauce, lime juice or country fish paste water if necessary. Finally, add the herbs and garnish with sliced fresh chili.

Serve with cucumber slices or strips, whole trimmed green beans; raw golf-ball eggplant, cut vertically one-third of the way down then turned 90 degrees and cut down again and soaked in cold water; some dill; and slightly bitter green leaves (*phak kadau*, green endive or radicchio leaves) and sticky rice.

LAP SIN DRESSED BEEF

In Laos this dish would usually be made using sliced or chopped raw buffalo meat and raw liver. Many people will find this lightly grilled version more palatable. This is the same dish as the northeastern Thai *lap* seen from the other side of the border.

3 tablespoons sticky rice
2 slices galangal, seared under the broiler until dry and finely chopped
7 oz (200 g) calf's liver (optional)
7 oz (200 g) cooked ox tripe (optional)
1¼ lb (600 g) rump or sirloin steak
3 tablespoons country fish paste water
1 tablespoon fish sauce
3 shallots, peeled and finely chopped
3–4 fresh red chilies, finely chopped
½ cup (125 g) sliced green onion
Handful of mint, chopped
½ cup (125 g) chopped fresh coriander leaves
Juice of 1 lime
Chopped mint and chili flowers (p. 21) for garnish

Roast the rice in a dry pan until it is brown then grind it with the galangal to the consistency of fine sand. Set aside.

If using less of the calf's liver or tripe, or omitting them altogether, increase the amount of other meat accordingly. Trim all skin and fat from the meat. Put it under the broiler until it is cooked rare to medium, then slice or chop it finely. Save the juices left in the broiler pan. Boil the liver (if using) in water until cooked and slice it finely. Boil the tripe (if using) and slice it finely.

Combine the meat juices from the pan, the country fish paste water and the fish sauce in a saucepan. Bring to a boil then take it off the heat and cool. In a bowl mix the steak, liver, tripe, shallots and the fish sauce mixture and toss them together. Add the roasted rice and mix thoroughly. Add the chilies, green onion, mint, coriander and lime juice and toss again. Garnish with additional mint leaves and chili flowers.

PON PA VEGETABLE SALAD WITH FISH DIP

This recipe bears a family resemblance to the northern Green Chili Dip and is served the same way.

1 lb (500 g) boneless, skinless fish fillets (bream, snapper, perch, catfish)
3–5 tablespoons country fish paste water
6 green golf-ball eggplant or 4 small purple cigar-shaped eggplant
5 fresh chilies
8–10 cloves garlic
5 green shallots
1 tablespoon fish sauce
3 green onions, sliced
¼ cup (60 g) coarsely chopped fresh coriander leaves

Combine the fish and the country fish paste water in a saucepan, add water to just cover and poach the fish until it is cooked. Flake the flesh, setting it aside and reserving the stock. Boil the eggplant until cooked and peel the skins. If using cigar-shaped eggplant, bake or grill rather than boil them. Put the chilies, garlic and the whole green shallots in the embers of a charcoal fire or under the broiler until the skins are dark brown. Peel the skins and slice them.

In a mortar or a food processor, grind the chilies, garlic and shallots to a smooth paste. Add the fish, eggplant and fish sauce and mash or blend further. Add some of the fish stock until you achieve the desired consistency. Add the sliced green onion and most of the coriander. Serve in a bowl garnished with the rest of the coriander and place on a platter accompanied by separate mounds of cucumber strips, lightly steamed trimmed green beans and any other raw or lightly steamed vegetables for dipping.

YAM KAI   CHICKEN SALAD

1 lb (500 g) boneless chicken
5 cups (1¼ liters) water
1 stalk lemongrass, bruised
Pinch of salt
1 tablespoon fresh lime juice
½ teaspoon sugar or to taste
2 tablespoons fish sauce or to taste
1 cup (250 g) green beans or celery, sliced diagonally
1 carrot, cut into matchsticks
1 cup (250 g) shredded cabbage
1 tablespoon toasted sesame seed
2 shallots, chopped
5 stalks fresh coriander leaves, chopped
Chopped fresh coriander leaves for garnish

Simmer the chicken in the water with the lemongrass and salt. Drain and reserve the stock for some other purpose. Slice the chicken into shreds. Combine the lime juice, sugar, fish sauce and salt in a small bowl. Mix the vegetables and chicken together and add the sauce, sesame seed, shallots and coriander. Toss well and serve garnished with a few extra coriander leaves.

SALAT   LAO-STYLE SALAD

2 tablespoons oil
3 cloves garlic, finely chopped
7 oz (200 g) lean ground pork
2 tablespoons palm or dark brown sugar
1 teaspoon salt (optional)
2 tablespoons fish sauce
3 hard boiled eggs, peeled, yolks mashed and whites
    chopped
2 tablespoons lime juice
Lettuce, washed and torn into pieces
Salad vegetables for six people (pickling cucumbers,
    sliced; whole green onions, cut into half lengthwise

and then into 1½-in [3-cm] lengths; tomatoes, sliced; radish or Chinese turnip, sliced; shallots or Spanish onions, sliced; mint leaves)

½ cup (125 g) peanuts, fried or roasted and coarsely ground

Heat the oil in a pan. Add the garlic and the pork and stir-fry until browned. Add the sugar, salt and fish sauce and stir. Take the pan off the stove and add the egg yolk and the lime juice. Taste and adjust the seasonings to achieve the right balance between sweet, salty and sour.

Arrange the lettuce on a plate and place the other vegetables decoratively on top. Sprinkle with peanuts, pour the dressing over and garnish with the chopped egg white.

TAM MAK HOUNG CHILI-PAPAYA SALAD

This is *som tam* Laos-style, not as sour as the version from northeast Thailand.

1 small green papaya
3 small carrots (optional—you may double the papaya instead)
4–6 red chilies, seeds intact
3–4 cloves garlic, sliced
3 tablespoons country fish paste water
1 teaspoon fish sauce
1–2 teaspoons palm or dark brown sugar
Juice of ½ a lime
1 very firm tomato, sliced into chunks

Shred the papaya as described on p. 47 and shred or grate the carrots, then mix together thoroughly. Grind the chilies and the garlic to a fine paste. Combine the country fish paste water, fish sauce, sugar and lime juice in a bowl. Taste and adjust the balance if necessary then add to the chili-garlic paste the papaya and carrot mixture and the tomato, mixing everything together thoroughly with the pestle as described for Pounded Green Papaya (p. 404).

Serve with dried beef (*sin*), pork crackling, grilled chicken or fried fish, sticky rice and a few fresh green salad vegetables such as cucumber slices, lettuce or green onion.

TAM MAK TAENG CHILI-CUCUMBER SALAD

3 cups (750 g) cucumber, cut into short strips
2 medium-length fresh chilies
1–2 teaspoons sugar
1 tomato, sliced into small wedges
Juice of ½ a lime
Fish sauce to taste
Country fish paste water to taste

Proceed according to the instructions in the recipe for Chili-Papaya Salad but add enough fish sauce and country fish paste water to suit your tastes.

ACCOMPANIMENTS

JIO BONG SPICY GARLIC SAUCE

This sauce, served with rice, is similar to the Chili Jam (p. 412) of Thailand. You can buy it in Asian food stores but here is a recipe to make your own.

Oil for deep-frying
1 large head of garlic, peeled and sliced
10 long red dried chllies, roasted in a dry pan until aromatic and seeded
4 slices galangal chopped
3 tablespoons dried shrimp, soaked in warm water and ground
3 tablespoons sugar
4 tablespoons fish sauce
2 oz (50 g) boiled pork skin, finely diced (available in Asian food shops)

Heat the oil in a small pan and fry the garlic slices until golden brown, taking care not to burn them. Lift them out and drain on paper towel. Grind the chilies to a powder in a food processor. Add the galangal, the dried shrimp and the garlic and grind everything to a paste.

Heat 4 tablespoons of oil in a pan over low heat, add the spice paste and stir-fry. Add the sugar and fish sauce to taste and stir until everything is brown. Add the pork skin at the end and mix well. Serve with rice or as an accompaniment to other dishes.

The sauce will keep in the refrigerator for some time.

JIO MAK PHET TIP FRESH GREEN CHILI SAUCE

6 large green chilies
6 cloves garlic
3 shallots
3 tablespoons fish sauce
1 teaspoon sugar, or more to taste
A few leaves of fresh coriander, chopped

Grill the chilies, garlic and shallots over charcoal or under the broiler until they are brown on the outside. Peel off the skins and grind the roasted ingredients in a mortar or a food processor. Add the fish sauce, sugar and chopped coriander, and blend well.

Serve with grilled fish or meat and sticky rice.

NAM BUDO COUNTRY FISH PASTE SAUCE

2 tablespoons palm or dark brown sugar
1 tablespoon white sugar
4 shallots, finely sliced
3–4 fresh chilies, sliced in rounds
1–2 teaspoons ground chili
2 tablespoons roasted ground rice
1 tablespoon chopped fresh ginger root
4 tablespoons country fish paste water

Mix everything together and stir until the sugar has dissolved. Serve as a dipping sauce with sliced green mango.

NOODLES AND ONE-DISH MEALS

KHAO PUN NAM JIO SPICY RICE VERMICELLI IN SOUP

This is the national dish of Laos.

6–8 shallots
3 cloves garlic
4 large red chilies
1 lb (500 g) belly pork in one piece, trimmed of fat
1 fresh pork hock or 2 lb (1 kg) pork bones
½ set pig's lungs (optional)
3 quarts (3 liters) water
10 slices galangal
6 kaffir lime leaves
4 tablespoons country fish paste water
Salt to taste
1 lb (500 g) fine-fleshed fish fillets
1–1½ lb (500–750 g) rice vermicelli
½ green papaya, peeled and shredded (p. 47)
1 can shredded bamboo shoots
½ banana blossom, thinly sliced across or 8 oz (250 g)
   bean sprouts
A few cabbage leaves, finely shredded
8 oz (250 g) green beans, cut into small rounds
½ –1 bunch water spinach (*phak bung*), cut into ¾–2-in
   (2–5 cm) lengths

Grill the whole unpeeled shallots, garlic and chilies either on a charcoal fire or under the broiler until they are seared and brown. Put the belly pork, pork hock or bones and lungs (if using) in 3 quarts (3 liters) of water with the shallots, garlic, chilies, galangal, lime leaves, country fish paste water and salt and bring to a boil, skimming any foam that forms off the top. Reduce the heat and simmer the stock until the broth is rich and the meat is coming off the bones.

Remove the meats and slice them—including the lung, if desired. Discard the bones, strain the stock into another saucepan and keep it hot. Add the fish fillets and poach until they are cooked. Remove and slice them. Return the meat and fish to the soup. Pour boiling water over the rice vermicelli, drain it and rinse in cold water. Cut it into manageable lengths with scissors and place on a platter. Arrange the separate piles of papaya and vegetables on another platter. Place several condiments in separate bowls on the table: ground dried chili, sugar, fish sauce, soy sauce, wedges of lime, fresh chilies, coriander leaves, Asian sweet basil and sliced green onion.

Pour the soup into a large tureen and place in the middle of the table with the platters of vermicelli and vegetables next to it and the bowls of condiments. Each diner puts vermicelli in their bowl followed by the vegetables of their choice and a ladle of meat and stock over the top. Diners help themselves to condiments and garnishes to taste.

KHAO PUN NAM YA RICE VERMICELLI AND FISH SAUCE

This dish should have a thick consistency. A similar version, known as *khanom jin nam ya*, is made in Thailand using shrimp paste instead of country fish paste.

2 tablespoons country fish paste water
2 teaspoons fish sauce
2 cups (500 ml) water
1 fish, about 1¼–1¾ lb (600–800 g) or 1 lb (500 g)
   boneless fish fillets
2 cups (500 ml) coconut milk
4 kaffir lime leaves
Sugar to taste (optional)
10 oz (300 g) rice vermicelli
½ banana blossom, sliced
2 cups (500 g) bean sprouts, washed and trimmed
8 oz (250 g) green beans, sliced into small rounds
2–3 cabbage leaves, finely shredded
Fresh coriander leaves or mint sprigs for garnish

Spice Paste
5 large dried chilies, seeded, soaked in warm water until
   soft then squeezed dry

1 stalk lemongrass, finely sliced
1 thick slice galangal, peeled and coarsely chopped
2–3 cloves garlic, peeled
10 shallots, peeled and sliced

Grind the chilies, lemongrass, galangal, garlic and shallots to a fine paste. Mix the country fish paste water, fish sauce and 2 cups (500 ml) of water in a saucepan, heat and add the fish. When the fish is cooked, remove it from the stock. Flake the flesh then pound it to a fine paste. Set the stock aside.

Bring 1 cup (250 ml) of coconut milk to a rapid boil in a saucepan and boil it, stirring constantly, until the water has reduced and the oil has come out. Add the Spice Paste and fry it in the coconut milk until fragrant, then add the fish, stir well and cook a few minutes more. Add the fish stock, the lime leaves and sugar. Taste and adjust the seasonings then add enough of the remaining coconut milk to achieve good flavor and consistency. Reduce the heat and cook uncovered a little longer.

Meanwhile cook the vermicelli and twirl it into a number of separate rounds if you can. Arrange these on a plate and the vegetables on another one. Pour the sauce into a bowl. Diners put a vermicelli round in their bowl together with a selection of vegetables then ladle the sauce over everything, garnishing with some coriander leaves or mint sprigs.

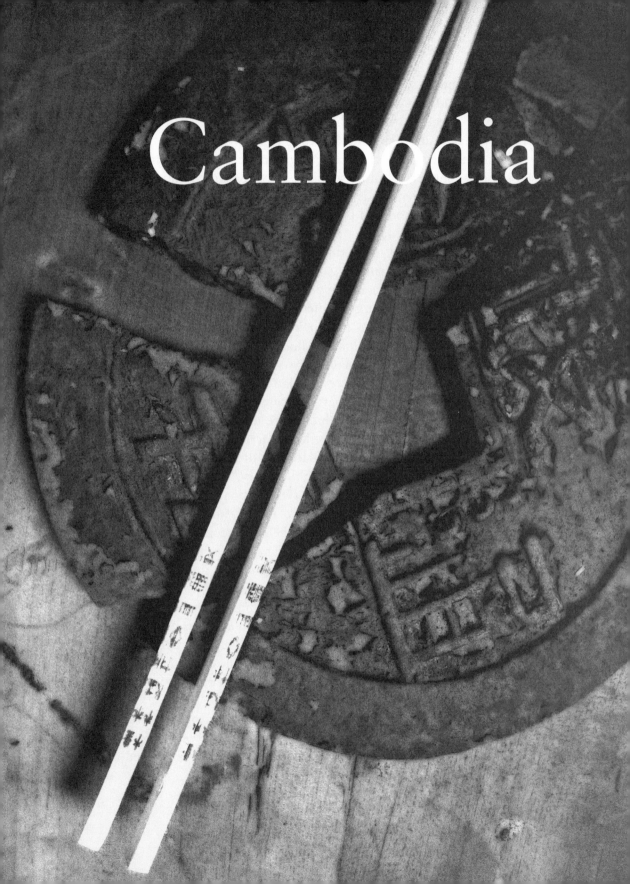

Cambodia

Given Cambodia's history and its geographical position, it is not surprising to find that many of its dishes are similar to those from other parts of Southeast Asia. Indeed the impressive reach of the Khmer Empire, based at Angkor during the 9th to 15th centuries, over large sections of modern Thailand, Laos and present day Vietnam, raises the possibility that several of these dishes may be Cambodian in origin.

There have been occasions too for culinary exchange in modern times. While Thailand and Cambodia have frequently confronted each other in history as enemies, they have nevertheless shared a familiar "Indianized" cultural tradition. The Thai court was often taken as a model for the Cambodian one, and the king of Cambodia at the end of the 19th century used Thai-born advisers. Then, too, the French encouragement of a large influx of Vietnamese workers and settlers into Cambodia in colonial times and their employment of Vietnamese to fill the lower ranks of their colonial administration there would also have contributed to some Vietnamese culinary influence.

These influences aside, however, Alan Davidson, in his book *Seafood of South East Asia*, remarks that "the capacity for taking pains and the highly developed techniques which were displayed by the builders of Angkor Wat could still be seen, reflected across the centuries . . . in the work done by the cooks of the Palace and of the aristocracy at Phnom Penh during the first half of [the 20th] century."

Davidson describes how at that time ordinary Cambodians would eat two meals a day, the first at around 11 a.m. and the second at dusk. The essential parts of the meal would be rice accompanied by a *samlaa* (wet dish: soup or stew), with other dishes, when available, from the general categories of *chha* (sauté or stir-fry), *aing* (a grill or roasted meat, poultry or fish) and *chion* (another kind of fried dish).

It would be useful to look at the culinary dynamics at work in Cambodia today, given the physical disruption and loss of tradition and cultural continuity that have been the sad legacy of its recent history. The opportunity has not been available to me, however, and the picture of Cambodian food that I give is derived from recipes learned from Cambodians living in Australia.

Most immigrant Cambodians are caught up in a nine-to-five workaday world, and their cooking and eating practices are very different from those described above. Their culinary efforts tend to be focused on the evening meal most days of the week, with any elaborate cooking con-fined to weekends. The dishes they most commonly cook understand-ably tend to be ones calling for the least amount of labor. Stir-fries and Chinese-derived dishes are the favorites, along with relatively unspiced sour soups and grills. It is the more complex dishes such as the *samlaa* and the *amok* that I suspect most closely reflect the Khmer tradition.

Everyday Cambodian cuisine is based heavily on fish, much of it freshwater. All of the recipes that follow work just as well, however, with fish from the sea and which type you use is a matter of personal conven-ience and access.

A fermented fish known as *prahoc*, which is virtually identical with the *pla ra* of northeastern Thailand or the Lao *padek*, is used in Khmer food. "Pickled Gourami Fish—Cream-Style" is the version of this coun-try fish paste available in Asian food shops that has been recommended by my Cambodian informants. Any of the versions I have named on p. 42 will do just as well, however, so use the one you have at hand.

Cambodians have traditionally used liquified pork fat as their frying medium, while butter came into fashion with French colonization. Recipes here mostly call for oil, which many Cambodians now use both for economic and health reasons.

The most common green herbs used in Cambodian cooking are ones that also appear in Thai and Vietnamese food: used as a garnish in soup are *eryngo* or long-leafed coriander (*chi rona* in Khmer, *pak chi farang*, *pak chi doi* in Thai or *ngo gai* in Vietnamese), or sometimes fish-cheek mint (*chi trey*); for use fresh in salads there are the Asian sweet basil of Thailand and Vietnam (*chi neangvong*), peppermint, spearmint (*chi mahao*) and Vietnamese mint (*sang hom*). *Mteh kraachaak neang*, the thin chili about 6-in (15-cm) long, and *mteh kmang*, the tiny bird's eye chili, are used fresh for flavoring, while the chili that goes into ground spice pastes is usually the dried large one.

In this chapter I have included Cambodian versions of some dishes which appear elsewhere when I have felt that they are significantly differ-ent. At the same time I have not included other recipes that have already been covered in much the same version in other chapters.

WET DISHES

SNGO CHROUK BANGKANG

TANGY SHRIMP SOUP

1½ cups (375 ml) water
8 oz (250 g) jumbo shrimp (3–4 large), deveined
½ teaspoon salt
1 large clove garlic, finely chopped
1 sprig Asian sweet basil, coarsely chopped
4 leaves of long-leafed coriander or a few fresh
   coriander leaves, coarsely chopped
Green part of a green onion, sliced
1 teaspoon fresh lime juice

Bring the water to a boil, add the shrimp and cook them, turning them once, for about 2 minutes or until they are pink. Remove the shrimp and set them aside. Add ½ teaspoon of salt to the stock and set it aside also. When the shrimp are cool peel them, including the head, retaining the tail and the head (optional). Save the coral liquid from the head in a soup bowl if you like it. Break the tails into 1-in (2½-cm) pieces and put these, together with the peeled heads (if using) into the bowl. Add the coral liquid (if using) and the garlic, reheat the stock and pour this over everything in the bowl. Add the herbs and the lime juice. Mix, adjust the seasonings and serve.

SNGO CHŒUNG CHAMNI CHROUK

PORK BROTH WITH GREENS

4 cups (1 liter) water
8 oz (250 g) belly pork, trimmed of excess fat, cut into
   strips then sliced
1 tablespoon dried shrimp, washed and drained
1 dried squid (optional—available in Asian food shops)
¼ teaspoon sugar
½ teaspoon salt or fish sauce to taste
5 oz (150 g) pork balls
10 oz (300 g) Chinese mustard greens or Chinese
   cabbage, washed and cut into strips

Put the water in saucepan and bring it to a boil. Add the pork, return the broth to a boil and skim the foam that forms off the top until clear. Add the dried shrimp. Peel the hard "quill" from the back of the squid (if using), wash the squid, tear it into pieces and add these. When the meat is cooked, add the sugar and salt or fish sauce to taste. Finally add the pork balls and when they rise to the surface add the greens and cook them briefly.

SAMLAA M'CHOU MOAN   SOUR CHICKEN SOUP

This dish is often cooked with fish but since it is very similar to the Vietnamese sour fish soup I have chosen to include a version with chicken here.

4 cups (1 liter) water
1½ lb (750 g) chicken pieces with bone or 1 small
    chicken, chopped into 2-in (5-cm) pieces
2 walnut-sized pieces of tamarind pulp
1 tablespoon fish sauce
¾ teaspoon salt
½ teaspoon sugar
1 can sliced unsweetened pineapple, cut into wedges or
    1 small fresh pineapple peeled, cored and similarly cut
8 oz (250 g) small tomatoes, each cut lengthwise into 4
    wedges
2 green onions—white part only—sliced diagonally into
    1½-in (3-cm) lengths
1 tablespoon oil
3 small cloves garlic, finely chopped
6 stalks fresh cumin leaves (optional), coarsely chopped
6 long-leafed coriander leaves or a handful of coriander
    leaves, coarsely chopped
10 Asian sweet basil leaves
1 chili, sliced diagonally

Bring the water to a boil, then add the chicken pieces and cook them, skimming any foam that forms off the top occasionally to ensure that the stock is clear. Meanwhile put the tamarind in a bowl, take out two ladlefuls of hot stock and pour them over, soaking the pulp. When the water is cool, knead the tamarind to mix and strain the water, discarding the pulp.

When the chicken is cooked add the fish sauce, salt, sugar, pineapple and tamarind water. Add the tomatoes and the white parts of the green onions. Heat 1 tablespoon of oil in a pan and fry the garlic until it is golden brown. Take the pan off the heat and add the herbs, the chili and the fried garlic and serve.

CHANG PLŒUNG CAMBODIAN STEAMBOAT

A similar dish to this one is popular in Vietnam as well.

4 cups (1 liter) chicken stock and ½ chicken breast or 1 small chicken

4 cups (1 liter) water

4 oz (125 g) squid tube

4 oz (125 g) lean ground pork

¼ teaspoon chopped garlic

¼ teaspoon salt

1 teaspoon sugar

1 small dried squid

1 tablespoon fish sauce or 1½ teaspoons salt

11 oz (325 g) Chinese celery cabbage (4 whole leaves)

7 oz (200 g) chicken livers, washed and sliced

7 oz (200 g) mixed prepared meat balls and fish balls (about 12 balls), sliced

½ tablespoon dried shrimp, rinsed, soaked in water for 30 minutes and drained

4 cups (1 kg) mixed vegetables, cut into 2-in (5-cm) lengths (Chinese mustard; Asian celery; any other Asian leafy green)

4 stems fresh coriander

If you are using a whole chicken, cut the breast off the bones and set it aside. Bring the water to a boil and add the rest of the chicken, skimming any foam that forms off the top as it comes to a boil. Cut the breast into 2-in (5-cm) strips and then across into slices. Cut the squid tube open and score it on the inside as described on p. 26, then cut it into strips and slice straight across into 1-in (2½-cm) pieces.

Combine the pork, garlic, salt and ¼ teaspoon of the sugar and roll the mixture into small balls. Take the quill off the dried squid, wash the squid and remove the skin. Break it into pieces and add it to the stock together with the fish sauce or salt and ¾ teaspoon of sugar. Wash the cabbage leaves, separate the hard stems from the leafy part and cut down the middle and across into cubes. Cut the leaves into strips.

Place the cabbage leaves in the bottom of the steamboat, stems first followed by the leafy part. Arrange the squid and chicken slices on top, the chicken livers, the meat and fish balls, then the dried shrimp. Add 4 cups (1 liter) of stock and put some red-hot charcoal or heat beads down the chimney. When the meat and fish balls float, the contents are cooked. Add the rest of the vegetables, including the coriander stems, and stir. Diners help themselves from the moat of the steamboat.

STEWS AND BRAISED DISHES

SAMLAA KAKO MIXED STEW

This dish, a very good one-dish meal, is one of the best known and most popular Cambodian dishes. You can make it without coconut milk and with any combination of vegetables. Ideally though the combination should include some pumpkin, beans, leafy greens and eggplant. Use roughly twice the weight of vegetables as meat.

½ medium-sized purple eggplant
2 golf-ball eggplants (optional—substitute by increasing the amount of purple eggplant)
6 oz (175 g) white or wax gourd or squash
14 oz (400 g) pumpkin

8 pumpkin flowers with 4 in (10 cm) of stem attached

1 oz (25 g) young pumpkin leaves from the tips of a
pumpkin vine or snowpea tips

2 oz (50 g) young leaves from the tips of a tomato plant

2 oz (50 g) spinach or silverbeet without stems

2 tablespoons uncooked rice

14 oz (400 ml) can coconut milk, unshaken, or ½ cup (125
ml) thick coconut milk and 1½ cups (375 ml) thin
coconut milk

1 tablespoon oil

8 oz (250 g) belly pork with lean meat, fat and skin, cut
into strips then sliced across

8 oz (250 g) chicken, cut into bite-sized pieces with or
without bone

1 teaspoon sugar

½ teaspoon salt

4 oz (125 g) green beans, trimmed and cut into 2-in
(5-cm) pieces

1 cup (250 g) shredded green papaya—about ½ of a long
green papaya, peeled

3 oz (100 g) zucchini, cut in half lengthwise then across
into ¾-in (2-cm) pieces

7 kaffir lime leaves

2½ cups (675 ml) or more water

Spice Paste

4 tablespoons of the green part of lemongrass, very finely
sliced

1-in (2-cm) piece galangal, peeled and coarsely chopped

¼ teaspoon chopped turmeric root or ⅛ teaspoon ground
turmeric

1 teaspoon country fish paste water or 2 teaspoons fish
sauce

4 small cloves garlic, chopped

Cut the purple eggplant into rounds and then into 1½-in (4-cm) wedges and soak them in water. Cut the golf-ball eggplants (if using) into 4 wedges and put them into a bowl of water to soak and to retain their color. Peel the gourd and cut it into 1-in (2½-cm) rounds then cut each round into 6 wedges. Peel and seed the pumpkin and cut it into 2 x 1½-in (5 x 3-cm) pieces. Pull the stems and the stamens off the pumpkin flowers, discarding the stamens. Peel the stems and break them into 2-in (5-cm) lengths. Pull the flowers apart into 3 pieces and set them aside in a bowl.

Pull the tendrils off the pumpkin shoots and discard them. Take the larger leaves off the main stems and tear them in two, rubbing each piece between your palms in order to bruise and dehair them as you go. Leave the young pumpkin leaves and tips on the stems but gently peel the skin off the stalks. Rub these between your palms as well. You should end up with about 1 cup (250 g) of leaves.

Wash the tomato tips, drain them and set them aside. Wash the spinach or silverbeet, cut the leaves in half and then into 1½-in (3-cm) strips.

In a mortar or a blender grind the lemongrass to a fine paste. Remove half of the paste and set it aside. To the half that remains add the galangal, the turmeric, the country fish paste water (if using) and the garlic and grind to a paste. Set aside.

Heat a heavy frying pan and roast the rice dry, stirring constantly, until it is light brown. Remove it and grind it in a blender or a spice grinder until it is the consistency of coarse sand.

If you are using canned coconut milk, scoop ½ cup (125 g) of the thick cream from the top. Heat 1 tablespoon of oil in a large pot and add the cream or ½ cup (125 g) of thick coconut milk. Stir the combination until most of the water has evaporated from the coconut milk and the oil is floating on top. Add the Spice Paste, the pork and the chicken and stir-fry until everything is aromatic. Add ¾ cup (175 ml) of the remaining coconut milk from the can and ¾ cup (175 ml) water or 1½ cups thin coconut milk and stir. Add the sugar, the fish sauce (if using) and the salt to taste, and simmer until the meat is cooked.

When the chicken is tender add the non-leaf vegetables, the ground rice and the lime leaves and 2½ cups (625 ml) of water and stir again. Simmer until the vegetables are sufficiently cooked, then add the leaves, the pumpkin flowers and the rest of the lemongrass. Stir, adjust the seasonings and serve. The stew should not be too thick and it should have a bright green color.

This dish can be made using either pork or chicken alone or fish such as catfish or other firm-fleshed fish, either freshwater or from the sea. If you use fish, add 1 teaspoon of chopped Chinese keys (*kcheay*) to the curry paste, if available.

SPICY CHICKEN STEW

This dish clearly shares inspiration with Thai red curry
though the method of cooking is slightly different.

14 oz (400 g) green or white golf-ball eggplant or long
   purple eggplant
1 chicken or 2 lb (1 kg) chicken pieces
2 cups (500 ml) thick coconut milk
1¼ cups (375 ml) thin coconut milk
1 teaspoon sugar
2 teaspoons fish sauce
3 kaffir lime leaves
A handful Asian sweet basil leaves

Spice Paste
14 large dried chilies, seeds and membranes removed,
   soaked in hot water for 30 minutes and squeezed dry
½ teaspoon salt
½ cup sliced lemongrass
1 slice galangal, peeled and coarsely chopped
1–2 coriander roots
¼ teaspoon chopped turmeric root or ½ teaspoon ground
   turmeric
1 slice of kaffir lime skin
1 teaspoon shrimp paste
5 cloves garlic
5 shallots, sliced

In an electric food processor or a mortar, grind the chilies and the salt to
a fine paste, then add the lemongrass, galangal, coriander, turmeric, lime
skin, shrimp paste, garlic and shallots and grind to a very fine paste.

Trim but do not peel the eggplant, cutting the golf-ball ones into quarters
or purple ones into wedges of similar size. Put them in cold water to soak.

Disjoint the chicken, cutting the breast in two lengthwise then cut
everything crosswise into 2-in (5-cm) pieces. Place the pieces in a large pot.
Mix the Spice Paste with 1 cup (250 ml) of thick coconut milk and add it
to the chicken. Put the pot on the stove over high heat, stirring until the
coconut milk has thickened, everything is mixed and the spices are fra-

grant. Add another cup (250 ml) of thick coconut milk and continue to cook, uncovered, on high heat, stirring occasionally, until the chicken is half-cooked. Add the thin coconut milk, the sugar and fish sauce and stir. Add the lime leaves and the eggplant, reduce the heat and simmer for another 10 minutes or until the chicken and the eggplant are cooked. Take the pot off the heat, add the basil and serve.

NGIEV KRŒUNG   SPICY SHELLFISH

2 lb (1 kg) small clams or cockles
½ cup (125 ml) water
1 tablespoon oil
½ cup (125 ml) thick coconut milk
1 cup (250 ml) thin coconut milk
Fish sauce to taste
Sugar to taste
Fresh coriander leaves for garnish

Spice Paste
3 large dried chilies, seeded and soaked in warm water
    for 30 minutes and squeezed dry
½ teaspoon salt
¼ teaspoon ground pepper
3 stalks lemongrass, finely sliced
4 coriander roots, chopped
12 small cloves garlic, sliced
8 shallots, sliced

Wash the clams and cover them in cold water and set them aside for 30 minutes to clear them of any sand. Put ½ cup (125 ml) of water in a saucepan and steam the clams until they open. Remove the meat from the shells and set it aside. Grind the chilies, salt, pepper, lemongrass, coriander roots, garlic and shallots to a fine paste.

Heat the oil in a wok or a pan and stir-fry the Spice Paste, adding ½ cup (125 ml) of thick coconut milk and stirring well until the liquid has reduced and everything smells fragrant. Add the thin coconut milk a little bit at a time, stirring constantly. Season with fish sauce and sugar, add the clam meat, bring back to a boil and serve garnished with coriander leaves.

SAMLAA SACH TIA NUNG PHLE

DUCK AND GRAPE CURRY

This recipe resembles the Thai Red Duck Curry with Lychees (p. 349), but uses grapes instead of lychees or tomatoes.

1 tablespoon oil
1 cup (250 ml) thick coconut milk
1 Chinese roast duck (already cooked), thickly sliced
2 cups (500 ml) thin coconut milk
Tamarind water or lime juice, to taste
Sugar to taste
Fish sauce to taste
4 kaffir lime leaves
1 lb (500 g) seedless white grapes

Spice Paste

1 teaspoon coriander seed
1 teaspoon cumin seed
5 large dried chilies, seeded, soaked in warm water for
   30 minutes and squeezed dry
1 slice galangal, peeled and coarsely chopped
4 stalks lemongrass, sliced
1 tablespoon shrimp paste
12 cloves garlic
8 shallots, sliced

In a mortar or a food processor grind the coriander and cumin seeds to a powder and set it aside. Grind the chilies, the galangal, lemongrass, shrimp paste, garlic and shallots to a fine paste, adding the coriander and cumin powder at the end.

Heat the oil in a saucepan, add the Spice Paste and fry until fragrant. Add the thick coconut milk and stir until the oil comes out. Add the sliced duck and mix well, then add the rest of the coconut milk, the tamarind water, sugar, fish sauce and 3 lime leaves and cook until the duck is heated and has absorbed the flavor. Add the grapes at the end and heat through. Garnish with the fourth lime leaf, thinly sliced.

STEAMED DISHES

TREY CHAMHOY STEAMED FISH

1 whole fish, about 1 lb/500 g (bream, snapper)
¼ cup (65 g) cloud-ear mushrooms
½ cup (125 g) mung-bean vermicelli, soaked in warm
    water for 5 minutes
4 thin slices fresh ginger root, cut into strips
1 tablespoon salted fermented soy bean (*tauco*)
¼ teaspoon sugar
Light soy sauce or fish sauce, to taste

Clean and scale the fish and slash it diagonally three times on each side. Soak the cloud-ear mushroom in warm water for 5 minutes, drain them, then pinch off and discard any hard bits. Drain the vermicelli, rinse it in cold water then cut it into 2-in (5-cm) lengths.

Put a covered pan with a steaming rack filled with water on the stove and bring it to a boil. Put the cloud-ear mushrooms, vermicelli, ginger, fermented soy beans and sugar in a wide bowl and mix them well. Roll the fish in this mixture, rubbing the juices into the slits in its sides. Place the fish into a shallow serving dish, spoon the mixture over the top, place the dish in the steamer and cover it. Steam for about 20–30 minutes or until the fish is cooked. Sprinkle light soy sauce or fish sauce over the top and serve.

STEAMED SPICED CHICKEN

AMOK

This dish appears in much the same form in Cambodia, Laos and Thailand but had its origin, I suspect, as a classic Khmer dish. Called *ho mok* in Thailand and *mawk* in Laos, it is often made there with egg to produce a savory custard. The egg version appears in Khmer cuisine too, but because I have covered the version with egg elsewhere I have chosen one without egg here.

½ cup (125 ml) thick coconut milk
1½ teaspoons sugar
1 tablespoon fish sauce
1 lb (500 g) boneless chicken breast, cut into 2-in (5-cm) strips then across
3 kaffir lime leaves, central rib removed and finely sliced
4 leaves silverbeet or 1 small bunch of spinach or Chinese broccoli

Spice Paste
14 dried chilies, seeded, soaked until soft and squeezed dry
½ teaspoon salt
½ cup (125 g) sliced lemongrass
1 slice galangal, peeled and coarsely chopped
1–2 coriander roots
1-in (2½-cm) piece turmeric root, peeled and coarsely chopped or ½ teaspoon ground turmeric
Piece of kaffir lime skin
1 teaspoon shrimp paste
5 cloves garlic
5 shallots, sliced

Grind the Spice Paste ingredients to a fine paste.

Combine the coconut milk, the Spice Paste, the sugar and fish sauce to taste in a bowl and mix well. The mixture should be discernibly sweet, spicy and salty. Add the chicken and mix, then add the lime leaves and mix everything together. You can use more coconut milk if you wish, although the mixture should not be too wet.

Remove the central rib from the silverbeet and cut the leaves into 2-in (5-cm) strips. Place the vegetable in the bottom of a soup bowl and spread the chicken on top. Put the bowl on a rack in a steamer and steam until cooked (about 25–30 minutes). Remove and serve in the bowl in which it was cooked.

Spicy Steamed Fish is made using 1 lb (500 g) of skinned thick fish fillets (such as ling or barramundi) cut into small pieces. Add 1 teaspoon chopped Chinese keys to the mixture if available.

FRIED DISHES AND GRILLS

CHION TREY CHAB ## FRIED POMFRET

> 1 small flat, fine-fleshed fish (pomfret, dart, bream,
>   flounder), cleaned and scaled
> 2 tablespoons oil
> 1 pickling cucumber
> 1 tablespoon dark soy sauce
> 1 green onion, green part only, curled (p. 22)
> 1–2 small red chilies for chili flowers (p. 21)

Wash the fish well, make three diagonal slashes across each side, and wipe it dry.

Heat a frying pan, add the oil and when it is hot, add the fish, frying it on high heat for 1 minute. Reduce the heat to medium-high and cook for 2 minutes or until the fish is cooked and crisp on one side. Turn the heat up again, flip the fish over and repeat the process on the second side. The fish should remain intact and crispy.

Meanwhile cut the cucumber in half lengthwise and cut two small ridges lengthwise in the skin to make the slices decorative. Slice the cucumber across into medium slices and fan the slices around one end of an oval plate large enough to accommodate the fish.

When the fish is brown and crisp, add the soy sauce to the pan and turn the fish once or twice to coat and flavor it. Place on the decorated plate and garnish with green onion curls and chili flowers.

CHION TREY I ## FRIED FISH I

> 2 bream or small snapper, about 1 lb (500 g) each,
>   cleaned and scaled
> 2–3 tablespoons oil
> 1 small clove garlic, chopped
> 3 tablespoons fresh lime juice
> 2 tablespoons water
> 2 tablespoons fish sauce
> 1½ tablespoons sugar

1 pickling cucumber, sliced in half lengthwise and across
    into half slices
2 red chilies, sliced diagonally

Make three diagonal slashes across each side of the fish and wipe them dry.

In a pan large enough to hold both fish, heat the oil and when it is hot add the fish and fry over medium heat until they are brown and crisp on one side (about 7–8 minutes). Turn the fish over carefully and cook on the other side.

Mix all the other ingredients except the cucumber and chilies together to make a sauce and when the fish are cooked, reduce the heat to low and pour the sauce over them in the pan. Arrange the cucumber slices on the edge of oval plates to fit the contours of the fish. When the sauce is hot lift the fish out onto the plates and cover with the sauce. Garnish with sliced chili.

CHION TREY II FRIED FISH II

2 bream or small snapper, about 1 lb (500 g) each
2–3 tablespoons oil
1 tablespoon chopped garlic
1 teaspoon finely chopped red chili
1 tablespoon finely sliced lemongrass
1 tablespoon fish sauce
1–2 tablespoons fish stock or water
1 teaspoon sugar
Fresh lime juice to taste (optional)
1 kaffir lime leaf, rib removed and thinly sliced
Sliced green onions and chopped fresh coriander leaves

Cook the fish according to the instructions in the recipe for Fried Fish I. When the fish are browned on both sides remove them from the pan on to the serving plate, leaving the oil behind in the pan. In the remaining oil fry the garlic, chili and lemongrass until they smell fragrant (add more oil if you have to). Add the fish sauce and the fish stock or water, sugar and lime juice to taste and then the lime leaf. Pour the sauce over the fish and garnish with green onions and coriander leaves.

LOCLAC SHAKING BEEF

This dish is a Cambodian version of the Vietnamese dish of the same name.

Lettuce
Cherry tomatoes, halved
1 medium-sized onion, sliced
10 oz (300 g) fillet or skirt steak, cut into 1-in (2½-cm) slices
3 teaspoons tomato purée
¼ teaspoon sugar
Salt to taste or 1 teaspoon fish sauce
¾ teaspoon flour
1 teaspoon oil
1–2 tablespoons oil
1–2 cloves garlic, finely chopped
3 teaspoons oil for dressing
1½ teaspoons white vinegar

Line a serving plate with lettuce at one end. Decoratively arrange a row of halved tomatoes and a few slices of onion on top of this.

In a bowl mix together the meat, the tomato purée, sugar, salt or fish sauce, flour and 1 teaspoon of oil and set aside to marinate for a few minutes.

Heat 1–2 tablespoons of oil in a heavy frying pan and add the garlic and the marinated beef and stir-fry over high heat until brown on the outside but still rare inside. Plate the beef on the other end of the decorated dish. Mix the 3 teaspoons of oil and the vinegar into a dressing and pour over everything.

CHHA SAKH KO KRŒUNG ## STIR-FRIED SPICY BEEF

1 tablespoon oil
1 lb (500 g) skirt steak, thinly sliced across the grain
1½ teaspoons sugar
½ teaspoon salt (optional)
1½ teaspoons oyster sauce
1 teaspoon fish sauce

Spice Paste
3 tablespoons sliced lemongrass (green part only)
1 thin slice galangal, peeled and coarsely chopped
1 very thin slice turmeric root, peeled and coarsely
  chopped or ¾ teaspoon ground turmeric
4 cloves garlic, chopped

Grind the lemongrass, galangal, turmeric and half of the chopped garlic to a fine paste and set aside.

Heat the oil in a wok or a pan over high heat. Add the rest of the chopped garlic and the meat to the pan and stir-fry until it changes color. Add the Spice Paste and stir-fry until the spices are fragrant. Season with the sugar, salt, oyster sauce and fish sauce and serve.

CHHA SAKH KO ## STIR-FRIED BEEF WITH TOMATOES AND CELERY

1 tablespoon oil
1 clove garlic, chopped
1 lb (500 g) skirt, blade or round steak, thinly sliced
  across the grain
1 teaspoon sugar
½ teaspoon salt
2 teaspoons oyster sauce
1 teaspoon fish sauce
5 tomatoes, cut into wedges
16 stalks and leaves Asian celery, cut into 1-in (2½-cm)
  lengths

Heat the oil in a pan add the garlic and the beef and stir-fry until the beef changes color. Add the sugar, salt, oyster sauce and the fish sauce and stir to mix. Add the tomato wedges and the celery stalks and stir-fry for 1 minute. Add the celery leaves and stir-fry for 1 minute then serve.

STIR-FRIED BEEF AND BROCCOLI

CHHA SAKH KO KHATNA

1 tablespoon oil
2 cloves garlic, chopped
8 oz (250 g) skirt, blade or round steak, thinly sliced across the grain
1 teaspoon sugar
Pinch of salt
1 teaspoon oyster sauce
7 oz (200 g) broccoli, broken into florets

Heat the oil in a pan or a wok over high heat. Add the garlic and the beef and stir-fry until the meat changes color. Add the sugar, salt and oyster sauce. When the meat is nearly cooked add the broccoli and stir-fry, covering the pan or wok with a lid to briefly steam the broccoli until it is tender-crisp.

STIR-FRIED PORK WITH TOFU AND BEAN SPROUTS

CHHA SAKH CHROUK, TAUHOU, SANDAEK BANDOH

1 tablespoon oil
1 clove garlic, chopped
4 oz (125 g) lean pork, thinly sliced or ground pork
¼ teaspoon salt
½ teaspoon sugar
1½ teaspoons soy sauce
1 teaspoon oyster sauce
3 oz (100 g) fried tofu cakes, cubed
2 oz (50 g) Chinese leeks, washed, trimmed and cut into 1-in (2½-cm) pieces
10 oz (300 g) bean sprouts, washed and trimmed

Heat the oil in a pan or wok, add the garlic and the meat and stir-fry until it changes color. Add salt, sugar, soy sauce and oyster sauce and stir. Add the tofu and stir-fry, then the harder ends of the Chinese leeks, then the bean sprouts and the rest of the Chinese leeks and stir-fry until the vegetables are tender-crisp.

STIR-FRIED PORK AND SNOWPEAS

CHHA SAKH CHROUK CHAMLOK HOLANTAV

Different combinations may be used in this recipe—sometimes just snowpeas, sometimes only snowpeas and cashews, and so on.

1–2 tablespoons oil

1 clove garlic, chopped

8 oz (250 g) lean pork, thinly sliced across the grain

1 teaspoon sugar

1 tablespoon oyster sauce

½ teaspoon fish sauce or ¼ teaspoon salt

8 oz (250 g) snowpeas, trimmed

1 can straw mushrooms

3 quail eggs, hard-boiled and peeled (optional)

2 tablespoons dried shrimp, rinsed

¼ cup (60 g) cashew nuts

Heat the oil in pan, add the garlic and the meat and stir-fry for one minute. Add the sugar, oyster sauce and fish sauce or salt. Add the snowpeas and stir, then drain and add the straw mushrooms, whole quail eggs (if using), dried shrimp and cashew nuts. Stir-fry until everything is cooked.

STIR-FRIED MUNG BEAN VERMICELLI

CHHA MII SU

1 tablespoon oil

2 small garlic cloves, chopped

8 oz (250 g) lean ground pork

1 small onion, sliced lengthwise

7 oz (200 g) mung-bean vermicelli, soaked in hot water for 5 minutes, then cut into bite-sized pieces

1 oz (25 g) cloud-ear mushroom, soaked in warm water for 5 mintues, stems and hard bits discarded

2–3 tablespoons dried shrimp, rinsed and soaked in cold
    water for 30 minutes
½ teaspoon sugar
1 teaspoon salt
1 tablespoon dark soy sauce

Heat the oil in a pan, add the garlic then the meat and stir-fry, breaking up the meat as you go. Add the sliced onion and the vermicelli and mix everything together. Add the cloud-ear mushroom, the shrimp together with the soaking water, the sugar, salt and the dark soy sauce and mix until everything is cooked. There should be enough water in the pan to to steam everything a little as it cooks, but add a spoonful of extra water if necessary.

CHHA DANGKEAB KDAM   STIR-FRIED CRAB CLAWS AND SHRIMP

1 tablespoon vegetable oil
1 clove garlic, chopped
8 oz (250 g) crab claws
½ teaspoon salt
½ teaspoon sugar
1 tablespoon oyster sauce
2 sponge gourds, peeled and cut into 2-in (5-cm) pieces
2 medium-sized onions, peeled and cut lengthwise
1 teaspoon fish sauce
8 oz (250 g) shrimp, peeled and deveined

Heat the oil in a pan, add the garlic, the crab claws, salt, sugar and oyster sauce and stir-fry over high heat. Add the sponge gourd, the onion and the fish sauce and stir well, cover for 1 minute and stir again. Add the shrimp and stir-fry until they are cooked.

CHHA TOMPANG STIR-FRIED ASPARAGUS

You can use sliced bamboo shoots instead of asparagus in this recipe.

1 tablespoon oil
1 clove garlic, chopped
8 oz (250 g) lean ground pork
½ teaspoon salt
½ teaspoon sugar
1 teaspoon fish sauce
1 tablespoon oyster sauce
1 bunch asparagus, washed, peeled and cut diagonally
    into 1-in (2½-cm) lengths
8 oz (250 g) shrimp, chopped

Heat the oil in a pan or wok, add the garlic, pork, salt, sugar, fish sauce and oyster sauce and stir-fry until the meat changes color. Add the asparagus and stir-fry until it is dark green. Add the shrimp, stir-frying until it is cooked and the asparagus is tender-crisp.

SAKH KO CHANGKAK GRILLED SKEWERED BEEF

1 teaspoon salt
2 teaspoons sugar
2 tablespoons oyster sauce
2 teaspoons oil
1 lb (500 g) skirt steak, cut across the grain into ½-in
    (1-cm) slices

Spice Paste

2 large dried chilies, seeded, soaked in warm water for
    30 minutes and squeezed dry
4 tablespoons finely sliced lemongrass (green part only)
1 very thin slice galangal, peeled and coarsely chopped
1 thin slice turmeric root, peeled and coarsely chopped
    or ½ teaspoon ground turmeric
2 cloves garlic, chopped

Soak bamboo skewers in enough water to cover to prevent them from burning during cooking. Grind the Spice Paste ingredients to a fine paste. Combine the Spice Paste with the salt, the sugar, the oyster sauce and the oil in a bowl. Add the meat to the bowl and mix everything together.

Thread the sliced beef onto the skewers across the grain and flatten them so that you have five flat pieces on each skewer. Place under the broiler or grill them over low heat, turning them so that they brown on both sides.

DRESSED DISHES AND SALADS

NHEAM MOAN ## CHICKEN SALAD

8 oz (250 g) boneless chicken thigh fillets or 12 oz (350 g) whole thighs
½ small head of cabbage, shredded
¼ pickling cucumber, skin intact, cut into very fine strips
¼ carrot (optional), cut into very fine strips
A handful of bean sprouts, washed
1 small bundle (1 cup/250 g) mung-bean vermicelli, soaked in hot water for 5 minutes then cut into 2-in (5-cm) lengths
1 tablespoon roasted peanuts, coarsely ground
1 tablespoon dried shrimp, rinsed, dried and ground
1 handful mint leaves

Dressing
1 clove garlic, finely chopped
2 tablespoons fresh lime juice
1 tablespoon water
1 tablespoon sugar
1½ tablespoons fish sauce
1 bird's eye chili, finely sliced

Put the chicken in a saucepan, cover with water and simmer until they are cooked.

Drain and cool the chicken, reserving the stock for some other use. Pull the chicken into rough shreds with your hands.

Put the chicken, shredded cabbage, cucumber, bean sprouts, carrot (if using) and vermicelli into a bowl and mix well. Add the peanuts and shrimp and mix. Roughly tear the mint leaves and add them, tossing everything together. Mix the dressing ingredients. Add dressing to suit your taste, toss well and serve.

BEEF AND LETTUCE SALAD
NHEAM SAKH KO SALAT

This salad can be plated Western-style or wrapped in a whole lettuce leaf and dipped into the dressing.

5 leaves Asian lettuce, washed, dried and torn into 3-in (8-cm) pieces
1 small onion, finely sliced
2 small tomatoes, sliced
2 hard-boiled eggs, peeled and cut into wedges
8 oz (250 g) skirt steak, finely sliced across the grain
1 teaspoon cornstarch
2 tablespoons oil
2 cloves garlic, chopped
Pinch of salt
½ teaspoon sugar

Dressing
1 small clove garlic, chopped
1 tablespoon fish sauce
½ teaspoon sugar
1 tablespoon fresh lime juice
2 teaspoons water
Pinch of black pepper

Line the edge of a serving plate with the lettuce. Arrange the onion on top of the tomatoes and the hard-boiled eggs on top of the onions.

Coat the beef with the cornstarch. Heat the oil in a pan or a wok, add the garlic and the beef and stir-fry for 1 minute. Add the salt and sugar and stir-fry until the meat is cooked.

Plate the beef in the center of the plate of salad. Mix the Dressing ingredients together and serve in a separate bowl or jug. Diners help themselves to salad and meat and pour dressing over everything to taste.

Vietnam

"Sinicized" culture in Vietnam and one categorized as "Indianized" in the rest of Southeast Asia. The style of cuisine follows this division.

Yet flashes of a recognizable Southeast Asian culinary pattern do exist in Vietnam and show up most evidently as regional variations. From the time of their independence from China in AD 939 the Vietnamese slowly but surely advanced southward into areas previously controlled by two heavily Indianized states: Champa on the central–south coast and by now Cambodia on the southern tip and the western hinterland. After 1630, moreover, the de facto southern leadership at Hue traded with the Portuguese in Macao, repeating a contact that was significant for all Southeast Asians. Legacies from both the earlier maritime contact of Champa had with the rest of Southeast Asia and from the Portuguese contact are to be found in Hue today in the use of shrimp pastes and chili in cooking.

The food of the south is characteristized by lemongrass, tamarind and coconut (most often in the form of coconut water rather than coconut milk squeezed from the flesh). Some features of cooking in the north are reminiscent of the cuisine of neighboring Laos—the use of galangal and of country fish paste for example, and a frequent resort to grilling over charcoal.

Ho Chi Minh City, where I commenced my journey, is now on the way to rapid modernity and globalization. Business and the free market thrive; shops, cars, motorbikes and consumer goods are everywhere, and each person you meet seems to be reaching for an opportunity. Markets and restaurants teem with the freshness as well as the variety that a tropical climate combined with a thriving economy can bring. Households still buy their food daily and cook it fresh but an increasing number of kitchens harbor open tiled benches around their charcoal stoves or electric hotplates, and sport refrigerators and sinks. Here a visitor is likely to encounter "party-style" food: four or five dishes containing multiple ingredients or those calling for considerable preparation such as battered deep-fried shrimp, mixed Vietnamese salads, Chinese-derived combination dishes, steamboats, and so on.

In Ho Chi Minh City I was able to devise recipes from both restaurant visits and from participating in the preparation of some home-cooked food. But my greatest familiarity with the food of the south came in the course of a very special train trip which lasted for nine days from Ho Chi Minh City up the coast to Hue, stopping off at Nha Trang and Danang on the way, and then on to Hanoi. A party of fifteen people occupied an old Romanian dining car and a French sleeping car dating from the 1930s. While other members of the group took in the country-side I spent my time in the galley watching two brilliant Vietnamese cooks performing their craft for the group's culinary enjoyment. It is hard to describe the feats these women performed, working in extreme temperatures without air conditioning in a narrow galley about 7 x 10 feet (3 by 2 meters) with a bench and sink down one side, a gas stove that did not appear to be working on the other and three portable charcoal grills on the floor supplemented by two kerosene stoves. My appreciation of the Buddhist approach to life grew daily as I watched the women spend hours calmly preparing huge bowls of seemingly random raw ingredients then transforming them into banquets of seven or eight dishes of steamed and fried fish, crab and shrimp with spring rolls, soups and braised meats for every lunch and dinner on the train. Their teamwork was brilliant, moving around each other cheerfully and effortlessly in that cramped space—always in the right place to steady precariously balanced woks full of boiling oil when the train lurched heavily or ground to a sudden halt and always willing to answer my questions as I struggled to note down what they were doing in logical Western fashion.

In Hanoi I was fortunate enough to spend time with a group of international Volunteer Service Officers and their Vietnamese friends. Again we visited modest restaurants serving local specialties where we identified ingredients and reconstructed recipes. There, too, the Hanoi Women's Association helped me with instructions for some of the dishes they use in cooking classes for local women, many of whom, due to years of separation from their families in war followed by periods of famine and shortage, never learned to cook in the traditional family way.

In the course of this experience I have come to appreciate the special lightness and delicacy of Vietnamese cuisine and to welcome its reliance on the individual adjustment of flavors. Vietnamese cooking incorporates a very Chinese pleasure in the texture of foods in the mouth. Great value is placed on the preparation of ingredients so that they are crunchy or full of texture, and this is a sign of real culinary refinement. Vinegar—though in Vietnam much softer than is common elsewhere (and I have adjusted for this by diluting vinegar with water)—is commonly used in cooking, as is tamarind water or fresh lime juice, and so is fish sauce and sugar (though more of the latter in the south than in the north). Dishes are always accompanied by a dipping sauce, of which there are various kinds, for adding more flavor if you need it. It is in these ways that flavor complimentary to the main ingredients is imparted rather than through the dried sea trade spices employed in much of Indianized Southeast Asia.

Vietnamese food is reminiscent of both Chinese and Thai cuisine—or at least those aspects of Thai food that do not owe their origin primarily to the spice trade. Chinese cooking techniques, the saltiness, the textures and the delicate aromas of Chinese food are present and so too are the fishy and sour flavors of Thai food, many common herbs and a similar use of sugar as a flavoring. But Vietnamese food is notably less oily than Chinese and it is a lot sweeter and less hot than Thai.

Like other Southeast Asian meals, a Vietnamese one will reflect both local resources and socio-economic status. Most Vietnamese earn modest incomes and live very simply. Meals generally consist of two dishes with rice (sometimes rice papers) and appropriate dipping sauces. One of the dishes is likely to be a soup—either a sour soup or a thin Chinese-style one containing fish, vegetable, a little meat or a combination—and it may be accompanied by something fried, grilled, steamed over rice or a simple raw vegetable with dipping sauce. More bountiful or expansive times might see a braised dish replace or accompany the soup, some meaty and more elaborate salads and more substantial amounts of fried, grilled or roasted meat or seafood.

Unless you remember that Vietnamese, like other Southeast Asians, are first and foremost eaters of rice and use other preparations merely as side dishes, Vietnamese cooks can sometimes seem prodigal with flavor additives. Lined up beside them as they cook are likely to be a large bowl of salt, one of sugar, one of MSG, and one of "chicken seasoning powder." All will have good-sized spoons in them. Alongside will be a bottle of fish sauce, one of soy sauce, and probably one of "seasoning sauce." Spoonfuls of everything—and usually more than one spoonful—will be added to a dish. On the table there may be hoisin sauce as well as dipping sauces.

In this they are not too different from some Thais, but I find that because of the relative lightness of the basic flavor in Vietnamese dishes, the use of too many additives can be overpowering. Though I am addicted to garlic, chilies and the flavors imparted by shrimp paste in cooking, I neither like nor react well to too much salt, sugar or chemical flavoring, especially when they are not neutralized in the company of large amounts of chili and spices. Most of my recipes, therefore, adopt a salt-sugar level at the lower end of the scale of Vietnamese possibilities although they attempt to maintain a general balance of flavors that is faithful to the one that might be encountered in Vietnamese homes or restaurants.

It is also important to remember some of the basic Vietnamese flavorings to achieve the right balance in individual dishes. Vietnamese vinegars, though generally, as I have noted before, softer and less acidic than ours, can still vary in strength and flavor according to where and how they were made. Fish sauce too, comes in different grades and qualities according to the "draw" it represents, and its price. In both cases some of those differences are apparent in brands of these items available overseas. The certain brand of Thai fish sauce I keep for everyday purposes may often be saltier and cruder than the most expensive Vietnamese fish sauce available here.

In Vietnam as in other parts of Southeast Asia it is usual for cooks to taste and adjust flavors frequently as they cook. Doing so is both a reflection of individual preference and an acknowledgement that the strength and quality of ingredients will vary. I cannot emphasize enough that my readers would be well advised to follow suit.

WET DISHES
Vietnamese Sour Soups

CANH CHUA CA SOUR FISH SOUP

Sour fish soup is the national dish of south Vietnam and a dish that echoes right across Southeast Asia. It is family food as familiar to a southern Vietnamese as fish and chips are to a someone from Britain or lamb chops to an Australian. In Vietnam taro stalk (*dot bac ha*) is always used in this soup. You can find this fairly readily in Asian food stores owned by Vietnamese, but stalks of celery would make an acceptable substitute. Some people also like to add 5 or 6 okra to this soup.

1 ¼ lb (600 g) whole fish, cleaned and scaled or fish
   steaks (freshwater perch, redfin, trout, pike or saltwater
   fish such as coral trout, sea perch, whiting)
2 cloves garlic, chopped (optional)
4–6 cups (1–1½ liters) water
3 green tamarind pods or tamarind water made from a
   walnut-sized piece tamarind pulp (p. 55) or 2 slices
   sour pineapple, sliced into small wedges
3 taro stalks, about 3 oz (100 g) or 2 large stalks celery
1 medium tomato, cut into wedges
3 tablespoons fish sauce
1 tablespoon sugar
Salt to taste
7 oz (200 g) bean sprouts, washed and trimmed
A handful of mixed green herbs: long-leaf coriander,
   sliced; coriander leaf, coarsely chopped; Asian sweet
   basil, torn; green onions, sliced
1 fresh chili, sliced

If using whole fish, rub it with garlic, and cut it into steaks about 2-in (5-cm) wide.

Put the head and tail in a saucepan, add the water and simmer for 20 minutes or so to make stock. When the water boils, add the tamarind pods (if using) and let them soften for 5–10 minutes. Remove the tamarind pods and mash them in a bowl with some stock added to moisten, then strain as much liquid as you want back into the stock, discarding the pulp.

Peel any tough skin off the taro stalks (if using) and cut them diagonally into bite-sized pieces. If you are using tamarind pulp, soak it in 3 oz (100 ml) of boiling water until it is soft, then squeeze it repeatedly with your fingers and strain it through a sieve, discarding the pulp and reserving the liquid.

Strain the stock and discard the solids. Return to a boil, add the tomatoes and cook for a minute, then add the pineapple or the tamarind water (if using), the fish sauce, sugar and salt (the broth should be a little sour and sufficiently but not excessively sweet). Add the taro stem, bring the soup back to a boil, add the fish steaks and simmer gently until cooked.

Place the bean sprouts in the bottom of a serving bowl, add the chunks of fish and sprinkle the herbs over them. Ladle the broth and the vegetable over the top and serve immediately.

Serve with a bowl of sliced fresh chili and one of fish sauce for diners to add if they wish.

Vietnamese families sometimes create two dishes instead of one here if they start with a substantial fish. They do not rub the fish with the garlic, but cut it into fillets. Some of the fillets are put aside. While the stock is cooking, 1–2 tablespoons of oil is heated in a pan, the garlic is added and then the fish fillets. The fish is fried gently until it is flavored and very lightly cooked without letting the garlic get too brown and bitter. The fried fillets are then taken out and set aside on a plate. The raw fillets are added to the soup and left to cook, while the fried ones are dipped in at the end for just enough time to heat them, they are removed and drained. They are placed on a plate and served as a separate dish with Basic Dipping Sauce (*Nuoc Cham*).

For vegetarians this soup may be made without the fish but with all the other vegetables. Soy sauce is used to flavor the broth in place of fish sauce.

CANH CHUA RAU MUONG — SOUR SOUP WITH WATER SPINACH

3 green tamarind pods or tamarind water made from a
  walnut-sized piece of tamarind pulp (p. 55)
2 small shallots or 1 small onion, finely chopped
2 tablespoons fish sauce
Pinch each of salt and pepper
10 oz (300 g) shrimp, peeled and deveined
1–2 tablespoons oil
6 cups (1½ liters) water
2 bunches water spinach, washed and cut into 3–4 in
  (8–10 cm) lengths, including leaves
1 heaping teaspoon sugar (optional)
Lime wedges

If you are using the green tamarind pods, boil them for 5–10 minutes then crush and strain them, reserving the water. Otherwise soak the tamarind pulp as described for Sour Fish Soup on page 489. Mix the shallots with a little fish sauce and salt and pepper and marinate the shrimp in this mixture for 15 minutes.

Heat the oil in a saucepan and stir-fry the shrimp for a few minutes. Add the water and bring to a boil. Add tamarind water to taste, then add the water spinach, salt, sugar (if using), and/or more fish sauce to taste.

Bring the soup back to a boil and simmer briefly for a few minutes, making sure that the water spinach does not lose its bright green color by overcooking. Serve hot, with wedges of lime.

Soups of Chinese Origin

CANH RAU CAI ## CHINESE CABBAGE SOUP (SOUTH)

1–2 tablespoons fish sauce
Freshly ground pepper
Pinch salt
1 teaspoon sugar
8 oz (250 g) or more pork bones
3 oz (100 g) lean pork, sliced into bite-sized pieces or lean ground pork
6 cups (1½ liters) water
3 thin slices fresh ginger root
1 lb (500 g) Chinese cabbage, preferably the green-stemmed variety (*rau cai*), cut into short lengths
Sliced green onions for garnish

Combine the fish sauce, pepper, salt and sugar and marinate the bones and the pork in this mixture for 30 minutes. Bring the water to a boil. Add the bones and the ginger to the pot and simmer for 45 minutes, skimming regularly to keep the stock clear. Remove the bones, add the cabbage and the pork and simmer for 5 minutes. Taste and adjust the seasonings, adding more sugar if you wish, then serve garnished with a sprinkling of freshly ground black pepper and some sliced green onions.

CANH NÀM GA ## CHICKEN AND MUNG-BEAN VERMICELLI SOUP

1 lb (500 g) chicken bones or giblets for stock
6 cups (1½ liters) water
3 oz (100 g) mung-bean vermicelli
1 chicken breast, finely sliced
1 small onion, sliced

2 tablespoons fish sauce, or to taste

2 dried Chinese mushrooms, soaked and thinly sliced

2 cloud-ear mushrooms, fresh or dried (soaked if dried),
   thinly sliced

½ teaspoon chicken seasoning powder or 1 chicken
   stock cube (optional)

Pepper to taste

Sliced green onions for garnish

Simmer the chicken bones in the water for 1 hour and skim any foam that forms off the top. Drain and discard the bones. Soak the vermicelli for 30 minutes in water and cut into bite-sized pieces. Add these to the soup stock.

Stir-fry the sliced chicken with the onion. Add 1 teaspoon of fish sauce and the mushrooms and continue to stir-fry for about 5 minutes. Add the chicken and onion to the soup with the seasoning powder, the rest of the fish sauce and pepper to taste. Serve garnished with green onions.

A complete meal may be prepared by using a small whole chicken to make the stock. When the stock is ready, remove the chicken and once it is cool, shred it. Put some of the shredded meat back into the soup, season and garnish and use the rest of the meat to make Chicken Salad (*Goi Ga*).

CANH THAP CAM COMBINATION SOUP

3 cups (750 g) pork bone stock (p. 20)

Water from 1 green coconut or 1 can (14 oz/400 ml)
   coconut juice

1½ cups (375 g) cauliflower, broken into small florets

1 medium carrot, cut into flowers (p. 22)

8 oz (250 g) shrimp, peeled and deveined

8 oz (250 g) squid tubes, prepared according to the
   instructions on p. 27 or 8 oz (250 g) baby octopus,
   cleaned

6 fish balls and/or pork balls, halved or sliced (optional)

1 tablespoon fish sauce or to taste

Salt to taste

1 heaping teaspoon sugar (optional)

2 fresh chilies, sliced in rounds

2 dill plants, cut into short lengths

Mix the stock with the coconut water and bring it to a boil. Add the vegetables to the soup and when they are partly cooked add the shrimp, the squid, the fish and pork balls, the fish sauce, salt and sugar to taste. Put the chilies and the dill in separate garnish dishes.

If you have used a young green coconut cut the top off it and flatten the bottom. Serve the soup in the hollowed coconut, on a plate in the center of the table. Otherwise serve in a tureen. Diners ladle a serving out into their individual soup bowls and add dill and chilies to taste. Other herbs such as coriander, green onion or long-leafed coriander may be used instead.

BRAISED DISHES

TOM KHO BRAISED SHRIMP

This dish comes from Hue, the old royal capital in central Vietnam. I ate it in a hotel overlooking the Perfumed River, a most appropriate setting. Shrimp are common Hue food, and here the markets display some of the ingredients that are familiar in other parts of Southeast Asia such as shrimp pastes and chili pastes.

1 tablespoon fish sauce
½ teaspoon sugar
¼ teaspoon refined shrimp paste (optional) (p. 531)
Salt to taste
½ teaspoon freshly ground pepper
1 lb (500 g) shrimp, peeled and deveined or with shells intact
2 tablespoons oil
1 clove garlic, chopped
4 shallots, finely chopped
½–1 teaspoon dried chili flakes

Mix the fish sauce, sugar, shrimp paste, salt and pepper and marinate the shrimp in this mixture for half an hour.

Heat the oil in a wok or pan, add the garlic, shallots and the chili flakes and stir-fry until fragrant. Add the shrimp and mix until they are coated with the spices. Add a splash or two of boiling water. Stir, cover the pan and cook for 2–3 minutes, by which time most of the liquid should have evaporated. If it has not, stir and cook, uncovered, a little longer. You should end up with a small amount of thick sauce.

Serve with rice and an Herb Salad Plate including fresh bean sprouts.

CA KHO THIT HEO BRAISED FISH WITH PORK

This dish may be cooked with sliced bamboo shoots rather than pork and with plain water instead of coconut water.

1 whole firm-fleshed fish, about 1¾ lb (800 g)
   (freshwater perch, barramundi, sea mullet, rock cod)
1 thin slice fresh ginger root, peeled and shredded
7 oz (200 g) belly pork or thick cured bacon
5 shallots, sliced or 1 medium-sized onion, finely
   chopped
1 fresh chili, sliced (optional)
½ teaspoon sugar
Pepper to taste
1 tablespoon fish sauce
Coconut water or canned coconut juice
2 teaspoons Caramel Coloring (p. 527), or to taste
1 tablespoon finely sliced Vietnamese mint (*rau ram*)

Clean and scale the fish and place a few shreds of ginger into the cavity. Cook it whole if you have a French fish kettle with a removable rack. Otherwise cut the fish into thick pieces and arrange them in the bottom of a saucepan. Cut the pork into thick slices and layer it on top of the fish. Grind the shallots and chili to a paste. Add the sugar, pepper and fish sauce, mix, pour this mixture over the fish, and marinate it for about 20 minutes. Add enough coconut water to cover half of the fish and carefully stir in the Caramel Coloring. Taste and adjust the seasonings to provide both the right combination of saltiness and sweetness and bring to a boil. Reduce the heat, cover and simmer gently for about 1 hour, adding more water if it is drying out. Serve hot, sprinkled with sliced Vietnamese mint, rice and an Herb Salad Plate.

Depending on the sweetness of any canned coconut juice you use, you may want to use less caramel. Also, if you substitute bacon for the belly pork you may want to use less fish sauce.

GA KHO XA GUNG ## CHICKEN BRAISED WITH GINGER AND LEMONGRASS

3 stalks lemongrass, finely sliced
3 cloves garlic, chopped
2-in (5-cm) piece fresh ginger root, peeled and chopped
2 lb (1 kg) chicken drumsticks, whole or chopped
2–3 tablespoons fish sauce
1–1½ tablespoons sugar
Salt and pepper to taste
3 tablespoons oil
1 cup (250 ml) water

Grind the lemongrass, garlic and ginger to a paste. Marinate the chicken in a mixture of 2 tablespoons fish sauce, 1 tablespoon sugar, pepper and salt for 20 minutes. Heat the oil in a pan. Add the chicken to the pan and stir-fry until it changes color. Add the lemongrass mixture and stir-fry until fragrant. Add the remaining marinade and the water, mix well, cover and simmer over low heat for about 30 minutes. Remove the lid, taste and adjust the seasonings, adding more fish sauce and sugar if you wish. Continue cooking until the chicken is done, the water is reduced and the sauce is thick.

GA NUOC COT DUA ## CURRIED CHICKEN IN COCONUT MILK

½ cup (125 ml) thick canned coconut milk
1½ cups (375 ml) thin canned coconut milk
1 tablespoon fish sauce, or more to taste
1 teaspoon sugar, or more to taste
Salt and pepper to taste
2 lb (1 kg) chicken, cut into bite-sized pieces
2 tablespoons oil
1 tablespoon curry powder (preferably Vietnamese)
Torn fresh coriander leaf
Asian sweet basil

Spice Paste

3 stalks lemongrass
1 fresh chili
3 cloves garlic, sliced
4 shallots, sliced

Open the can of coconut milk without shaking it and set aside ½ cup (125 ml) of the thick milk at the top. Combine the fish sauce, sugar, salt and pepper and marinate the chicken in this mixture. Grind the lemongrass, chili, garlic and shallots to a fine paste. Heat the oil in a wok and fry the paste until it smells fragrant, add the chicken and the curry powder and stir-fry until the chicken has changed color. Add thin coconut milk to cover, stir and cook uncovered until the chicken is tender and the gravy has reduced. Add fish sauce and sugar to taste. Add the thick coconut milk and stir. Serve garnished with fresh coriander leaf and basil.

BRAISED PORK CHOPS IN COCONUT WATER

THIT HEO KHO NUOC DUA

4 cloves garlic, chopped
1 tablespoon fish sauce (optional)
1 heaping teaspoon sugar (optional)
Freshly ground black pepper to taste
1½ lb (750 g) thin loin pork chops
3 tablespoons oil
Water from 1 young coconut or 1 can (14 oz/400 ml)
   coconut juice
Chopped fresh coriander for garnish

Combine the garlic, fish sauce, sugar and pepper and marinate the chops in this mixture for 30 minutes. Heat the oil in a frying pan. Add the chops and fry them gently until they are golden brown on both sides. Pour off any excess oil, add the coconut water, cover the pan and simmer gently until the chops are tender. Remove the lid, turn the heat to high and continue cooking until the juice has reduced to a few tablespoons (you may need to keep turning the chops at the end to prevent them from burning). You can serve the chops whole or slice them. Either way, serve them on a platter with the remaining juice poured over and garnish with chopped coriander leaf.

THIT HEO KHO TAU # BRAISED PORK WITH BOILED EGGS

3 cloves garlic, chopped

2 tablespoons fish sauce, or more to taste

1 heaping teaspoon sugar

1 lb (500 g) boned pork belly, cut into bite-sized pieces

1–2 tablespoons oil

2 shallots or 1 small onion, chopped

Juice from 1 green coconut or 1 can (14 oz/400 ml)
   coconut juice or water

1 teaspoon Caramel Coloring (p. 527) or to taste

4 hard-boiled eggs, peeled

Combine the garlic, fish sauce and sugar and marinate the pork in this mixture. Heat the oil in a saucepan, add the shallots and stir-fry until they are soft. Add the pork and stir-fry until it is brown on the outside. Add the remaining marinade, enough coconut juice (or water) to just cover, and the Caramel Coloring. Taste and adjust the seasonings. Bring to a boil, reduce the heat and simmer, covered, about 1 hour. By this time the gravy should have reduced somewhat. Add the hard-boiled eggs and simmer for another half hour, until the meat is very tender. Remove and halve the eggs and serve with the meat and an Herb Salad Plate, Pickled Bean sprouts and rice.

CHAN GIO NAU KIEU BCC # NORTHERN BRAISED PORK

This northern version of braised pork leg incorporates some of the flavorings used in other countries of Southeast Asia but that are not common in the south of Vietnam. The northern Vietnamese have a rather "refined" way of extracting the juices of very young galangal and turmeric roots and using them as ingredients in a marinade.

1 lb (500 g) boned pork leg, skin and fat intact

3 cloves garlic, sliced

1 shallot, sliced

1-in (2-cm) piece galangal, peeled and chopped

½ teaspoon ground turmeric

1 teaspoon refined shrimp paste (p. 531)

2 teaspoons sugar

1½ tablespoons fish sauce

1 tablespoon oil

3 oz (100 g) cooked or canned whole bamboo shoots,
  cut into chunks (optional)

¾ teaspoon vinegar mixed with ¾ teaspoon water

Pepper to taste

Sliced green onions for garnish

Grill the boned pork leg skin side down over charcoal or under the broiler until it is browned on the outside. Turn and grill the other side until brown. Cut the meat into cubes and put these into a bowl. Mash the garlic and shallot to a paste, add the galangal and ground turmeric, shrimp paste, sugar and fish sauce and mix well. Combine this mixture with the meat and set it aside to marinate for 1 hour.

Put the oil in a saucepan, remove the meat from the marinade and stir-fry it until it is browned all over. Add the rest of the marinade and stir-fry for 1 minute. Add sufficient water to just cover, the bamboo shoots and enough diluted vinegar to produce a slightly sour taste. Bring to a boil, cover and simmer over low heat for at least 1 hour or until the meat is tender and the sauce has thickened. Remove the lid at the end to thicken the sauce, if necessary. Sprinkle with pepper, add sliced green onions to garnish and serve accompanied by an Herb Salad Plate and rice.

BO KHO XA BEEF BRAISED WITH LEMONGRASS

2 tablespoons fish sauce

1 tablespoon dark soy sauce

1 tablespoon sugar

3 cloves garlic, chopped

1 thick slice fresh ginger root, peeled and chopped

1 teaspoon five-spice powder

1 lb (500 g) lean beef, cubed

2 stalks lemongrass, bruised and cut into 2-in (5-cm)
  pieces

2 tablespoons oil

4 shallots or 1 small onion, finely chopped

2 carrots, thickly sliced (optional)

2 oz (50 g) roasted peanuts, coarsely chopped

Combine the fish sauce, soy sauce, sugar, garlic, ginger and five-spice powder in a shallow dish and marinate the beef in this mixture. Put the lemongrass in the bottom of a saucepan or a Chinese claypot. Heat the oil in a heavy pan and sauté the shallots and carrot until the shallots are soft. Add the beef and sauté until it is browned on all sides.

Add the sautéed shallots, carrot and beef to the saucepan or claypot, along with the remaining marinade and enough water to just cover the beef. Cover and simmer, stirring occasionally until the beef is tender (at least an hour, possibly two depending on the cut of meat). Remove the lid and cook on high heat until the liquid has reduced a little. Add enough of the peanuts to make a thick sauce, return to a boil and serve with the rest of the peanuts sprinkled over the top.

The dish can also be cooked in a casserole dish in the oven on low heat.

STEAMED DISHES

TRUNG CHUNG THAP CAM ## STEAMED EGGS

¼ cup (65 g) mung-bean vermicelli, soaked in warm
  water until soft then drained
2 large or 4 small cloud-ear mushrooms
3 large eggs
3 oz (100 g) lean ground pork
Salt and pepper to taste
2 shallots or ½ small onion, finely chopped
2 small tomatoes, seeds removed and coarsely chopped
1 tablespoon fish sauce

Cut the vermicelli into bite-sized lengths. Soak the cloud-ear mushrooms in hot water until they are soft. Drain and cut off any hard stem pieces and slice the rest into thin strips.

Break two whole eggs and one egg white into a bowl, setting the spare yolk aside. Beat the two eggs and the egg white lightly to just mix them. Add the ground pork, salt and pepper, shallots, mushrooms, tomatoes, vermicelli and fish sauce and mix well. Transfer the mixture to a lightly oiled bowl for steaming.

Bring water to a boil in a steamer. Place the bowl on a rack inside the steamer, cover and steam for 10 minutes. Beat the remaining egg yolk and pour over the top of the mixture in the bowl. Cover and steam for another 10 minutes or until cooked through. Remove the bowl from the steamer and set it aside to rest. Cut the steamed egg into wedges and serve with rice, a braised dish and an Herb Salad Plate.

MAM RUOC CHUNG STEAMED EGGS WITH SHRIMP

This dish can be steamed inside a pot of cooking rice. Once the water has evaporated from the surface, rest the bowl on top of the rice and replace the lid. When the rice is cooked the egg will be too.

2 eggs
½ teaspoon sugar
Salt and pepper to taste
2 green onions, finely sliced
1 teaspoon refined shrimp paste (p. 531)

Beat the eggs in a small bowl with the sugar, salt and pepper and green onions. Add the shrimp paste and mix well. Steam the mixture for 10 minutes or until cooked through, or fry it as an omelette. Cut it into slices and serve with the rice.

CHA TOM SHRIMP PÂTÉ

Shrimp Pâté can also be served as an appetizer.

1 lb (500 g) shrimp, peeled and deveined
2 oz (50 g) piece pork fat
2 cloves garlic, chopped
1 teaspoon fish sauce
1 teaspoon sugar
Salt and pepper to taste
4 shallots, finely chopped
3 cloud-ear mushrooms, soaked until soft, drained and finely chopped
1 egg, separated

Refresh the shrimp according to the instructions on p. 25 and then refrigerate them for 30 minutes. Mash them to a fine paste in a mortar or a food processor.

Boil the piece of pork fat for 10 minutes, drain it thoroughly and dice it into tiny pieces. Combine the shrimp, pork fat, garlic, fish sauce, sugar, salt and pepper and knead it with your hands to thoroughly combine the ingredients. Add the shallots and the cloud-ear mushrooms. Lightly whisk the egg white and add enough of it to the mixture to make it light but not too wet.

Spread the mixture in a greased shallow baking dish and steam the dish on a rack in a covered steamer for 10 minutes. Beat the egg yolk and pour it over the top. Replace the lid of the steamer and steam for another 5 minutes. Set the dish aside to rest for 5 minutes then cut it into pieces and pile them onto a serving dish. Serve with rice, Basic Dipping Sauce (*Nuoc Cham*) and an Herb Salad Plate.

FRIED DISHES
Stir-fries

TOM RIEM ## CARAMEL SHRIMP

This dish is usually very sweet and is eaten in small quantities with lots of rice. Use less sugar or caramel if you prefer it less sweet.

1 lb (500 g) shrimp, peeled and deveined
Salt
1 tablespoon oil
4 shallots, finely chopped
3 cloves garlic, chopped
1 heaping teaspoon sugar
2 tablespoons fish sauce
2 teaspoons–1 tablespoon Caramel Coloring (p. 527),
    or increase quantity of white sugar to 1 tablespoon

Refresh the shrimp according to the instructions on p. 25. Heat the oil in a pan. Fry the shallots and garlic until golden then add the sugar, stirring until it dissolves. Add the shrimp and stir-fry until almost cooked then add the fish sauce and sufficient Caramel Coloring. Reduce the heat and stir until the sauce is thick and the shrimp are cooked.

If you don't have Caramel Coloring on hand, add 1 tablespoon of sugar to the pan after the shallots and garlic are golden and the shrimp have been lightly stir-fried, then stir over high heat until the sugar turns brown and caramelizes. Add the fish sauce, reduce the heat and stir-fry until the shrimp are cooked and the sauce is thick.

TOM XAO STIR-FRIED SWEET SHRIMP

1 lb (500 g) shrimp, peeled and deveined
Salt
1 teaspoon cornstarch
Pinch of freshly ground pepper
1 young plant Chinese celery or 1 small stick celery, cut
  into matchsticks
1 carrot, finely sliced into flowers (p. 22)
1 small Chinese turnip (the same size as the carrot),
  finely sliced into flowers
Vinegar
Pinch of sugar
2–3 tablespoons oil
3 cloves garlic, chopped
1 medium-sized onion, thickly sliced lengthwise
1 tablespoon fish sauce
2 teaspoons sugar
1 tablespoon rice wine or sherry
½ cup (125 ml) light chicken stock or water
Chopped fresh coriander leaves and sliced green onions
  for garnish

Refresh the shrimp according to the instructions on p. 25 then refrigerate them for 20 minutes. Combine the cornstarch and pepper and dust the shrimp lightly with this mixture.

If using Chinese celery, cut it into 1½-in (4-cm) lengths; if using celery cut it into matchsticks. Soak the carrot and turnip flowers in water with a dash of vinegar and a pinch of sugar added to it. Drain well and set aside.

Heat 2 tablespoons of oil in the wok. Add the shrimp and stir-fry until they are cooked. Remove and set them aside.

Add more oil to the pan if necessary. Add the chopped garlic and fry until it is light brown, then fry the sliced onion, carrot, turnip and celery and stir-fry until tender-crisp. Add the fish sauce, sugar, rice wine and stock and mix well. Return the shrimp to the pan, mix, taste and adjust the seasonings (it should be noticeably sweet) and serve garnished with chopped fresh coriander leaves and sliced green onions.

MUC XAO STIR-FRIED SQUID

2 cucumbers, about 8-in (20-cm) long, peeled
2 medium-sized tomatoes
3 oz (100 g) mung-bean vermicelli
14 oz (400 g) small squid rings
1–2 tablespoons fish sauce
2 cloves garlic, chopped
Salt and pepper to taste
Pinch of sugar
2 tablespoons oil
1 medium-sized onion, sliced lengthwise into thick strips
Chopped fresh coriander leaves or sliced green onions
   for garnish

Cut the cucumbers in four lengthwise, remove the seeds and slice diagonally into strips. Cut the tomatoes into wedges and remove seeds. Soak the mung-bean vermicelli in hot water for 5 minutes, rinse under cold water and cut it into 2-in (5-cm) lengths. Combine 2 teaspoons of fish sauce, 1 clove of chopped garlic, salt and pepper and a pinch sugar in a bowl and marinate the squid in this mixture.

Heat the pan and when it is hot, add 1 tablespoon of oil. When the oil is hot add the squid and its marinade and stir-fry until the squid is cooked but not tough. Remove it from the pan and keep it warm.

Add another tablespoon of oil to the pan, heat and add the remaining garlic and the sliced onion and stir-fry for 1 minute. Add the cucumber and stir-fry and then the tomatoes and stir-fry, then add the vermicelli and more fish sauce to taste. Stir well to mix everything together, return the squid to the pan and stir until the vermicelli is cooked but the tomatoes are still firm. Garnish with chopped fresh coriander leaves or sliced green onions and serve.

GA XAO XA OT STIR-FRIED CHICKEN WITH LEMONGRASS AND CHILI

1–2 tablespoons fish sauce
Pinch each of salt and pepper

1–2 teaspoons sugar

1 lb (500 g) boneless chicken thighs, sliced

2 tablespoons oil

2 oz (50 g) roasted peanuts, coarsely chopped

Spice Paste

2 stalks lemongrass, sliced

4 shallots, sliced

2 cloves garlic, sliced

2 fresh chilies, chopped

Combine 1 tablespoon of fish sauce, salt and pepper and 1 teaspoon of sugar in a bowl and marinate the chicken in this mixture. In a mortar or a food processor, grind the lemongrass, shallots, garlic and chili to a fine paste. Heat the oil in a wok. Fry the Spice Paste until fragrant. Add the chicken and stir-fry until it is golden brown. Add any leftover marinade together with another splash of fish sauce and another teaspoon of sugar if desired, more salt and pepper if necessary and a splash of water. Stir, cover for a minute to steam, then uncover and cook until the liquid has reduced to a thick sauce and the chicken is tender. Serve garnished with peanuts.

CHICKEN GIBLETS WITH DRIED VEGETABLES

LONG GA XAO DO TAU

Dried tofu twists lend a more interesting texture to this dish than the dried tofu skins I call for in this recipe but you have to soak them for some hours or overnight beforehand.

1 oz (25 g) mung-bean vermicelli, soaked in hot water for 5 minutes

1 oz (25 g) dried tofu sheet, soaked in hot water for 15 minutes

1 oz (25 g) cloud-ear mushroom, soaked in warm water until soft

1 oz (25 g) dried lily buds, soaked in warm water until soft

1 tablespoon oil

2 cloves garlic, sliced

1 medium-sized onion, thickly sliced lengthwise

8 oz (250 g) chicken giblets or liver or heart or
  combination of the three
1 tablespoon light soy sauce
½ teaspoon sugar, or more to taste
Splash chicken stock or water
Salt to taste

Drain the vermicelli and cut it into bite-sized lengths. Cut the tofu sheet into square pieces, and the mushroom into quarters if it is large. Tie a knot in the middle of each lily bud to retain some texture through cooking.

Heat the oil in a wok. Add the garlic and the onion and stir-fry until fragrant. Add the giblets and stir-fry until they change color, then add the tofu, cloud-ear mushroom and lily buds. Mix and stir-fry for 1 minute. Add the soy sauce and sugar, a splash of chicken stock or water and salt, if necessary, then stir-fry until everything is cooked. Add the vermicelli and mix until it is heated through before serving.

BO XAO STIR-FRIED BEEF

2 tablespoons fish sauce
2 teaspoons sugar
Pinch each of salt and pepper
1 lb (500 g) lean beef, thinly sliced
1 tablespoon oil
3 cloves garlic, chopped
3 small onions, quartered lengthwise and separated into
  petals
2 oz (50 g) roasted peanuts, coarsely chopped

Combine the fish sauce, sugar, salt and pepper in a bowl and marinate the beef in this mixture. Heat the oil and fry the garlic and the onion until they are partially cooked, then add the beef and stir-fry until the meat is cooked through. Serve garnished with crushed peanuts.

BO XAO XA BEEF STIR-FRIED WITH LEMONGRASS

3 stalks lemongrass, sliced finely
4 shallots, chopped finely
3 cloves garlic, chopped

2 tablespoons fish sauce
2 teaspoons sugar, or more to taste
Salt and pepper to taste
1 lb (500 g) lean beef, thinly sliced
1–2 tablespoons oil
2 oz (50 g) roasted peanuts, coarsely chopped

In a mortar or a food processor, grind the lemongrass to a fine paste and set it aside. Pound or grind one shallot and the garlic and add the fish sauce, sugar, salt and pepper. Marinate the beef in this mixture.

Heat 1 tablespoon of oil in a wok or a pan and stir-fry the lemongrass and the remaining shallots. Add the beef and its marinade, mix well and cover the pan for 5 minutes. Remove the lid and stir-fry until the beef is tender. Garnish with the chopped peanuts.

This dish and Stir-fried Beef (p. 121) can be served with lettuce leaves, a plate of Rice Noodle Cubes, an Herb Salad Plate and individual bowls of Basic Dipping Sauce (*Nuoc Cham*). Diners take a lettuce leaf on to their plate, place a cube of the noodle cake, a couple of beef slices and some herbs on one end, fold in the sides and roll it up into a cigar shape, dipping the end in the sauce with each mouthful. It can also be served with noodles. Put some sliced or torn lettuce in the bottom of a rice bowl with noodles and meat on top. Add sliced cucumber and herbs, garnish with extra peanuts and eat with Basic Dipping Sauce (*Nuoc Cham*).

BO LUC LAC SHAKING BEEF

This is the Vietnamese version of a dish found in many parts of Southeast Asia. It appears to be a local adaptation of the French beef sauté, using Vietnamese seasonings and beef cut into chopstick-sized pieces. The reason for the title is shrouded in mystery but it could refer to the French practice of shaking the pan in the sautéing process.

15 shallots or 2 small onions
2 tablespoons white vinegar diluted with 2 tablespoons
   water
Salt and pepper to taste
Pinch of sugar
1 tablespoon fish sauce

1 teaspoon sugar

6 cloves garlic, chopped

Pinch of dried chili (optional)

1 tablespoon oil and 1 teaspoon butter

1 lb (500 g) beef fillet or rump steak, cubed

1 head of lettuce (mignonette or bibb)

Peel the shallots and slice them thickly lengthwise or slice the onions into very fine rings. Combine the diluted vinegar, the salt, pepper and a pinch of sugar in a bowl and soak the shallots or onions in this mixture for at least 1 hour.

Combine the fish sauce, sugar, garlic, pepper, chili and 1 teaspoon of the oil in a bowl and marinate the beef in this mixture for 30 minutes.

Wash and dry the lettuce leaves and arrange them around the edge of a plate with the drained vinegared shallots arranged decoratively on top. Heat the 2 teaspoons of oil and 1 teaspoon of butter in a pan until it is very hot. Add the beef and cook quickly, stir-frying or shaking it in the pan until it is cooked on the outside but still pink inside. Serve in the center of the lettuce plate.

BO XAO THOM STIR-FRIED BEEF WITH VEGETABLES AND PINEAPPLE

1 cucumber, 8-in (20-cm) long, peeled, seeded and cut into 2-in (5-cm) chunks

1 medium-sized onion, peeled and cut lengthwise into ½-in (¾-cm) wedges

4 small plants Chinese celery, stems and leaves cut into pieces

2 cloves garlic, chopped

1 teaspoon sugar

Salt and pepper to taste

2 tablespoons seasoning sauce or light soy sauce

13 oz (375 g) beef topside or silverside, thinly sliced across the grain

2 tablespoons oil

½ small pineapple, cut into 2-in (5-cm) chunks

Put all the vegetables in separate piles on a big round tray or plate near the stove.

Combine half of the garlic, the sugar, salt and pepper and seasoning sauce and marinate the beef in this mixture.

Heat 1 tablespoon of oil in a wok and fry the rest of the chopped garlic. Add the pineapple, cucumber and onion then the celery (stalks only) and stir-fry until everything is lightly cooked. Add the celery leaves and mix until slightly wilted. Lift out and set aside.

Heat the remaining oil and stir-fry the beef until cooked. Return the pineapple and vegetables to the pan and mix until heated through. Adjust the seasonings and serve.

BO XAO DAU STIR-FRIED BEANS WITH BEEF

This dish can be made with pork or shrimp instead of beef, or a combination of both. Bean sprouts or a mixture of vegetables can be susbstituted for the green beans. Note, however, that bean sprouts will take less time.

1 clove garlic, chopped
2 teaspoons fish sauce
Salt and pepper to taste
7 oz (200 g) lean beef, sliced
1–2 tablespoons oil
14 oz (400 g) French green beans, washed and cut into
    bite-sized pieces
Chopped fresh coriander leaves for garnish

Combine the garlic, fish sauce, salt and pepper in a bowl and marinate the beef in this mixture for 15 minutes.

Heat the oil in a wok or a pan. Add the beans and stir-fry until they are coated in oil. Cover the pan and cook for 10 minutes until the beans are tender-crisp, lifting the lid regularly and stirring to prevent them from burning. Take the lid off, add the beef and stir-fry until everything is cooked. Taste and adjust the seasonings—add an extra splash of fish sauce during this final stage if you like. Serve garnished with chopped fresh coriander.

THIT HEO XAO ## STIR-FRIED PORK WITH VEGETABLES

Different meats and vegetables can be cooked using this recipe. Try shrimp alone or with pork, sliced zucchini and bean sprouts, or a combination of green beans, carrots, cabbage, cauliflower or broccoli.

1 tablespoon fish sauce
1 clove garlic, chopped
Pepper to taste
Pinch of sugar
8 oz (250 g) lean pork, thinly sliced
2 tablespoons oil
8 oz (250 g) cauliflower, cut into small florets
3 oz (100 g) baby corn, sliced into two lengthwise
1 medium-sized onion, cut lengthwise into 8 wedges
Sliced green onion for garnish

Combine the fish sauce, garlic, pepper and sugar in a bowl and marinate the pork in this mixture for 15 minutes. Heat 1 tablespoon of oil in a wok, add the cauliflower and the corn and stir-fry until coated with the oil. Add a splash of water and cover for a few minutes to steam then take the lid off and stir-fry until all the water has evaporated and the vegetables are tender-crisp. Remove them and set them aside.

Heat another tablespoon of oil in the wok. Add the onion and stir-fry until coated with oil, then the meat and its marinade and stir-fry until cooked through. Add the vegetables and a splash of water and cook until everything is heated through.

Pan-fries

CA CHIEN SOT CA CHUA ## FRIED FISH FILLETS WITH TOMATO SAUCE

3 medium-sized fish fillets (kingfish, Spanish mackerel, blue-eye)
3–4 tablespoons oil

2 cloves garlic, chopped

3 shallots or 1 small onion, finely chopped

3 cups (750 g) peeled and diced fresh tomatoes

Salt and pepper to taste

2–3 tablespoons white vinegar, diluted with an equal
amount of water

Sugar to taste (up to 1 tablespoon)

Pat the fish fillets dry with paper towel. Heat the oil in a pan, add the fillets and fry them over medium heat until brown on both sides. Remove them from the pan and keep warm.

Drain the pan of all but 1 tablespoon of oil and add the garlic and the shallots and fry until soft. Add the tomatoes, salt and pepper, diluted vinegar and sugar to taste, and cook down into a smooth sauce, tasting and adjusting the flavorings. Pour over the fish and serve.

FRIED STUFFED SQUID
MUC CHIEN NHOI THIT

Replace the pork with two tomatoes, seeds removed and chopped, and more mung-bean vermicelli for a vegetarian alternative.

2 tablespoons mung-bean vermicelli, soaked in warm
water until soft

8 oz (250 g) lean ground pork or a combination of pork
and shrimp

3 large fresh or dried cloud-ear mushrooms, soaked in
warm water until soft (if dried) or 3 Chinese
mushrooms, soaked in warm water and stems
removed, caps sliced

1 lb (500 g) small or medium-sized squid, cleaned,
tentacles finely chopped

2 cloves garlic, finely chopped

4 shallots or 1 small onion, finely chopped

Salt and pepper to taste

Chopped fresh coriander leaves

6 tablespoons oil

Drain the mung-bean vermicelli and cut it into bite-sized pieces. Combine the pork, mushrooms, squid tentacles, garlic, shallots, salt and pepper, vermicelli and a pinch of the chopped coriander and mix well. Stuff the mixture into the squid bodies, leaving some room at the open end for expansion. Close the end with a toothpick.

Heat the oil in a wok and fry the squid, turning frequently until they are brown, then cover, reduce the heat and cook for about 10–15 minutes more. Remove and drain.

Pull out the toothpicks. Slice the squid into rings and serve on a bed of lettuce, garnished with chopped coriander and accompanied by Basic Dipping Sauce (*Nuoc Cham*).

The squid can also be steamed in a small amount of boiling water in a saucepan or on a rack in a covered steamer. Turn the squid over once to cook both sides.

Deep-fries

TOM CHIEN BOT ## DEEP FRIED SHRIMP IN BATTER

Boiled quail's eggs and bite-sized cauliflower pieces can be susbstituted for the shrimp for a vegetarian alternative. Soak the cauliflower pieces in salted water, rinse and dry them well before battering and frying them.

¾ cup (175 g) self-rising flour and ¾ cup (175 g) rice
   flour
Pinch each of salt and pepper
3 egg yolks
¾ cup (175 ml) water
Oil for deep-frying
6 cloves garlic, finely chopped
1 lb (500 g) jumbo shrimp, peeled and deveined
Sea salt, freshly ground white pepper and lime wedges
Lettuce leaves or watercress and tomato wedges

Sift the flours together with the salt and pepper. Beat the egg yolks in a bowl. Add the sifted and seasoned flour and the water to the egg, a little at a time, mixing and beating in between each addition. You should end up with a batter the consistency of thick but pourable cream. Set aside for at least an hour.

Heat a sufficient amount of oil for deep-frying the shrimp in a wok until hot. Add the garlic to the batter and whisk it to aerate it once again. Place one shrimp on a large serving spoon and dip it into the batter, filling the spoon completely with batter. Carefully push the shrimp and the batter into the oil so that the batter surrounds the shrimp and does not drip into the oil in strings. Cook only 3–4 shrimp at a time, turning each one until it is light brown and cooked. Lift out and drain well.

Prepare individual dip plates for each diner containing a mound of rough sea salt and one of freshly ground white pepper together with some wedges of lime. Small bowls of Basic Dipping Sauce (*Nuoc Cham*) are also a nice accompaniment. Put a layer of lettuce or watercress on a plate, arrange the shrimp in the center and decorate with tomato wedges around the edge.

GRILLS AND ROASTS

CHA TOM NUONG SUGARCANE SHRIMP

Sugarcane skewers impart a luxurious flavor to this dish.

1 lb (500 g) shrimp, peeled, deveined and tails removed
2 oz (50 g) pork fat
3 cloves garlic, chopped
1 teaspoon fish sauce
1 teaspoon sugar
Salt to taste
1 egg white, lightly whisked
Sugarcane or bamboo skewers cut into 6-in (15-cm)
   lengths and soaked

Refresh the shrimp according to the instructions on p. 25 then refrigerate them for 30 minutes. Grind the shrimp to a fine paste in a mortar or a food processor. Boil the piece of pork fat for 10 minutes, drain it thoroughly and dice it into tiny pieces. Combine the shrimp, pork fat, garlic, fish sauce, sugar, salt and pepper and sufficient egg white to bind the mixture without making it too sloppy. Knead the mixture to combine it.

Peel the sugarcane (if using) and cut it into 4–5 in (10–12 cm) lengths then split it lengthwise into 4–6 very thick skewers. Wet your fingers, and mold some shrimp paste onto one end of the skewer about halfway down, smoothing the surface with freshly wet fingers (the thickness should be plump but manageable). Brush with oil and cook on an oiled grill or on an oiled piece of aluminum foil under the broiler, turning it so that it browns all over.

Serve the skewers with Prepared Rice Papers (p. 528), an Herb Salad Plate and individual bowls of Basic Dipping Sauce (*Nuoc Cham*). Diners place a rice paper on their plate, select a little salad and place it near one edge, folding the edge over it. They then take a shrimp skewer, cutting pieces of shrimp meat off the skewer onto the top of the fold, tuck in the sides of the rice paper and roll it forward to form a cigar-shaped packet.

Frozen crab claws (available in Asian food stores) are a nice alternative to the sugarcane skewers. These are already shelled to the degree necessary—just remember to make sure they are defrosted by the time you are ready to do the grilling. Mold the shrimp paste around and over the shelled part of the crab claw, leaving the nipper exposed as a handle.

CHA CA GRILLED FISH
(North)

There is one restaurant left in Hanoi on a street that was once called Cha Ca Street that serves nothing but this specialty. Unfortunately one of its most impor-tant flavorings, the juice extracted from a particular bug, is not available outside Vietnam. The dish, however, is still interesting without it.

3 shallots, sliced
2 cloves garlic, chopped
2 teaspoons ground turmeric
1 tablespoon refined shrimp paste
1 tablespoon fish sauce
1 tablespoon white vinegar diluted to half strength with
    water or 1 tablespoon white wine
Pepper to taste
2–3 tablespoons oil

2 lb (1 kg) small, thin fish fillets (bream, sea perch), cut
   into pieces
1 bunch dill, cut into bite-sized lengths
Green part from 4 green onions, sliced into bite-sized
   lengths
Bamboo skewers

Accompaniments
7 oz (200 g) roasted peanuts, coarsely chopped
3 medium-sized onions, peeled and halved lengthwise,
   finely sliced into rings and then marinated in vinegar
   diluted with an equal quantity of water, or Sweet
   Pickled Spring Onion Bulbs
Rice noodles, cooked and drained
Herb Salad Plate
Dipping Sauce with Shrimp Paste (p. 531)

Mash the shallots and garlic to a paste. Combine the turmeric, shrimp
paste, shallots and garlic, fish sauce, vinegar, pepper and 1 tablespoon of
oil in a bowl and marinate the fish in this mixture for 2 hours or overnight. Soak the skewers in water.

Thread two pieces of fish lengthwise onto one end of a skewer and
grill them lightly under the broiler, turning once as they cook.

Meanwhile mix the dill and green onions and spread a layer of this
on each diner's plate. Gently remove the fish from the skewers and slice
them. Layer the fish and the herbs on the plate and drizzle with the rest
of the oil and serve with a bowl of chopped peanuts, a bowl of marinated
onion slices or sweet pickled green onions, a plate of cooked and drained
rice noodles, an Herb Salad Plate and Dipping Sauce with Shrimp Paste.

CA NUONG CHARCOAL-GRILLED FISH

The dish is good with rice and Pomelo Salad.

1 whole fish about 1¾–2 lb (800 g–1 kg) (freshwater
   perch, morwong, snapper, trevally)
Banana leaf or aluminum foil, to wrap the fish
1 thin slice fresh ginger root, peeled and shredded
3 shallots, sliced

2 teaspoons light soy sauce

Pepper to taste

1 teaspoon fresh lime juice

2 tablespoons oil

10 green onions, cut into bite-sized lengths

2 oz (50 g) roasted peanuts, coarsely chopped

Clean and scale the fish and make three slashes across each side. Oil the inside of the aluminum foil or banana leaf and lay the fish on it. Stuff the fish with the shredded ginger and sliced shallots and sprinkle it lightly with soy sauce, pepper and lime juice. Wrap up securely and cook over a medium-hot grill until the banana leaf is brown. You could also cook the fish in the oven or, if the fish is an oily one such as mackerel or bonito, you could cook it in an oiled fish grill over low heat.

Heat 2 tablespoons of oil in a wok or a pan and stir-fry the green onion until coated with oil. Cover and cook a minute or two to soften a little.

When the fish is cooked unwrap it and place it on an oval dish. Pour the fried green onions over the fish and sprinkle the peanuts over and around it.

Serve with a Sour Fruit Plate as well as the usual Herb Salad Plate, a Tamarind Dipping Sauce (*Nuoc Cham Me*) and a plate of Prepared Rice Papers (p. 528). Diners layer pieces of lettuce on the edge of a rice paper, remove small pieces of fish with their chopsticks and place them on top with a selection of sour fruits and herbs, roll the rice paper into a cigar shape and eat, dipping the roll in their dipping sauce at each mouthful.

BO NUONG GRILLED BEEF
(North)

This dish can also be made with larger steaks grilled on a barbecue.

1 lb (500 g) lean beef, cut into escalopes

1 tablespoon sesame seed

2 stalks lemongrass, sliced

1 chili, seeded and chopped

4 cloves garlic

1 tablespoon fish sauce

1 tablespoon dark soy sauce

1 teaspoon sugar (optional)

1 teaspoon oil

1 bunch of Asian sweet basil

Roast the sesame seeds in a dry pan until they are brown. In a mortar or a food processor, grind the lemongrass, chili and the garlic to a fine paste. Combine the paste with the fish sauce, soy sauce, sugar (if using) and oil in a bowl and marinate the beef in this mixture for half an hour.

Brush a cast-iron grill pan with oil and heat it until very hot. Grill the beef until brown on one side then turn and grill the other side.

Arrange the beef on a bed of Asian basil and scatter the sesame seeds over the top. Serve either with noodles or lettuce rolls as in the recipe for Stir-fried Beef (p. 507) or as a rice paper dish. Place an Herb Salad Plate and a bowl of Dipping Sauce with Shrimp Paste made with chilies rather than sesame seeds.

THIT NUONG LA LOT GRILLED MEAT IN BETEL-LEAF PACKETS

12 oz (350 g) lean ground beef

5 oz (150 g) ground pork

4 shallots or 1 small onion, finely chopped

3 cloves garlic, chopped

1½ tablespoons fish sauce

1½–2 teaspoons sugar, or more to taste

Salt to taste

⅛ teaspoon freshly ground white pepper

2 bunches betel leaves (*la lot*), bok choy or chard leaves

2 tablespoons oil

Mix the beef and the pork, shallots, garlic, fish sauce, sugar, salt and pepper together. Cut the betel leaves (if using) off their stems cleanly and wash and dry them well. Lie a leaf flat, put a spoonful of meat mixture on it, form the meat into a roll, turn the edges of the leaf in and roll the whole thing into a thumb-sized roll. Repeat until all the meat is used up. Brush the rolls with oil, put them in a flat fish grill and grill over low heat or under the broiler. Turn the leaves before they turn black. Cook the other side and serve with Basic Dipping Sauce (*Nuoc Cham*) or Anchovy Dipping Sauce (*Nuoc Cham Voi Mam Nem*).

GA ROTI POT-ROASTED CHICKEN PIECES

2 lb (1 kg) chicken, or 8 chicken thighs
3 cloves garlic, sliced
4 shallots or 1 small onion, chopped
1½ teaspoons sugar, or more to taste
1½ tablespoons fish sauce
1 tablespoon soy sauce
3 tablespoons oil

If using a whole chicken, cut it into big pieces—half breasts, whole wings, thighs and drumsticks. Grind the garlic and shallots, sugar, fish sauce and soy sauce to a paste. Marinate the chicken pieces in this mixture overnight.

Heat the oil in a pan. Dry the chicken pieces and fry them over high heat, turning them constantly, until they are browned. Reduce the heat to low, add the leftover marinade and a very small amount of water, cover and cook until the chicken is tender and the sauce is thick (about 40 minutes). If the liquid is drying out as the chicken cooks, add a splash of water to the pan and mix well. Turn the pieces of chicken over after 20 minutes. Serve with Tomato Rice.

CA CHUA NHOI THIT BAKED STUFFED TOMATOES

5 shallots or 1 large onion, finely chopped
4 green onions, finely sliced
2 cloves garlic, finely chopped
1 lb (500 g) lean ground pork
Pinch each of salt and pepper
1 tablespoon fish sauce
5 large firm but ripe tomatoes
1 tablespoon oil
Pinch of sugar
Chopped fresh coriander leaves

Combine the shallots, the green onions, half of the garlic, the pork, salt and pepper and fish sauce and set aside.

Preheat the oven to 300°F (150°C). Cut the tomatoes in halves across, remove and discard the seeds and scoop out the pulp, setting it aside.

Stuff the tomato halves with the meat mixture, place them in a greased baking dish and bake until the meat stuffing is cooked through.

Meanwhile heat the oil in pan and brown the rest of the garlic. Add the tomato pulp and fry until it is soft. Season with salt and pepper. Take the stuffed tomatoes out of the oven and pour the sauce from the pan over them. Sprinkle each tomato half with a pinch of sugar and return them to the hot oven to caramelize. Serve garnished with chopped coriander.

RICE PAPER DISHES

Vietnamese rice paper dishes are unlike anything else in Southeast Asia, except perhaps Popiah in Malaysia. They may owe their origin either to China or to the French crêpe and are often combined with the elegant Chinese steamboat-style of cooking. Serving these dishes to your guests will make them feel very pampered. Rice papers are also good for turning leftovers into an elegant family meal.

Some of the dishes dealt with elsewhere in this chapter are also often treated in this way—to contribute the meat- or fish-based components combined with herbs and salad ingredients in rice paper rolls. See in particular, Sugarcane Shrimp and Charcoal-grilled Fish.

To prepare dried rice papers for the table see p. 528.

BO DO BIEN NHUNG GIAM ## VINEGAR-DIPPED BEEF AND SEAFOOD

The double quantity is provided here for serving this dish at a party. For an ordinary meal you could select either beef or seafood only and cook in half the liquid.

1 lb (500 g) beef fillet
3 thin slices fresh ginger root, peeled and finely chopped
2 tablespoons sesame seed, roasted in a dry pan until brown
1 small egg
2 medium-sized onions, peeled and sliced lengthwise
8 oz (250 g) shrimp, peeled and deveined
1 small clove garlic, chopped

Pepper to taste

8 oz (250 g) squid tubes

Green part of 1 green onion, sliced

Coconut water from 2 green coconuts or 2 14 oz
  (400 ml) cans coconut juice

10 oz (300 ml) rice vinegar

¼ teaspoon salt or to taste

1–1½ teaspoons sugar to taste (if the coconut water is
  sweetened use less or none at all)

Slice the beef into paper-thin slices and arrange them in the center of a serving plate. Scatter the ginger and sesame seeds over the beef and break the egg on top, taking care not to break the yolk. Arrange the sliced onion in a circle around the edge.

Refresh the shrimp according to the instructions on p. 25. Combine the garlic and pepper in a bowl and toss the shrimp with this mixture. Cover and refrigerate. Wash the squid, score them diagonally (p. 26) and cut them into bite-sized pieces.

Arrange the shrimp in the middle of another serving plate, scattering a little sliced green onion over the top. Arrange the squid in a circle around the edge.

Put a steamboat or a chafing dish with its own source of heat on the table.

In a saucepan combine the coconut water and the vinegar. Add salt to taste and a little sugar (the liquid should be distinctly sour). Bring the mixture to a boil on the stove then transfer it to the steamboat, putting hot coals down the chimney to keep it boiling. If you are using a chafing dish, pour the liquid from the saucepan into it and light the attached heat source.

Put a plate of Prepared Rice Papers (p. 528), a Sour Fruit Plate, a plate of Lightly Pickled Salad with Vegetables and an Herb Salad Plate on the table. Provide individual dishes of Basic Dipping Sauce (*Nuoc Cham*) and Anchovy Dipping Sauce as well.

Using chopsticks, break the egg and mash it into the beef until mixed. Diners select one or two pieces of meat and some onion from the meat plate or some shrimp and squid and drop them into the bubbling vinegar mixture until they are cooked to taste. They place a rice paper flat on a plate in front of them, putting a small piece of lettuce, some bean sprouts and a selection of sour fruits, pickled vegetables and/or herb salad on one edge and fold the rice paper once over the vegetables. The pieces of meat and onion or seafood are arranged on top of the fold, the sides of the rice paper are tucked in and everything is rolled up into a parcel the shape of a fat cigar.

These dipped meats and the vegetables can also be served with noodles. Serve according to the instructions provided in the recipe for Rice Noodles with Marinated Pork.

GOI CUON TOM THIT MEAT AND SHRIMP RICE PAPER ROLLS

7 oz (200 g) pork loin or boneless chicken thigh or a
  mixture of both
½ packet rice papers, prepared (p. 528)
½ bunch Chinese leeks or Chinese chives, cut into 4-in
  (10-cm) lengths
2 cups (500 g) shredded lettuce
1½ cups salad herbs (Vietnamese mint, coriander leaves,
  mint)
7 oz (200 g) bean sprouts, trimmed
1 cup (250 g) rice vermicelli, already cooked, rinsed in
  cold water and left to thoroughly drain and dry
12 oz (350 g) medium-sized cooked shrimp, peeled,
  deveined and cut in half lengthwise
1 cup (250 g) roasted peanuts, coarsely chopped

Boil the meat(s) separately, cool and slice them into rough shreds. Set some stock aside for the sauce. Take a prepared rice paper, put a little bit of lettuce, some herbs, bean sprouts and a small amount of vermicelli on one edge and roll once tightly. Add a few pieces of pork, shrimp and some peanuts, turn the edges in and roll up into a cigar shape, letting a Chinese leek protrude slightly at one end for show. Pile the rolls on a plate and cover until you are ready to serve them.

Serve with individual dishes of Basic Dipping Sauce (*Nuoc Cham*) or a meatless dipping sauce such as Bean Sauce (*Nuoc Tuong Cham*).

GRILLED BEEF AND RICE PAPER ROLLS

Grilled Beef (p. 517) can also be served as a rice-paper dish. Cut the beef into paper-thin slices and, after marinating, arrange them on a plate on the table. Grill them quickly in a cast iron grill pan. Serve with a plate of Prepared Rice Papers, an Herb Salad Plate and Dipping Sauce with Shrimp Paste or Anchovy Dipping Sauce. Diners take a rice paper, place a layer of lettuce and herbs on one edge, top this with grilled beef, roll everything into a cigar-shaped packet and eat with the dipping sauce.

DRESSED DISHES AND SALADS

GOI GA CHICKEN SALAD

This salad is traditionally served with Shredded Chicken Rice Porridge but it is good with other dishes too.

8 oz (250 g) banana blossom, cabbage or iceberg lettuce
1 carrot, finely shredded or grated
Vinegar
1 teaspoon sugar
2 whole chicken breasts, poached and shredded
4 shallots, finely sliced or 1 small onion, finely sliced lengthwise
½ cup (125 g) finely shredded Vietnamese mint leaves
Coarsely chopped roasted peanuts for garnish

Dressing
2 small cloves garlic, chopped
1–2 fresh chilies, finely chopped
2 tablespoons fish sauce diluted with 2 tablespoons water
1 tablespoon rice vinegar, or to taste
2 tablespoons fresh lime juice, or to taste
2 teaspoons sugar, or to taste

Remove the tough outer leaves from the banana blossom, cabbage or lettuce, wash and shred them. Soak the lettuce and shredded carrot in water with a dash of vinegar and a teaspoon of sugar added to it for 1 hour. Drain, rinse and dry. Mix the shredded chicken, soaked vegetables, sliced shallots or onion and shredded Vietnamese mint in a serving bowl.

To make the Dressing, mash the garlic and chili together to a paste. Combine the paste with the diluted fish sauce, vinegar, lime juice and sugar to taste. Toss however much dressing you want into the salad and scatter peanuts over the top.

If you are eating the salad as an accompaniment to Shredded Chicken Rice Porridge, do not dress it, but serve a bowl of Basic Dipping Sauce (*Nuoc Cham*) on the side.

GOI TOM THIT PORK AND SHRIMP SALAD

¼ cup (60 ml) white vinegar

½ cup (125 ml) water

1 tablespoon sugar

Mixed vegetables (1 small carrot, cut lengthwise into thin pieces or shreds; 1 pickling cucumber, seeded and cut into thin strips; ½ cup [125 g] young lotus stems in brine, halved lengthwise and cut into bite-sized lengths, or celery cut into strips)

7 oz (200 g) shrimp, peeled, deveined and tails removed

7 oz (200 g) pork

3 oz (100 g) roasted peanuts, coarsely chopped

½ cup (125 g) fried onion flakes

Handful of Vietnamese mint or other salad herb

1 packet shrimp crackers

Dressing

2 shallots, sliced

1 clove garlic, chopped

1 teaspoon sugar, or more to taste

1 tablespoon fish sauce diluted with 1 tablespoon water

1 tablespoon fresh lime juice

Salt and pepper to taste

Combine the vinegar, water and sugar in a bowl and soak the vegetables in this mixture for at least an hour.

Poach the shrimp and boil the whole piece of pork separately. Drain, slice the shrimp in half lengthwise, slice the pork and set them both aside to cool.

Drain the vegetables and mix them with half the pork and half the shrimp. Combine the Dressing ingredients, pour a generous amount over the meat and vegetable mixture and toss. Add the chopped peanuts and toss again.

Serve the salad in the center of a large plate and arrange the remaining shrimp around the edge and the remaining slices of meat over the top. Garnish with fried onion flakes and chopped Vietnamese mint. Serve surrounded by shrimp crackers.

POMELO SALAD

This is a great salad if you can find pomelo. It is very popular in restaurants in Ho Chi Minh City.

1 pomelo
5 oz (150 g) squid tubes
12 oz (350 g) small shrimp, peeled and deveined
3 shallots or 1 small onion, finely chopped
½ cup (125 g) fried onion flakes
¼ cup (125 g) roasted peanuts, coarsely chopped
leaves of 8–10 sprigs Vietnamese mint, finely sliced
Sugar to taste
Lettuce leaves (butter, mignonette, bib)
1 packet shrimp crackers

Dressing

2 small cloves garlic, chopped
1–2 fresh chilies, chopped
2 tablespoons fish sauce diluted with 2 tablespoons
    water
1 tablespoon rice vinegar, or to taste
2 tablespoons fresh lime juice, or to taste
2 teaspoons sugar, or to taste

To make the Dressing, mash the garlic and chili together to a paste. Add the diluted fish sauce, vinegar, lime juice and sugar and mix well.

Peel the pomelo. Pull the membrane off the segments as cleanly and completely as possible. Discard the seeds, pull the flesh apart into small flakes and set it aside.

Cut the squid tubes into pieces with a diamond pattern (p. 26). Put the pieces into a strainer and dip this into a pot of boiling water just until the pieces curl up and are cooked and white, with an attractive patterned surface. Remove the strainer and drain the squid thoroughly. Boil a new pot of water and cook the shrimp until they turn pink. Drain and cool them.

Combine all the ingredients except the shrimp crackers and the lettuce. Toss well with Dressing to taste, adding extra sugar if you wish. Serve in a lettuce-lined bowl placed in the center of a flat platter. Surround the bowl with shrimp crackers.

BASICS AND ACCOMPANIMENTS

NUOC MAU CARAMEL COLORING

5 tablespoons sugar
4–5 tablespoons boiling water

Place the sugar in a heavy-bottomed saucepan over high heat until it starts to dissolve and stir until it is a light brown syrup. Lift the saucepan off the stove and continue stirring until the syrup has turned dark brown. You can return it to the stove from time to time for another burst of heat if it does not seem hot enough but do not leave it there or it may burn. Add the boiling water a little at a time, stirring vigorously. Return the saucepan to the heat to mix evenly into a dark thick syrup. Cool and pour into a jar or other container to be stored until needed.

RAU SONG HERB SALAD PLATE

Wash some tender lettuce and dry it. Arrange this on a plate accompanied by a row of peeled, sliced cucumber and a handful of whole stems of washed herbs such as Vietnamese mint, coriander, perilla, Asian sweet basil, fish-cheek mint, or common mint. Also include a pile of washed, trimmed bean sprouts.

CHUOI, THOM, KHE SOUR FRUIT PLATE

¼ small pineapple, peeled and cut lengthwise as a wedge
2 star fruit, washed
1 tropical green sour banana, peeled and sliced, or
 substitute slices of other tart fruit such as green
 mango or tart apple

Slice the pineapple, the star fruit and the green banana across into very thin slices. Arrange in separate rows on a plate.

BANH TRANG — PREPARED RICE PAPERS

Fill a wide shallow dish with warm water and spread a clean kitchen towel out beside it. Carefully slide a single rice paper out of the packet and dunk it quickly in the water. Drain and transfer it to the towel, dipping your hand in the water and gently rubbing each side of the rice paper, taking care not to tear it or get it too wet. Repeat until there are no longer any brittle patches and the whole paper is soft, with its excess water having been soaked up by the towel. Transfer the rice paper very carefully on to a dinner plate and repeat the process, making a pile of them. Cover the plate to prevent the papers from drying out as you prepare them.

Alternatively, put a large bowl of warm water on the table for diners to prepare their own, dunking in the water and simply shaking off any drips.

BANH HOI — RICE NOODLE CUBES

Boil rice vermicelli for 5 minutes, drain it and spread it out in a shallow dish in an even layer about ¾ in (2 cm) thick. Once the vermicelli has cooled it will stick together. Cut the cake of noodles into cubes and serve.

DAU RANG — ROASTED PEANUTS

To avoid scorch marks it is better to use small raw peanuts complete with their red skins. Heat a heavy pan until hot, add the peanuts and stir continuously until the skins are black. Cool and remove the skins by rubbing vigorously between the palms of your hands. Peanuts freshly roasted in this way are much better than store-bought roasted peanuts.

You can also fry the peanuts (p. 51).

DUA GIA CHUA PICKLED BEAN SPROUTS

2 teaspoons salt
6 teaspoons sugar
7 oz (200 g) bean sprouts
3 Chinese leeks, cut in two lengthwise and then into
    1½-in (4-cm) pieces
1 small carrot, shredded (optional)

Put enough water to cover the bean sprouts into a saucepan. Add the salt and sugar and heat it until the sugar has dissolved. Set aside to cool—or leave it a bit warm if you want it to pickle more quickly.

Wash, trim and drain the bean sprouts and mix them with the leeks and the carrots (if using). Put the vegetables into a large jar and just cover with the seasoned water. Put something heavy on top of the vegetables so that they are compressed and leave them, unrefrigerated, for 3–4 days.

The pickle will keep in the refrigerator for a month or more.

HANH CHUA SWEET PICKLED GREEN ONION
BULBS

2 oz (50 ml) white vinegar
3–4 tablespoons sugar
5 oz (150 ml) water
8 oz (250 g) white ends from young green onions with
    plump bulbs
3 whole small chilies

Combine the vinegar, sugar and water in a saucepan and heat it until the sugar dissolves. Put the green onion bulbs in a bowl or a jar with the chilies on top and pour the syrup over. The pickle will keep for a long time in a covered jar or plastic container.

DUA CHUA LIGHTLY PICKLED CARROT AND
DAIKON

These pickled vegetable flowers make a wonderful decoration when
arranged in a row around the edge of a serving plate.

> Carrots
> Daikon
> 1½ cups (375 ml) water
> ¼ cup (60 ml) rice vinegar or white distilled vinegar
> 1 tablespoon sugar, or more to taste
> 1 fresh chili, chopped (optional)
> Sliced green onion (optional)

Peel the vegetables and cut three or four small furrows at equal distances
along their length. Slice them across into flower shapes. Heat the water
and dissolve the sugar in it. Set aside to cool. Combine the vinegar, sugar,
water and chili (if using) in a bowl. Add the sliced vegetables and set
aside for a few hours. Strain the vegetables, arrange them on a platter
and garnish with sliced green onion, if desired.

RAU CHUA LIGHTLY PICKLED SALAD WITH
VEGETABLES

These pickled vegetables are very good wrapped in
rice paper rolls with Sugarcane Shrimp, barbecued
meats or in spring rolls together with pieces of noodle cake and salad herbs.

> Lotus stems or celery, cut in two lengthwise and into
>   bite-sized pieces
> Cucumber, peeled, halved lengthwise, seeded and sliced
>   diagonally
> Carrot, cut into thin strips
> Daikon, cut into thin strips

The method is the same as for Lightly Pickled Carot and Daikon, above.

Dipping Sauces

NUOC CHAM   ## BASIC DIPPING SAUCE

Sometimes coconut water is used instead of plain water in this dipping sauce.

2½ tablespoons water
1–2 teaspoons sugar, or to taste
1 fresh chili, finely chopped
2 small cloves garlic, chopped
2–3 teaspoons fresh lime juice
1 teaspoon white vinegar or rice vinegar
2½ tablespoons fish sauce
2 teaspoons peeled and shredded carrot

Heat the water and sugar until the sugar has dissolved and set aside to cool. Mash the chili and garlic to a paste. Combine the paste with the sugar water, lime juice, vinegar and fish sauce to taste. Mix well and add the grated carrot for color.

NUOC CHAM VOI MAM TOM   ## DIPPING SAUCE WITH SHRIMP PASTE

Sesame seed, roasted and crushed or fresh chili, finely shredded
2 tablespoons fresh lime juice
2 tablespoons refined shrimp paste (labeled Fine Shrimp Sauce or Sauce de Crevette Raffinée)
½–1 chili, chopped
3 tablespoons water or beer
½ teaspoon sugar

Heat a dry pan and roast the sesame seeds (if using) until they are brown. Remove and set aside.

Pour the lime juice over the shrimp paste and stir until it is mixed. Mash the chopped chili to a paste. Add the shrimp paste mixture, water and sugar and mix. Serve the sauce sprinkled with the sesame seeds or shredded chili.

ANCHOVY DIPPING SAUCE
NUOC CHAM VOI MAM NEM

1 tablespoon water
2 teaspoons sugar, or more to taste
½ –1 red chili, chopped
3 cloves garlic, sliced
2 tablespoons anchovy sauce (*Mam Nem*)
1 tablespoon fresh lime juice
½ teaspoon fish sauce
Roasted crushed sesame seed for garnish

Heat the water and sugar until the sugar has dissolved and set aside to cool. In a mortar mash the chili and the garlic to a fine paste. Add the anchovy sauce, lime juice and fish sauce and mix well. Pour into sauce dishes and garnish with crushed sesame seeds.

BEAN SAUCE
NUOC TUONG CHAM

Be sure to select a Vietnamese soy bean paste that is not too salty.

2 cloves garlic, chopped
3 shallots, sliced or ½ small onion, finely chopped
1 tablespoon oil
4 tablespoons Vietnamese soy bean paste (*tuong*)
Coconut water or water to moisten
Sugar to taste
Vinegar to taste (optional)
Coarsely chopped roasted peanuts for garnish

Mash the garlic and shallots to a paste. Heat the oil in a wok or a pan, add the garlic paste and stir-fry until it is fragrant. Add the bean paste and mix well. Add the coconut water (or plain water) to moisten, add the sugar and vinegar to taste and mix well. Pour into individual sauce dishes and garnish with chopped roasted peanuts.

This bean sauce can also be made with meat. Add 4 oz (125 g) of ground pork to the frying garlic paste. Stir-fry until cooked, add the bean paste and continue according to the instruction provided above, adding chicken or pork stock to moisten.

TAMARIND DIPPING SAUCE

1 fresh chili, chopped
2 cloves garlic, sliced
½ –1 teaspoon sugar
3 tablespoons tamarind water
1 tablespoon fish sauce diluted with an equal amount of
water, or more to taste

Mash the chili, garlic and sugar to a paste. Add the tamarind water and the diluted fish sauce to taste and adjust the other flavors, if necessary. Serve in individual sauce bowls.

NOODLES, RICE AND ONE-DISH MEALS

The soups in this section are one-dish meals, especially favored for late breakfast or lunch. They each use a different kind of rice noodle, available in Vietnamese food stores.

HU TIEU SOUTHERN RICE NOODLE SOUP

This soup was probably borrowed from China. Sour fish soup is the traditional soup of South Vietnam, with noodle soups existing traditionally only in central and northern Vietnam.

13 oz (375 g) packets dried rice noodles
7 oz (200 g) pork or fish balls
8 oz (250 g) Chinese barbecued pork (*cha siew*) or pork shoulder
3 oz (100 g) lean ground pork
8 oz (250 g) shrimp, shelled and deveined
3 oz (100 g) squid tube, treated according to the instructions on p. 26
14 oz (400 g) bean sprouts
15 Chinese leeks, cut into short lengths or 5 stems Chinese celery cabbage, thinly sliced across
Sliced green onion
2 limes, quartered
2 chilies, sliced in rings
Vietnamese mint, long-leaf coriander, Asian sweet basil and coriander for garnish

Stock
¼ cup (60 g) dried shrimp
1 dried squid
2 small daikon
2 lb (1 kg) pork or chicken bones
5 quarts plus 1 cup (5 liters) water
Pinch of salt
2 tablespoons fish sauce, or to taste

To make the Stock, wash the dried shrimp and soak them in water for 30 minutes. Remove the quill from the dried squid, wash the squid and peel off the skin. Break the squid into pieces. Peel the daikon. If you are using pork bones, wash them to remove loose bits, put them in a large saucepan, cover with cold water and bring to a boil. Boil until the water is frothy then drain, rinse the bones and wash the pan. Return the bones to the pan, add the water and bring to a boil, skimming until the water is clear. Add the daikon, dried squid, dried shrimp and a little salt. Simmer over low heat for 4 hours. If you are using pork shoulder rather than barbecued pork, add it into the stock as it simmers and cook until done. Remove the pork and set it aside. Strain the stock into another saucepan, discarding the bones, dried shrimp, squid and daikon, and add fish sauce to taste. Keep the stock hot on the stove.

Meanwhile, soak the rice noodles in hot water for 5–8 minutes just until they soften, then drain, rinse and set them aside in the colander. Fry the pork or fish balls until brown. Slice them and set them aside. Slice the barbecued pork or cooked shoulder thinly.

Put some noodles into a strainer, suspend this in the soup for a moment to heat them (they should still be a bit chewy), then place enough for one serving in the bottom of as many individual soup bowls as you need, repeating as necessary. Put the meat- or fish-ball slices in the strainer, suspend in the stock until they cook and divide these between the bowls. Next suspend the ground pork, shrimp, squid and meat—all separately—in the stock and divide among the bowls. Wash the bean sprouts and put a handful of these in each bowl.

Divide the Chinese leeks or the celery cabbage between the bowls. Pour boiling stock over the contents of each bowl, garnish with sliced green onions and serve immediately. Serve with a plate of lime wedges, a dish of sliced chili and the sprigs of herbs, together with a bowl of extra fish sauce.

PHO BO HANOI BEEF NOODLE SOUP

Hanoi is full of small restaurants specializing in this common breakfast or snack. People have their favorites and patronize them regularly, becoming attached to particular flavors. The recipe that follows is a fairly basic one—feel free to add beef balls or thinly sliced beef tripe, if you wish.

2 lb (1 kg) beef soup bones
3–4 quarts (4–5 liters) water
2 thumb-sized pieces of fresh ginger root, bruised
2 onions
2 small daikon or carrots
Salt to taste
4 whole star anise
1 whole cinnamon stick
2 Chinese or Thai cardamom pods, broken open (p. 36)
8 cloves
½ teaspoon peppercorns
8 oz (250 g) beef tendon
1 lb (500 g) beef brisket, trimmed of fat or a thick piece of trimmed chuck
1 lb (500 g) fillet steak or silverside
2 tablespoons fish sauce
1½ teaspoons sugar
2 x 375 g (13 oz) packets dried rice sticks (*banh pho*)
2 oz (50 g) cooked beef tripe, sliced finely (optional)
½ cup (125 g) sliced green onions
12 oz (350 g) bean sprouts, washed
Long-leaf coriander and Asian sweet basil leaves
Chilies, sliced into rounds
Lime wedges

Wash the bones to remove loose bits, put them in a large pot, cover with cold water and bring to a boil. Boil until the water is frothy, drain, rinse the bones and wash the pot. Return the bones to the pot and add 3–4 quarts (4–5 liters) of water. Grill or broil the ginger and the onion until brown on the outside. Add the ginger, the onions, the daikon or carrots and salt to taste to the stock and bring to a boil, skimming for a while if necessary. Break the star anise and the cinnamon roughly and add them along with the cardamom pods, cloves and peppercorns. Add the beef tendon and the brisket or chuck, reduce the heat and simmer gently for 3 hours, skimming again when necessary. Remove the stewing beef and tendon from the stock, slice the meat into thin slices and cut the tendon into chunks. Slice the fillet into paper-thin slices and keep this separate. Add fish sauce and sugar to the stock to taste.

Meanwhile, prepare the rice sticks by soaking them in cold water for 30 minutes. Bring a large pot of water to a boil. Drain the rice sticks and dip them in the boiling water for a minute to soften. Drain and rinse under cold water then put sufficient amounts into individual Chinese soup bowls. Put a little cooked beef, beef tripe and tendon on top, then some slices of raw beef. Strain the boiling stock (liquid only) on top of this, garnish with green onion and carry to the table.

Serve with a plate of washed bean sprouts together with the herb leaves, a bowl of sliced fresh chili, some lime wedges and some fish sauce. Once the sliced beef has poached in the stock, diners add bean sprouts, herbs and other flavorings to taste.

BUN THIT NUONG RICE NOODLES WITH MARINATED PORK (North)

1 lb (500 g) boneless pork belly spareribs or butterfly
  steaks
3 cloves garlic, chopped
2 tablespoons fish sauce
Freshly ground pepper to taste
2 teaspoons sugar
Cooked fresh rice noodles
Lettuce leaves

Slice the pork into pieces. Crush the garlic in a mortar then add the fish sauce, pepper and sugar or blend all these ingredients together in a food processor. Marinate the meat in this sauce for 30 minutes to 1 hour.

Cook the pork slices on the grill, on a griddle or under the broiler, turning to brown on both sides. Slice, pile on a plate and serve hot with a bowl of cooked fresh rice noodles, an Herb Salad Plate, a plate of Lightly Pickled Carrot and Daikon and some Basic Dipping Sauce (*Nuoc Cham*). Diners tear some lettuce into the bottom of an individual rice bowl, put some noodles on top, add meat, herbs and pickled vegetables and eat with the dipping sauce.

SOUTHERN VERSION

Slice lean pork into strips and then across into thin slices. Marinate the slices in the sauce used in the Northern Version. Heat 1 tablespoon of oil in a pan and stir-fry the pork until it is cooked. Serve garnished with coarsely chopped roasted peanuts and with Rice Noodle Cubes.

Diners take a whole lettuce leaf from the Herb Salad Plate, place on one end a piece of noodle cake, a couple of pork slices, some pickled vegetable and some herbs, roll everything up into a cigar shape and dip it into the sauce as they eat.

CHAO GA SHREDDED CHICKEN RICE PORRIDGE

This dish is served for breakfast or for a light but comforting meal at any time.

2 lb (1 kg) chicken
2 quarts (2½ liters) water
Salt to taste
8 oz (250 g) short-grain rice
Chopped fresh coriander and sliced green onion
Pepper to taste

Wash the chicken and put it in a saucepan with the water and some salt. Bring it to a boil and simmer gently, covered, until the chicken is cooked and tender. Remove the chicken, and once cool, shred the flesh finely. Set a little of the chicken aside to put on top of the porridge and use the rest for making Chicken Salad (p. 524).

Wash the rice until the water runs clear, return the chicken stock to a boil, add the rice and cook over very low heat until it is a soft porridge (about 1½ hours).

Serve garnished with a spoonful of shredded chicken, some chopped coriander, sliced green onion and freshly ground pepper. Serve Chicken Salad on the side and some Basic Dipping Sauce (*Nuoc Cham*).

COM SOT CA CHUA   TOMATO RICE

2 tablespoons oil
5 shallots or 1 medium-sized onion, finely chopped
2 cloves garlic, chopped
2–3 tomatoes, peeled and finely chopped
Pinch of sugar
4 cups (1 kg) cooked white rice
6 green onions, sliced
Salt and pepper to taste
Chopped coriander leaves for garnish

Heat the oil and fry the shallots and the garlic until soft. Add the tomatoes and the sugar and cook until the mixture is thick. Add the cooked rice and mix thoroughly, then add the green onion, salt and pepper and mix again. Serve garnished with chopped coriander.

BANH XEO   VIETNAMESE PANCAKE

2½ cups (375 g) rice flour
½ teaspoon ground turmeric
Salt to taste
2 cups (500 ml) coconut milk
2 cups (500 ml) water (enough to make a thin batter)
1 lb (500 g) belly pork
2 teaspoons fish sauce
Pepper to taste
10 oz (300 g) shrimp, peeled and deveined
8 oz (250 g) bean sprouts, trimmed
½–1 tablespoon oil
1 medium-sized onion, thinly sliced lengthwise
7 oz (200 g) mushrooms, thinly sliced

The batter for these pancakes needs to be made ahead of time. Sift the flour into a bowl with the turmeric and salt. Make a well in the middle and add the coconut milk, a little at a time, and enough water to produce a thin, smooth batter. Set aside for a few hours.

Cut the pork into thin slices. Season it with fish sauce and pepper. Rub the shrimp with salt, rinse well and dry them thoroughly with paper towels. Wash and dry the bean sprouts.

Set all of the ingredients on separate plates around the stove. Heat a frying pan to hot. Add the oil, a few of onion slices, 4–5 slices of pork and 4 shrimp. Stir-fry for a minute, then cover for a minute until cooked. Take the cover off, add a ladle of batter (enough for a thin pancake only) and spread it out over the surface of the pan. Place a few mushroom slices and a spoonful of bean sprouts on top, cover for another minute or two until the pancake and the vegetables are lightly cooked. Uncover and cook until the edges curl up and the pancake is brown and crunchy but not burned on the bottom.

For the southern version of this dish lift the pancake out and serve on a plate accompanied by an Herb Salad Plate and Basic Dipping Sauce (*Nuoc Cham*). Pieces of pancake are often rolled up with herbs in lettuce and eaten by hand, dipping in the sauce between mouthfuls.

I prefer to make this dish like an omelette—it is often served this way in central Vietnam. Add the bean sprouts and mushrooms on one side of the pancake. At the last stage of cooking, when the pancake is crunchy on the bottom, carefully fold the empty half over the half containing the mushrooms and bean sprouts.

NIBBLES AND APPETIZERS

BANH BEO TOM KHO STEAMED RICE WITH DRIED SHRIMP

This dish is a recreation of one I had in Hue. The topping also goes nicely on toast, store bought rice crackers or water biscuits.

2 oz (50 g) dried shrimp
½ teaspoon dried chili flakes
2 tablespoons oil for frying and more for oiling bowls
6 shallots or 1 medium-sized onion, finely chopped
4 oz (125 g) crab meat or 4 oz (125 g) shrimp, finely chopped
½ teaspoon sugar, or more to taste
1 teaspoon fish sauce, or more to taste
8 oz (250 g) rice flour, sifted
Water
3–4 pieces pork cracklings, chopped into coarse crumbs (optional)
Pepper to taste

Soak the dried shrimp in warm water for 10 minutes then drain. Grind the chili flakes in a food processor, add the dried shrimp and process together coarsely.

Heat a wok or a pan to hot. Add the oil and when it is hot, reduce the heat to medium. Add the shallots or onion and fry until golden brown. Add the dried shrimp and chili and fry them until brown. Add the crab or chopped shrimp, the sugar and the fish sauce and stir-fry until everything is mixed well, has absorbed all the flavors and the mixture is dry. Cool and set aside.

Mix the flour and water to a smooth batter in the proportion of 1 part flour to 2 parts water. Oil the inside of 6 small bowls or ramekins. Pour enough batter to cover the bottom of each dish to a thickness of about ¼ in (½ cm). Put the bowls in a steamer on a rack over boiling water and steam gently for about 5 minutes or until cooked. Remove the bowls and cool, putting a second batch into the steamer if you have them. If not, use the same bowls again after the next step.

When the bowls are cool, loosen the steamed rice circles and slide them out. Mix the crackling crumbs and pepper into the crab mixture and spoon a little on top of each rice circlet. Arrange the circles on a plate and serve with Basic Dipping Sauce (*Nuoc Cham*)

CHA CIO VIETNAMESE SPRING ROLLS

For speed and convenience many people use the prepared Chinese spring roll skins that are available in most well-stocked supermarkets instead of rice papers. These are made from wheat flour, however, and are not as fine as rice papers.

1 egg, separated
1 lb (500 g) lean ground pork
5 oz (150 g) shrimp, finely chopped
3 oz (100 g) crab meat, finely flaked
½ cup (125 g) cloud-ear mushrooms, soaked or 2 oz
  (50 g) fresh mushrooms, finely chopped
1 medium-sized onion, finely chopped
5 green onions, finely sliced
4 cloves garlic, chopped
2 oz (50 g) mung-bean vermicelli, soaked then cut into
  short lengths
Salt and pepper to taste
1 packet rice papers, preferably small ones
Oil for deep-frying

Set some of the egg white aside for sealing the wrappers. Beat the rest of the white and the yolk separately.

In a bowl, combine the pork, shrimp, crab, mushrooms, onion and green onions, garlic, vermicelli, salt, pepper and beaten egg. Set aside for 30 minutes.

In the meantime prepare the rice papers (p. 528).

To fill the rice papers, fold over one part of the curved edge of a small rice paper to make a straight edge. Place about 2 heaping teaspoons of the filling on top of the fold in a roll shape, fold in the sides, roll up and seal with egg white.

Remember that Vietnamese spring rolls should be small and thin. If the papers are big, cut each one into four. Fold in the curved edge as before, place meat mixture on it, fold over the sides and roll up, sealing the end with egg white.

Deep-fry the rolls in plenty of hot oil until golden brown and drain. Serve with an Herb Salad Plate and Basic Dipping Sauce (*Nuoc Cham*). Pickled Bean sprouts are also a nice accompaniment. A whole leaf of butter lettuce layered with cucumber slices, herbs of your choice and a spring roll, rolled into a packet and dipped into sauce is a good combination.

CHA GIO HUE HUE SPRING ROLL

These spring rolls feature more shrimp than pork and are served with a classic Hue sauce.

1 lb (500 g) shrimp, peeled and deveined
8 oz (250 g) lean ground pork
½ cup cloud-ear mushroom, soaked in warm water until
   soft, hard bits cut off, then finely chopped
2 oz (50 g) mung-bean vermicelli, soaked in warm water
   until soft and then cut into short lengths
5 green onions, finely sliced
2 cloves garlic
3 oz (100 g) bean sprouts, coarsely chopped
Salt and pepper to taste
1 packet rice papers (preferably the small ones)

Wash and dry the shrimp thoroughly with paper towel. Grind them in a food processor, add the ground pork and mix to a rough paste. Mix together with the cloud-ear mushroom, vermicelli, green onions, garlic, bean sprouts, salt and pepper.

Prepare the rice papers (p. 528), then fill and deep-fry according to the instructions provided for Vietnamese Spring Rolls. Serve with an Herb Salad Plate and Bean Sauce (*Nuoc Tuong Cham*), which is the classic Hue dipping sauce.

A Few Desserts

Main meals in Southeast Asia do not normally include desserts. Many kinds of sweets and rice flour cakes are made there but they are largely sold on the streets and eaten as snacks between meals. Dessert, if it is eaten at all, is confined to fresh fruit.

Some well-known Southeast Asian sweets, particularly ones made with coconut milk, do lend themselves well to desserts, however. Many readers will have encountered them in Southeast Asian restaurants in the West. For those who wish to try them, here are a few favorites from throughout the region.

CHA HOUY TOEUK   SEAWEED JELLY IN COCONUT MILK (Cambodia)

½ packet agar-agar powder
2½ quarts (3 liters) boiling water
6 cups (1½ liters) coconut milk
½ teaspoon salt
1 cup (250 g) sugar, or more to taste
1 can palm seeds
1 can lotus seeds (lotus nuts)

Dissolve the agar-agar powder in the boiling water. Pour into a flat tray to a depth of 2 in (5 cm) and set aside to cool and set.

Bring the coconut milk to a boil with salt and sugar to taste. Set aside to cool.

Cut the agar-agar jelly into matchstick strips and put these into a serving bowl. Add the palm seeds, drained, and the lotus seeds with half the syrup from the can. Add the coconut milk, mix and serve.

KHAO NIAO MAMUANG   MANGOES AND STICKY RICE (Thailand)

This combination of mangoes and sweet and salty sticky rice is quite compelling.

2 cups (500 g) sticky rice
Pandan leaf (p. 51) or pandan essence (optional)
1 cup (250 ml) coconut milk

1 tablespoon sugar

½ teaspoon salt

4 tablespoons very thick coconut milk

4 ripe mangoes, peeled and cut into thick slices

Cook the sticky rice according to the instructions on p. 15, adding a piece of pandan leaf or a drop of pandan essence to the water (if using).

Combine the coconut milk, sugar and salt in a bowl and when the rice is cooked to the paddling stage add this mixture and mix well. Put the rice in a bowl, cover with a cloth and a lid and set aside for 20–30 minutes.

Unmold the rice into the center of a plate, spooning the very thick coconut milk on top. Surround with thick slices of ripe mango.

COCONUT CUSTARD

**SANG KHAYA/
(Thailand)
SRIKAYA/
(Indonesia)**

12 small hen's eggs or 9 duck eggs

1–2 cups (250–500 g) palm or dark brown sugar to taste (Thais and Indonesians might use 3 cups/750 g)

3 cups (750 ml) thick coconut milk

Japanese pumpkin or green coconut

2 pandan leaves or 2 drops pandan essence (optional)

Beat the eggs and the sugar together. Gradually add the coconut milk, mixing thoroughly. Cut the top off a Japanese pumpkin or a green coconut and remove the seeds or the juice to make a container for the custard. Alternatively use a greased dish. Pour the mixture in, cover and steam over boiling water in a covered steamer for about 30 minutes or until the custard is set.

If you have used pumpkin, try cutting it into wedges with the custard attached. You could also add 2 pandan leaves, knotted, or a couple of drops of pandan essence to the custard for flavor.

SAGO IN COCONUT MILK WITH PALM SUGAR SYRUP
(Malaysia)

SAGU GULA MELAKA

7 oz (200 g) palm or dark brown sugar

1 cup (250 ml) water

2 pandan leaves or 2 drops pandan essence (not green
pandan paste) (optional)

8 oz (250 g) fine pearl sago

2 cups (500 ml) medium-thick coconut milk or 14 oz
(400 ml) can of "pure" coconut milk

Pinch of salt

Break up the palm sugar and bring it to a boil with the water, dissolving the sugar into a syrup. Add one knotted pandan leaf or a drop of pandan essence. Pour into a jug and set aside to cool.

Fill a large saucepan with water and bring it to a boil. Wash the sago well and drain it. Cover the sago with more cold water and soak it for a few minutes then drain it again. Put the sago into the boiling water and cook until it is transparent, stirring to prevent sticking. When it is cooked, strain it through a colander and rinse thoroughly under a cold tap, draining well. Put the sago into rinsed single-serve pudding molds or into one big bowl and set aside to cool and set.

Bring the coconut milk to a boil with a knotted pandan leaf or a drop of pandan esssence and a pinch of salt and cook, stirring, until it thickens. Remove and set aside to cool. To serve, unmold or spoon the sago into stemmed glasses and pour syrup and coconut milk over it to taste.

For an interesting contrast try pouring warm syrup and coconut milk over chilled sago or vice versa.

BLACK RICE PUDDING
(Bali)

BUBUR KETAN HITAM

The white coconut milk looks very dramatic against the purple-black background of the rice.

10 oz (300 g) black sticky rice

7 cups (1½ liters) water, or more to taste

5–7 oz (150–200 g) Indonesian or Malay palm sugar,
broken up

2 pandan leaves or 2 drops pandan essence (not green
   pandan paste)
Pinch of salt
2 cups (500 ml) thick coconut milk
Fresh coconut for garnish (optional)

Wash the rice and soak it in cold water overnight. Drain the rice and put it in a saucepan with 6 cups (1½ liters) of water and bring to a boil. Simmer, stirring occasionally, until the rice is soft. Add the sugar to taste, one pandan leaf, knotted, and 1 cup (250 ml) of water. Continue cooking until the sugar has dissolved and the porridge is the right consistency (add more water if you want). Take the pan off the stove, remove the pandan leaf, put the rice in a serving bowl and set it aside to cool (it may be served hot, room temperature or cold).

Add a pinch of salt to the coconut milk and bring it to a boil with the other pandan leaf, stirring constantly. Cook until thick and serve in a sauceboat for diners to pour over the porridge. Finish with a garnish of fresh grated coconut.

GOLAK BANANA, PUMPKIN AND SWEET POTATO IN COCONUT MILK (Indonesia)

6 cups (2 liters) coconut milk
1 large pumpkin, peeled and cubed
4 long white yams, peeled, halved lengthwise and cubed
1 pandan leaf or 1 drop pandan essence
10 oz (300 g) palm or dark brown sugar, or to taste
1 teaspoon salt
7 bananas, peeled and sliced

Bring the coconut milk to a boil in a large saucepan. Add the pumpkin and the yams, cover and bring back to a boil. Add the pandan leaf, knotted, and simmer for about 20 minutes.

Ladle about 2½ cups (675 ml) of the coconut milk into a second saucepan, add the palm sugar and salt and stir over medium heat until the sugar is dissolved. Add the sliced bananas and cook for 10 minutes. Add this to the pumpkin mixture, mix and serve.

Bibliography

Reference and Background

Andaya, B. W. & Andaya, L. Y. *A History of Malaysia*. Macmillan, London, 1982.

Becker, E. *When the War Was Over: The Voices of Cambodia's Revolution and its People*. Simon & Schuster, New York, 1986.

Bongsprabandh, H. R. H. Prince W. W. K. N. *Romanization of Thai Names and Their Pronunciation*. The Rotary Club of Dhonburi, Dhonburi.

Brickell, C. (ed.) *The Royal Horticultural Society Gardener's Encyclopedia of Plants and Flowers*. Dorling Kindersley, London, 1989.

Brissenden, R. L. "Patterns of Trade and Maritime Society Before the Coming of the Europeans," in *Studies in Indonesian History*. Ed. E. McKay. Pitman, Melbourne, 1976.

Burkill, I. H. *A Dictionary of the Economic Products of the Malay Peninsula: Vols. I & II*. Malaysian Ministry of Agriculture and Co-Operatives, Kuala Lumpur, 1966.

Cady, J. F. *Southeast Asia: Its Historical Development*. McGraw-Hill, New York, 1964.

Chan, M. *Foodstops: A Guide to Food and Good Eating in Singapore*. Landmark Books, Singapore, 1992.

Coedès, G. *The Indianized States of Southeast Asia*. Trans. S. B. Cowing. Australian National University Press, Canberra, 1968.

Covarrubias, M. *The Island of Bali*. Oxford University Press, Petaling Jaya, 1972.

Creber, A. *A Multitude of Fishes: The Complete Australian and New Zealand Fish and Seafood Cookbook*. William Heinemann and René Gordon, Melbourne, 1987.

Davidson, A. *Seafood of South-East Asia*. Federal Publications, Singapore, 1976.

de Josselin de Jong, P. E. *Minangkabau and Negri Sembilan: Socio-Political Structure in Indonesia*. Martinus Nijhoff Uitgeverji, Den Haag, 1980.

Downie, S. *Down Highway One: Journeys Through Vietnam and Cambodia*. Allen & Unwin, Sydney, 1993.

Ebihara, M. *Svay: A Khmer Village in Cambodia*. (Ph.D. thesis from Columbia University). University Microfilms, Ann Arbor University, Michigan, 1968.

Evans, G. *Lao Peasants Under Socialism*. Yale University Press, New Haven, 1990.

Evans, G. & Rowley, K. *Red Brotherhood at War: Indochina Since the Fall of Saigon.* Verso, London, 1990.

Geertz, C. *The Religion of Java.* The Free Press of Glencoe, Glencoe, Illinois, 1960.

Griswold, A. B. & na Nagara, P. "The Inscription of King Rama Gamhen of Sukhodaya (1292 A.D.)." Epigraphic and Historical Studies No. 9, *Journal of the Siam Society,* Vol. 59, Part 2, July 1971.

Gullick, J. M. *Malaya.* 2nd edn. Ernest Benn Ltd, London, 1964.

Hong, L. *Thailand in the Nineteenth Century: Evolution of the Economy and Society.* Institute of Southeast Asian Studies, Singapore, 1984.

Jacquat, C. *Plants from the Markets of Thailand.* Editions Duang Kamol, Bangkok, 1990.

Kailola, P. J. et al. *Australian Fisheries Resources.* Bureau of Resource Sciences and the Fisheries Research and Development Corporation, Canberra, 1993.

Keyes, C. F. *The Golden Peninsula: Culture and Adaptation in Mainland Southeast Asia.* Macmillan, New York, 1977.

Khonkhai, K. *The Teachers of Mad Dog Swamp.* Trans. G. Wijeyewardene. University of Queensland Press, St Lucia, 1982.

Krongkaew, M. "Thailand's Internationalisation and its Rural Sector." Paper presented at the Conference on the Globalisation of Thailand, organised by the ANU Thai Studies Group, Australian National University, November 1993.

la Loubere, S. de. *A New Historical Relation of the Kingdom of Siam, 1688.* Ed. and intro. J. Villiers. Bangkok, 1986.

le Bar, F. M. & Suddard, A. *Laos: Its People, its Society, its Culture.* 2nd edn. HRAF Press, New Haven, 1963.

McPhee, C. *A House in Bali.* Oxford University Press, Kuala Lumpur, 1979.

Moerman, M. "Meaning and Magnitude: Some Changes in How Ban Ping Farms." Paper presented at the International Conference on Thai Studies, Australian National University, July 1987.

Molesworth Allen, B. *Malayan Fruits: An Introduction to the Cultivated Species.* Donald Moore Press, Singapore, 1967.

Ochse, J. J. *Vegetables of the Dutch East Indies.* Australian National University Press, Canberra, 1977.

Osborne, M. *Before Kampuchea: Preludes to Tragedy.* George Allen & Unwin, London, 1979.

Osborne, M. *Southeast Asia: An Introductory History.* 2nd edn. George Allen & Unwin, Sydney, 1983.

Proyek Sumber Daya Ekonomi, Lipi (Bogor). *Sayur-Sayuran*. Balai Pustaka, Jakarta, 1980.

Purcell, V. *The Chinese in Malaya*. Oxford University Press, London, 1948.

Purseglove, J. W. *Tropical Crops: Dicotyledons*. (Low-priced Edition. Vols I & II combined.) The English Language Book Society and Longman, Essex, 1974.

Purseglove, J. W. *Tropical Crops: Monocotyledons*. (Low-priced Edition. Vols I & II combined.) The English Language Book Society and Longman, Third ELBS Impression, Essex, 1983.

Raffles, S. *The History of Java*. Black, London, 1817.

Reid, A. *Southeast Asia in the Early Modern Era*. Cornell University Press, Ithaca, 1993.

Ripe, C. *Goodbye Culinary Cringe*. Allen & Unwin, Sydney, 1993.

Skinner, G. W. *Chinese Society in Thailand: An Analytical History*. Cornell University Press, Ithaca, 1957.

Steinberg, D. J. (ed.) *In Search of Southeast Asia: A Modern History*. Rev. edn. Allen & Unwin, Sydney, 1987.

Thirabutana, P. *Little Things*. William Collins, Sydney, 1971.

Wall, K. *A Jakarta Market*. American Women's Association, Jakarta, 1983.

Winstedt, R. *The Malays: A Cultural History*. (Updated and rev. T. Seong Chee). Graham Brash, Singapore, 1981.

Cookery Books

The following books on the food and cookery of Southeast Asia have influenced my perspective over the years.

Abdulkadir, B. *Buku Masakan*. Hoofd Agent Pertjetakan Republik Indonesia, Djokjakarta, 1957.

Anwar, Z. *The MPH Cookbook*. MPH Distributors, 1978.

Bhumichitr, V. *The Taste of Thailand*. Pavilion Books, London, 1988.

Brennan, J. *Thai Cooking*. Futura, London, 1984.

Chaslin, P., Canungmai, P. & Invernizzi Tettoni, L. *Discover Thai Cooking*. Simon & Schuster, Brookvale, 1987.

Chu Duc Thang. *Ky Thuat Nau An*. NhaXuat Ban Quan Doi Nhan Dan (Armed Forces Publishing House), Hanoi, 1992.

Goldrick, R. (ed.) *The Best of Thai Seafood*. Sangdad Publishing Co., Bangkok.

Freeman, M. & Le Van Nhan. *The Vietnamese Cookbook*. Viking, Ringwood, 1995.

Handy, E. *My Favourite Recipes*. 2nd edn. The Malaya Publishing House, Singapore, 1963.

Hanum, Z. *Masakan Tradisional Utara*. Berita Publishing, Kuala Lumpur, 1991.

Holzen, H., Arsana, L. & Hutton, W. *The Food of Bali*. Viking Penguin Books, Melbourne, 1993.

Hutton, W. *The Food of Malaysia: Authentic Recipes from the Crossroads of Asia*. Viking Penguin Books, Melbourne, 1994.

Johns, Y. *Dishes from Indonesia*. Thomas Nelson (Australia) Ltd, Melbourne, 1971.

Kahrs, K. *Thai Cooking*. New Burlington Books, London, 1992.

Kongpan, S. *The Best of Thai Cuisine*. Sangdad Publishing Co., Bangkok.

Latief, A. A. *Resep Masakan Daerah*. CV Atisa, Jakarta, 1988.

Lee, C. K. *Mrs Lee's Cookbook: Nonya Recipes and Other Favourite Recipes*. 1974 (reprinted 1975).

Marahamin, H. & Djalil, R. *Indonesian Dishes and Desserts*. Gaya Favorit Press, Jakarta, 1990.

Ngo, B. & Zimmerman, G. *The Classic Cuisine of Vietnam*. Barron's Woodbury, New York, 1979.

"Njonja Rumah." *Pandai Masak 1*. Kinta, Jakarta, 1965.

"Njonja Rumah." *Pandai Masak 2*. Kinta, Jakarta, 1965.

Owen, S. *The Rice Book: The Definitive Book on the Magic of Rice Cookery*. Doubleday, London, 1993.

Owen, S. *Indonesian Regional Food and Cookery*. Doubleday, London, 1994.

Sing, P. *Traditional Recipes of Laos*. Eds A. & J. Davidson. Prospect Books, London, 1981.

Sonakul, S. *Everyday Siamese Dishes*. 6th edn. The Pracand Press, Bangkok, 1971.

Stuart, A. T. *Vietnamese Cooking: Recipes My Mother Taught Me*. Angus & Robertson, Sydney, 1986.

Suyono, R., Pangemanan, C. & Tjakrawati, H. (eds) *Puspasari Jamuan Makan Indonesia*. Gaya Favorit Press, Jakarta, 1991.

Tan, C. *Penang Nyonya Cooking: Foods of My Childhood*. Times Books International, Singapore, 1992.

Tan, T. *Straits Chinese Cookbook*. Times Books International, Singapore, 1981.

Thompson, D. *Classic Thai Cuisine*. Simon & Schuster, East Roseville, NSW, 1993.

Traditional Malaysian Cuisine. Berita Publishing House, Kuala Lumpur, 1983.

Van Chau (ed.) *Mon An Viet Nam*. 2nd edn. Nha Xuat Ban Phu Nu (Women's Publishing House), Vietnam, 1992.

Yew, B. *Rasa Malaysia: The Complete Malaysian Cookbook*. Times Books International, Singapore, 1982.

Zainu'ddin, A. G. *How to Cook Indonesian Food*. The Australian Indonesian Association of Victoria, Melbourne, 1965.

Zucchi, H. *Indonesian Cuisine*. William Heinemann, Melbourne, 1989.

Index